Founding Faith

founding faith

PROVIDENCE, POLITICS, AND THE BIRTH
of RELIGIOUS FREEDOM IN AMERICA

—◆—

STEVEN WALDMAN

RANDOM HOUSE
New York

Published in the United States by Random House, an imprint of The Random House Publishing
Group, a division of Random House, Inc., New York.

RANDOM HOUSE and colophon are registered trademarks of Random House, Inc.

LIBRARY OF CONGRESS CATALOGING-IN-PUBLICATION DATA
Waldman, Steven.
Founding faith : providence, politics, and the birth of
religious freedom in America / Steven Waldman.
p.   cm.
Includes bibliographical references and index.
ISBN 978-1-4000-6437-3
1. Freedom of religion—United States.   2. United States—Religion—History.   I. Title.
BL640.W35 2008   323.44'2097309033—dc22   2007021710

Printed in the United States of America on acid-free paper

www.atrandom.com

2 4 6 8 9 7 5 3 1

Resources on religious freedom: www.beliefnet.com/foundingfaith

FIRST EDITION

Book design by Casey Hampton

The cover background uses an image of the actual Jefferson Bible. Around 1819, Jefferson cut
passages from the Gospels—in Greek, Latin, French, and English—and pasted them side by side
onto loose sheets. He then had them bound into a volume, with a red leather binding and gilt
lettering. The full title was "The Life and Morals of Jesus of Nazareth, Extracted Textually from the
Gospels in Greek, Latin, French and English." Passed down through several generations of Jefferson
descendants, the book now resides in the Smithsonian Institution. Cover artist Kathleen DiGrado
enhanced the color to approximate how it would have looked in Jefferson's time.

For Amy, Joseph, and Gordon

contents

introduction

THOMAS JEFFERSON STOOD IN A BLACK SUIT AT THE DOORWAY OF
the White House, watching a bizarre spectacle. It was New Year's Day
1802, and two horses were pulling a dray carrying a 1,235-pound cheese—just
for him. The work of nine hundred cows, the cheese measured four feet in di-
ameter and seventeen inches in height. As impressive as the size of the cheese
was its eloquence. Painted on the red crust was the inscription: REBELLION TO
TYRANTS IS OBEDIENCE TO GOD. The cheese was a gift from a Baptist church
in western Massachusetts.

It might seem perplexing that religious leaders would be paying tribute to
Jefferson, who just a year earlier had been attacked as an infidel and atheist.
John Adams's campaign operatives during the 1800 presidential election had
suggested that the Francophile Jefferson would destroy America's Christian
heritage just as the French revolutionaries had undermined their own. Quoting Jefferson's line that he didn't care whether someone believed in one god
or twenty, a Federalist newspaper had posed the election as a cataclysmic
choice: "God—And a religious president . . . [or] Jefferson—and no God."

But in a modern context, what made the cheese remarkable is that it
came from evangelical Christians.[1] It was the brainchild of the Reverend
John Leland, a Baptist and, therefore, a theological forefather of the Reverend Jerry Falwell. Though considered anti-religion by some, Jefferson had

become a hero to evangelicals—not despite his advocacy of separation of church and state, but because of it. Baptists believed state-supported religion violated Jesus's teachings and deeply appreciated Jefferson's efforts to keep government and religion far apart.

Are we surprised that some of the most important advocates for separation of church and state were evangelical Christians? If so, it may be because we too often view our history through the lens, darkly, of today's culture wars. In battles over prayer in school, courtroom displays of the Ten Commandments, and other emotional issues, both sides follow a well-worn script: The "religious" side wants less separation of church and state, and the "secularists" want more. Straightforward. And from these baseline assumptions flow many others. For starters, many conservatives believe that if they can show that the Founding Fathers were very religious, they thereby also prove that the Founders abhorred separation of church and state. "Any diligent student of American history finds that our great nation was founded by godly men upon godly principles to be a Christian nation," Falwell wrote.[2] If the Founders were devout Christians, then activists can claim their endorsement for their agenda of inserting more religion into the public square. Tim LaHaye, co-author of the blockbuster apocalyptic *Left Behind* series, declared in his book *Faith of Our Founding Fathers* that these men had "beat back the attempts of the secularizers 200 years ago. If they were living today, I know whose side they would champion."[3] Some liberals, meanwhile, feel the need to prove that the Founders were irreligious or secular—and therefore, of course, in favor of separation. In *The Nation* magazine, Brooke Allen maintained that "the Founding Fathers were not religious men."[4] If they were irreligious, then surely they would oppose letting faith infiltrate the halls of government.

But in the heat of this custody battle over the spiritual lives of the Founding Fathers, both sides distort history. Each has embraced a variant of the same non sequitur.[5] In the eighteenth century, it did not follow that one's piety determined one's views about separation of church and state. Being pro-religion didn't mean one was anti-separation. And being pro-separation didn't mean one was anti-God. In fact, the culture wars have so warped our sense of history that we typically have a very limited understanding of how we came to have religious liberty. Freedom of conscience, as the Founders liked to call it, is one of the most important characteristics of American democracy, and yet the real story of how it happened is rarely told. That's what this book will attempt to do.

Along the way, we will by necessity trample on some common myths:

- *America was settled as a bastion for religious freedom.* Actually, it was settled primarily by people who wanted rule of one religious denomination over others.
- *The Founding Fathers were mostly rebelling against the religious tyranny
in Europe.* Actually, they were rebelling as much against the religious
tyranny they saw among their colonial neighbors.
- *The Founding Fathers wanted religious freedom because they were
Deists.*[6] Few of them were true Deists—people who believed that God
had created the universe and then receded from action. Most of the
Founding Fathers at one point believed in a God who intervened in the
lives of Americans.
- *The Founding Fathers wanted religious freedom because they were devout
Christians.* Most of them disliked much about organized Christianity,
the clerical class, and its theology, especially the common Calvinist
doctrine that salvation came only from expressed faith in Jesus—or
from being among God's select—rather than through good works.
- *Evangelical Christians invariably want more government support for religion and less separation of church and state.* In fact, separation of
church and state would not exist if not for the efforts of eighteenth-
century evangelicals.
- *The American Revolution was fought solely over economic and philosophical issues.* One of the most important factors was religion.
- *The United States was founded as a Christian nation.* North America
was settled as a Christian realm, and many states did promote Christianity even after the nation's founding, but the United States of America
was not established as a "Christian nation."
- *The First Amendment was designed to separate church and state throughout the land.* Actually, the Founders only intended it to apply to the federal government, not the local governments that regulate schools, local
courthouses, and town squares.

But this book is not, for the most part, about myth busting or mocking the
different sides in the culture wars. In fact, I hope you'll discover that both
sides actually have brought some keen insights and can learn from each
other. Though I will occasionally tie the history back to contemporary con-

flicts, and I do return to those issues in the concluding chapter, this book aspires mostly to simply describe the dramatic birth of religious freedom without the distortions introduced by either a heavy ideological agenda or romantic wishful thinking.

Why *do* we have religious freedom? How did it happen? And therefore, how do we preserve and treasure it?

The first part of the story, the first 150 years, is ugly. Most colonies were established to promote particular religious denominations—with brutal results. The martyrs for religious freedom in America include: the Quakers hung from trees in the Boston Common; the Baptist minister in Virginia, imprisoned for preaching without a license, who stood powerless as a heckler urinated in his face through a jailhouse window; and the Catholics who fought in the Continental army even though some Revolutionary leaders considered them in league with Satan. Eventually, homegrown persecution helped discredit the idea that government should promote particular religions.

It was not just religious excess that stimulated the move toward freedom. Religious revivalism—the passion of true believers who felt vivified by faith—fueled the drive for liberty, too. To a degree rarely acknowledged, the American Revolution and the new approach to church and state that resulted were powerfully shaped by the Great Awakening, a period of evangelical resurgence in the mid–seventeenth century led by a crosseyed preacher named George Whitefield. Whitefield and his Great Awakening brethren encouraged colonists to challenge authority. Though their first target was the Miter, the Scepter was not far behind.

Religion helped cause and sustain the American Revolution. The efforts to break from the Crown became inextricably tied to the drive to undermine the Church of England, and vice versa. The role of religion could sometimes be grotesque, as when patriots used fear of Catholics to incite rebellion. Other times, faith ennobled. George Washington articulated a vision that called on the active intervention of God in the war but also embraced a broad religious tolerance that transformed the Continental army.

After the war, Americans, possessed by the spirit of liberty, pressed to expand freedom of conscience. But they discovered that they disagreed over what that meant. Clearly, the state shouldn't make particular religions illegal anymore. Almost everyone accepted *that* principle. But could the state help some denominations a bit more than others? For that matter, could government help religion at all? Some of the most important battles were fought in the newly minted states, where men such as Madison and Adams first began articulating their answers to these questions. During this period, a powerful alliance formed between evangelical Christians and some Enlightenment intellectuals. Jefferson and Madison teamed up with fire-and-brimstone preachers like Leland and Isaac Backus to fight the status quo (defended, ironically, by Patrick Henry). The philosophers and the preachers sometimes approached the issue from different directions but sought the same result: a ban on religious oppression and a separation of church and state. They viewed both concepts as connected, challenging the prevailing sentiment that for religion to thrive, it would need state help.

The Founders went straight from these local battles into the writing of the US Constitution and the Bill of Rights, around which many of today's church–state battles revolve. Crèches at city hall, "under God" in the Pledge of Allegiance, tax credits for parochial schools—all of these fights stem from a larger battle over what the Founders meant when they wrote that "Congress shall make no law respecting an establishment of religion, or prohibiting the free exercise thereof." My view is this: The conservatives are wrong when they assert that separation of church and state was a "myth" perpetuated by twentieth-century courts. James Madison *was* a strict separationist. We can see it in his writings, and we can see it in his actions—in Virginia, as a member of Congress, and as president of the United States. But this doesn't matter as much as we might think. For one thing, Madison reluctantly had to concede that the First Amendment would only apply to the federal government, not to state or local governments, which could aid—or even oppress—religion as much as they wanted. We tend to forget (now that these men are demigods) that they were also politicians. Madison's task was to assemble a coalition, and if we look at the other men who shaped the Constitution and the First Amendment, we find a wide variety of views, including some strong *advocates* of government-supported churches. In the Constitution, the original intent was, intentionally, murky.

Fortunately for our efforts to decipher the Founders' views on church–state issues, four of the key figures in defining religious freedom during the Revolutionary period then served as president of the United States. We therefore can see them apply in practice those inspiring-but-vague concepts. And what did they conclude? That they disagreed with one another. In that sense, it's misleading even to speak about "the Founding Fathers" as if they were a unitary bloc. They, too, struggled to figure out some of the Constitution's original intent, and they were the ones who had done the intending!

This book has five main characters: Benjamin Franklin, John Adams,

George Washington, Thomas Jefferson, and James Madison. Each contributed different insights.

Benjamin Franklin forged a personal hybrid between the morality-focused Puritan theology of his youth and the reason-based Enlightenment philosophy of his adulthood, thereby bridging the generation of the early eighteenth century and that of the Revolutionary period.

George Washington's importance began before he was president. As leader of one of the first truly national institutions, the Continental army, he concluded that religious tolerance was a practical and military necessity. By one day banning the practice of soldiers burning effigies of the pope and another declaring that God was helping them win the war, Washington set what became a classically American tone, liberality mixed with a chauvinistic conviction that God favored America. He also established a tradition of public rhetoric that was both inclusive and explicitly religious.

John Adams's pungent views on religion—hatred of the Church of England and distrust of Roman Catholics—affected both his Revolutionary fervor and his strategy. Born and bred a Puritan, Adams accepted more government role in promoting religion, but also used the fear of some types of state-supported faith to energize patriots fighting Great Britain.

Thomas Jefferson's seminal contributions—the Declaration of Independence and the Virginia Statute for Religious Freedom—are usually explained as the outgrowth of his Enlightenment-era rationalism. But there's another part of the story. Jefferson loved Jesus but hated organized Christianity, a tension most dramatically illustrated by his astonishing effort to create his own Bible purged of miracles and supernaturalism. He was spiritual and heretical, a combination that helped define his radical, and historic, approach to religious freedom.

The least charismatic founder, James Madison, was the most important. Diminutive and soft-spoken, Madison nonetheless appeared Zelig-like in the key battles for religious freedom. As a delegate in the Virginia assembly, he led the forces of freedom in one of the most important political fights in American history: over whether tax dollars could aid religion in Virginia. He ushered through Jefferson's Statute for Religious Freedom. As a member of the Constitutional Convention, he played a decisive role in birthing the "Godless Constitution." As a leader in the first House of Representatives, he led efforts to write the First Amendment, then personally chaperoned its passage. And as president, he took the hardest line of all in applying the First Amendment to practical cases. Along the way, Madison offered the most integrated vision of how to build a set of institutions and rules that would both prevent tyranny and encourage religious vibrancy. Where did this drive come from? To a degree rarely explored, Madison's passion for religious freedom came from a quirk of history: He happened to live in a particular region of Virginia that experienced a brutal wave of religious persecution against Baptists. Madison's transformational ideas about religious freedom grew in part from disturbing incidents in his backyard.

Though this book is a history of religious freedom, not a biography of the Founding Fathers, it's impossible to understand why they behaved the way they did without also understanding their own spiritual journeys. In chapters 3, 5, 7, 9, and 11, I break from the chronological narrative to probe their faith lives, the goal being to understand their spiritual state of mind as they became central players in the battle to redefine the relationship between religion and government. We then learn more about their religious lives in subsequent chapters and, finally, assess where they ended up spiritually at the close of their lives. Though whole books can be (and have been) written on the beliefs and practices of each Founder, my focus has been specifically on how their personal spiritual journeys might have influenced their approach to religious freedom.

Since each evolved throughout his lifetime—and differed from his comrades in significant ways—it is nonsensical to generalize too much about what "the Founding Fathers believed." However, they did share several common traits: Each felt religion was extremely important, at a minimum to encourage moral behavior and make the land safe for republican government; each took faith seriously enough to conscientiously seek out a personal path that worked for him; each rejected major aspects of his childhood religion; and none accepted the full bundle of creeds offered by his denomination. In other words, they were spiritual enough to care passionately about religious freedom, but not so dogmatic that they felt duty-bound to promote a particular faith. This combination led them to promote religious freedom rather than religion.

Other, less familiar figures played crucial roles in the fight: George Whitefield, the evangelical preacher who revolutionized faith in America and shook the foundation of established religion; Mary Dyer, the Quaker martyr whose courage in the face of death helped shame the Puritans into change; Isaac Backus and John Leland, who rode hundreds of miles on horseback to spread their vision of religious liberty and provided Madison and Jefferson with their political shock troops; and, most paradoxically,

Patrick Henry, who championed freedom at one point in his career, then later became Madison's thuggish nemesis.

The birth of religious freedom was not inevitable. The Founding Fathers contemplated the approach taken by their grandfathers for more than a century—and rejected it. Through a variety of battles—some local, some national, some born of enlightenment and some of parochialism—these men and women helped create a radical new three-part creed:

- Religion is essential to the flourishing of a republic.
- To thrive, religion needs less help, not more, from the state.
- God gave all humans the right to full religious freedom.

The Founding Faith, then, was not Christianity, and it was not secularism. It was religious liberty—a revolutionary formula for promoting faith by leaving it alone.

Founding Faith

1

christian america

SETTLERS TRY TO PLANT PROTESTANTISM
AS THE OFFICIAL FAITH—AND FAIL

———

THE NEW WORLD WAS SETTLED TO PROMOTE CHRISTIANITY. FOR more than 150 years, colonial governments actively supported the dominant faith. Less acknowledged today is a point well understood by the Founding Fathers: Nearly all of these experiments in state encouragement of religion failed.

———

Christopher Columbus believed the world would soon end. In the year 1652, to be exact, Christ would return and usher in a glorious new Kingdom—*if* certain prophecies were fulfilled before then. Columbus's arrival in the New World in 1492 was one such event, he wrote later, a clear "fulfillment of what Isaiah had prophesied." He was quite certain that God had guided him. "With a hand that could be felt, the Lord opened my mind to the fact that it would be possible to sail from here to the Indies." Another precondition for Jesus's return was the conquest of Jerusalem, which was held by the Muslims. His voyages to the New World would help with that, too, providing a glorious model to inspire Christian warriors, and the gold to pay their way. Finally, his discovery of the new lands would enable Christians to fulfill another essential requirement, the spreading of the Good News to all corners of the world.

"The Gospel must now be proclaimed to so many lands in such a short time," Columbus explained to Queen Isabella and King Ferdinand.[1]

After encountering hospitable natives in the Caribbean, he had become quite optimistic that he would indeed be able to bring these generous but unsaved souls to God, plus get some cheap labor. "If one asks for anything they have they never say no," he wrote.[2] "They should be good servants . . . and I believe they would easily be made Christians, for they appear to have no religion."[3]

Though he declared a desire to convert them "by love and friendship rather than by force," the Europeans did not have a light touch with the natives. Those in the Caribbean who rejected or destroyed statues of Christian saints were burned at the stake. Slaughter and European-borne disease killed all but a few thousand Indians.[4] But the Spaniards persisted and their missions eventually made their way to current-day Florida and Mexico.

While the Spaniards did not ultimately win control of the land that became the thirteen American colonies, fear of Catholic Spain's expansion helped prompt England to get serious about settling America in the early 1600s.[5]

VIRGINIA'S LAWES DIVINE

The twin goals of converting Indians and defeating Catholics provided a strong rallying cry for Virginia's settlers. Prospective settlers were instructed to bring "no traitors, nor Papists that depend on the Great Whore."[6] An Anglican promotional booklet argued that if the Spanish had so much luck pressing their corrupt religion, imagine how successful the English could be with their noble goals of saving "those wretched people," drawing them from "darkness to light, from falsehood to truth, from dumb idols to the living God, from the deep pit of hell to the highest heaven."[7] King James's charter for Virginia in 1606 made it official: The mission was to promote Christianity to those living "in darkness and miserable ignorance of the true knowledge and worship of God."[8]

The faiths of the settlers were tested even before they landed in Virginia. One-third of the immigrants on the *Godspeed*, the *Discovery*, and the *Susan Constant* in 1607 died en route. Once in America, their goal of converting Indians soon took a backseat to survival. In 1609 and 1610, the period known as "the starving time," the colony almost perished. Settlers ate dogs, cats, rats, and one another in order to survive. One man was executed for killing his wife for food.[9]

To try to salvage the colony, the Virginia Company in May 1611 sent Lord Thomas de la Warr and Thomas Dale, who swiftly issued a new set of laws to bring order, in part through forced religiosity. The laws declared that the job of the king is "principal care of true Religion and reverence to God"[10] and that the settlers themselves were "especial souldiers in this sacred cause." The new "Lawes Divine, Morall and Martiall" required worship twice each Sunday. Those who failed to do so would lose their daily allowance; a second infraction would draw a whipping, and the third offense would put them in the galleys at sea for six months. Settlers who failed to observe the Sabbath lost provisions for a week (first offense), received a whipping (second offense), or were executed (third offense). Women convicted of sexual misdeeds were required to wear white gowns, hold white wands, and "stand on chairs or stools during public worship."[11] Blasphemy—the use of "unlawful oaths" and "taking the name of God in vain"—was a serious crime, sometimes punishable by having a hot iron plunged through the tongue, and sometimes by execution.[12] Eight settlers were put to death in Jamestown for violations of Dale's laws. Though alien to us, the idea behind forced worship was practical: Pervasive worship would secure God's favor and give settlers the strength and moral wherewithal to cope with the crushing burdens of disease, Indian attacks, and internal squabbling.

As in England, clergy were to be supported by taxes and public funds, or, to be more precise, ten pounds of tobacco and a bushel of corn per settler. A special patch of farmland, a glebe, was also set aside for the parson.[13] Despite these provisions, there was a severe shortage of clergy. By 1662, there were only ten ministers serving forty-five different parishes.[14] Since there was no ecclesiastic church structure to monitor religious matters and manage clergy, the state accepted that role, even disciplining clergy who hadn't preached at least one sermon each Sunday.[15]

The settlers did survive, in part because of their strong faith. This alone prompted wonder. John Rolfe, an early Jamestown resident credited with the introduction of tobacco, wrote that the settlers were "chosen by the finger of God."[16]

In surviving, they prevented encroachment from French and Spanish Catholics who settled west and south of Virginia. At that moment in history, the Catholic Church was viewed in England not as a competing form of Christianity but as a fraudulent faith. It was called "the Whore" because it had prostituted itself by selling indulgences (the promise that for a fee, the church would make sure that the soul of a loved one wouldn't be stuck in purgatory). Protestants believed Catholics should be called papists, not Christians, because they had substituted worship of the pope for devotion to Christ. And only the Antichrist, it was thought, would use the trappings of faith to so distort the message of Jesus. Not surprisingly, the Virginia government attempted to squelch Catholicism within the colony. In 1640, it prohibited Catholics from holding public office unless they "had taken the oath of allegiance and supremacy" to the Church of England. It decreed that any "popish priests" who arrived in Virginia "should be deported forthwith."[17]

The settlers' other religious goal—that of pulling the Indians from the deep pit of hell—proved harder to meet. Pocahontas's conversion to Christianity was much celebrated and, indeed, is depicted in a painting in the US Capitol to this day. But mostly the settlers just viewed the Indians as untamable savages, and vice versa.[18] Moreover, Virginia certainly didn't limit itself to punishing just Catholics and Indians. In 1660, it forbade ship captains from importing Quakers;[19] Puritan clergy were banished; and Jews were kept out entirely for two generations.[20]

As the economy developed and the population grew, the Church of England became more powerful throughout Virginia. By the 1740s, the church had become a place of social and spiritual nourishment for the gentlemen farmers who came to run the colony. Though it became more genteel and less coercive, Anglicanism remained the legally established, official religion of the colony. Taxpayers financed the salaries of the Anglican ministers in their area, as well as the construction of new Anglican churches. During some of this time, other religious bodies were simply not allowed to erect churches at all. Up through the 1740s, it was clear in Virginia that there was one church, one spiritual style, one faith—not just by custom but by law.

THE HOLY COMMONWEALTH OF MASSACHUSETTS

While religion was *a* factor in Jamestown, it was *the* impetus for Pilgrims who landed in Plymouth and the Puritans who settled in Massachusetts Bay. Again, the motivation was not promotion of Christianity in general but Protestantism specifically. Puritans believed that despite Henry VIII's split with Rome, the Church of England had retained too many vestiges of the Catholic Church. "Kneeling at the Sacrament, bowing to the Altar and to the name of Jesus, Popish holy days, Holiness of places, Organs and Cathedral Musick, The Books of Common prayer, or church Government by Bishops . . . They are nothing else but reliques of Popery, and remnants of Baal," sniffed one prominent Puritan.[21] They viewed the Anglican ministers as ungodly and incompetent. In a petition to Parliament, one Puritan called the clergy "Dumme Dogs . . . Destroying Drones, or rather Caterpillars of the Word."[22] Worst of all, the Church of England seemed to let in as a congregant any damned sinner who requested entry.

King James found the Puritans annoying. While passing through Lancashire one day in 1618, he noticed that the Puritans had even prohibited sports and recreation. He explicitly prevented them from banning "maygames, Whitsun-ales, Morris-dances, and the setting up of Maypoles"—all activities that Puritans regarded as pagan.[23] Though we tend to think of those who settled in New England as fleeing severe religious persecution, it might be more precise to say most were avoiding the harassment of a government that wanted the Puritans to be more liberal. Frustrated by the relentless protests of the Puritans about the church, King James declared, "I shall make them conform themselves, or I will harry them out of the land, or else do worse."[24]

The Pilgrims were Puritans who had become "Separatists" because they believed that the Church of England was so corruptly entangled with Catholicism that nothing short of a clean break would suffice. They had left England and sought religious refuge in Holland. Their sense of mission was biblical: William Bradford, in his journal from Plymouth Plantation, compared these settlers to those cast out of Israel. "Our fathers were Englishmen which came over this great ocean, and were ready to perish in this wilderness; but they cried unto the Lord, and he heard their voice, and looked on their adversity."[25] Sailing aboard the *Mayflower* in 1620, the Pilgrims wrote the Mayflower Compact, committing themselves to "ye glory of God, and advancement of ye Christian faith."

Though the Pilgrims landed the starring roles in future Thanksgiving celebrations, it was the Puritans who thrived economically, took over Massachusetts, profoundly influenced American religious history. (One historian estimated that in all thirteen colonies, Puritanism "provided the moral and religious background of fully 75% of the people who declared their independence in 1776.")[26] In 1628, the "great migration" of Puritans from England began. They came for "liberty," said the Massachusetts minister John Cotton—the freedom to practice their religion *precisely*—"not of some ordinances of God, but of all, and in all purity."[27] It was with tongue not in cheek that Richard Mather explained his motives for immigrating: the opportunity "to censure those who ought to be censured."[28]

In spring 1630, John Winthrop, an influential Puritan, boarded the *Ar-bella* and headed toward the New Israel. On board, he gave what would be-come one of the most famous sermons in American history. They were "God's chosen people," required by covenant to lead exemplary Christian lives. "We shall be as a City upon a Hill," he declared. "The eyes of all peo-ple are upon us." This passage has been used by many a politician since, evoking the idea that America would become a model of freedom for the world. But the rest of the sermon bore a darker message. If they *didn't* succeed in providing a Christian model, God would show his wrath—"we shall be made a story and a by-word through the world."[29]

The Puritans left us many ennobling legacies. They set up Congrega-tional churches that stressed simplicity, local control, and a direct connection to God. Because reading the Bible was so central, they established a remark-able system of schools and pressed for widespread literacy. They outlawed usury and promoted the dignity of work, even to the point of endorsing trade guilds. But this book, by necessity, will focus on how they mixed church and state, and how they used power.

Like the Anglicans who settled in Virginia, the Puritans in Massachusetts viewed church and state as fully entwined—a "Holy Commonwealth." "Theocracy, or to make the Lord God our governor, is the best form of gov-ernment in a Christian commonwealth," wrote John Cotton. If it seems shocking to read one of our forefathers so boldly employ a word today associ-ated with Islamic fundamentalists, we ought to remember that it was a typical approach at the time. Since Constantine made Christianity the official reli-gion of the Roman Empire, Western Christian leaders had believed that, thanks to Adam's bite of the apple, man was so inherently depraved, a strong one–two punch of church and state working together would be required to tame his evil impulses.

The Puritans believed that civil authorities, bound by the same Bible as they, could be responsible for creating a godly society.[30] This wasn't to be state manipulating church but rather church shaping state. According to Puritan theology, drawn from French theologian John Calvin, they had an obligation to create a kingdom of God on earth—a society and a church of mostly "visi-ble saints" that would make the worldly kingdom resemble heaven as much as possible. This church was to comprise a limited number of Christians se-lected by God to receive saving grace.[31]

Figuring out who was favored by God was no easy task. It helped if you were well behaved and prosperous, but that was no guarantee. A candidate for membership in a church would present him- or herself before the elders for examination. He would have to demonstrate facility with scriptures and provide a chronicle of how "God's saving Grace came to him." The mission was not to save sinners but to eject them, protecting the saints from corruption. Thomas Shepard, the pastor of the church in Cambridge, Massachusetts, explained that "if we could be so Eagle-eyed, as to discern them now that are hypocrites, we should exclude them now." Why? Because "one man or woman secretly vile, which the church hath not used all means to discover, may defile a whole church."[32]

The church was composed of the saved, and the state would be governed by members of the church. Only full members of the Congregational churches could vote in civil elections. One Puritan named Robert Child suggested that the limitations on the franchise and church membership be abolished. The Massachusetts General Court rejected his request, and had him arrested for good measure.[33] Of course, Catholics were not allowed. (Since the Puritans tried to embody the compassion of Jesus, they did allow that any "Jesuits" who had ended up in their midst due to a shipwreck need not be killed.)[34] In 1644, the Massachusetts General Court banned Baptists, too.[35] Increase Mather, a Boston Puritan leader, later declared that "the Toleration of all Religions and Perswasions, is the way to have no Religion at all."[36] Puritans did not hunt the eastern seaboard for deviants, but tried to keep their own communities spiritually pure. "The government of Massachusetts, and of Connecticut as well, was a dictatorship, and never pretended to be anything else," wrote Perry Miller, the foremost historian of the Puritans. "It was a dictatorship, not of a single tyrant, or of an economic class, or of a political faction, but of the holy and regenerate."[37]

Two of the most famous to be purged for faulty theology were Anne Hutchinson and Roger Williams. Hutchinson was a reputable Boston matron who began holding meetings after church to discuss the day's sermons or the Bible. It was deemed a direct assault on the official church. Theologically, she believed that the Puritans emphasized good works *too much* and put insufficient emphasis on grace. She was brought before the general court, where her accusers were also her judges. She declared that the local clergy lacked inspiration from God, and asked what laws she'd broken. The fifth commandment, they said, since she was disobeying the church and state and therefore, metaphorically, her father and mother. When she retorted that even children should disobey parents when they are immoral, Governor John Winthrop responded, "We do not mean to discourse with those of your sex." They became more enraged when she told them that she had directly heard the voice of God.[38] She was banished—first by the church, then by the civil magistrate—and moved to New York, where she died during an Indian massacre.

Roger Williams was, in many ways, just as conservative as those in Massachusetts's ruling order. But he believed that the church had become corrupt in a number of ways. The settlers had been unfair to the Indians, he said, and while he shared the desire to convert them, the New Englanders had simply stolen their lands. Second, he said that church and state needed to be separated or else men of faith would lose their way. Like Hutchinson, he was expelled from Massachusetts for heresy and later became a leader of the Baptists in Rhode Island. And these were just the most famous to be punished. A catalog of judicial rulings in Salem, Massachusetts, in 1644 shows that even small instances of inappropriate speech or thought drew sanctions: A Miss Alice George of Gloucester was to be whipped for calling a fellow a "wicked wretch"; Mr. William Hewes and his son John were fined fifty shillings each for deriding those who sang in the congregation and "for saying that Mr. Whiting preached confusedly."[39]

"NOT A WOMAN CHILD, BUT A MONSTER"

It was to the Quakers that the Puritans showed their sharpest fangs. Quakers were Christians who believed that each person had to rely for spiritual guidance on the Inner Light more than scripture. The Congregational Church viewed this as blasphemous. In seventeenth-century New England, it was *illegal* to be a Quaker.[40] For the crime of being a Quaker who refused to leave Massachusetts, the punishment on the first offense was usually whipping; on the second offense, an ear was cut off. For a third offense, the criminal would be executed. In a 1703 book called *New England Judged by the Spirit of the Lord*, George Bishop, an English Quaker, cataloged some of the punishments inflicted on New England Quakers, sometimes for intentionally defying banishment orders and sometimes for just worshipping privately. Behold the sheer viciousness of the Puritan approach:

- William Brend, "a man of years," was locked in irons for sixteen hours and then whipped 117 times with a pitched rope, "so that his flesh was beaten black and as into a jelly, and under his arms the bruised flesh and blood hung down, clotted as it were into bags; and it was so beat into one mass, that the sign of one particular blow could not be seen."

- Josiah Southwick compounded the crime of being a Quaker with refusal to remove his hat in the presence of a magistrate (Quakers kept their heads covered in deference to God). The General Court directed "the executioner" to strip him from the waist up, "tie him to a cart-tail, and whip him ten stripes out of Boston and deliver him to the Constable of Roxbury" who was, in turn, supposed to repeat the procedure and deliver him to the constable of Dedham, who would do it again.[41]
- Alice Ambrose, Mary Tomkins, and Ann Coleman had taken to preaching their gospel at the Piscataqua River. They were arrested, "stripped naked, from the middle upward, and tied to a cart, and after a while cruelly whipped . . . , whilst the priest stood and looked on, and laughed at it."[42]

This makes for depressing reading, but please bear with me for one more case, for the story of Mary Dyer should be known by any American who loves religious freedom.

A young mother living in Boston, Dyer in 1637 had been attending Anne Hutchinson's Sunday meetings. Viewing the group as heretical, the Puritans saw an opportunity to send a message after Dyer gave birth to a deformed stillborn baby. Her minister, the Reverend Joseph Wilson, preached from the pulpit: "We have been visited of late by the admonition of the Lord. One Mary Dyer of our midst, who has lately become addicted to heresy, has produced not a woman child but a monster. God himself has intervened and pointed His finger at this woman at the height of her sinful opinions."

She was banished from Boston. In later years, during a trip to England, Dyer met George Fox, the founder of the Quakers, and became one herself. When she returned to Massachusetts Bay in the fall of 1656, she was arrested and taken to the prison yard. As several men watched, she and another Quaker woman were stripped to the waist, tied to a whipping post, and flogged until blood flowed from wounds on their back and breasts. On October 27, 1659, Dyer was convicted of defying an order of banishment and sentenced to death along with two friends. She watched as her friends' necks snapped, and then was given a last-minute reprieve. That had been the court's intention all along: They wanted her to witness her friends' execution before letting her go.

A year later, she defied the law again and was brought before the General Court, with Governor John Endicott presiding.

"Do you consider yourself to be a prophetess?" the governor, who was also the judge, asked.

"I speak only the words that the Lord speaks in me," Dyer replied.

"Away with her!" shouted Governor Endicott. "Away with her."

On June 1, 1660, wearing a plain gray dress, cloak, and bonnet, Dyer walked from prison to the Boston Common. Sixty armed soldiers and drummers lined her route, ready to play—and drown out her words—if she attempted to speak to the crowd. Her old pastor, the Reverend Wilson, came forward to challenge her. "Repent, Mary Dyer . . . Repent! Continue not this wicked delusion. You have indeed been carried away by the deceit of the Devil. Repent!"

"Nay, man, I am not now to repent. I do only what the Lord God requires of me. Do not mourn of my passing, for I am filled with happiness."

A rope had been wrapped around the horizontal branch of a great elm. She climbed a ladder, allowed the noose to be placed around her neck, and was executed by the Holy Commonwealth of Massachusetts—the very government that had been set up by Puritans who had fled England to avoid religious persecution.[43]

Suffice it to say, the Puritan goal of creating a kingdom of God on earth by purging its church of heretics did not succeed. In the 1630s, 70 to 80 percent of taxpayers belonged to a church; by the 1670s, half that many did. In Salem, only about 30 percent belonged to a congregation in 1690.[44] The grip of the Congregational leadership was further weakened as European immigration brought the region Baptists, Presbyterians, French Protestants, Scots-Irish, and Welsh. In 1684, King Charles II—deciding that he no longer wanted the holy commonwealth to exclude Anglicans or Catholics— rescinded the charter and decreed that Anglicans should be allowed to worship in the Massachusetts colony.[45]

Historians speculate that these conditions laid the groundwork for the Salem witch trials of 1692. Though the most famous example of Puritan excess, the witch trials bear less on church-state issues than does the persecution of the Quakers but, for several reasons, are still worth a quick review. The episode began when some local girls accused an Indian slave, Tituba, of casting spells. The girls said some of the townspeople were witches whose spirits had come to their homes to entrance and torment them. These visitations by ghosts—known as "spectral evidence"—were considered attacks no less real than if a physical body had struck them. During the trials, accused witches were chained to the walls so their specters couldn't escape. Wardens searched their bodies for witches' teats. "Much of the searching was in and around the accused's genitals," noted Salem scholar Frances Hill.[46] Dorcas Goode, the four-and-a-half-year-old daughter of one accused witch, Sarah Goode, was imprisoned for seven or eight months. After refusing to confess, Giles Corey was crushed under a gradually increasing pile of stones.[47] In all, 150 people were arrested and twenty executed.

Some of what makes the Salem witch trials well studied—the phenomenon of mass hysteria, the absurd standards of legal evidence—does not relate to the topic of this book. But there are two points of relevance. First, it was the Puritan theology that a few sinners (or demons) could pollute and destroy the whole church that made persecution of the witches seem urgent. Some historians have argued that the Puritans viewed themselves as players in an apocalyptic drama. If they succeeded, Christ would come again; if they failed, "allowing heresy to spread," God would "punish them just as he had the Israelites of the Old Testament."[48]

Second, this inquisition wasn't driven merely by a few village zealots; it was supported by the top leaders of Puritan society, Increase Mather and his son, Cotton Mather. One alleged witch, George Burroughs, almost avoided execution by giving an earnest speech and reciting the Lord's Prayer to the crowd that had assembled for his hanging. According to one account, "It seemed as if the spectators would rise to hinder the execution." Then, wrote historian George Bancroft, "Cotton Mather, on horseback among the crowd, addressed the people, caviling at the ordination of Burroughs, as though he had been no true minister; insisting on his guilt, and hinting that the devil could sometimes assume the appearance of an angel of light: and the hanging proceeded."[49]

Mather's involvement in the witch trials came at the beginning of a long career of Puritanical preaching. And although he eventually mellowed, his basic theology remained harsh. In 1708, for instance, he wrote a message to children: "Ah, children; be afraid of going prayerless to bed, lest the devil be your bedfellow. Be afraid of playing on the Lord's Day, lest the devil be your play fellow. Be afraid of telling lies, or speaking wickedly, lest that evil tongue be one day tormented in the flames, where a drop of water to cool the tongue will be roared for."[50] He lived until 1729, and was therefore a dominant figure in Boston during the childhood and early adulthood of Benjamin Franklin.

REPUGNANT JEWS AND DEMONIC CATHOLICS

Though Virginia and Massachusetts were especially important, every colony experimented with a different relationship between church and state. With the exception of Rhode Island, all colonies had official or semi-official churches that promoted the glory of Jesus Christ. Most defined Christianity as being Protestantism, and most discriminated blatantly against Catholics and Jews. Beyond that, there were important differences. The New England colonies—Massachusetts, Connecticut, New Hampshire—were dominated by Puritans and their Congregational churches. They disliked the Anglicans. Virginia, North Carolina, South Carolina, and Georgia were at one point or another dominated by the Church of England. They disliked Puritans.

Four colonies followed more distinctive paths. Rhode Island, led by Roger Williams, established something close to the modern American approach to tolerance (though even there, Jews didn't have full rights). Williams had urged tolerance even for "popish and Jewish consciences" and, in *The Bloudy Tenent of Persecution for cause of Conscience*, set out concepts that have hardened into gems over time: that religious wars were not "required nor accepted by Jesus Christ the Prince of Peace"; that non-Christians be battled only with "the Sword of Gods Spirit, the Word of God"; that "inforced uniformity" of religion has caused "hypocrisie and destruction of millions of souls"; and, most important, that the sacred roles of spiritual leadership and the secular missions of civil leadership were different and must be kept separate.[51]

Pennsylvania established a "Holie Experiment" that gave protection to Quakers and most other minorities but ran into troubles that will be described in the next chapter. And Maryland and New York offer their own captivating, unique, and disheartening lessons, to which we now turn.

New York, of course, originated under the Dutch, not the English. Neither the propaganda designed to draw settlers nor the official chartering documents emphasized religion as much as the English had. Amsterdam, as a trading center of Europe, embraced religious tolerance earlier than most; those values were partly transmitted to their new settlements.[52] And New Amsterdam (later called New York) became overwhelmed so quickly by such a wide variety of different sects that efforts to establish the Dutch Reformed Church as the official church were ineffective.

But that didn't mean religious tolerance reigned. In 1654, a group of Jews who had been kicked out of Brazil (when the Portuguese regained control from the Dutch) arrived in New Amsterdam seeking freedom, and were promptly thrown in jail for not having the money to pay for the ship ride.[53] Johannes Megapolensis, a Dutch Reformed minister in New Amsterdam, explained the difficulties that might arise from allowing Jews entry: They were "godless rascals" who "have no other God than the unrighteous Mammon, and no other aim than to get possession of Christian property."[54] New Amsterdam's administrator, Peter Stuyvesant, asked the Dutch West India Company to rule that the "very repugnant" Jews not be allowed to "infect" the colony. Stuyvesant also warned that tolerating Jews, bad in itself, created worse problems since, by "giving them liberty, we cannot refuse the Lutherans and Papists."[55]

But the company informed Stuyvesant that he *had* to welcome the Jews, since "many of the Jewish nation are principal shareholders in the company."[56] Stuyvesant grudgingly followed orders but harassed the Jews by restricting their ability to buy homes or cemetery plots,[57] preventing them from opening retail shops, and banning them from practicing any crafts (except being a butcher) as well as from conducting public synagogue services.[58] In 1655, authorities barred Jews from military service—then put a special tax on them because they were not serving in the military.[59] In 1658, the citizens of Flushing on Long Island wrote the Flushing Remonstrance, which declared that religious freedom was a blessing that should be protected. Stuyvesant responded to this inspiring call for liberty by having the man who delivered it, Tobias Feake, arrested and banished.[60]

As with most of the colonies, there were occasional breaks in either the repression or the exclusive control of one faith. For a brief period from 1682 to 1688, New York actually had a Catholic governor.[61] Then, in 1689, a man named Jacob Leisler took over, spread rumors that French Catholics and Indians were conspiring to attack, and called for the arrest of "all reputed papists." Their franchise was suspended, and priests were ordered out within three months.[62] Eventually, New York moved toward a more pluralistic approach, but only after demonstrating the tyranny of both Dutch and English establishments.

Then there's the sad saga of Maryland, established explicitly as a refuge for Catholics. An English Catholic convert named George Calvert, aka Lord Baltimore, was given the land grant by King Charles I in 1632. He told his brother Leonard, who would be the first governor, to "treat the Protestants with as much mildness and favor as justice will permit."[63] But enemies of Lord Baltimore, who resented his medieval way of running the colony, laid claims on Maryland's land. In 1644, an influential Virginian, William Claiborne, launched a military attack and captured Kent Island in the name of fighting the "Papist devils."[64] Eventually, Baltimore recovered the land and resumed efforts to create a religious safe haven. In part to prove that he was not establishing the Catholic Church as the official religion, he worked with the assembly to pass in 1649 a law allowing tolerance of all (except, of course, for "blasphemers and Jews").[65] The Act Concerning Religion declared that no one "professing to believe in Jesus Christ shall from henceforth be in any ways troubled, molested or discountenanced for or in respect of his or her religion. . . ." The lofty spirit of tolerance faded from the document in the penalty section, which prescribed capital punishment for anyone who blasphemed God, denied or criticized the divinity of Christ, or criticized any component of the Trinity.[66] While the death penalty for non-Christians might strike some of us today as a bit extreme, Baltimore's more pressing problem was trying to appease Protestants, who had come to outnumber Catholics in Maryland. In one sense, this gesture of tolerance worked — in 1649, several hundred Puritans, oppressed in Virginia by the Anglicans, fled to the freedom of Maryland. But with no good deed going unpunished, the Puritans soon allied with Lord Baltimore's enemies and claimed that *he* was "professing an establishment of the Romish Religion only," "suppressing poor Protestants," and making citizens swear to "uphold Antichrist."[67]

By 1681, Protestants outnumbered Catholics thirty to one in Maryland. In 1689, the Glorious Revolution was under way in England, and rumors of Catholic-Indian plots now spread rapidly. In July, a group calling itself the Protestant Association again seized the Maryland government.[68] After that, the Church of England was established and followed patterns similar to those in Virginia, using taxes to build churches, set up vestries, and compensate the Anglican clergy.[69] In 1700, the colony prevented Catholics from inheriting or purchasing land and established life imprisonment for priests. Informants who spotted priests saying Mass could get a one-hundred-pound reward. In 1704, it prohibited Catholic worship. In 1715, it required that children of a Protestant father and Catholic mother be forcibly removed from the mother if the father died. The next year, public officeholders were required to swear allegiance to the Church of England; in 1718, Catholics were denied the vote unless they took the same oath.[70]

So ended Maryland's experiment in religious tolerance.

It must always be remembered that for most people of faith in the colonies, religion was a source not of discord but of strength. Countless settlers created families, grew communities, and survived against great odds in large part because of their faith in Jesus Christ. These stories do not generally make the history books because they deal with the mundane, and awesome, power of God in people's lives. It's quite possible none of us would be here today if their religious beliefs and practices hadn't enabled the Puritans, Pilgrims, and Jamestown settlers to persevere against gruesome odds. They were not for the most part hypocrites or sadists. In most cases, they tried to create a world that would bring them closer to God, following his commandments as best they knew how.

But the colonies struggled mightily to establish the proper relationship between church and state. Instances of repression were persistent and often grounded in law. And let's be clear: These laws were not intended to promote "Judeo-Christian values," as is sometimes claimed. Jews were not included, nor were most Catholics. The laws aimed to advance first Protestantism and then, depending on the colony, a particular Protestant denomination. Obviously, none of the colonies resembled the model enshrined in the US Constitution in 1787. Forced worship, taxpayers paying ministers' salaries, voting rights limited to certain religious denominations, brutal punishments for worshipping in a different manner—these are all behaviors that today's liberals and conservatives would together abhor. Yet they were common in the colonies, and it's worth noting that the victims of these practices were not atheists or secularists. The victims of these efforts to promote religion were people of faith.

How did this ancient history affect the Founding Fathers and their views on religious liberty? Of course, to some of them, these events were not of the distant past. For instance, Benjamin Franklin's father immigrated to Massachusetts nine years *before* the Salem witch trials, and Cotton Mather was still preaching in the small town of Boston until Ben was twenty-two. The world of the founding grandfathers shaped the attitudes of the Founding Fathers. So, let us now turn to our first Founder, who was born an old-fashioned Puritan and evolved into a historically important hybrid—a religious freedom fighter with Puritan DNA.

benjamin Franklin

THE PURITAN NEW AGER

———◆———

OON AFTER BENJAMIN FRANKLIN WAS BORN IN JANUARY 1706, HE
was carried across the street to be baptized at Boston's South Church, a
Puritan house of worship dedicated to the idea that God divides humans at
birth into two groups, those who are designated for heaven and those who are
not. Franklin's father, Josiah, had come to Massachusetts from England in
1683 in part to flee harassment of Puritans, but mostly to get better work.[1]
Within two years, he was given full church membership, allowing him to participate in the Lord's Supper (or take communion). By 1697, he was helping
enforce Sunday attendance and watch out for "nightwalkers, tipplers, Sabbath breakers . . . or whatever else tending toward debauchery, irreligion, pro-
faneness and atheism."[2]

This was not a time of glory for Puritanism in Boston, then a town of eight
thousand people.[3] The grand patriarch, Increase Mather, believed that after
the pious generation had died off, a "more sinful generation [rose] up in their
stead."[4] His son, Cotton Mather, complained that Harvard, training ground
for future clergy, had taken into its stacks so many liberal tomes that it was
now "Satan's Library."[5] Only one of twenty New Englanders belonged to
churches.[6]

In his attitudes toward the Puritans, Franklin was like a child who both respects the integrity and hates the narrow-mindedness of his stodgy parents.

He admired Cotton Mather's emphasis on personal virtue.[7] "Frequent *self-examination* is the duty of all," Mather wrote, laying out a series of moral rules and tips that would influence Franklin.[8] But he also rebelled against the Puritan clergy early and often. At fifteen, Franklin—in the guise of his fictitious alter ego, Silence Dogood—declared in his regular newspaper column, "It is the obligation of all good citizens to criticize hypocritical clergy."[9] As word spread that Silence was actually Benjamin, "my indiscreet Disputations about Religion began to make me pointed at with Horror by good People, as an Infidel or Atheist."[10] Working in his brother's print shop, he came across all manner of religious writings, including some attacking Deism, the increasingly popular doctrine that God had created the universe and then receded from the action. Because it denied the legitimacy of the biblical revelation, Deism was viewed as hostile to institutional Christianity. But the anti-Deism books backfired with Franklin, who concluded that Deist principles were "much Stronger than the Refutations." It was the perfect theology for someone like him, because it imagined a Holy Inventor who wrote the natural laws and then gave humans the brains to master nature. "In short," Franklin later recalled, "I soon became a thorough Deist."[11]

To escape the oppressive control of his brother, to whom he was apprenticed, Franklin in 1723 moved to Philadelphia, where his spiritual seeking continued. At the age of twenty-two, he attempted to spell out a full theology. "I believe there is one Supreme most perfect Being, Author and Father of the Gods themselves," he wrote. Yes, *Gods*, as in more than one. Franklin had difficulty imagining that the Supreme Being could possibly be interested in the petty needs—or prayers—of earthlings. Yet he believed that humans have a powerful need "to pay Divine Regards to SOMETHING." So, ever the engineer, Franklin concluded that God created a system of deputy gods. "The INFINITE has created many Beings or Gods"—one, apparently, for each solar system—to more directly attend to the inconsequential humans.[12] The God of *our* solar system, he said, pays attention to our behavior: "He is not above caring for us, being pleas'd with our Praise, and offended when we slight Him, or neglect his Glory." In this creative solution, we can see Franklin trying to reconcile his two worlds: the Calvinism that evoked an involved God and the Enlightenment-based Deism that didn't. His compromise enlisted a distant God of the Deists—"infinitely above it"—overseeing a squad of Calvinist helper-gods who *do* intervene. Despite his Puritan upbringing, he envisioned a warm, loving God. "I should be happy to have so wise, good and powerful a Being my Friend."

Franklin developed a theology emphasizing the cultivation of virtue. God wants us to be happy, and to be happy, we must be good. He customized a liturgy of prayers, poems, and readings that served these ends. One self-composed prayer evoked a God who relishes the joy of His subjects, reveals His power in the laws of science, and cares most that we behave well:

> *Powerful Goodness, &c.*
> *O Creator, O Father, I believe that thou art Good, and that thou art*
> *pleas'd with the Pleasure of thy Children.*
> *Praised be thy Name for Ever.*
>
> *By thy Power hast thou made the glorious Sun, with his attending Worlds;*
> *from the Energy of thy mighty Will they first received their prodigious*
> *Motion, and by thy Wisdom hast thou prescribed the wondrous Laws by*
> *which they move.*
> *Praised be thy Name for ever.*
>
> *Thou abhorrest in thy Creatures Treachery and Deceit, Malice, Revenge,*
> *Intemperance and every other hurtful Vice; but Thou art a Lover of Justice*
> *and Sincerity, of Friendship, Benevolence and every Virtue. Thou art my*
> *Friend, my Father, and my Benefactor.*
>
> *Praised be thy Name, O God, for Ever.*

His focus on good works put him in conflict with Calvinists, who believed that we could not do-good our way out of damnation if we were marked from the start. Franklin thought this doctrine created an ineffective system of carrots and sticks, which possibly accounted for Christianity's mixed record in promoting positive behavior. "I wish it were more productive of good works, than I have generally seen it," he wrote to a Calvinist preacher. "I mean real good works; works of kindness, charity, mercy, and public spirit; not holiday-keeping, sermon-reading or hearing; performing church ceremonies, or making long prayers. . . ." Jesus, he declared, cared less about liturgy than action: "He preferred the doers of the word, to the mere hearers." [13] His critique of religious hypocrisy was usually more wry than angry. "Serving God is doing good to man, but praying is thought an easier service and therefore is more generally chosen." [14] But it was radical, inverting traditional Protestant doctrine by declaring that "Morality or Virtue is the End, Faith only a Means to obtain that End: And if the End be obtained, it is no matter by what Means."[15]

With one question in mind—*Is virtue being promoted?*—Franklin sampled a variety of worship services. Soon after arriving in Philadelphia, he visited a Quaker meeting, which gave him such a sense of peace that he promptly fell asleep.[16] He paid dues at the local Presbyterian church but rarely showed up on Sundays, a pattern noticed by the minister, Jedediah Andrews. He chided Franklin, who finally consented to show up for five straight Sundays. The experience only reinforced his negative view, as Andrews's sermons were "very dry, uninteresting and unedifying," rarely taught moral values, and focused largely on "explications of the peculiar Doctrines of our Sect." Their aim, he said, was "rather to make us good Presbyterians than good citizens." He stopped going. Some time later, a young minister named Samuel Hemphill arrived from Ireland as an assistant to Andrews. What a difference! He drew on a wide range of philosophies, chastised the current church for depicting God as overly stern, and preached the practice of "virtue." Smitten, Franklin was furious when, within six months, Andrews— feeling upstaged and angry at Hemphill's newfangled worldview—brought his assistant up on charges before a tribunal of Presbyterian leaders. Franklin wrote four not-very-subtle attacks on these "Rev. Asses" who recited scripture to avoid rational thought. They were, he said, "grave and dull Animals."[17]

Franklin marveled at how, despite being the objects of persecution themselves, Christians were inexorably drawn toward oppressing others. His frustration turned to disgust in 1764 when a group known as the Paxton Boys massacred a community of Indians. "These poor defenceless creatures were immediately fired upon, stabbed, and hatcheted to death!" he said—yet the Paxton Boys claimed to be inspired by God. "With the Scriptures in their hands and mouths," they likened themselves to Joshua trying to destroy the heathen. "Horrid perversion of the Scripture and of religion! To father the worst of crimes on the God of peace and love!" He wrote acidly that Christians declare themselves better than other faiths, and then offered examples of pagans, heathens, and Muslims who were more generous than Christians. He concluded, "Our frontier people call themselves Christians! They [the Indians] would have been safer, if they had submitted to the Turks."[18]

Not surprisingly, one part of Puritan doctrine he did embrace was the idea that human beings were lazy, malicious, egotistical, and prone to a "life of ease."[19] Therefore, despite his complaints about Christianity-as-practiced, he concluded that religion was quite useful, especially for *other* people. As he wrote later in life to a friend who was apparently a well-behaved atheist, "You yourself may find it easy to live a virtuous Life without the Assistance afforded by Religion. . . . But think how great a Proportion of Mankind consists of weak and ignorant Men and Women." And then there were the lascivious youths "who have need of Motives of Religion to restrain them from Vice, to support their Virtue, and retain them in the Practice of it till it becomes *habitual*." Thus Franklin reconciled his conviction that much religion is horrendous with his equally powerful belief that it is essential. "If Men are so wicked as we now see them *with Religion* what would they be *without it?*"[20]

At least that was his approach for the riffraff. For the motivated and self-disciplined, Franklin had a different plan. Around the time he was battling the "Rev. Asses" of Philadelphia, he conceived "the bold and arduous Project of arriving at moral Perfection." Since human misconduct was not based on original sin, we could reform ourselves through training, without even having to attend church. He was far more optimistic about the perfectability of man than his ancestors. Franklin wrote a list of virtues, and each day would assess how well he practiced them:[21] Temperance, Silence, Order, Resolution, Frugality, Industry, Sincerity, Justice, Moderation, Cleanliness, Tranquility, Chastity, and Humility ("Imitate Jesus and Socrates"). Franklin credited the regimen with helping him to develop some of the characteristics that we do, indeed, now ascribe to him. (On Humility, he confessed, "I cannot boast of much success in acquiring the *reality* of this virtue, but I had a good deal with regard to the *appearance* of it.")

At first blush, it seems as if Franklin held a cynical double standard: religion for the ignorant masses and a secular program of moral self-improvement for elites such as himself. But Franklin was more spiritual than that. Rather than rejecting religion, he customized it. He didn't attend church but continued to write prayers for himself. In 1768, Franklin even rewrote the Lord's Prayer to make it more streamlined and clear. His new version: "Heavenly Father, may all revere thee, and become thy dutiful Children and faithful Subjects; may thy Laws be obeyed on Earth as perfectly as they are in Heaven: Provide for us this Day as thou hast hitherto daily done: Forgive us our Trespasses, and enable us likewise to forgive those that offend us. Keep us out of Temptation, and deliver us from Evil."[22]

Like Jefferson later, Franklin tended to strip the miracles from his personal liturgy. When he and a friend edited the Apostles' Creed, he sliced out the supernatural and downgraded the importance of the church but retained a clear Theism:

I believe in God, the Father almighty,
creator of heaven and earth.

I believe in Jesus Christ, God's only Son, our Lord,
who was conceived by the Holy Spirit,
~~*born of the Virgin Mary,*~~
~~*suffered under Pontius Pilate,*~~
~~*was crucified, died, and was buried;*~~
~~*he descended to the dead.*~~
~~*On the third day he rose again;*~~
~~*he ascended into heaven,*~~
~~*he is seated at the right hand of the Father,*~~
~~*and he will come again to judge the living and the dead.*~~

I believe in the Holy Spirit,
~~*the holy catholic church,*~~
~~*the communion of saints,*~~
the forgiveness of sins,
the resurrection of the body,
and the life everlasting. AMEN. [23]

Franklin rejected claims that the Bible was penned by the Almighty and, although he admired Jesus's teachings, said that "I have, with most of the present Dissenters in England, some Doubts as to his Divinity."[24] This has led some to say he was an atheist, which he was not. That he would go through the trouble of writing his own prayers showed a real spiritual conscientiousness. He spent countless hours trying to find a path that connected him with the divine while avoiding the parts of organized religion he found repellent.

Although he once described himself as a Deist, at other times in his life he embraced the very non-Deistic view that God intervened in the lives of human beings. His system of deputy gods for each solar system implied active divine involvement, as did his later comments at the Constitutional Convention that "God governs in the affairs of men." Acknowledgments of God's power were routinely inserted in his letters as subordinate clauses, as in, "if it please God that I live long enough"[25] or "thanks to God, who has preserved all our family in perfect health."[26] Each person's talents were "the gift of God" that ought to be used "as if he heard a voice from heaven."[27] He appeared to believe in an afterlife. In a condolence note to a friend, he wrote, "Why then should we grieve that a new child is born among the immortals?"[28] And, at least later in life, he felt certain he was the beneficiary of God's love. "And, if he loves me, can I doubt that he will go on to take care of me, not only here but hereafter?"[29]

His true faith was religious pluralism. He wanted a society that was religiously dynamic and relentlessly accepting of differences. This practical — and some would say relativistic — worldview was captured by Franklin in a parody he wrote called "Remarks Concerning the Savages." As he spun the tale, a Swedish diplomat was attempting to teach some Susquehanna Indians stories from the Bible. It seems the Indians listened politely and expressed their appreciation. They then told the diplomat *their* creation story, prompting the minister to declare it a mere "fable." The Indians, according to Franklin, then accused the Swedish official of lacking "common civility." "You saw that we, who understand and practice those Rules, believed all *your* stories," the Indians said. "Why do you refuse to believe ours?"[30]

BATTLING THE QUAKER PACIFISTS

Another set of events — involving the rise and fall of the Quakers in Pennsylvania — likely shaped Franklin's views on the role of faith in government in a more practical way. Pennsylvania had been established by William Penn, a Quaker, as a "Holy Experiment" in religious tolerance. But contrary to popular impressions, the colony was not secular; the "Quaker Party" controlled the legislature. Pennsylvania therefore tested an interesting hypothesis: Could one merge church and state if those in power were religious pluralists rather than exclusivists, as they had been in Massachusetts and Virginia?

On many of the issues that tripped up other colonies, the Quakers did well. They did not force people of other faiths to pay taxes to support Quaker meetinghouses. Ministers could criticize politicians without being thrown in jail. Philadelphia had the only Catholic church in all the colonies protected by authorities, and diversity flourished.[31] As one traveler wrote in 1750, "Sects of every belief are tolerated. You meet here Lutherans, Reformed, Catholics, Quakers, Mennonites, Herrenhuter or Moravian Brethren, Seventh Day Baptists, Dunkers, Presbyterians, the New Born, Free Masons, Separatists, Free Thinkers, Negroes and Indians." Franklin admired the Quakers for their tolerance and lack of clergy (and didn't mind getting their printing contracts either).[32] Compared with other colonies, Pennsylvania managed its diversity well—and the other Founding Fathers repeatedly pointed to Pennsylvania's thriving economic and cultural life as evidence that religious tolerance was smart as well as right.[33]

Ironically, the main flaw was the Quaker commitment to pacifism. Throughout the colony's history, Quaker lawmakers had adamantly refused to create militias or arm soldiers, in keeping with the religion's view that one of Jesus's most central teachings was nonviolence. When pressed by the British Crown to pay for colonial defense, the Quakers would concoct indirect ways of doing so, such as when they approved funds for "other grains" and didn't object when the governor interpreted that to mean gunpowder. This don't-ask-don't-tell approach worked fine while times were relatively calm. Quakers had built good relations with Indians on the western frontier of the colony and believed that the resultant peace proved that God was providing His special protection.[34]

But by the summer of 1747, French and Spanish privateers were raiding towns along the Delaware River,[35] and rumors spread that they would attack Philadelphia the following summer. The Quakers who controlled the assembly refused to engage in military action. Non-Quakers accused them of imposing their faith on them, and jeopardizing their physical safety. Franklin, then a member of the assembly, wrote an article, signed "a Tradesman of Philadelphia," warning that "fortunes, wives and daughters shall be subject to the wanton and unbridled rage, rapine and lust" of the enemy.[36] His other newspaper articles, while respectful of the Quaker position, argued that self-defense was essential. He raised money privately for weapons in part by establishing a lottery, selling ten thousand tickets for two pounds each.[37]

On November 15, 1755, a group of 120 Indians near present-day Reading, Pennsylvania, murdered fifteen settlers and scalped three children.[38] The Germans began to abandon the frontier. On November 25, 1755, four hundred wagons carrying eighteen hundred angry and weary settlers poured into Philadelphia and headed to the governor's residence. There, on the sidewalk in front of the house, they displayed the scalped, mutilated, blackened bodies of a dozen friends and relatives. A few days later, the assembly approved a defense commission to supervise the war effort, and the Quakers' theological control was effectively ended.

Given the Quakers' historic suffering in Massachusetts, it must have seemed to them a terrible irony that the other faiths in Pennsylvania viewed *them* as oppressors. Though the Pennsylvania experiment failed for different reasons than those of Massachusetts, Maryland, or Virginia, Franklin could not help but observe that any government dominated by a particular religious faction—even one committed to tolerance—would struggle if it tried to legislate religious views.

He also could not help but notice some of the positive influences that religion was having in the land. For Franklin had a front-row seat for a Christian religious revival that would transform American culture and pave the way for religious freedom. Franklin—the ultimate Enlightenment scientist-philosopher—not only witnessed the Great Awakening but helped push it along as well.

3

the evangelical revolution

A CROSS-EYED PREACHER FUELS THE DRIVE FOR
INDEPENDENCE AND RELIGIOUS FREEDOM

———◆———

IN 1775, GENERAL BENEDICT ARNOLD WAS PREPARING TO LEAD
troops up to Quebec to enlist Canadians in the colonial cause—or failing
that, simply to conquer them. Before leaving, Arnold's chaplain, Samuel
Spring, had a morbid idea for motivating the troops. He marched them to
Newburyport, Massachusetts, to the grave of a preacher named George
Whitefield. They dug up the casket, broke it open, and removed from the
skeleton Whitefield's clerical collar and wristbands. Spring cut them up and
distributed them to the troops for inspiration.

Why did Spring choose this particular preacher to disturb? Whitefield was
the most important leader in the period known as the Great Awakening, and
Spring undoubtedly wanted help from the preacher's divine connections
when the men faced combat. Moreover, it was fitting that Whitefield, or bits
of him, would be dragged into battle because—to a degree seldom acknowledged in textbooks—the evangelical revival he led helped lay the groundwork for American independence and the triumph of religious liberty.

The dramatic wave of religious activity dubbed the Great Awakening
started in New Jersey and western Massachusetts, where ministers such as
Gilbert Tennent and Jonathan Edwards were preaching about the importance of personal born-again experiences. They believed that New England
was especially sinful but that God would be offering a new wave of dispensa-

tions.[1] These isolated revivals became a mass movement in fall 1739 with the arrival from England of Whitefield, who was a friend of John and Charles Wesley, the founders of Methodism. Whitefield had developed a following in England after writing about his conversion experiences and travels from depravity to salvation. Just twenty-five years old, his voice was powerful and hypnotic. He was described as handsome, even though one of his eyes was crossed inward—which some viewed as a divine mark.[2] He attacked the Church of England for its lethargy and failure to emphasize the idea that only God's mercy keeps us from damnation. Anglican churches banned him from their pews, so he went into the fields, where he drew worshippers by the thousands.

When he arrived in the colonies, Whitefield declared that they were fortunate enough to be in the midst of a special outpouring of grace from God, a rare moment when He expanded the pool of the saved—and pity the poor fool who was not paying enough attention to accept the gift. He moved crowds to tears or gasps or silence. His arrival in a town was an *event.* "I was in my field at Work," a farmer in Middletown, Connecticut, wrote in a journal. "I dropt my tool that I had in my hand and ran home to my wife telling her to make ready quickly to go and hear Mr. Whitfield preach." Breathless, he arrived in time to see the preacher—"young, slim, slender . . . almost angelical," and looking as if "cloathed with the authority from the Great God."[3]

Like modern evangelists, Whitefield used the latest media innovations to spread the gospel far and wide. In his case, that meant tapping into a burgeoning network of newspapers that had sprung up in the colonies—one of the most important being *The Pennsylvania Gazette,* a small publication purchased in 1729 by Benjamin Franklin. For six months before his arrival in the colonies, the *Gazette* printed dispatches about Whitefield's preaching in England—the twenty thousand who showed up at Kensington commons; the time he delivered a sermon on a tombstone; how he used tree limbs as pews. Once Whitefield arrived, Franklin offered saturation coverage of his every move, including the huge crowds in Charleston and Wilmington and the money he was raising for an orphanage in Georgia. Apparently skeptical of some early crowd estimates, Franklin conducted an experiment while Whitefield was preaching from the top of the courthouse steps at the intersection of Market and Second streets in Philadelphia. Franklin walked backward down Market Street and kept going until he could no longer hear the sermon. He then imagined a semicircle with himself as one of the outermost points. From that he calculated that Whitefield was speaking to thirty thousand people.

Keep in mind that the populations of Boston, New York, and Philadelphia were each between ten and fifteen thousand at the time.[4] Historian Frank Lambert, in *"Pedlar in Divinity,"* has estimated that 75 percent of the *Gazette's* issues during the fourteen months Whitefield was in America carried pieces about the preacher. On eight occasions, Franklin devoted the entire front page to Whitefield.[5] The two even collaborated on a popular subscription series based on his talks, and Franklin helped connect Whitefield with the publishers of other colonial newspapers.

In describing one of Whitefield's sermons, Franklin's bemusement over the preacher's message but admiration for his salutary impact both shone through:

> The multitudes of all sects and denominations that attended his sermons were enormous, and it was a matter of speculation to me . . . to observe the extraordinary influence of his oratory on his hearers, and how much they admir'd and respected him, notwithstanding his common abuse of them, by assuring them that they were naturally half beasts and half devils.
>
> It was wonderful to see the change soon made in the manners of our inhabitants. From being thoughtless or indifferent about religion, it seem'd as if all the world were growing religious, so that one could not walk thro' the town in an evening without hearing psalms sung in different families of every street.

In some parts of America, Whitefield reported finding a hollow and superficial faith. In his journal during his trip to Boston in October 1740, Whitefield wrote that "it has the form of religion kept up, but has lost much of its power." Mark Noll, one of the preeminent historians of this period, has noted that Whitefield's efforts did result in a dramatic increase in the number of people "making personal profession of faith in order to join a church." From 1730 to 1740, before the Great Awakening, Congregational churches in Connecticut had recorded an average of eight new members per year. In 1741 and 1742, during the height of the revival, the average was four times that.[6] More broadly, the Great Awakening divided many American churches into "New Lights," who embraced the new evangelical spirit, and "Old Lights," who were more traditional. Certain new denominations—especially the Baptists—grew rapidly. New universities sprouted up to promote the approach, including Princeton, Brown, Rutgers, and Dartmouth. In colony after colony, these proto-evangelicals turned against the dominant religious hierarchies.

Why was Whitefield embraced by someone like Franklin, an Enlightenment thinker, who strongly disagreed with Whitefield's view that salvation was based on faith rather than good behavior? Franklin clearly thought Whitefield was good for business; he charged more for a collection of Whitefield's sermons than for his own *Poor Richard's Almanack*. But there was more to his admiration. For one thing, Whitefield was a small-*d* democrat whose style and tone challenged traditional forms of social organization and authority. He denounced the mistreatment of slaves, endorsed education for Negroes, and established several charities.[7] He believed that each person, no matter how well educated or wealthy, could make a choice for Jesus. And Franklin must have loved the way Whitefield mocked denominational differences. In the first sermon he preached in Philadelphia, Whitefield offered an imaginary conversation in Heaven:

> Father Abraham, who have you in heaven? Any Episcopalians?
>> No!
> Any Presbyterians?
>> No!
> Any Baptists?
>> No!
> Have you any Methodists, Seceders or Independents there?
>> No, no, no!
> Why, who have you there?
>> We don't know those names here. All who are here are Christians, believers in Christ—men who have overcome by the blood of the Lamb, and the word of his testimony.[8]

When local clergy stopped giving Whitefield a place to speak, Franklin helped build a new hall for him, *and* clergy of any other religion. Franklin boasted that it was "expressly for the use of any preacher of any religious persuasion who might desire to say something to the people at Philadelphia; the design in building not being to accommodate any particular sect, but the inhabitants in general; so that even if the Mufti of Constantinople were to send a missionary to preach Mahometanism to us, he would find a pulpit at his service."[9] A church for the leading evangelical—and the Mufti of Constantinople? Franklin viewed Whitefield's cause and that of religious pluralism as tightly joined.

Most important, Whitefield was brutal in his criticism of the Church of England and its colonial outposts. He challenged their pettiness, stodginess, and lethargy about moral evils. "The reason why congregations have been so dead," he declared, "is because they have dead men preach them."[10] So as the New Lights multiplied, the colonies began to fill with men and women hostile to one of the most visible institutions of England. And what started as enmity toward the connection between a particular church and a particular state led naturally to a reassessment of the traditional assumption that church and state must be connected. As noted earlier, most of the colonies had imported the idea that an official "established" church was an absolute necessity for promoting religion. In the South, it was the Anglican Church, while in the North, the Puritan-influenced Congregational Church was dominant. In both cases, colonial elites mostly accepted that established churches were traditional and sensible. But evangelicals of the Great Awakening viewed these official and semi-official churches as the ones keeping them from worshipping as they saw fit.

Many historians have argued that it was through the revivals that colonists gained practice in challenging authority in general. Whitefield believed that "God's grace made it possible for even the humblest individual to take a place alongside the greatest of saints," wrote Mark Noll, Nathan Hatch, and George Marsden. "This spirit—a frank expression of popular democracy and the sharpest attack yet on inherited privilege in colonial America—probably had much to do with the rise of a similar spirit in politics later on." New Light Baptists in Massachusetts refused to pay religious taxes. Throughout the colonies, evangelicals flouted church and legislative laws requiring preachers to have special licenses and limit their work to predetermined boundaries. Theologically, average colonists were taught that they needn't rely on experts to translate their conversations with God; they had the insight, and right, to connect directly and interpret God's will. The dominant institutions of community life need not be heeded; if people in authority were limiting your freedom, you had the right to ignore them. "Defiance of authority was infectious," wrote William G. McLoughlin.[11]

In other words, it was in part from the evangelicals that many colonists learned how to be revolutionaries.

Of course, not all Americans needed the New Light spirit to fuel antagonism to Great Britain. It was, after all, in the traditional Puritan strongholds of New England that rebellion's fire burned first. So to understand the drive toward independence—and religious freedom—we must now turn to Boston, and to the religiously complex John Adams.

4

john adams

THE ANGRY UNITARIAN

———•———

THE MEETINGHOUSE IN BRAINTREE, MASSACHUSETTS, WAS SO cold in the winters that the communion bread would sometimes freeze solid. But the Adams family rarely missed services each Sunday, one in the morning and one in the afternoon. Because John Adams's father was a deacon, young John marched straight to the front, sitting just to the left of the pulpit, a place of honor.[1]

Though Puritanism's hold on Massachusetts had weakened by the time of John Adams's birth in 1735—twenty-nine years after Franklin's—it still powerfully shaped him. By law, the local schools were required to teach the Westminster Catechism, the core of the Congregational Faith, which declared with precision the correct doctrines about the Trinity, original sin, the Ten Commandments, and 104 other points.[2] Religion jumped from every page of textbooks such as *The New England Primer*, showing the tenderness of Puritanism ("HUSH my dear, lie still and slumber, holy angels guard thy bed") as well as the harsher side ("There is a dreadful fiery hell / Where wicked ones must always dwell"). Through school, church, and family, Adams came to revere God and his ancestors. To be sure, he acknowledged, the Puritan fathers might have occasionally exhibited excessive "enthusiasm"—a Quaker hanging here, a witch stoning there—but they were just reflecting the behavioral norms of their day. On balance, the Puritans had founded the colonies on "wise, humane and benevolent principles," bequeathing a system of universal education, care for the poor, and a free press—and, most important, demonstrating the power of faith through their courage in the face of punishing odds.[3] Adams had no doubt about the source of the Puritans' strength: It was their faith, "without which they would have been rakes, fops, sots, gamblers, starved with hunger, or frozen with cold, scalped by Indians."[4]

But it was also in Braintree that Adams became disgusted with many facets of religion. One reason was the case of Lemuel Briant. In 1744, while John was off at Harvard, town minister the Reverend John Hancock Sr. died and was replaced by a young preacher who believed, controversially, that good works could play a major role in determining the soul's fate. After preaching a sermon called "The Absurdity and Blasphemy of Depreciating Moral Virtue" in 1749, he was accused of being an "Arminian"—a reprobate who rejected Calvinist ideas of predestination and believed that individual behavior could affect salvation. The town splintered into camps. Pamphlets were written. Ecclesiastical councils were convened, some at the Adams house, to pick over Briant's ideas and behavior. He's a heretic! A troublemaker! An *Arminian*! Adams thought Briant was obviously correct and became dismayed by the ugliness of the conflict. "I saw such a spirit of dogmatism and bigotry in clergy and laity," Adams would recall later, that he decided not to become a minister, which "would involve me in endless altercations, and make my life miserable, without any prospect of doing any good to my fellow-men."[5]

The incident occurred at a time when Adams was spending countless hours exploring religion and philosophy, first as a student at Harvard and then as a teacher in Worcester. He seemed especially influenced by enlightened theists such as John Locke, who argued that reason applied to faith would enhance, not obliterate, Christianity. Like Locke, Adams believed that since God created the laws of the universe, the scientific study of nature would help us understand His mind and conform to His wishes.[6] He became convinced that while God loved a good argument, Christian leaders didn't, preferring to rule through intimidation rather than persuasion. "Ever since the Reformation, when or where has existed a Protestant or dissenting sect who would tolerate A Free Inquiry?" While church leaders hypocritically forgive immoral behavior when exhibited by one of their own, they react violently if one of their truths is even questioned. "The blackest billingsgate, the most ungentlemanly insolence, the most yahooish brutality is patiently endured, countenanced, propagated, and applauded. But touch a solemn truth in collision with a dogma of sect, though capable of the clearest proof, and you will soon find you have disturbed a nest, and the hornets will swarm about your legs and hands and fly into your face and eyes."[7]

Adams came to reject major parts of orthodox Christian theology. He was unwilling to accept that Adam's bite of the apple "damned the whole human Race, without any actual Crimes committed by any of them."[8] After hearing a dinner companion defend as "mysterious" the idea that Jesus's crucifixion saved us from our sins, Adams wrote in his diary, "Thus mystery is made a convenient cover for absurdity."[9] The idea of the Trinity was illogical. "Miracles or Prophecies might frighten Us out of our Witts; might scare us to death; might induse Us to lie; to say that We believe that 2 and 2 make 5. But We should not believe it."[10] The First Parish Church of Quincy, which Adams attended his whole life, would eventually become officially Unitarian.[11]

He believed Christianity was based on "a revelation" from God but that the true parts have been mixed with "millions of fables, tales, legends" to create "the most bloody religion that ever existed." So grumpy was he about Christianity-as-often-practiced that he even criticized distribution of Bibles to other lands: "Would it not be better, to apply these pious Subscriptions, to purify Christendom from the Corruptions of Christianity; than to propagate those Corruptions in Europe Asia, Africa, and America!"[12]

Most of all, like Franklin, he was repulsed by the fundamental Protestant doctrine that salvation was determined by only faith—acceptance of Christ as personal savior—rather than deeds. This doctrine was "detestable," "invidious," and "hurtful"—and would "discourage the practice of virtue."[13] He, too, believed that Christianity ought not be focused on making "good Riddle Solvers or good mystery mongers," but rather creating "good men, good majestrates and good Subjects, Good husbands and good Wives, good Parents and good Children, good masters and good servants." He knew full well that he was abjuring the dominant theology of New England and his childhood, including the Calvinists. "Howel. Snarl, bite, Ye Calvinistick!" he wrote in old age. "Ye will say, I am no Christian: I say Ye are no Christians. There the Account is balanced. Yet I believe all the honest men among you, are Christians in my sense of the Word."[14]

His disdain for Calvinists was surpassed only by his contempt for Catholics. If spoken by a contemporary politician, many of Adams's comments about Catholics would render him or her unelectable. In 1765, he wrote that the "whore of Babylon" had falsely grabbed the "keys to heaven"; blasphemously claimed to convert wine into the blood of the Lord; and sur-

vived by keeping subjects in "sordid ignorance and staring timidity." It's hard
to recognize freedom's champion in a letter to Abigail in which he described
a visit to St. Mary's Catholic Church in Philadelphia. His pen dripping with
contempt and pity, Adams cataloged the repellent customs: "The poor
wretches fingering their beads, chanting Latin, not a word of which they understood, Their holy Water—their Crossing themselves perpetually—their
Bowing to the Name of Jesus, wherever they hear it—their Bowings, and
Kneelings, and Genuflections before the Altar." He marveled at the power of
the gaudy ritual to hypnotize. "But how shall I describe the Picture of our
Saviour in a Frame of Marble over the Altar at full Length upon the Cross, in
the Agonies, and the Blood dropping and streaming from his Wounds . . .
Here is everything which can lay hold of the Eye, Ear, and Imagination.
Every Thing which can charm and bewitch the simple and ignorant."[15]

Those hoping to prove the irreligiousness of the Founders have no trouble finding ammunition from Adams. The liberal magazine *The Nation* and
the website www.deism.org both homed in on this comment from Adams:
"Twenty times in the course of my late reading, have I been upon the point
of breaking out, 'this would be the best of all possible worlds, if there were no
religion in it.' "[16] But in typical culture-war behavior, neither *The Nation* nor
deism.org included the rest of the quote, in which Adams explained that the
negative sentiment *soon passed* and was replaced by his realization, "Without
religion this world would be something not fit to be mentioned in polite society, I mean hell."[17] When we view the totality of Adams's writings, instead of
cherry-picking quotes, it becomes clear that, like Franklin, Adams believed
religion has its problems, but we'd all be worse off without it.

As an adult, Adams attended church regularly—he called himself a
"meeting going animal,"[18] but in a liberal church that would eventually become Unitarian. Unitarians, as they came to be called by the early 1800s, considered themselves thoroughly Christian, though they rejected Trinitarian
doctrine and emphasized Christ's moral teachings more than his gift of salvation. Despite his many complaints about Christianity-as-practiced, Adams
effusively praised it as the embodiment of "the eternal, self-existent, independent, benevolent, all powerful and all merciful creator, preserver and father
of the universe, the first good, first perfect, and first fair." In fact, he said,
Christianity's core principles were so perfect, they must have been of divine
origin. "Neither savage nor civilized man, without a revelation, could ever
have discovered or invented it."[19] He disliked secular humanism and feared

that a world without faith would lead to moral mayhem. Commenting on the Deistical writings of Tom Paine, Adams wrote in his diary, "The Christian religion is, above all the religions that ever prevailed or existed in ancient or modern times, the religion of wisdom, virtue, equity and humanity, let the blackguard Paine say what he will."[20] Despite his more-than-occasional frustration with religion, Adams never lost a sense of profound idealism about Christianity's potential. If ever a people would actually live by the tenets of the Bible, kindness would prevail; drunkenness, lust, and gluttony would decline, men would not waste time on cards or "trifling amusements," and peace would light the land. A "rational and manly" piety would reign. "What a Eutopia; what a Paradise would this region be!"[21]

Adams's love of Christianity went beyond the theoretical. He believed that God was dictating events. The settlement of America, for instance, was divinely orchestrated, "the opening of a grand Scene and Design of Providence."[22] Those who criticize recent presidents for imagining a divine calling might be surprised to learn that Adams thought God had chosen him for his political career and the presidency. "I have been called by Providence to take a larger share in active Life, during the Course of these Struggles, than is agreeable to my Health, my Fortune or my Inclination." After his election to the presidency in 1796, he told Abigail that the results reflected "the voice of God."[23]

Clearly Adams balanced a noisy mix of feelings about religion. As the colonies became estranged from Great Britain, he focused on another facet of faith: the important role it must play if America were to become an independent republic. Under monarchy, wickedness can be controlled by force. But in a democracy, the goodness of ordinary people becomes essential. "The best republics will be virtuous," he wrote in his *Defence of the Constitutions of Government of the United States.*[24] And without religion, virtue could not flourish—because, while Adams didn't believe in original sin, he surely did believe in sin. "When men are given up to the rule of their passions, they murder like weasels for the pleasure of murdering, like bulldogs and bloodhounds in a fold of sheep," he wrote.[25] Religion was the only thing that could tame our savage natures. "I look upon Religion as the most perfect System," he wrote Abigail.[26]

Its perfection as a "system" derived from its capacity to regulate behavior cradle-to-grave. Christianity takes the "great principle of law of nature and nations"—namely, "Love your neighbor as yourself"—and spreads it to all manner of people, "children, servants, women and men." Religion makes *good citizens.* "No other institution for education, no kind of political discipline could diffuse this kind of necessary information, so universally among the ranks and descriptions of citizens." It wasn't just a matter of repetition or exhortation. Religion had the most effective system of incentives ever invented, the promise of salvation for those who followed the golden rule and damnation for those who didn't. "Prudence, justice, temperance, and fortitude, are thus taught to be the means and conditions of future as well as present happiness."[27] (Conversely, he believed that without an afterlife, this life would be meaningless. "Let it once be revealed or demonstrated that there is no future state, and my advice to every man, woman, and child, would be, as our existence would be in our own power, to take opium.")[28]

Careening through Adams's contradictory writings on religion, we are reminded that just because the man was great does not mean he was coherent. He thought Christianity perfect, except for many of its most important teachings. He loved his Puritan ancestors except for their core beliefs. He hated religion's tendency to squelch rational thought but admired its effectiveness at instilling morality. The Founding Fathers were brilliant but, like all mortals, changed over time, and Adams in particular had no shyness about expressing his views in certain terms, even as he was still figuring them out. Some of Adams's views, however, only seem contradictory when seen through the prism of our current beliefs. His contempt for hypocritical clergy was not a sign of secularism; his belief in an omnipotent God was not a sign of evangelicalism.[29] It's just the way militant Unitarians were back then.

Still, there were two inconsistencies that we must return to, because they affected the course of religious freedom. Adams so revered his ancestors that he did not appreciate the contradiction between his love of freedom and their love of repression. As a result, he never fully turned against state-supported religion as the other Founders did. Less than a year before the Declaration of Independence, he wrote to Abigail that he was proud of the New England system of taxpayer-financed religion. The "institutions in New England for the Support of Religion, Morals and Decency, exceed any other," he noted, "obliging every Parish to have a Minister, and every Person to go to Meeting."[30] Then there is the question of how one of the most articulate fighters for liberty could be such an anti-Catholic bigot. We need not defend his views to remember that Adams was raised in a Puritan family for whom Catholicism wasn't merely an inferior religion, but in fact the enemy—indirectly, the very reason they had come to America in the first place. For them, Catholicism *was* tyranny. New England was settled in part by people who thought the Church of England had become too Catholic. Adams's antagonism toward Catholicism was emotionally connected to his suspicion of the Church of England. And as we'll soon see, it was the Church of England that fueled some of his rage against the king of England.

5

the godly roots of rebellion

FEAR OF ANGLICANS AND CATHOLICS
HELPS CAUSE THE AMERICAN REVOLUTION

—➤—

NO TAXATION WITHOUT REPRESENTATION. THAT'S WHAT THE American Revolution was about—the fight for political and economic liberty, or so we're taught in school.

Not according to John Adams. He believed that *religion* was one of the major causes of the Revolution. Fear of British religious meddling, Adams wrote, contributed "as much as any other cause, to arouse the attention not only of the inquiring mind, but of the common people." This was, he said, "a fact as certain as any in the history of North America."[1]

Not only did religion help trigger the Revolution, it did so in ways with profound implications for the later fights over separation of church and state. The colonists became convinced that political liberty and religious liberty were intertwined. To earn one, they would need to win the other.

Those clergy who were aligned with the patriot cause, including most of those in New England, provided religious justification for rebellion. This is not as easy as it sounds, since the Bible explicitly requires obedience to civil authority. The Reverend Jonathan Mayhew, a Boston minister who greatly in-fluenced Adams, took a shot. He recalled that King Charles had allowed crimes against God, such as sports on the Sabbath or having "encouraged pa-

pist, and popishly effected clergymen in preference" to more Puritan ministers. When a king "turns tyrant and makes his subjects his prey to devour and
to destroy, instead of his charge to defend and cherish, we are bound to throw
off our allegiance to him, and to resist."[2] Therefore, he and the other patriot
clergy preached, God sanctioned war against Britain because He wants us to
be free. The fight for liberty was God's fight. And let there be no doubt that
the Prince of Peace would want colonists to take up their muskets. In a sermon to commemorate the Boston Massacre, Nathaniel Whitaker of Salem
declared that their cause was so just that, should the British again use force
against them, "the spirit of Christian beneficence would animate us to fill our
streets with blood."[3]

If they were aligned with God, then the British were, by definition, in
league with Satan. "It is the cause of justice . . . and the cause of heaven and
against hell—of the kind Parent of the universe, against the prince of darkness, and the destroyer of the human race," declared the Reverend Abraham
Keteltas in 1777.[4] Historians believe that this period saw a resurgence of "millennial" thinking—many were convinced that the apocalypse and Christ's return were near. Prior to 1763, the part of the Antichrist in this script was
played nicely by the French, a Catholic nation.[5] With the end of the French
and Indian War, many colonists saw the British as taking up the satanic role.
The Reverend Samuel Sherwood of Weston, Connecticut, declared in 1776
that the seven-headed beast mentioned in chapter 13 of the Book of Revelation was "the corrupt system of tyranny and oppression, that has been fabri-
cated and adopted by the ministry and parliament of Great Britain."[6]
Connecticut minister Ebenezer Baldwin said the revolution was "preparing
the way for this glorious event."[7] Some political cartoons suggested that the
stamps colonists were required to use under the unpopular Stamp Act were
actually "marks of the beast."[8]

The aggressiveness of the patriot clergy prompted one British loyalist to
refer to the patriot ministers as the "Black Regiment" because of their important role in agitating for American independence. "It is absolutely certain,"
said Charlis Inglis, the rector of Trinity Church in New York, "that on the
part of many, the present is a Religious War."[9]

It wasn't just the preachers who attempted to make the Revolution into a
holy war. To a degree rarely mentioned in our textbooks, many Founding Fathers used religious language and ideas to justify rebellion and rally the people to the cause. For instance, Tom Paine, who would later be attacked by
religious leaders for his Deistic manifesto *The Age of Reason*, cast his call for

rebellion in at least partially biblical terms. The title notwithstanding, Paine's influential polemic *Common Sense* relied heavily on the argument that the Old Testament had discredited the validity of royal rule. In antiquity, there were no wars until monarchies were established, he wrote. "Government by kings was first introduced into the world by the Heathens, from whom the children of Israel copied the custom. It was the most prosperous invention the Devil ever set on foot for the promotion of idolatry." Paine then reviewed the rule of kings among the Jews and concluded that, "The will of the Almighty, as declared by Gideon and the prophet Samuel, expressly disapproves of government by kings." Indeed, he proclaimed, "Monarchy is ranked in scripture as one of the sins of the Jews."

Nor is it usually mentioned that in his most famous speech, Patrick Henry also relied on God to clinch his argument. "We shall not fight our battles alone," he declared on March 23, 1775. "There is a just god who presides over the destinies of nations, and who will raise up friends and fight our battles for us." Arguing that Virginians must prepare militarily because the British had begun to use coercion against them, he declared to the gathered assemblage of Virginia leaders, *"There is no longer any room for hope. If we wish to be free, we must fight! I repeat it, sir, we must fight!* An appeal to arms and to the God of Hosts, is all that is left us." The assembly was mesmerized as Henry grew more impassioned. War is inevitable, he informed them. "Let it come!" Referring to those who wished to remain loyal or passive, he declared, "Is life so dear, or peace so sweet, as to be purchased at the price of chains and slavery?

"Forbid it, Almighty God!" he concluded, raising his head and arms toward the ceiling of the church where the meeting was being held. "I know not what course others may take, but as for me—give me liberty, or give me death."[10]

There was no doubt whose side God was on. Sam Adams declared from the steps of the State House in Philadelphia in 1776 that "the hand of heaven appears to have led us on to be perhaps humble instruments and means in the great providential dispensation which is completing." Elbridge Gerry agreed that "the hand of Heaven seems to have directed every occurrence."[11] The Continental Congress produced a steady stream of documents, declarations, and manifestos invoking God in their cause. Historian Derek Davis reviewed all of the paper flow and found that they had invoked: God, Nature's God, Lord of Hosts, His Goodness, Providence, Creator of All, Greater Governor of the World, Supreme Judge of the Universe, Supreme Disposer of All

Events, Jesus Christ, Holy Ghost, and Free Protestant Colonies. "So powerful were the religious influences on the independence movement that it becomes possible to say that those in the Continental Congress who made the political decision to separate from Great Britain did so only because they fully believed with the majority of the American people that such a monumental act was their religious duty," wrote Davis.[12]

In striking contrast with twentieth- and twenty-first-century invocations of God—which mostly assume Americans to be inherently meritorious—the colonials believed that they needed to prove themselves worthy of God's help. That's why in 1774, Congress resolved to "discourage every species of extravagance and dissipation, especially all horse-racing, and all kinds of gaming, cockfighting, exhibitions of shows, plays and other expensive diversions and entertainments."[13] If they wanted divine help, they'd better shape up.

A DIVERSITY OF CHRISTIANS

By the time of the Revolution, religious minorities were in the majority. Before 1690, 90 percent of churches were affiliated with the dominant sects—Congregationalism or Anglicanism. By 1770, only 35 percent were. First, the Great Awakening had fueled growth in dissenting sects; then immigration brought a new wave of souls. From 1776 to 1820, roughly 250,000 people arrived, bringing a wide range of religious practices.[14] Scottish and Scots-Irish Presbyterians poured in, often carrying with them an antagonism toward Britain. (A Hessian soldier fighting for the British, wrote in January 1778 that the war was "nothing more or less than an Irish-Scotch Presbyterian Rebellion.")[15] German-speaking immigrants—Lutherans, Reformed, Mennonites, Moravians, Baptists, and Catholics—concentrated in Pennsylvania, Maryland, West Virginia, North Carolina, and New York. Catholics, Methodists, and Jews settled in Savannah, Philadelphia, Charleston, and other cities. French Protestants called Huguenots congregated in Boston, New York, and South Carolina. Some, like the Huguenots, fled religious persecution; others came for more secular reasons. They brought with them different theologies. Germans from the Church of the Brethren were dubbed "Dunkers" because they believed in full-immersion baptism. Methodists stressed regular prayer, devotional reading, and contemplation, and rejected Calvin's views about human depravity and predestination.[16] Quakers abjured hymns, sermons, and liturgy. Some denominations shared theology but disagreed about church governance. These denominations would invariably splinter and, crucially, because of the ready availability of new frontier land, they would often press westward rather than staying in a community to fight the control of the majority faith.

To modern eyes, colonial America might seem uniform. Except for an inconsequential smattering of Jews, everyone was Christian. But to the colonists, the influx of exotic new faiths and the schisming of old meant a highly fragmented religious landscape. It would take a while to sink in, but patriot leaders came to understand the new facts on the ground: There was no dominant faith, and there likely never would be one.

With all the religious activism, it's easy to forget that while most of the colonial elites were churchgoers, the majority of the population was not. Historian W. W. Sweet estimated that only one in eight were full members of churches;[17] another set of historians placed "religious adherence" rates in 1776 at only 17 percent. To some extent, this is because transportation difficulties made church attendance far more difficult.[18] And for years, Congregational churches were deliberately set up as exclusive enclaves of the most pious, starkly different from the come-one-come-all approach most houses of worship take today. So it should not be assumed that the low church membership numbers meant a rampant lack of religiosity. Still, measured in terms of church attendance, the colonials were *less* religious than Americans now. Non-churchgoing Christians were naturally resistant to a government overly influenced by a particular faith.

The growth of religious pluralism meant that while the Revolution might be a holy war, it couldn't be one led by one particular denomination or it would alienate rather than energize the populace. This would have to be a holy war like few others—religiously fueled but nonsectarian.

PATRICK HENRY AND THE RAPACIOUS HARPIES

The rise of evangelicalism, religious diversity, and the theological recasting of Britain as a satanic force—all of these factors increased antagonism to the Anglican Church in the colonies. One of the earliest illustrations involved Patrick Henry many years before his immortal "Give Me Liberty or Give Me Death" speech, in what came to be known as "the parsons' cause." Though the principles involved were lofty, the facts of the case revolved around taxes, tobacco, and bad weather. In those days, the local Anglican clergy were paid through public taxation, but the currency was tobacco. Under a 1696 law, each parson got sixteen thousand pounds of tobacco a year. In normal years this system worked well, but farmers figured out that in the event of a bad crop—and therefore rising tobacco prices—that same sixteen thousand pounds of tobacco would be worth a lot more. In 1757, drought hit, which meant that while the planters suffered, the pastors made out very well. In the first sign that they needed help with their public relations strategy, some pastors boasted that their good fortune was fair because it was clearly gifted by Providence.

The planters didn't see it that way, and got the Virginia House of Burgesses to pass a law setting the tobacco price at two pence per pound, eliminating the parsons' windfall. The clergymen were outraged, with one declaring that burgesses who voted for the Two Penny Law were "scoundrels" who ought to be hanged. Failing to persuade the House of Burgesses, a number of parsons appealed to the king. The Privy Council agreed, invalidated the law, and suggested to the ministers that they sue to get the extra pay that was due them.[19]

It's worth remembering that Anglican ministers did not enjoy universal respect. Those sent to the New World to preach were often considered second-rate. Anglican lay leaders complained "about clergy that left England to escape debts or wives or onerous duties, seeing Virginia as a place of retirement or refuge," according to historian Edwin Gaustad.[20] The House of Burgesses early on felt compelled to stipulate in legislation that the ministers "shall not give themselves to excess in drinking or riot, spending their time idle by day or night playing at dice, cards or other unlawfull game."[21] What's more, this Tidewater area of Virginia had been stirred by the visits of Whitefield and had a growing number of anti-Anglican dissenters. Patrick was nine when Whitefield imposed himself on St. Paul's Church over the resistance of its esteemed pastor, the Reverend Patrick Henry, young Patrick's uncle. The pastor's sister, Sarah—mother of the soon-to-be-renowned patriot leader—had an emotional and spiritual connection with the evangelicals and dissenters. Her father, Isaac Winston, had actually been fined by the General Court for allowing "unlicensed" religious meetings in his house. And she used to take her son to the church of one of the leading New Lights ministers, Samuel Davies, and then challenge him, during the ride back, to recount the minister's points.[22]

So when the ministers did bring suit in 1763 to get their extra pay—"the parsons' cause"—they were not necessarily the crowd's favorites. The specific case that drew Patrick Henry into prominence involved the Reverend James Fontaine Maury, rector of Fredericksville in nearby Louisa County. He was a respected man who ran a boys' school that had taught the likes of young Tom Jefferson—and with twelve children, he probably needed the money. The judge, John Henry—Patrick's father!—ruled that as a matter of law, Maury was correct: The Privy Council had indeed stricken down the Two Penny Law. He encouraged the pastors to claim damages.

The second phase of the trial was merely to establish the amount Maury would be paid. Patrick Henry was hired by the tax collectors to argue against Maury. His first victory came when he succeeded in getting several anti-Anglican New Lights churchmen put on the jury, including one man who had started the first dissenting meetinghouse and another who had referred publicly to the Reverend Henry as an "unconverted wretch."[23] Maury would later complain that the sheriff had plucked these jurors from "among the vulgar Herd."[24] The parson's lawyer, Peter Lyons, reiterated the legal points, calculated the amount that the parsons were owed—and then made a tactical blunder. To render the jury more sympathetic to granting a windfall to the parsons, he attempted to remind them of the parsons' virtues—their concern for the souls of the common people, their hard work and strong character.

Henry pounced. Instead of focusing on the particulars of this case, he dramatically expanded the argument, claiming that it was inappropriate for the king to void a law of the colonies and that local communities should be able to control and regulate their own ministers.

This was treason being spoken! Maury's lawyer declared.

But Henry pressed on. Roaming the room with a slight stoop, he declared that the vestries shouldn't have to pay a dime more to the clergy than they were worth, which, by the way, was *not much*:

> We have heard a great deal about the benevolence of our reverend clergy. But how is this manifested? Do they manifest their zeal in the cause of religion and humanity by practicing the mild and benevolent precepts of the Gospel of Jesus Christ? Do they feed the hungry, or clothe the naked? Oh no, Gentlemen. Instead of feeding the hungry and clothing the naked, these rapacious harpies would, were their powers equal to their will, snatch from the heart of their honest parishioner his last hoe-cake, from the widow and her orphan children their last milch cow, and the last bed—nay, the last blanket—from the lying-in woman.[25]

Sitting in the front of the court, in places of honor, were some twenty parsons in black cloaks from throughout the area. Outraged, they stood up and walked out.

The jury deliberated for just five minutes before returning a judgment that the Reverend Maury should be paid one penny.

INVASION OF THE BISHOPS

Only in the context of this increasing antagonism to the Anglican Church—and the linkage in the public mind of church oppression and political tyranny—does another controversy makes sense: By the early 1760s, many colonists were becoming nearly hysterical over the possibility that England would send bishops to live in the colonies.

Because the church had been struggling, a number of Colonial and British officials pushed the idea of having a Church of England bishop stationed in America. They believed that the Church suffered from structural problems. Those wishing to be ordained as ministers needed to travel to Great Britain; and if ministers strayed, there was no one on the ground in the colonies to impose discipline. In the January 1761 issue of *The Boston Gazette*, an anonymous author made the case for a bishop. He decried the proliferation of "sects" and called for unification behind a single, tidy faith: "We shall all call aloud with one Heart and Voice, for One way (and if it be not inconsistent with my Character, I would speak in Time for the *Established Way*)."[26] According to historian Carl Bridenbaugh, these Anglican parries were often inept and countered by clever colonial responses. For instance, the Reverend East Apthorp, possibly in line to be one of the first bishops, insulted New Englanders by writing that the presence of the Anglicans had "manifestly improved" the religious condition, especially compared with those dour Puritans.[27] "Religion no longer wears among us that savage and gloomy appearance, with which Superstition has terribly arrayed her," he wrote.[28]

Patriot clergy looking to stir the pot had a field day after the construction of a large house in Cambridge, Massachusetts, rumored to be Apthorp's "palace."[29] On April 21, 1763, Boston minister Jonathan Mayhew published a pamphlet bitingly citing the house as proof that the Episcopal Church—with all its garish, Romish trappings—would soon be erecting a *"super edifice"* to serve as a *"Palace* of one of the *humble successors* of the apostles."[30] Mayhew recalled that it was the Church of England that had driven many of the early settlers to the New World in the first place.[31] "Will they never let us rest in peace, except where all the weary are at rest? Is it not enough that they persecuted us out of the old world? Will they pursue us into the new to convert us here?"

Patriots equated the practices of the Church of England with those of the Catholic Church. On August 12, 1765, *The Boston Gazette* published an essay again linking the two churches to each other, and to tyranny. The essay argued that religious canon law—"extensive and astonishing"—was created by "the Romish clergy for the aggrandizement of their own order." Church law enslaved people by "reducing their minds to a state of sordid ignorance and staring timidity" and warned that only an educated populace could thwart the "direct and formal design on foot, to enslave America."[32] Though it was not known at the time, the author was twenty-nine-year-old lawyer John Adams.

Some colonists even associated the bishops with that outrage of outrages: higher taxes. Establish a system of bishops and, before long, new taxes would be levied to support their lavish lifestyles. Charles Chauncy of Boston said a "large revenue" would be needed to support a "complete church hierarchy, after the pattern of that at home."[33] The negative reaction against the Townshend Duties flowed in part from Americans who feared that the tax on tea, glass, and paper implied the power to appoint bishops. Antagonism to the church grew when it was noticed that the Anglican missionaries were among the strongest supporters of the much-reviled Stamp Act of 1765, which required the colonists to pay a small tax for legal notices and correspondences. The link between small bits of political or economic tyranny and large principles of religious oppression became strong, at least for some rebels. "The religion and public of liberty of people are so intimately connected, their interests are interwoven, and cannot exist separately," wrote Sam Adams in 1772.[34] The main threat to the colonies, he said, was "the utter loss of those *religious rights*, the enjoyment of which our good forefathers had more especially in their intention, when they explored and settled this new world."[35]

The hapless Anglicans tried to assuage colonial fears. Thomas Bradbury Chandler was commissioned by a convention of clergy to explain to the public that the plan would not involve tax support and would constitute "no Invasion of the civil or religious Privileges of any, whether Churchmen or Dissenters."[36] Alas, he then undercut his argument by noting that a mere four pence for every thousand pounds would suffice to support the episcopacy, "no mighty hardship."[37] Their propaganda was relentlessly ham-handed. Take, for instance, the comments of John Ewer, bishop of Llandaff, who on February 20, 1767, declared that the Puritans had flubbed their grand exercise of bringing Christianity to the wilds of the New World: "Instead of civilizing and converting barbarous Infidels, as they undertook to do, they became themselves Infidels and Barbarians."[38] So much for winning the hearts and minds.

The Church of England never did land a bishop in America—and evidence is that the rebels greatly exaggerated the threat all along—but fear of their arrival persisted right up until the Revolution. American anger at the Church of England hierarchy became ever more fused with anger at the Crown. "They demonstrated to the public satisfaction that bishops represented incipient tyranny," wrote Bridenbaugh.[39]

FREEDOM TO HATE CATHOLICS

Part of the hatred of the Church of England—both when the Puritans were still in England and in the century since they had emigrated—stemmed from the belief that it too closely resembled the Catholic Church. The anti-Catholic credentials of the British were strong enough when they were busy warding off the Catholics in the French and Indian War, but after that ended in 1763, suspicions resumed that the British might be soft on the Catholic menace. In the late 1760s and early 1770s, colonists celebrated "Pope Day," an anti-Catholic festival derived from the English Guy Fawkes Day (named for a Catholic who attempted to assassinate King James I). "Orations, cartoons, and public hangings of effigies depicted royal ministers as in league alternately with the pope and the devil," wrote historian Ruth Bloch.[40] Hatred of Catholics at that point was widespread. Roger Sherman and other members of the Continental Congress wanted to prohibit Catholics from serving in the Continental army. Only three of the thirteen colonies allowed Catholics to vote. Most of the New England colonies and the Carolinas prohibited Catholics from holding office; Virginia would have priests arrested for entering the colony; Catholic schools were banned in all colonies except Pennsylvania.[41]

In 1774, Parliament passed the Quebec Act, taking the enlightened position that the Catholic Church could remain the official church of Quebec. This appalled and terrified many colonists, who assumed it to be a

British attempt to subjugate them religiously by allowing the loathsome Catholics to expand into the colonies. Colonial newspapers railed against the popish threat. *The Pennsylvania Gazette* said that the legislation would now allow "these dogs of Hell" to "erect their Heads and triumph within our Borders."[42] *The Boston Evening Post* reported that the act was "for the execution of this hellish plan" to organize four thousand Canadian Catholics for an attack on America.[43] In Rhode Island, every single issue of the *Newport Mercury* from October 2, 1774, to March 20, 1775, contained "at least one invidious reference to the Catholic religion of the Canadians," according to historian Charles Metzger.[44]

Protestant clergy fanned the flames. The Reverend John Lathrop of the Second Church in Boston said Catholics "had disgraced humanity" and "crimsoned a great part of the world with innocent blood."[45] The Reverend Samuel West of Dartmouth declared the pope to be "the second beast" of Revelation,[46] while Joseph Perry warned his Connecticut neighbors that they would soon need to swap "the best religion in the world" for "all the barbarity, trumpery and superstition of popery; or burn at the stake, or submit to the tortures of the inquisition." Indeed, English lawmakers were being controlled by the devil; the Quebec Act "first sprang from that original *wicked politician.*"[47] Commenting on anti-Catholic fervor, historian Alan Heimert wrote that there was "a special and even frenetic urgency to their efforts to revive ancient prejudices by announcing that the Quebec Act—and it alone—confronted America with the possibility of the 'scarlet whore' soon riding 'triumphant over the heads of true Protestants, making multitudes drunk with the wine of her fornications.' "[48] The 1774 Pope Day was one of the grandest in years; in Newport, two large effigies of the pope were paraded.[49] In New York, a group marched to the Financial Exchange carrying a huge flag inscribed GEORGE III REX, AND THE LIBERTIES OF AMERICA. NO POPERY. Later that day, a pamphlet that had been distributed urging tolerance toward the Catholics of Canada was smeared with tar and feathers and nailed to the pillory.[50]

Even some of our most respected Founding Fathers echoed these views. Alexander Hamilton decried the Quebec Act as a diabolical threat. "Does not your blood run cold to think that an English Parliament should pass an Act for the establishment of arbitrary power and Popery in such an extensive country? . . . Your lives, your property, your religion are all at stake." He warned that the Canadian tolerance in Quebec would draw, like a magnet, Catholics from throughout Europe, who would eventually destroy America.[51] Sam Adams told a group of Mohawk Indians that the law "to establish the religion of the Pope in Canada" would mean that "some of your children may be induced instead of worshipping the only true God, to pay his dues to images made with their own hands."[52] The silversmith and engraver Paul Revere created a cartoon for *The Royal American Magazine* called "The Mitred Minuet." It depicted four contented-looking mitred Anglican bishops dancing a minuet around a copy of the Quebec Act to show their "approbation and countenance of the Roman religion." Standing nearby are the authors of the Quebec Act, while a devil with bat ears and spiky wings hovers behind them, whispering instructions.

The Continental Congress took a stand against the Catholic menace. On October 21, 1774, it issued an address "to the People of Great Britain," written by John Jay, Richard Henry Lee, and William Livingston, which expressed shock that Parliament would promote a religion that "disbursed impiety, bigotry, persecution, murder and rebellions through every part of the world."[53] It predicted that the measure would encourage Canadians to "act with hostility against the free Protestant colonies, whenever a wicked Ministry shall choose to direct them."[54] Once Americans were converted to Catholicism, they would be enlisted in a vast popish army to enslave English Protestants.[55]

For some, the resistance to Catholicism carried a special urgency: Christ's return depended on it. "It was not uncommon for colonists to believe that the pope was the Antichrist and that America, surely the location of Christ's coming millennial reign, needed a purging of Catholic influences that were undoubtedly responsible for delaying the onset of the millennium," historian Derek Davis has explained. The New England Congregationalist James Dana, for example, preached in 1770 that the decline of the papal Antichrist since the Reformation was nearly complete and that in a very short time, "The millennium will come and true Christianity will prevail."[56] Defeat of the Quebec Act, on the other hand, might hasten the Messiah's arrival. Revelation 12:6 14 indicated that the "flight of the woman into the wilderness" would signal his return. "These violent attacks upon the woman in the wilderness, may possibly be some of the last efforts, and dying struggles of the man of sin," wrote Samuel Sherwood, a New England minister.[57]

If it seems today a bit strange that a war against a Protestant King George III could be cast as a fight against Catholicism, this was a paradox apparent to some British at the time. Describing the Quebec Act as the turning point, General Thomas Gage puzzled over how colonists had become convinced that Britain would eliminate their religious freedom. When they could not "be made to believe the contrary . . . the Flame [of rebellion] blased out in all

Parts." Ambrose Serle, who served as secretary to Admiral Lord Richard
Howe from 1776 to 1778, reported to his superiors that "at Boston the war is
very much a religious war." Not surprisingly, over the years some Britons have
chafed over the idea that the Revolution was about lofty concepts of freedom.
In 1912, the English cardinal Gasquet flatly declared that "the American Revolution was not a movement for civil and religious liberty; its principal cause
was the bigoted rage of the American Puritan and Presbyterian ministers at
the concession of full religious liberty and equality to Catholics of French
Canada." Yes, he noted, people were upset by taxation, but that could have
been resolved if not for the "Puritan firebrands and the bigotry of the people."[58]

SEGUE INTO RELIGIOUS FREEDOM

The Revolutionary War's religious dimensions had specific implications for
the later fights over separation of church and state. Not only did the episcopacy controversy fuel anti-royal sentiment, it also helped reinforce the growing
view that the mingling of church and state was antithetical to the new American principles.[59] It would become difficult for patriots to attack the evils of the
Anglican establishment, then turn around and defend the maintenance of an
official state church—especially over the objections of religious minorities
such as Baptists.

Religious minorities went out of their way to make this point—as we can
see in the inspiring tale of Isaac Backus, one of the true heroes of American
liberty. A minister in Middleborough, Massachusetts, Backus had become a
"Separate" or New Light Baptist in part because he believed that the dominant church had become too permissive, allowing participation of all manner
of men and women who had not yet been "regenerate" or born again. "At all
times the doors of the church should be carefully kept against such as cannot
give a satisfactory evidence of the work of God upon their souls, whereby they
are united to Christ," he wrote.[60] In 1734, Massachusetts had ostensibly exempted Anabaptists and Quakers from taxation to support the Congregational Church but made them jump through many hoops to avoid the taxes.
Separate Baptists had to submit documents verifying Baptist heritage, gain
certification from a *traditional* Baptist church, and prove they regularly attended church.[61] They must have built an appropriate meetinghouse and
hired an "able, learned and orthodox" minister. Backus's mother, Elizabeth,
a Separate Baptist in Connecticut, refused to pay taxes on the grounds that

she should not be forced to support the minister of the traditional church with which she did not agree. For so doing, she "was taken and, though a weakly woman, was carried to prison in a dark rainy night," Backus wrote. His brother and uncle were also imprisoned.[62] In Ashfield, Massachusetts, the Baptists refused to pay the taxes, and the town responded by selling some of their land.[63]

These and other indignities prompted Backus, the head of the Warren Grievance Committee in Boston, to seek help elsewhere—and to reprimand non-Baptist patriots for their hypocrisy in fighting British tyranny while imposing their own. In a letter to the other Baptist churches in Massachusetts, Backus wrote, "Liberty of conscience, the great and most important article of liberty, is evidently not allowed as it ought to be in this country, not even by the very men who are now making loud complaints of the encroachments upon their own liberties [by Parliament]."[64] His most important tract was *An Appeal to the Public for Religious Liberty Against the Oppression of the Present Day*, which historian William McLoughlin called the "pietistic America's declaration of spiritual independence."[65] Backus pointed out that the Massachusetts law requiring infant baptism went directly against the Baptist belief that the practice was not authorized by the Bible. He attacked the educational and training requirements for ministers as ignoring the possibility that God granted ministerial gifts to all manner of people. And he noted that forcing the Baptists to pay taxes that helped another denomination could go by another name: taxation without representation.[66]

Backus extended the argument beyond the persecution of the Baptists, declaring that all state laws regulating religion perverted Christianity. "Bringing in an earthly power between Christ and his people has been the grand source of anti-Christian abominations," he wrote. "Now who can hear Christ declare that his kingdom is NOT OF THIS WORLD, and yet believe that this blending of church and state together can be pleasing to him."[67] Backus and other Baptists even went so far as to argue that religion that is forced or even cajoled simply doesn't count. "Nothing can be true religion but a voluntary obedience unto his revealed will, of which each rational soul has an equal right to judge for itself," he later wrote.[68]

Backus pressed his case with Revolutionary leaders, figuring that their love of freedom would surely make them allies to his cause. After the Boston Tea Party, Parliament had passed the Coercive Acts, which, along with the Quebec Act had prompted the creation of the First Continental Congress. Backus led a delegation in fall 1774 to Philadelphia to meet with members of

Congress. The mission was complicated by Backus's tactical error of including in the group Quaker leaders, who had similar religious grievances but
also tended to be royalists. On October 14 in Carpenters Hall, they met with
the Massachusetts delegation plus delegates from other colonies. Backus's
Baptist colleague James Manning began the meeting by reading a long statement linking religious and political liberty and reviewing the record of religious persecution of Baptists. Faith was, he said, "a concern between God
and the soul with which no human authority can intermeddle."

John Adams felt ambushed. Who were these men to form this "self-
created tribunal" designed to impune the laws of the great Commonwealth
of Massachusetts? Sam Adams bristled at the speech and, for a full hour, he
and Robert Treat Paine defended the Massachusetts way—including the establishment of Congregationalism as the official faith of the state. "There is
indeed an ecclesiastical establishment in our province," John Adams said.
"But a very slender one, hardly to be called an establishment."[69] The Massachusetts government was "clear of blame" and always open to legitimate concerns, they maintained. Sam Adams suggested that the "regular" Baptists
seemed happy enough and suggested that trouble was being stirred by the
"enthusiasts," who seemed to find value in suffering persecution. Paine complained that this problem stemmed from the Baptists' refusal to turn in their
certificates, and suggested that the whole affair was really not about liberty
but rather "only a contending about paying a little money."

Backus resented the implication, angrily declaring, "It is absolutely a
point of conscience with me." A somewhat diffident man, Backus had an odd
habit of closing his eyes when preaching or conversing on important subjects, but with the Adams cousins he was stern: "I cannot give in the certificates they require without implicitly acknowledging that power in man
which I believe belongs to God."[70]

John Adams gruffly denied Massachusetts had a problem and said that liberty of conscience allowed residents to write their own rules about religion,
without meddling from other states or religions. In his own diary, Adams
recorded his suspicion that one of the Quaker delegates, Israel Pemberton,
was an "artful Jesuit" (apparently a generic insult) attempting to "break up
the Congress."[71]

After four hours, the meeting broke up with Adams telling Backus, "We
might as soon expect a change in the solar system" as to expect the state to
give up Congregationalism as its official religion.

Adams was wrong, of course. The establishments would eventually fall, even in Massachusetts, in part because the very process of becoming a single nation would change the way leaders handled religious diversity. Though it took many years for nationalism to fully transform the fight for religious liberty, dramatic changes in attitude became apparent almost as soon as the first national institutions were created—and the first truly national leaders emerged.

6

george washington

PROTECTED BY GOD

———◆———

O N THE CEILING OF THE US CAPITOL'S ROTUNDA IS A PANTHEON
of gods. Minerva stands on the perimeter with helmet and spear, sym-
bolizing science. Neptune rides a chariot led by seahorses, while Vulcan, the
god of the forge, stands imposingly atop a cannon. And in the center of the
dome is the greatest god of them all. No, not Zeus — Washington.[1] Called *The
Apotheosis of Washington* (*apotheosis* meaning "elevation to the status of a
god"), the painting points up a peculiar difficulty in assessing Washington
and religion. He ascended to such a godly status himself that religious leaders have been jockeying to define him as one of theirs since the day he died.
Washington, said conservative minister D. James Kennedy, had a "fervent
evangelical faith."[2] Tim LaHaye declared in his book *Faith of Our Founding
Fathers* that the first president was a "devout believer in Jesus Christ and had
accepted Him as His Lord and Savior."[3] LaHaye predicted that "were George
Washington living today, he would freely identify with the Bible-believing
branch of evangelical Christianity that is having such a positive influence on
our nation."[4] Both cited many examples of Washington's piety, including the
well-known, and oft-painted, story of the Pennsylvanian who came upon
Washington on his knees praying at Valley Forge. Secularists, on the other
hand, point to Washington's unwillingness to speak about Christianity and

other Deistic tendencies he exhibited throughout his life. "Religion seems to have played a remarkably small role in his own life," wrote Brooke Allen.[5]

Because the mythologizing began so quickly, it's hard to unravel fact from fiction. For instance, it turns out that the source for the story about Washington on bended knee at Valley Forge was the biography by Parson Weems, the same creative fellow who made up the tale about young George chopping down the cherry tree. Weems described a witness, Isaac Potts, coming upon Washington near the camp. "As he approached the post with a cautious step, whom should he behold, in a dark natural bower of ancient oaks, but the commander in chief of the American armies on his knees at prayer! Motionless with surprise, friend Potts continued on the place till the general, having ended his devotions, arose, and, with a countenance of angel serenity, retired to headquarters."[6] Later historians discovered that Potts hadn't begun working at Valley Forge until several years later. On the other hand, there is plenty of evidence that Washington prayed, so Weems may have concocted a story that captured some actual Washingtonian quality.

What do the knowable facts show? A portrait not likely to satisfy either extreme in the culture war—a deeply spiritual man who believed God was protecting him and the nation, and who yet showed disinterest in and sometimes disdain for important facets of Christianity. Most important, he exhibited an unusual—and world-historic—sense of tolerance that would have a profound impact on the evolution of religious freedom.

THE CUNNING OLD FOX

Washington was raised in an Anglican family along the Potomac River in Virginia. His father was a vestryman in the church and his mother, pious. Shortly before her death, she supposedly said to him, "Go, George, fulfill the high destinies which Heaven appears to have intended for you."[7] Washington married in the Anglican Church and owned two pews in Pohick Church, seven miles from Mount Vernon, as well as one in Christ Church in Alexandria. He was one of twelve vestrymen in the Truro parish, Virginia—active from 1763 to 1774 and less so after, according to Paul Boller, who wrote one of the most balanced assessments of Washington's religious life. He served on the building committee, helped with collections, and performed other requisite duties. His church attendance seemed to average about once a month. According to Washington's diaries, he attended services four times in the first five months of 1760 and fifteen times in the year 1768. Sometimes bad weather prevented him from making the lengthy trip, but there's also evidence that Washington visited friends, traveled, or went foxhunting instead of to church.[8] One has the sense that were he alive today, he absolutely would head to church, unless there was a really good football game on.

While at church, Washington was "always serious and attentive," reported William White, the minister at Christ Church in Philadelphia during and after the Revolution—but he never kneeled. More significant, Washington did not generally take communion, perhaps the most deeply spiritual act in the Anglican Church. In fact, he would generally leave services before his wife, Martha, who often did take the sacrament. The Reverend White explained, "Truth requires me to say, that General Washington never received the communion, in the churches of which I am parochial Minister. Mrs. Washington was a habitual communicant."[9] Dr. James Abercrombie, assistant rector of Christ Church, acknowledged that Washington was "a professing Christian" who attended regularly but added, "I cannot consider any man as a real Christian who uniformly disregards an ordinance so solemnly enjoined by the divine Author of our holy religion, and considered as a channel of divine grace." So disappointed was Abercrombie that he made a not-so-veiled reference to Washington's behavior in a sermon. "I considered it my duty, in a sermon on Public Worship, to state the unhappy tendency of *example*, particularly those in elevated stations, who invariably turned their backs upon the celebration of the Lord's Supper," Abercrombie later wrote. "I acknowledge the remark was intended for the President." A senator soon thereafter heard Washington comment on having been so reproached and explain that if he were to suddenly start taking communion, after years of not doing so, it would be viewed as "an ostentatious display of religious zeal." Significantly, Washington's solution, then, was not to start taking communion—but rather to avoid church on the Sundays when communion was being offered.[10]

Washington rarely referred to Jesus Christ or Christianity in his writings. He often spoke of God, Providence, the Great Architect, and other formulations for the deity, but to Christ in only a handful of instances, which have been widely quoted. At one point, Washington said he hoped the Continental army would consist of people acting like "good Christian soldiers"; on another occasion he told some Indian chiefs that they would do well to follow "the religion of Jesus Christ."[11] The most famous Christian invocation seemed to be in his last communication as commander of the army on June 8, 1783, when he wrote the governors that they should all "do Justice, to love mercy, and to demean ourselves with that Charity, humility, and pacific temper of mind, which were the Characteristicks of the Divine Author of the blessed Religion, and without an humble imitation of whose example in these things, we can never hope to be a happy nation." *Subsequent* reproductions of the letter mysteriously added the phrase "through Jesus Christ Our Lord" and dubbed it "Washington's Prayer."[12]

James Madison's view was that Washington was spiritual but not interested in the theological particulars of the Christian faith. Compared with the other Founding Fathers, Washington spent little time on religious exploration or debate, acting, in effect, more like a general than a philosopher. Madison did "not suppose that Washington had ever attended to the arguments for Christianity, and for the different systems of religion, or in fact that he had formed definite opinions on the subject. But he took these things as he found them existing, and was constant in his observance of worship according to the received forms of the Episcopal church in which he was brought up."[13]

That Washington was reluctant to speak about Jesus or even Christianity was not lost on others. The Reverend Samuel Miller of New York wondered how it could be that "a true Christian, in the full exercise of his mental faculties, [would] die without one expression of distinctive belief, or Christian hope."[14] Ashbel Green, one of the ministers of the Second Presbyterian Church in Philadelphia and the chaplain in the House of Representatives, attempted to prod Washington into a public embrace of Christianity. He and twenty-three other Protestant clergymen in the Philadelphia area issued an address thanking Washington on the occasion of his retirement from public service. Hoping they could get him to counter the Deistic influences of Tom Paine, they praised Washington for being a good Christian: "We are more immediately bound to acknowledge the countenance which you have uniformly given to his holy religion." Surely, they figured, Washington would respond to the missive by revealing his love of Christ. But Washington responded more generally about the importance of faith — "religion and morality are the essential pillars of civil society" — and went on to praise toleration. He concluded by referring to the "Divine Author of life and felicity." A colleague of Green's reported that the minister was disappointed with the response: "The old fox was too cunning for us."[15]

Was Washington a "good Christian"? By the definition of Christianity offered by contemporary *liberal* Christians, he would pass muster. He believed in God, attended church, endorsed the golden rule, and valued the behavioral benefits of religion. More conservative Christians, however, generally believe that being a good Christian means accepting Jesus Christ as personal savior and the Bible as God's revelation. By those standards—those of twenty-first-century conservative evangelical Christianity—Washington was not Christian.

THE GOD OF ARMIES

Still, he wasn't a Deist, either. He believed in an omnipotent and constantly intervening God—one who seemed to protect the nation as a whole and him in particular. As a colonel during the French and Indian War, Washington was in a particularly brutal gun battle, had two horses shot out from under him, and later discovered four bullet holes in his jacket—and yet he had not a scratch. Devout Christians then and now have cited this as evidence of his special place in the eye of God, a view Washington shared:[16] "By the all powerful dispensations of Providence, I have been protected beyond all human probability or expectation."[17]

As we'll see in the next chapter, Washington ascribed many battle successes to God and beseeched the troops to attend worship in order to draw the "Smiles of Providence." After victories in Saratoga and Montreal, he thanked God for His interventions. In his farewell orders on November 2, 1783, he wrote that the "singular interposition of Providence in our feeble condition were such, as could scarcely escape the attention of the most unobserving." He thanked "the God of Armies"[18] and, when he resigned his commission, turned away the compliments about his own skill by saying that his efforts resulted in part from "the support of the Supreme Power of the Union, and the patronage of Heaven."[19] He issued many orders calling for days of prayer, was heard to pronounce or call for prayers at meals, and—most important—seemed to believe that God could be influenced by the prayers and behavior of men.

The second aspect of Washington's spiritual life bound to disappoint some ardent secularists is that he, like Franklin and the other Founding Fathers, considered religion essential to the creation of a democracy. He made several comments to this effect, the most famous being his farewell address. After describing the perils of political factions and internal strife, and praising the system of checks and balances designed to ameliorate those tensions, he said that the *most* important safeguards were religion, morality, and virtue. "Of all the dispositions and habits which lead to political prosperity, religion and morality are indispensable supports. . . . Reason and experience both forbid us to expect that national morality can prevail in exclusion of religious principle."[20]

Washington's most significant contribution was his commitment to religious tolerance. Time and time again, he chose to promote an almost twenty-first-century vision of spiritual pluralism. As we'll see in the next chapter, his liberal attitude was largely prompted by the realities of war. Washington led one of the only truly national institutions, the Continental army, and had to grapple earlier than others with the practicalities of nationhood—which principles would unite, and which would divide. Bigotry, in his view, was impractical.

Though I do believe that his role as commander of the Continental army was the most important factor shaping his vision of tolerance, there may have been one other influence: He was a Mason.

Freemasonry began as an association of bricklayers and craftsmen but, in the 1720s in England, evolved into "speculative Masonry," connecting non-craftsmen and elites from a variety of callings.[21] Masonry became quite important in the colonies in the period just before, during, and after the American Revolution, providing a way for social elites from different realms to gather, form bonds, complete business deals, and promote common values. The Founding Fathers were fairly obsessed with the question of how to instill enough virtue into citizens that a republic could flourish. Institutions that could imbue personal and communal values—such as Masonic lodges and churches—were viewed as essential building blocks for democracy. "Every character, figure, and emblem, depicted in a Lodge has a moral tendency, and inculcates the practice of virtue," declared one Masonic handbook.[22] As De Witt Clinton, a prominent New York politician and Mason, put it, the "principal attention" of the order was the "cultivation of morality."[23] The Masons also emphasized science, created museums, and helped finance the construction of local schools.[24]

Though they renounced claims to being a religious organization, the Masons did have a distinct attitude about faith. First, Masonry maintained substantial symbolic ties to biblical Judaism. The original Masons claimed to have descended from Hiram Abiff, the master bricklayer for King Solomon's Temple, allegedly murdered during construction. "Rituals firmly placed Jewish biblical tradition at the heart of all Masonry," historian Steven Bullock has written.[25] In one ritual, Masons were supposed to embrace each other according to the "five Points of Fellowship"—hand to hand, foot to foot, cheek to cheek, knee to knee, and hand in back—to symbolize the raising of Hiram

Abiff's corpse from the Temple's bowels using a similar "lion's grip."[26] By the 1700s, Masonic lodges required members to believe in a Supreme Being—what they called "the Grand Architect." In the years before and after the Revolution, temples typically kept a Bible in a place of honor and used scriptural passages in their rituals.[27] For example, during a 1755 procession in Philadelphia opening the first Masonic hall in America, Benjamin Franklin's son and another Mason carried crimson cushions bearing an open Bible and the Masonic Book of Constitutions.[28]

Later, the Masons became even more explicitly and exclusively Christian—and later still were attacked by evangelicals as anti-Christian[29]—but during the period when Washington was most involved, the Masons stressed a broad religious tolerance. One central Masonic "constitution" of 1723 decreed that members were bound to "that religion in which all men agree."[30] Philadelphia's St. John's Lodge included Baptists and Presbyterians; the lodge in Newport, Rhode Island, even included Jews.[31]

To what degree was Washington influenced by Masonry? He was open about his involvement, having joined the Fredericksburg lodge in 1752 and become "Charter Worshipful Master" of Alexandria Mason Lodge No. 22 in 1788. He apparently attended few private meetings, but did participate in public Masonic rituals.[32] "Being persuaded that a just application of the principles on which the Masonic Fraternity is founded must be a promotive of private virtue and public prosperity, I shall always be happy to advance the interest of the Society and be considered by them as a deserving brother," he wrote.[33] Most dramatically, in 1793 Washington led the ceremony laying the cornerstone of the US Capitol: He wore an ornate Masonic apron and sash, placed a silver plate on the stone, and then baptized it with the Masonic symbols of corn, oil, and wine. (Depending on the interpretation, these either symbolized nourishment, refreshment, and joy; or Masonry, science, and virtue.)[34] In comments to the Pennsylvania Grand Lodge, Washington reportedly declared Masonic goals fully in sync with those of the new republic, which itself needed to become "a lodge for the virtues."[35] In one letter to a Masonic leader, Washington prayed "that the Great Architect of the Universe may bless you and receive you hereafter into his immortal Temple."[36] He was sworn in as president on a Bible borrowed from a New York Masonic temple, was surrounded in the Continental army and in his government by other Masons, and was buried with full Masonic rites. There is no direct evidence that Masonry influenced Washington's approach to tolerance—perhaps Washington developed the sensibility on his own and was attracted to the Masons because they shared his views—but at a minimum it reinforced Washington's desire for nonsectarianism.

Whatever the cause, Washington's approach to religious tolerance represented a significant departure from earlier generations. At one point, he surveyed all the possible causes of America's greatness and highlighted just two. The first was the "cheapness of land," which allowed for much of the population to become property owners. The second was "civil and religious" liberty, which "stand perhaps unrivalled by any civilized nation of earth."[37] Long before Emma Lazarus welcomed the tired and poor, Washington declared that the "bosom of America [was] open to receive, the oppressed and persecuted of all Nations and Religions, whom we shall welcome to a participation of all our rights and privileges."

7

holy war

GEORGE WASHINGTON USES RELIGIOUS TOLERANCE,
AND APPEALS TO GOD, TO WIN THE WAR OF INDEPENDENCE

———◆———

A S THE WAR BEGAN, MANY PERSISTED IN SEEING CATHOLICS AS excellent scapegoats. American clergy, newspapers, and politicians had used anti-Catholic rhetoric to stir opposition to the British. They had declared that the Quebec Act would lead to a Catholic invasion. They had claimed that the posting of Anglican bishops bore the dark influence of popery.

George Washington, however, rejected the Catholic-bashing, not so much on philosophical grounds as for practical reasons. As commander of the Continental army, he believed that unless he could neutralize Canada, he couldn't protect New England and New York from British invasions from the north. Washington hoped he could cut off this British northern front by rallying the Canadian people—especially the French Canadians living in Quebec—to a continentwide democratic revolt against the British Crown. He therefore launched an "expedition" (sometimes referred to as an "invasion") to Canada under the command of Colonel Benedict Arnold.

These particular troops had not fully mastered the art of wooing Catholics. One military chaplain on the campaign confided to his diary the thrill of attempting to destroy Catholicism to the north: "Had pleasing views of the glorious day of universal peace and spread of the gospel through the vast extended country, which has been for ages the dwelling of Satan, and the reign of the Antichrist."[1] Washington knew he had to damp down the anti-Catholicism. On September 14, 1775, he banned the practice of burning effigies of the pope once a year.[2] Moreover, he told Arnold, the troops had to move considerably beyond keeping their bigotry under wraps; they had to convince Catholics that they'd be *welcomed* into the colonial union and would flourish under the American approach to religious freedom. "Prudence, Policy and true Christian Spirit, will lead us to look with Compassion upon their Errors without insulting them," Washington wrote. His condescending comment about Catholic "errors" notwithstanding, Washington was one of the first to recognize that a revolution based on "liberty" would need to encompass a new approach to religious freedom. "While we are contending for our own Liberty," he wrote, "we should be very cautious of violating the Rights of Conscience in others, ever considering that God alone is the Judge of the Hearts of men, and to him only in this Case, they are answerable."[3]

Washington was not done purging anti-Catholic bias from the ranks. On November 5, 1775, he scolded troops in Cambridge, Massachusetts, for celebrating Pope Day. He told them of his "surprise that there should be Officers and Soldiers in this army so void of common sense" as to encourage such a "ridiculous and childish custom," especially when the colonies were soliciting aid from Canadian Catholics. "At such a juncture, and in such Circumstances, to be insulting their Religion, is so monstrous, as not to be suffered or excused."[4] Washington may also have been concerned about troop morale. Among the soldiers who had gone to aid Boston in its hour of need were Catholics from Maryland and Pennsylvania.[5] Washington's tolerance initiative succeeded. The practice of burning effigies of the pope apparently disappeared from the colonies as a result of his decree, and newspaper attacks on Catholics dwindled.[6]

The Continental Congress, which had earlier attacked the Quebec Act for helping Catholics, flip-flopped and tried to assist Washington. Just five days after issuing its attack on Catholicism, Congress fired off a letter beseeching the French Canadians to join them in the cause of freedom. The letter urged the Canadians to be suspicious of the Quebec Act's new guarantees of religious liberty for the Catholics. "What is offered to you by the late Parliament?. . . Liberty of conscience in your religion? No. God gave it to you."[7] On May 29, 1775, Congress—filled with delegates who hated

Catholicism—concluded that "we perceived the fate of the protestant and catholic colonies to be strongly linked together."[8] It was a hilariously abrupt about-face, and the Canadians were suspicious.

To be taken more seriously, in 1776 Congress sent a delegation consisting of Benjamin Franklin, Samuel Chase, and Charles Carroll, a Catholic representative from Maryland. Carroll convinced his cousin John Carroll, a Catholic priest, to join the group. But the priests they met in Montreal told the delegation that the British had indeed lived by the spirit of the Quebec Act and treated them well (in fact, much better than Catholics were treated in most of the American colonies). Furthermore, the Canadians said, they could not easily forget or ignore the hostile views expressed about Catholics after the passage of the Quebec Act.

In the course of the Revolution, Washington and Congress also became acutely aware that Catholic soldiers were shedding blood for the American cause. The Maryland militia was brimming with Catholics who helped thwart British raids from Virginia.[9] Stephen Moylan, a prominent Catholic in Pennsylvania, recruited a group of volunteers in March 1776 to rush to Boston when it was under siege. He would over time become muster-master general of the Continental army, quartermaster general, a brigadier general, George Washington's personal secretary, and commander of his own cavalry unit called the Fourth Continental Dragoons.[10] In response to a letter from notable Catholics in 1790, Washington praised "the patriotic part which you took in the accomplishment of [the] revolution."[11]

Part of the sudden appreciation of Catholics stemmed from the desire to win France as an ally. Congress heaped praise on France; even John Adams, in correspondence with his wife, began to admit grudging admiration for their religion. He'd attended Catholic Mass in Brussels and concluded that he might have been a tad "rash and unreasonable" earlier in "cursing the knavery of the priesthood and the brutal ignorance of the people."[12] Governor Greene of Rhode Island declared a public day of prayer for France, and Massachusetts followed suit. When French officials invited members of Congress to attend services at the new Catholic church in Philadelphia, several did their duty.[13] When a Catholic Spanish agent died while visiting Washington's headquarters, officials were even invited to assist at Mass. Though some objected—Benjamin Rush "declined attending as not compatible with the principles of a Protestant"—others did, and one participant, Ebenezer Hazard, described excitedly that the service included "not only Papists but Presbyterians, Episcopalians, Quakers etc. . . ." Hazard enthused that he'd witnessed "the minds of people so unfettered with the shackels of bigotry."[14] On May 5, 1778, after the alliance with France was finalized, Washington declared that it was God's work.[15]

There was one other way that military necessity spawned tolerance. Roughly one-third of the British ground troops were Hessian mercenaries. They came from a number of principalities in Germany and included Calvinists, Lutherans, Unitarians, and Roman Catholics. Congress adopted a strategy of encouraging defections among the Hessians by promising them citizenship, fifty acres of land, *and* religious freedom. A congressional resolution pointed out that "after they have violated every Christian and moral precept, by invading, and attempting to destroy, those who have never injured them or their country, their only reward, if they escape death and captivity, will be a return to the despotism of their prince." Alternatively, they could leave the military, settle in a colony, and "be protected in the free exercise of their respective religions."[16] On August 14, 1776, Congress approved this resolution and distributed thousands of copies, in German, among the troops and on the backs of tobacco wrappers. One historian estimated that somewhere between five and twelve thousand German soldiers defected.[17]

The Quebec situation was not the only time when Washington viewed religious tolerance warmly as a result of his unique vantage point atop a national institution. In 1775, the Rhode Island brigade appointed as chaplain John Murray, the founder of American Universalism, a brand of Christianity that denied the divinity of Jesus and believed that all men and women would gain salvation. Orthodox Christian clergymen loathed Universalism because they believed that removing the threat of hell undercut the basic enforcement mechanism for moral behavior. The other chaplains stationed in Cambridge petitioned Washington to have Murray fired. In September 1775, Washington responded tersely, "The Revd. Mr. John Murray is appointed Chaplain to the Rhode-Island Regiments and is to be respected as such."[18] Washington was not intending to make a particular statement about Universalism but recognized that his troops, and his nation, comprised different religious "sects" that ought to be able to choose their own religious leaders. For the same reason, Washington opposed a proposal from the Continental Congress to appoint chaplains on a brigade level, instead of based on smaller regimental groups, a system that would have made it less likely that the chaplain would represent the denominations of the soldiers to which he was ministering. Such an approach, he explained, "would compel men to a mode of Worship which they do not profess." Instead, having chaplains matched to local sensibilities was "founded on a plan of more generous toleration."[19]

In that sense, the inherent pluralism of the Continental army helped spread tolerance throughout the colonies. Neighbors formerly viewed as "dissenters" or heretics—on the other side of a divide—were now sharing common cause in a holy struggle against a common enemy. The Continental army consisted of Baptist Rhode Islanders, Dutch Reformed New Yorkers, New Jersey Presbyterians, Connecticut Congregationalists, and even Maryland Catholics.[20] They fought and slept alongside one another, or traveled to new parts of the land where they were fed and cared for by locals of different religious and cultural backgrounds. They observed as patriot clergy of different faiths offered spiritual and physical shelter. The Presbyterian and Baptist churches in Morristown, New Jersey, turned over their buildings to the army for use as hospitals,[21] while in Pennsylvania support was offered by Lutherans, Reformed, and even German mystical sects.[22] As veterans, the men who witnessed this behavior would later constitute the leadership of the nation.[23]

NEUTRAL BUT NOT SECULAR

Washington was a strong believer in the importance of religion as a force to improve conduct and obedience—and he was not shy about using the power of his military office to promote religion for those purposes. Earlier in his career, he had argued for chaplains on the grounds that they would "improve morale and discourage gambling, swearing and drunkenness."[24] On July 9, 1776, he issued the order authorizing military chaplains for the Continental army. Washington hoped the chaplains would encourage morality and virility. He praised one Reverend Abiel Leonard as typifying the ideal chaplain who helps "animate the Soldiery and impress them with a knowledge of the important rights we are contending for,"[25] as well as for "holding forth the Necessity of courage and bravery and at the same time of Obedience and Subordination to those in Command."[26] Washington viewed religion partly as a disciplinary tool and made it clear to the officers that attendance at services was part of good command and control. It "will reflect great credit on the army in general, tend to improve the morals, and at the same time, to increase the happiness of the soldiery."[27]

Washington also believed that they could only win if God was on their side, nothing being more important in victory than the "favour of divine providence."[28] To secure God's support, the soldiers would not only have to fire their muskets well but also behave in a way that the Lord would admire. Referring to himself in the third person, he wrote, "The General hopes and trusts, that every officer and man will endeavor to live and act as becomes a Christian soldier, defending the dearest rights and liberties of his country."[29] When the chaplains were not having quite the desired effects, Washington huffily issued a new order reporting, "The General is sorry to be informed that foolish and wicked practice of profane cursing and swearing (a vice hitherto little known in the American Army) is growing into fashion"; he urged a crackdown lest the army lose divine support. "We can have but little hopes of the blessing of heaven on our Arms, if we insult it by our impiety and folly," he said. On May 2, 1778, he required chaplain-led services to be held each Sunday at eleven. The goal: "To the distinguished character of a Patriot, it should be our highest glory to add the more distinguished character of a Christian."[30] He thought it important that the soldiers and the rest of the citizenry embrace special days of fasting. These, he said, would "incline the Lord, and Giver of Victory, to prosper our arms."[31]

Time after time, Washington ascribed battlefield developments to God's intervention. On September 13, 1777, he praised soldiers for their fight a few days earlier and said that with "another Appeal to Heaven" they would win again.[32] After General Horatio Gates's victory over General John Burgoyne in Saratoga the next month, Washington ordered thanksgiving services and declared: "Let every face brighten, and every heart expand with grateful Joy and praise to the supreme disposer of all events, who has granted us this signal success."[33] After victory at Yorktown, on October 20, 1781, Washington urged troops to attend a special service to show gratitude for the "astonishing interpositions of Providence" during the war.[34]

This sense of holy war helped energize and motivate some of the troops. "Most revolutionary spokesmen believed that service in the Continental army had a clear religious meaning for the soldier," wrote historian Charles Royster. "A recruit could enlist in two armies at once—the continental Army for the salvation of his country and Christ's army for the salvation of his soul."[35] On the standards carried by the Third Connecticut Regiment was the motto AN APPEAL TO HEAVEN. "Resistance to Tyrants Is Obedience to God" was carried by Pennsylvania troops.[36] The pastors' influence was not limited to words spoken from the pews. Yale president Ezra Stiles wrote in his diary of military marches at least partly organized by the ministers: "East Guilford—83 armed, with Mr. Todd their pastor. Haddam—100 armed—

animated by Rev. Mr. May. Chatham—100 marched with Rev. Mr. Board-
man, Pastor."[37] Millennial fervor continued as the war progressed. In praying
for the Sixth Pennsylvania Battalion in March 1776, Chaplain William Linn
asked for their safety and added, "Above all, may the peaceful reign of king
Jesus soon commence, when the earth shall be filled with the knowledge of
the Lord, and the inhabitants thereof learn war no more."[38]

American victories against the mighty British army and navy led many to
invoke not only the armies-of-Israel metaphor but also that of David and Go-
liath. In 1779, the Continental Congress reminded Americans how the nation had "without arms, ammunition, discipline, revenue, government or
ally, with a 'staff and a sling' only, dared, 'in the name of the Lord of Hosts,'
to engage a gigantic adversary."[39] In his most bitter moments, Washington de-
spaired that he must surely rely on God because he wasn't going to be able to
count on his poorly trained and occasionally mutinous army. "Providence
has heretofore saved us in remarkable manner and on this we must principally rely."[40]

Since the leaders assumed that God's favor needed to be earned, they
sometimes ascribed defeats not to bad soldiering but to immorality. At some
points during the war, John Adams feared that the cause would fail because
he saw too much greed and commercialism in the colonies. "I have seen all
my life such selfishness and littleness even in New England, that I sometimes
tremble to think that, although we are engaged in the best cause that ever employed the human heart, yet the prospect of success is doubtful not for want
of power or wisdom but of virtue." During the Revolution, Adams, evoking
the manner of his Puritan ancestors, told his friend Benjamin Rush that the
colonials would only have a chance of winning "if we fear God and repent
our sins."[41] He even speculated that God might intend for America to be defeated so that its "vicious and luxurious and effeminate appetites, passion and
habits" would be cleansed, laying the foundation for a better deserved victory
in the future. Adams wasn't alone in seeing the events on the ground as a reflection—positive *and* negative—of God's assessment. One minister ascribed
the Continental army's difficulties to the presence of slavery.[42] Noting the
brutal winter, the poor crops, the loss of cattle, and the seemingly imminent
collapse of the army, a Quaker farmer speculated that it was part of a divinely
ordained set of plagues.[43] When on July 20, 1775, the Continental Congress called for a day of prayer, it was accompanied by a call for fasting, self-
reflection, and a unified effort to "unfeignedly confess and deplore our many
sins."

Given the tremendous debate in recent years over whether the Founders believed America was a "Christian nation," it's worth noting that, at this particular moment, the Continental Congress seemed to view it that way. Most public declarations simply assumed a Christian audience and vocabulary. On November 1, 1777, representatives approved a resolution to celebrate December 18 as a time of thanksgiving and call for acts to "please God through merits of Jesus Christ" and to nourish "the means of religion, for the promotion and enlargement of that Kingdom, which consisteth 'in righteousness, peace and joy in the Holy ghost.' "[44]

Were there cynical motives to all the invocations of God? Were they merely using whatever language was most likely to rally colonists? It does not appear that Washington viewed it that way. But perhaps a few others did. Thomas Jefferson wrote that in 1774 he had "rummaged" through Puritan writings and "cooked up" a resolution for a day of fasting, humiliation, and prayer "under the conviction of the necessity of arousing our people from the lethargy into which they had fallen."[45] The edge of cynicism in Jefferson's comment serves as a reminder that while the nation's birth was profoundly influenced by the passions of the two former Puritans, Adams and Franklin, and the visionary farsightedness of Washington, it was also shaped by the more radical vision—and the furious spiritual journey—of the sage of Monticello.

8

thomas jefferson

THE PIOUS INFIDEL

———◆———

To UNDERSTAND THOMAS JEFFERSON—AND THE RELIGIOUS CON-
cepts embodied in the Declaration of Independence—we must flash
forward to 1803. There sat Jefferson in the new presidential mansion in Washington City. Done with his official work for the day, he opened his Bible—
not to pray, but to cut. He scoured the text for Jesus's greatest teachings, sliced
out his favorite portions, and glued them into an empty volume. He called it
"The Philosophy of Jesus." In 1819, he started over and created a new version
called "The Life and Morals of Jesus of Nazareth," often referred to now as
the Jefferson Bible. In Jefferson's version, Jesus was not divine.

The virgin birth—gone.

Christ's bodily resurrection—gone.

The miracles of the loaves, walking on water, raising Lazarus—none of
them made Jefferson's book.

He transformed the Bible from the revelation of God into a collection of
teachings of a brilliant, wise religious reformer—author of "the most sublime
and benevolent code of morals which has ever been offered to man." Conservatives who can't bear to think that the Declaration of Independence was
written by a Bible defacer have spread the rumor that Jefferson did this to create an ethical guide to civilize American Indians. "The so-called 'Jefferson
Bible' was really a tool to introduce the teachings of Jesus to the Indians," de-

clared the Reverend D. James Kennedy.[1] Actually, Jefferson's editing of the Bible flowed directly from a well-thought-out, long-stewing view that Christianity had been fundamentally corrupted—by the Apostle Paul, by the early church, by great Protestant reformers such as Martin Luther and John Calvin, and by nearly the entire clerical class for more than a millennium. Secularists love to point to the Jefferson Bible as evidence of his heathen nature, but that misses the point, too. Jefferson was driven to edit the Bible the way a parent whose child had been kidnapped is driven to find the culprit. Jefferson *loved* Jesus and was attempting to rescue him.

Most historians who study the Declaration of Independence and Jefferson's ideas look to the philosophers who influenced him most, some emphasizing John Locke,[2] others the Scotsman Frances Hutcheson. And there's no question that these men shaped Jefferson's approach to knowledge, reason, and freedom of religion. But reading through Jefferson's writings on faith reveals not only an idealistic philosophy but a deep rage as well. To understand his views on liberty, we must tap into this fury. Jefferson believed that a secret to religious freedom was destroying the concept of heresy, the crime of expressing unauthorized religious thought. And he cared deeply—personally, passionately—about heresy because, in the context of his times, Thomas Jefferson was a heretic, and wanted to live in a nation that tolerated men like him.

DIAMONDS AND DUNG

Jefferson had studied early Christian history and was particularly influenced by Joseph Priestley's book *The History of the Corruptions of Christianity*, which he read "over and over again."[3] In Jefferson's view, Christianity was ruined almost from the start. "But a short time elapsed after the death of the great reformer of the Jewish religion, before his principles were departed from by those who professed to be his special servants, and perverted into an engine for enslaving mankind, and aggrandizing their oppressors in church and state." The authors of the canonical Gospels were "ignorant, unlettered men" who laid "a groundwork of vulgar ignorance, of things impossible, of superstitions, fanaticisms, and fabrications."[4] The Apostle Paul made things worse. "Of this band of dupes and imposters, Paul was the great Coryphaeus, and first corrupter of the doctrines of Jesus."[5]

Then the Council of Nicaea and other clerical bodies designed elaborate doctrines that abandoned Jesus and brought great harm to the world, Jefferson believed. Take, for instance, the concept of the Trinity. "Ideas must be distinct before reason can act upon them; and no man ever had a distinct idea of the trinity," he declared. "It is mere Abracadabra of the mountebanks calling themselves the priests of Jesus"[6] and the "hocus-pocus phantasm of a god like another Cerberus, with one body and three heads."[7] The immaculate conception was preposterous, too, Jefferson believed, and would someday be "classed with the fable of the generation of Minerva in the brain of Jupiter."[8]

The Protestant Reformation made things no better. John Calvin stressed the idea of predestination: that God had chosen some to be saved, and their behavior couldn't alter their fate. This idea—at the heart of the faiths practiced by a majority of Americans at the time—disgusted Jefferson. "Calvinism has introduced into the Christian religion more new absurdities than its leader [Jesus] had purged it of old ones," he explained.[9] What would have been the proper response to the "insanities of Calvin"? The "strait jacket alone was their proper remedy."[10] Like Adams, Jefferson was most bothered by this philosophy because it undermined morality. Any religion that eliminated good behavior as the path to salvation merited no respect, and any God who picked the favored few without considering the lives they led was an imposter, in Jefferson's view. Therefore, he said, Calvin "was indeed an atheist, which I can never be; or rather his religion was Daemonism. If ever man worshiped a false god, he did."[11]

Jefferson did not believe Jesus was divine. "That Jesus did not mean to impose himself on mankind as the son of god physically speaking I have been convinced by the writings of men more learned than myself," he wrote. But he added that Jesus "might conscientiously believe himself inspired from above"; because his milieu of Judaism stressed that leadership was invariably based on divine revelation, Jesus might have breathed "the fumes of the most disordered imaginations."[12]

The entire ministerial class—the "priests," as he called all clergy and theologians—was pervasively corrupt, having a vested interest in making Christianity opaque. "Sweep away their gossamer fabrics of fictitious religion, and they would catch no more flies."[13] The history of clerical leadership was a relentless, obsessive, and wicked focus on peripheral matters for the purpose of dividing and oppressing—"vestments, ceremonies, physical opinions, and metaphysical speculations, totally unconnected with morality, and unimportant to the legitimate objects of society."[14] He noted the centuries of bloodshed justified in the name of the Prince of Peace, declaring that Protestant catechisms and creeds have "made of Christendom a slaughter-house, and at this day divides it into castes of inextinguishable hatred to one another."[15] Year after year, priests managed to take the "purest system of morals ever before preached to man," and twist it into a "mere contrivance to filch wealth and power to themselves."[16] He was convinced that the obfuscation was often deliberate, since the "mild and simple" principles of Jesus required little explanation. Priests therefore had to "sophisticate it, ramify it, split it into hairs, and twist its texts till they cover the divine morality of its author with mysteries, and require a priesthood to explain them."[17]

To an extent rarely acknowledged, Jefferson also despised Jews—or at least the Jews of the Old Testament and the religion it seemed to spawn. The "vicious ethics" of the Jews[18] were "irreconcilable with the sound dictates of reason & morality," encouraged poor relationships among people, and were downright "repulsive and anti-social, as respecting other nations." When he began to sketch out a "syllabus" about the life of Jesus, Jefferson explained that the Jewish God bore attributes that "were degrading and injurious."[19] This God was depicted as "cruel, vindictive, capricious and unjust."[20] Though his negative attitude about Judaism seemed mostly confined to antiquity, he occasionally revealed an up-to-date bias. Referring to irksome New England Federalists, Jefferson declared that "they are marked, like the Jews, with . . . a perversity of character."[21] Referring to the Quaker tendency to support the British, he said contemptuously, "Dispersed, as the Jews, they still form, as those do, one nation, foreign to the land they live in."[22]

In contrast with Adams, Jefferson was convinced that organized religion invariably opposed freedom. "In every country and in every age, the priest has been hostile to liberty," he said. The dynamic repeated itself throughout history: Unable to spread their principles through persuasion, religious leaders instead relied on the power and support of the state, in exchange for offering the ruler the legitimacy and moral authority of the church. "He is always in alliance with the despot, abetting his abuses in return for protection to his own."[23] These alliances of government and clergy—a "loathsome combination of church and state"—brutalized the people throughout history.[24] While James Madison focused on the threat to religion from government, Jefferson wrote more about the effects of religion, and religious leaders, on government, not only in ancient history but in contemporary America as well. By getting themselves "ingrafted into the machine of government," he said, the New England clergy "have been a very formidable engine against the civil and religious rights of man."[25] The priesthood discouraged *thinking*, which was essential for republicanism, so a powerful church hierarchy—especially one entangled with or supported by government—was a great threat to liberty.

The more one reads Jefferson railing against the "priests," the more one is struck by how personal it seems. It is not merely Jesus who was maligned by the priests, but Jefferson. The opinions reviewed above—against the Trinity, the virgin birth, the divinity of Christ, Calvin, and so on—were violently at odds with orthodox Christianity in Jefferson's time. And Jefferson was conscious of how the clerical class punished such heresies. In *Notes on the State of Virginia*, for instance, he reviewed the penal laws governing religious belief. "According to an act of 1705, those who don't believe in the Trinity or that scriptures are of 'divine authority' are punishable in the first instance by being banned from holding public office; on the second, a father may lose custody of his children and be sentenced to three years in jail." It was after summarizing these horrors that Jefferson wrote the words that would get him in trouble during the 1800 presidential election: "The legitimate powers of government extend to such acts only as are injurious to others. But it does me no injury for my neighbour to say there are twenty gods, or no god. It neither picks my pocket nor breaks my leg."

I'm certainly not arguing that Jefferson wanted to change the laws because he feared imminent arrest. But I do believe that for him, the idea that people with unorthodox views should be tolerated was no mere abstraction. During the 1800 campaign, the *"genus irritable vatum"*—irritable tribe of priests—were "all in arms against me" and "printing lying pamphlets against me" and spreading "absolute falsehoods." They wanted to preserve or extend their religious establishments—government support of religion—and Jefferson opposed them. "They believe that any portion of power confided to me, will be exerted in opposition to their schemes. And they believe rightly; for I have sworn upon the altar of god, eternal hostility against every form of tyranny over the mind of man."[26]

Indeed, after reading several letters in which he described how Jesus was maltreated by the priestly class and other letters in which Jefferson described how *he* was abused by the clergy, one cannot help but wonder whether Jefferson identified his own plight with that of the earlier misunderstood sage. In August 1801, soon after the bruising election, Jefferson wrote to his attorney general, Levi Lincoln, about how the New England clergy was showing him "no mercy." Unself-consciously, he declared that while "they crucified their Savior," the "laws of the present day withhold their hands from blood"—but that "lies and slander remain to them."[27] Was he writing about Jesus, or himself, when he declared: "The office of reformer of the superstitions of a nation is ever dangerous"? Jesus's efforts to reform religion, he said, were perilous. "A step to right or left might place him within the grip of the priests of the superstition, a blood thirsty race."[28] Same for Jefferson.[29]

His counterattacks defended himself and Jesus at the same time. "While I have classed [the priests] with soothsayers and necramancers, I place him among the greatest of the reformers of morals, and scourges of priest-craft that have ever existed," he wrote. "They felt him as such, and never rested until they had silenced him by death."[30]

RESCUING JESUS

It was during the 1800 election that Jefferson's faith was attacked most stridently (more on that in chapter 15). In the second year of his presidency, he sensed the criticisms rising again, in part because Tom Paine, now famous for his Deist writings, had returned to America from France. Jefferson's first efforts to slice up the Bible were, to some degree, about justifying his own life and faith. Of his first Jesus book, "The Philosophy of Jesus," Jefferson wrote: "It is a document in proof that I am a real Christian, that is to say, a disciple of the doctrines of Jesus, very different from the Platonists, who call me infidel and themselves Christians."[31] In a separate letter, he asserted again the authenticity of his faith: "I am a Christian, in the only sense he wished any one to be; sincerely attached to his doctrines, in preference to all others; ascribing to himself every <u>human</u> excellence; & believing he never claimed any other."[32]

So Jefferson set out to create a Bible as he thought Jesus would have wanted it. This meant pulling "diamonds" (the wisdom of Jesus) from the "dunghill" (the conglomeration of lies and fiction that made up the rest of the Bible). Poor Jesus, he said, had for centuries "been inveloped by Jugglers to make money of him" who have "dressed up in the rags of an Imposter."[33] Jefferson's task was to remove the artifice to reveal that "a more precious morsel of ethics was never seen."[34] So in 1803, he created a "syllabus" outlining the key points about Jesus's story and teachings. In May, he got from Joseph Priestley copies of a Unitarian analysis of the Bible called *A Harmony of the Evangelists in English and A Harmony of the Evangelists in Greek*.[35] Initially, he had hoped to get Priestley—who had fled Britain to escape religious persecution for his Universalist views—to undertake the task of creating an authentic Bible. But Priestley died before making much progress.

In February 1804, Jefferson received two Bibles in English and two in Greek and Latin. He clipped his favorite passages and pasted them in double columns on forty-six "octavo sheets."[36] "It was the work of 2 or 3 nights only, at Washington, after getting thro' the evening task of reading the letters and papers of the day," he wrote years later.[37] He did not end up using the Greek; in fact, the forty-six-page book was lost to history. Historian Dickinson Adams recently reconstructed the document by taking copies of the sliced-up Bibles—which *had* been saved—and studying the holes. The book, which Jefferson never showed anyone, was called "The Philosophy of Jesus of Nazareth extracted from the account of his life and doctrines as given by Matthew, Mark, Luke, & John. Being an abridgement of the New Testament for the use of the Indians unembarrassed with matters of faith beyond the level of their comprehensions."[38]

Jefferson returned to the project in 1819. His goal was still to "justify the character of Jesus against the fictions of his pseudo-followers" in order "to rescue his character."[39] This time, he used Greek, Latin, French, and English translations, pasting the key passages in four vertical columns on loose sheets. Once bound, the book was eight and a quarter inches tall and five inches wide; its red leather cover has "The Morals of Jesus" engraved in gilt on its back. While "The Philosophy of Jesus" included only moral precepts, "The Life and Morals of Jesus of Nazareth" included some of his actions as well.

This book offered a religion sans miracles or supernatural interventions. Jefferson deleted Gabriel's explanation that the Holy Ghost would be coming to Mary. He placed Jesus in the manger but skipped the angels appearing to the shepherds. Jesus's baptism was mentioned, but the heavens didn't open and God's spirit didn't descend like a dove. Portions of Jesus's story that dealt with morality—kicking the money changers out of the Temple and the Sermon on the Mount—received great attention. Jesus was extraordinary but not holy. In presenting the Beatitudes, Jefferson passed over Matthew's line "Be ye perfect even as your Father in heaven is perfect" and instead used "Be ye, therefore, merciful, as your Father in heaven also is merciful."

The best explication of the theological implications of Jefferson's choices comes from historian Edwin Gaustad, who summarized: "If a moral lesson was embedded in a miracle, the lesson survived in Jeffersonian scripture, but the miracle did not. Even when this took some rather careful cutting with scissors or razor, Jefferson managed to maintain Jesus' role as a great moral teacher, not as a shaman or faith healer." A most dramatic example: In Matthew 12:9–10, a man with a withered hand approached Jesus. Jesus responded to the Pharisees' questions about the lawfulness of healing on the Sabbath, and then healed the man. Jefferson kept the disquisition on the Sabbath—"The Sabbath was made for man, and not man for the Sabbath"—but left the hand unhealed. Gaustad made an insightful comparison between the messages of Jesus and Jefferson. In the Gospels, he said, Jesus "distinguished between what was centralized and what was peripheral in the moral life. A man was defiled not because of what he ate but because of what he said and, even more, what he did." Jefferson, he continued, "merely carried the principle of the essential versus redundant further," by eliminating material that obscured the essential truths. "Too much dross concealed the gold; too much dung buried the diamonds." Jefferson deleted all passages that asserted Jesus's divinity, many of which are in the Gospel according to John. "When quoting from John," Gaustad noted, "Jefferson kept his blade busy."[40] Tellingly, the Jefferson Bible ends with the line from Matthew, after Jesus is laid to rest. "There laid they Jesus, And rolled a great stone to the door of the sepulchre, and departed." In Jefferson's Bible, Jesus never rises.[41]

In further writings, Jefferson elaborated on what he loved about Jesus. While other philosophers, such as Socrates, focused on how humans could govern their passions to procure "our own tranquility," Jesus forced people to connect to a larger whole.[42] While the early Jews thought like a parochial tribe, Jesus extended the principles of neighborliness to "all mankind, gathering all into one family, under the bonds of love, charity, peace, common wants and common aids." Jewish law focused on actions, but Jesus "pushed his scrutinies into the heart of man; erected his tribunal in the region of his thoughts, and purified the waters at the fountain head."[43] Moses had "bound the Jews to many idle ceremonies, mummeries, and observances, of no effect towards producing the social utilities which constitute the essence of virtue. Jesus exposed their futility and insignificance. The one instilled into his people the most anti-social spirit toward other nations; the other preached philanthropy and universal charity and benevolence."[44] Though he did excise the miracles from the Bible, Jefferson praised Jesus for teaching "the belief of a future state."[45] (Note, however, that Jefferson mostly applauded the idea of heaven's existence because of the practical effect it would have on temporal human behavior.) Jefferson was an optimist. In Jesus, he found a man who called upon the best of human nature, not one who harped upon the worst. Shortly before he went to bed each night, Jefferson made a practice of spending a half hour to an hour reading "something moral, whereon to ruminate in the intervals of sleep." Scholars believe that this handcrafted volume of teachings from the man he considered the most masterly moral teacher in history was one of the books Jefferson used to infuse moral wisdom into his dreams.[46]

For those who think that Jefferson was indifferent about which kind of religion was practiced (be there "twenty gods, or no god"), it's worth noting that he clearly viewed the message of Jesus as superior to all others. In fact, he thought that if people could just see Jesus's unadulterated teachings, Christianity would conquer the world. "Had the doctrines of Jesus been preached always as pure as they came from his lips, the whole civilized world would now have been Christian."[47]

And yet despite his clear love of Jesus, Jefferson was desperate to keep this Bible project secret. Each friend he showed it to was cautioned to practice discretion. Don't show it; don't discuss it; and whatever you do, don't let it get published, he said. "Every word which goes forth from me, whether verbally or in writing, becomes the subject of so much malignant distortion, and perverted construction, that I am obliged to caution my friends against the possibility of my letters getting into the public papers."[48] After his friend Benjamin Rush died, Jefferson actually went to the trouble of asking the surviving family to return any letters in which he had expressed his views about Jesus.[49] In explaining why he refused to make public his ethics-of-Jesus document, Jefferson wrote, "I was unwilling to draw on myself a swarm of insects, whose buzz is more disquieting than their bite." In showing the syllabus to Attorney General Levi Lincoln, he warned that should it become public, he "would become the butt" of endless priestly attacks.[50]

How sad that Jefferson believed—accurately, no doubt—that he did not yet live in a country free enough that he could publish his real views on religion without it leading to relentless attacks on his character. When one of his friends, Charles Thomson, broke the vow and showed some of Jefferson's Jesus work to acquaintances, a rumor spread that Jefferson had altered his religious views and become more orthodox. He sternly wrote to one woman who had inquired about the change, "A change from what? The priests indeed have heretofore thought proper to ascribe to me religious, or rather antireligious sentiments, of their own fabric." Referring to himself in the third person, he continued, "They wished him to be thought Atheist, Deist, or Devil"—but no curious onlooker could possibly know his heart. "I have ever thought religion a concern purely between our god and our consciences, for which we were accountable to him, and not the priests. I never told my own religion, nor scrutinized that of another." And then the man who had been labeled an "infidel" throughout his life declared, "My opinion is that there would never have been an infidel, if there had never been a priest."[51]

THE SCIENCE OF GOD

All these anti-Christian comments by Jefferson have led to some comic contortions on the part of Christian conservatives reluctant to completely give up on such an important Founding Father. Conservative minister D. James Kennedy, for instance, noted that Jefferson attended church regularly, gave donations to ten different churches, and, as we'll see later, allowed for some government support of religion. A glass-half-full kind of preacher, Kennedy asserted that the man who put razor to Scripture was, in his dedication to understanding the text, "a Bible scholar." As for the unfortunate matter of Jefferson rejecting Jesus's divinity, Kennedy forgivingly wrote, "He faithfully studied it, but apparently, there was no one there to guide him, and he came to a rejection of the deity of Christ."[52] But the most creative rationalization for how we could have such an anti-Christian Founding Father has come from Tim LaHaye, who declared simply that Jefferson wasn't really a Founding Father. "Thomas Jefferson, the closet Unitarian who had nothing to do with the founding of our nation (he was in France being humanized by the French skeptics of the Enlightenment at the time), was no friend of faith."[53]

LaHaye need not despair, for there was another facet to Jefferson's theology.

Though one of the most Deistic of the Founding Fathers, even Jefferson was not a full-fledged Deist if we accept that philosophy as having had two fundamental tenets: a rejection of biblical revelation *and* a conviction that God, having created the laws of the universe, had receded from day-to-day control and intervention. Jefferson clearly did agree with the first part of Deism. But he did not agree with the second.

Jefferson seemed to believe in a God who was still present in, and intervened in, the lives of men and nations. After having read Jefferson attack so many of the legs of religion, it might seem jarring to now read his regular invocations of God as a personal force in life—sometimes in terms so direct and literal, they surpass those of today's politicians. In his first inaugural address, he declared that we should be "acknowledging and adoring an overruling Providence, which by all its dispensations proves that it delights in the happiness of man here and his greater happiness hereafter."[54] In his first message to

Congress, in 1801, he thanked the "beneficent Being" who instilled in the warring politicians a (temporary) "spirit of conciliation and forgiveness."[55] In his second message, he credited the "smiles of Providence" for economic prosperity, peace abroad, and even good relations with the Indians. He never stopped asserting the importance of separating church and state, but he did this in the context of repeated public pronouncements about the powerful role of an intervening God in the fate of America. These two somewhat contradictory themes came together most directly in his second inaugural address. In the first part of the speech, he defended his practice of not issuing days of fasting or thanksgiving proclamations. But toward the end, he said that to avoid making the mistakes to which he, as a human, was prone, "I shall need, too, the favor of that Being in whose hands we are, who led our fathers, as Israel of old, from their native land and planted them in a country flowing with all the necessaries and comforts of life."[56]

Some look at Jefferson's public pronouncements and sense cynicism. Recall his comment about "cooking up" an effective prayer proclamation to rally lethargic Americans. Perhaps he was just being a pol, using the language he thought would most appeal to his audience. But the evidence is stronger that Jefferson genuinely believed in a personal God and a spirit life. For one thing, he went much further in his public pronouncements than he needed to, attributing a wide range of events and policies to God's "smiles." More important, his private letters reflected a similar view about the nature of God. In a letter to Eliza Trist, he declared that "it is not easy to reconcile ourselves to the many useless miseries to which Providence seems to expose us. But his justice affords a prospect that we shall all be made even some day."[57] In 1763, he wrote John Page that if we hope to fortify ourselves from misfortunes, "The only method of doing this is to assume a perfect resignation to the Divine will, to consider whatever does happen, must happen."[58] In 1801, he commended one's "endeavours to the Being, in whose hand we are."[59] When Napoleon was defeated, he wrote to a friend: "It proves that we have a god in heaven. That he is just, and not careless of what passes in the world."[60]

How could this ultra-rationalist—a believer in science and reason—so fully embrace a supernatural God watching over our lives? This is another case in which today's activists and scholars, by applying the standards and definitions of our time, misunderstand the ideas of a Founding Father. Remember: In this era before Charles Darwin, most of the Enlightenment leaders were *not* arguing against the existence of God. On the contrary, they argued that the laws of science actually *proved* the existence of God, if one knew how to look at it the right way.

Jefferson believed that our spiritual journeys must be led by reason, not faith. In a letter to his nephew Peter Carr, he urged rigorous application of scientific principles to the Bible. For instance, he encouraged Carr to look at the story of Joshua making the sun stand still and then added, "You are astronomer enough to know how contrary it is to the law of nature that a body revolving on its axis, as the earth does, should have stopped" without then having "prostrated animals, trees, buildings." Jefferson conceded that such an investigation might take the young man away from God. "Do not be frightened from this inquiry by any fear of its consequences. If it ends in a belief that there is no God, you will find incitements to virtue in the comfort and pleasantness you feel in its exercise, and the love of others which it will procure you." If, on the other hand, "you find reason to believe there is a God," you will find comfort and happiness in that, too. And you should not feel badly or anti-God should your mind take you away from the church, since "your own reason is the only oracle given you by heaven."[61]

It's not absurd to read such passages and conclude that Jefferson was a relativist. If it's up to everyone's individual reasoning process to determine religious truth, then is there any genuine reality? This impression was reinforced by his statement in *Notes on the State of Virginia* that "it does me no injury for my neighbour to say there are twenty gods, or no god."[62] But Jefferson did believe in religious truth; he just had an overriding conviction that it was reason, acting in a marketplace of ideas, that would lead people to find it. "It is error alone which needs the support of government. Truth can stand by itself."[63]

Jefferson himself was *not* an agnostic on this point. He applied reason and critical scientific thought to the world and concluded that God *does* exist. Read this extraordinary letter from Jefferson to John Adams on April 11, 1823, and it's possible to see how his anti-Christian, rationalist approach nonetheless led him to a deep love of God.[64]

I hold (without appeal to revelation) that when we take a view of the Universe, in its parts general or particular, it is impossible for the human mind not to perceive and feel a conviction of design, consummate skill, and indefinite power in every atom of its composition. The movements of the heavenly bodies, so exactly held in their course by the balance of centrifugal and centripetal forces, the structure of our earth itself, with its distribution of lands, waters and atmosphere, animal and vegetable bodies, examined in all their minutest particles, insects mere atoms of life, yet as perfectly organised as man or mammoth, the mineral substances, their generation and uses, it is impossible, I say, for the human mind not to believe that there is, in all this, design, cause and effect, up to an ultimate cause, a fabricator of all things from matter and motion, their preserver and regulator while permitted to exist in their present forms, and their regenerator into new and other forms.

We see, too, evident proofs of the necessity of a superintending power to maintain the Universe in its course and order. Stars, well known, have disappeared, new ones have come into view, comets, in their incalculable courses, may run foul of suns and planets and require renovation under other laws; certain races of animals are become extinct; and, were there no restoring power, all existences might extinguish successively, one by one, until all should be reduced to a shapeless chaos. So irresistible are these evidences of an intelligent and powerful Agent that, of the infinite numbers of men who have existed thro' all time, they have believed, in the proportion of a million at least to Unit, in the hypothesis of an eternal pre-existence of a creator, rather than in that of a self-existent Universe.

Yes, Thomas Jefferson—hero of modern liberals—believed in intelligent design.

Even though most of Jefferson's important actions on behalf of religious liberty took place from 1776 to 1809, the quotations in this chapter are taken from throughout his life. His anger at the priesthood intensified as he aged, and his focus on Jesus sharpened, but the basics of Jefferson's views were there all along. What emerges is a picture of Thomas Jefferson that belies stereotypes created by modern culture warriors. He was anti-Christian and pro-Jesus. He was anti-religion and pro-God. He was against blind faith and in favor of reason-based belief. He turned to the power of science to explain the world, and to prove the existence of God. As he put it later, he was a "sect by myself."[65]

How does this all relate to the history of religious freedom in America? What it shows is that the classical view of how Jefferson came to support the separation of church and state and fight for religious freedom—that his views grew out of his study of Locke and other thinkers—misses one part of the picture. The author of the Declaration of Independence was on a personal spiritual journey that took him outside the mainstream. He resented being considered a heretic, because he believed that his approach to God and Jesus was more faithful to both of them. He believed that oppression of "the mind" not only led to persecution but also constrained the process of rational exploration that would lead to religious truth. This was no mere abstraction for him. He knew that had he been forced to believe the official line, he would have been deprived of an unobstructed journey to God. Jefferson wanted religious freedom in part because he wanted to be, religiously, free.

9

nature's god meets the supreme judge

THE DECLARATION OF INDEPENDENCE AND
THE GOD COMPROMISE

◆

WHEN CONGRESS DECLARED INDEPENDENCE ON JULY 2, 1776,
Jefferson and the other delegates had just recently heard about George
Washington's smashing success in driving the British from Boston. A few
might even have heard of America's defense of Fort Moultrie in South Carolina from British attack in late June. But by August 2, 1776, when they finally
gathered in Independence Hall to sign the document, the tide had shifted.
Some thirty-two thousand British troops, thirty battleships, and twelve hundred cannon had gathered in New York Harbor to take control of New York
and cut the North from the South. In that darkening context, the delegates to
the convention affixed their names and pledged their lives, fortunes, and sacred honor—"with a firm reliance on the protection of Divine Providence."

Who was this Divine Providence that would be protecting them? As they
scratched their names below that phrase, did the delegates imagine the aloof
god of the Deists, who had created the laws of nature but did not meddle in
the lives of mortals? Or was He the God of the Bible, poised to protect them
in their coming ordeal?

The members of Congress probably had a sense of what Thomas Jefferson
believed on the matter. Though the full depth of his antagonism toward "the

priests" would not become known until later, Jefferson had shared with his congressional colleagues some of his irreligious views. Remarkably, according to an eyewitness account from Benjamin Rush, Jefferson had come right out and voiced his "objections to Christianity" in the very session of the Continental Congress in which he would author the Declaration of Independence. And in another stunning moment in their complicated relationship, it was John Adams who then gently chastised Jefferson for "cast[ing] aspersions on Christianity." To be sure, Adams said, softening the blow, this was the only time he could remember that this man of "sound sense and real genius" had made such a blunder, by appearing to be "an enemy to Christianity."[1]

Jefferson wasn't the only one in the group who resisted biblical religion. His comrade on the Declaration drafting committee, Benjamin Franklin, was the very symbol of scientific, rationalistic thinking. The roles of Jefferson and Franklin—combined with the fact that the Declaration did not once mention or promote Christianity—prompted law professor Alan Dershowitz to write, "The Declaration of Independence was a resounding defeat for organized religion in general and traditional Christianity in particular."[2]

Yet we cannot consider only the views of Franklin and Jefferson. Most of the other men in that hall likely imagined something different when they read the phrase *Divine Providence*—not the god of nature but the God of scriptures. John Hancock, the first to sign, had served as president of the Massachusetts Provincial Congress when it declared that "it becomes us, as Men and Christians," to rely on "that GOD who rules in the Armies of Heaven."[3] George Read, one of Delaware's delegates, had written the Delaware constitution, which required legislators to take an oath to "God the Father, and in Jesus Christ his only Son, and in the Holy Ghost."[4] New Jersey's delegate was the Reverend John Witherspoon, the president of Princeton, which trained young men to become evangelical ministers. It was Witherspoon who had authored a resolution the year before, on July 20, 1775, calling for a continentwide day of fasting and prayer, and he was hardly a Deist: "I entreat you in the most earnest manner to believe in Jesus Christ, for there is no salvation in any other [Acts 4:12]," he had written.[5] Richard Henry Lee of Virginia, who offered the resolution on independence, would a year later propose one creating a national day of prayer in which the people "may join the penitent confession of their manifold sins, whereby they had forfeited every favor, and their humble and earnest supplication that it may please God, through the merits of Jesus Christ, mercifully to forgive and blot them out of remembrance."[6] Sam Adams, the influential Boston radical, had called for "bringing in the holy and happy period when the kingdoms of our Lord and Saviour Jesus Christ may be everywhere established, and the people willingly bow to the scepter of Him who is the Prince of Peace."[7]

And by this point, John Adams was viewing the American Revolution as being, at least in part, a religious war—fought over religious causes and, more important, only winnable with the active assistance of God. It is well known that he wrote presciently to Abigail that July 2 ought to be "celebrated by succeeding generations as the great anniversary festival," chock-full of "games, sports, guns, bells, bonfires and illuminations." Less well known was the passage from the very same letter in which he suggested that "it ought to be commemorated as the day of deliverance, by solemn acts of devotion to God Almighty"—yes, that independence should be celebrated as a quasi-religious holiday. Despite the obstacles they faced, John told Abigail, he trusted that God would not let them fail: "Through all the gloom, I can see the rays of ravishing light and glory."[8]

It was the Christian background of these men that prompted the Reverend Jerry Falwell to write, "Any diligent student of American history finds that our great nation was founded by godly men upon godly principles to be a Christian nation. The founders actually included their Christian beliefs in their Declaration of Independence."

Which God was in the Declaration—the god of Jefferson or the God of Hancock?

CARVED IN STONE

First, let us consider why the rationalist Jefferson would write those words in the Declaration that the Revolution's success would rest on the "protection of divine Providence." Or why he would write that to assess the "rectitude of our intentions," Congress was "appealing to the Supreme Judge of the world"—a classically biblical vision of God's stature, disposition, and involvement.

The best explanation as to why he wrote those words is that he probably didn't. Though DIVINE PROVIDENCE is carved in the wall at the Jefferson Memorial, it was not in Jefferson's draft, nor was the invocation of the Supreme Judge. Both were added by Congress. Jefferson had taken a different approach to the divine. The rights to which men were entitled were provided by "the Laws of Nature and of Nature's God" and by "their Creator." This was the language of the Enlightenment theology that grew up in the eighteenth century as a result not only of philosophical innovations—John Locke, David Hume, and others—but also, more important, of scientific innovations. Through simple observations of the world around—an apple dropping from a tree—Isaac Newton had shown the world that man could understand the grand laws of the physical universe. Hostile to organized religion and supportive of science, Jefferson chose the in-vogue term of Deists and liberal Christians.

The *Supreme Judge* language came from a different tradition. We don't know who exactly proposed the language—some suggest it was John Witherspoon—but at some point during the debates someone in that room felt that invoking Nature's God was insufficient and added an explicit appeal to a biblical God.[9] When the parchment entered the room, it invoked only a Deistic God. When it left, it called upon the Supreme Judge.

At first glance, this seems a rather comical and incoherent compromise. If you can't decide between a biblical, interventionist God and an aloof Deistic God, simply appeal to both! But while theologians clashed passionately on these matters, there was more room for common ground than might now be supposed. Jeffrey Morrison, a biographer of John Witherspoon, has noted that a variant on *all four* phrases—even Nature's God and the "Creator"—could be found in the Westminister Confession of Faith of 1647, a classical Christian document. After all, while many orthodox Christians disliked Deism's attacks on the Bible, the laws of nature themselves were thought to be *God's* laws. Most people who used such phrases did so to prove God, not disprove Him. Nature's God was certainly not the preferred appellation of evangelicals, but it was at least theistic and not as heretical as we might now suppose. Conversely, the term *Divine Providence* was one the Deists could accept, because it left the door open for God to work either directly and personally or through the laws of nature. And as we saw earlier, even Jefferson seemed to believe that God was present, not aloof. History sometimes sharpens lines that are meant to stay blurry: At that time, Deists were using Christian language, and vice versa. All four phrases, therefore, were acceptable to the full Congress. As contemporary scholar Michael Novak put it, "Our founders learned—and taught—a *twofold* language. The language of reason *and* the language of biblical faith. They did not think that these two languages— at least as regards principles of liberty—were in contradiction. These two languages form a union. The Creator spoke both languages, and so can we."[10]

CONGRESSIONAL CONSCIOUSNESS RAISING

The God compromise in the Declaration was but one occasion when
Congress had to confront the spiritual diversity of the new nation. The
delegates—often parochial men who came from colonies that were viewed as
virtually separate nations—were forced by circumstance to approach religion
in a new way. For instance, on September 6, 1774, in one of its first acts, the
Continental Congress had considered a resolution that the next day's session
be opened with a prayer read by the Reverend Jacob Duche, an Anglican. According to John Adams, the resolution "was opposed by Mr. Jay of New York
and Mr. Rutledge of South Carolina because we were so divided in religious
sentiments, some Episcopalians [Anglicans], some Quakers, some Anabaptists, some Presbyterians, and some Congregationalists, that we could not join
in the same worship." Astonishingly, it was Sam Adams—the man who had
attacked the Church of England for its alliance with demonic "Popery"—
who declared that he would be fine with having a prayer offered by an Anglican. According to cousin John's account, "Mr. Samuel Adams arose and said
that he was no bigot, and could hear a Prayer from any gentleman of Piety
and virtue, who was at the same time a friend to his country." The next day,
Duche prayed that the new nation prosper and that its people be crowned
"with everlasting Glory in the world to come." All this, he concluded, "we ask
in the name and through the merits of Jesus Christ, Thy Son and our Saviour, Amen."[11]

Part of Congress's evolution toward pluralism probably resulted from the
simple fact that it was the most religiously diverse body most of the delegates
had ever encountered. It included Episcopalians, Congregationalists, Quakers, Presbyterians, Universalists, Dutch Reformed, Lutherans, Baptists, Methodists, and even a Catholic. They sometimes worshipped—as a body—at the
Episcopalian, Lutheran, Presbyterian, and Congregational churches. Amazingly, they even went to an occasional Catholic Mass, escorted by the
Catholic delegate, Charles Carroll.

It's worth appreciating that there *was* even a Catholic delegate to the Continental Congress. Charles Carroll, from a wealthy Maryland family, had to
be educated in France because Catholic schools were illegal in Maryland
when he was a boy. And some didn't much appreciate his presence in Congress. The Reverend Duche, for instance, wrote to George Washington com-
plaining about the participation of a Catholic representative.[12] Once in

Congress, Carroll came to impress Adams and others with his passion for the patriot cause. Adams noted to his friend James Warren on February 18 that through his "zeal, fortitude and perseverance," Carroll, a wealthy man, was jeopardizing his fortune and life for the cause. Franklin developed a strong friendship with the Carrolls that grew out of the tenderness shown by Charles Carroll's cousin, John Carroll, a priest, during an illness Franklin fought during that period.[13]

Thus, the God compromise embedded in the Declaration of Independence reflected a new reality that was dawning on the members of the Continental Congress: To defeat Great Britain, they would need to put aside certain theological disagreements and seek language that would unite rather than divide. As a Catholic member of the Congress later wrote, "When I signed the Declaration of Independence, I had in view, not only our independence from England, but the toleration of all sects professing the Christian religion, and communicating to them all equal rights."[14]

A DECLARATION OF RELIGIOUS FREEDOM

On June 24, 1826, the nation was getting ready to celebrate the fiftieth anniversary of the Declaration. In declining an invitation to participate in festivities, an eighty-three-year-old Jefferson said that he hoped the regular July 4 celebrations would "forever refresh our recollections of these rights, and an undiminished devotion to them."

What rights was he referring to? The pursuit of happiness? No taxation without representation? In these weeks before his death, those were not the rights Jefferson was thinking of most. "May it be to the world, what I believe it will be, (to some parts sooner, to others later, but finally to all,) the signal of arousing men to burst the chains under which monkish ignorance and superstition had persuaded them to bind themselves," he wrote. And it was this rejection of old-fashioned religion—"monkish ignorance"—that allowed Americans "to assume the blessings and security of self government." Thomas Jefferson then summarized the essence of the Declaration of Independence as being the establishment of "the free right to the unbounded exercise of reason and freedom of opinion." He continued, "The general spread of the light of science has already laid open to every view the palpable truth, that the mass of mankind has not been born with saddles on their backs, nor a favored few booted and spurred, ready to ride them legitimately, by the grace of God."[15] This seems to be a reference both to divine-right-based monarchical tyranny in general and to Calvinism in particular ("a favored few" empowered "by the grace of God").

Jefferson is surely a good authority on the meaning of the Declaration, but it's not exactly clear what he's referring to. Oddly, the Declaration of Independence—the nation's seminal expression of freedom's characteristics—does not explicitly mention religious liberty at all.[16] Yet as Jefferson recognized, there were concepts embedded in the Declaration that would indeed feed the mighty current sweeping religious liberty through the nation. These concepts can be found primarily in the document's first two sentences: "When in the Course of human events it becomes necessary for one people to dissolve the political bonds," those citizens are merely claiming the gifts "to which the Laws of Nature and of Nature's God entitle them." Then, "We hold these truths to be self-evident, that all men are created equal, that they are endowed by their Creator with certain unalienable Rights, that among these are Life, Liberty and the pursuit of Happiness."

In terms of the history of religious freedom, the most important words in the Declaration are *endowed by their Creator,* for they imply a powerful idea about the nature of freedom. After all, God is *not* the only possible source of rights. Earlier philosophers had viewed rights as coming from a king. But Jefferson couldn't well describe as the source of rights the very king they were rebelling against. Other philosophers and statesmen had invoked "positive law"—the idea that the people created the great legal principles by mutual consent. But Jefferson couldn't take that approach, either. The Declaration was extralegal, a document describing why normal laws of Parliament were illegitimate. He had to call upon a higher source.

Jefferson genuinely believed that rights came from above. The "God Who gave us life," he wrote, "gave us liberty at the same time."[17] We need to embrace these gifts and never let anyone else claim authority over them. "Our rulers can have authority over such natural rights only as we have submitted to them," he wrote in the *Notes on the State of Virginia.* "The rights of conscience we never submitted, we could not submit. We are answerable for them to our God." In that same work, and referring to the problem of slavery, he declared that "these liberties are of the gift of God."[18] This idea—that freedom comes from God—was the foundation for a new American conception of rights. If rights resulted from a social compact—a practical way of allowing for mutual survival—then they certainly could be altered by the majority when it seemed practical or convenient. If they came from God, however, they were immutable and inviolate, whether you were in the majority or not. This had particularly important implications for those wrestling with how to define and protect religious liberty. Toleration assumed that the state was generously choosing to do the tolerating. As Thomas Paine put it later, "Toleration is not the *opposite* of intolerance but the *counterfeit* of it. Both are despotisms: the one assumes to itself the right of withholding liberty of conscience, the other of granting it."[19] A God-given right is something quite different.

It is in contemplating the idea that rights come from a creator that conservative Christians have their best argument that Judeo-Christian tradition influenced the creation of our nation. Divinely ordained rights grew in part from the biblical injunction that God created man in his own image. Jefferson might not admit to having been so influenced. But when he told the world that liberties came from the "Creator," he knew full well that while he might imagine that deity as Nature, many others in America would envision Jesus or Yahweh. Either way, if rights came from God, they were sacrosanct.

This powerful idea was given the most famous expression by Jefferson's quill. But another young man had codified it even earlier. A few months before the Declaration of Independence was approved, James Madison and George Mason were working in Virginia on a similar document. Mason's draft of the Virginia Declaration of Rights had called for religious "toleration." The twenty-five-year-old Madison changed it to "free exercise of religion, according to the dictates of conscience." This simple edit gives the first clue that Madison was not merely Jefferson's sidekick in the fight for religious liberty. In fact, as we shall soon see, no one did more to secure religious freedom than the shy, sickly man his friends called Jemmy.

10

james madison

THE RADICAL PLURALIST

———◆———

A S A CHILD, JAMES MADISON NEEDED ONLY TO LOOK ACROSS THE
dinner table to see the Anglican establishment. His father, James Madison Sr., was a vestryman in the Brick Church, the Anglican house of worship in Orange County, Virginia. The church lay leaders (the vestry) had not only religious powers but also the authority to collect taxes and enforce moral laws. It was they who would declare punishments for those who rode on horseback on the Sabbath or drank too much or cursed.

Religion pervaded Madison's childhood.[1] Each Sunday, the family rode on horseback or one-horse chair to the church, where relatives and friends gathered to pray and exchange gossip and news. When James Madison Sr. died, most of the eighty-five titles in his library were about religion or medicine.[2] And one of James Madison Jr.'s teachers from age sixteen until he went to college was the local pastor, the Reverend Thomas Martin. But there was a big difference between the education that the future president received and that of his father or grandfather. By the 1750s, many Christian teachers believed that the tools of the Enlightenment were compatible with faith.

So, for instance, Madison's primary teacher as a child, Donald Robertson, taught Horace, Justinian, Homer, Demosthenes, and Ovid—New Testament *and* geography, geometry, Latin, Greek, and science.[3] A fifteen-year-old Madison kept a notebook he called "James Madison his Book of Logick," which recorded his lessons in deductive and inductive reasoning. Therein can be found long references to Locke, Plato, and an elaborate astronomical chart, with the sun blazing in the center, as Copernicus had declared in defiance of church teachings.[4]

Most up-and-coming boys of the Virginia gentry at that time would have gone to college at William and Mary. Madison went instead to the College of New Jersey, later known as Princeton. His official explanation was that the "climate" of William and Mary was "unhealthy for persons going from a mountainous region."[5] Though partly plausible, given Madison's tendency toward either illness or hypochondria, most scholars focus on other explanations. William and Mary's reputation had gone downhill, with stories spreading that the teachers "played all Night at Cards in publick Houses in the City, and . . . often [were] seen drunken in the street."[6] Still others maintain that Madison turned from the school because it had become intoxicated by something worse than liquor: rampant Deism.[7] Madison said he was influenced by his tutor's brother, Alexander Martin, who was, significantly, a strong defender of Baptist dissenters in North Carolina. Biographer Irving Brant has speculated that Madison may have already been aware of the persecution of Baptists near his home—the Great Awakening had spawned a wave of "dissenters" in the area—and perceived Princeton as a school more devoted to religious liberty.[8]

Whatever the reason, his decision to go to Princeton was momentous, for at the time, it was an *evangelical* Christian school. It was founded by New Light Presbyterians, the faction that had arisen during the Great Awakening to emphasize adherence to the Bible and passionate evangelism—to churn out evangelists. Its first president was Jonathan Edwards, the Billy Graham of his day.

By the time Madison arrived in 1769, the school was headed by the Reverend John Witherspoon, who would become one of the most important religious figures of the Revolutionary era. He healed the rift between Old Lights (the traditionalists) and New Lights (the evangelicals) within the Presbyterian Church, and helped marry the Enlightenment with the evangelical impulse. While he temperamentally disliked the emotional tenor of revivalism, he maintained a powerfully traditional view of God's role and a healthy respect for the evangelical emphasis on experience over doctrine. He championed what was known as the Scottish Common Sense philosophy, which advocated an integration of classical piety with commonsense observations about how the world works.

The school's curriculum melded evangelicalism and science, scriptures and the classics: Greek, Latin, Hebrew, Horace, Homer, science, math, geography, ethics, history, logic—and the Bible.[9] Today Witherspoon would be considered a theological conservative. "Nothing can be more absolutely necessary to true religion, than a clear and full conviction of the sinfulness of our nature and state," he preached.[10] But he also articulated the classically Christian view that man, being in the image of God, had inherent worth—and therefore human rights came as a gift from God, not a king. Most important, Witherspoon supported the revolutionary view that political and religious freedom were entwined. "There is not a single instance in history in which civil liberty was lost, and religious liberty preserved," he said.[11] He could not understand why the power of the state need be employed against false religious ideas, which would, left alone, collapse from their own hollowness. "Such as hold absurd tenets are seldom dangerous," he noted. "Perhaps they are never dangerous, but when they are oppressed."[12]

Madison was likely also influenced by his fellow college students, albeit in complicated ways. Two religious revivals took place at Princeton while Madison was there, one in 1770 and one in March 1772. Letters from students described the fervor: Nathan Perkins of Norwich, Connecticut, had to be helped from class after "his mind was suddenly relieved of its burden and filled with unspeakable joy"; Samuel Spring "was so overcome by his religious thoughts that he burst into tears while reciting in class."[13] Lewis Wilson "is said to have got religion," and the "formerly abandoned Glover is seeking the way to heaven."[14]

The revivalism helped cleave the student body into two groups, one called the Cliosophical Society, which was more evangelical, and the other, more cerebral, American Whig Society. Madison was in the latter. "The American Whigs, though devoted to religious studies, were inclined to feel aloof, sophisticated and intellectually superior," Irving Brant has explained. "The Whigs felt superior, not to religion, but to religious enthusiasm and extreme piety."[15] Madison was not, it appears, swept up in the revival. One bit of evidence: When his friend William Bradford reported to Madison that one of the evangelical (Cliosophical) students had gotten a girl pregnant and then married her—"put the cart before the horse" in Bradford's wry words— Madison replied cattily, "I agree with you that the world needs to be peopled but I should be sorry it should be peopled with bastards as my old friend Dod and _____ seem to incline. Who could have thought the old monk had been so lecherous." Perhaps, Madison joked, their passionate piety had stimulated other passions. "I hope his religion like that of some enthusiasts was not of such a nature as to fan the amorous fire."[16] The collegiate rivalries played out in a series of dueling poems the students wrote about one another, including this one that Madison offered about a classmate, indicating Madison's apparent sensitivity to hypocrisy among the devout:

> The lecherous rascal there will find
> A place just suited to his mind,
> May whore and pimp and drink and swear,
> Nor more the garb of Christian wear.[17]

In general he referred to the Cliosophical society members—five out of six of whom became ministers—as "sons of screech owls." He seemed uncomfortable with them, not for their faith but for their fervor.

Still, while Madison clearly did not *become* an evangelical, he did retain a tremendous amount of respect for them and their calling—including the decision of some of them to proselytize in Virginia.[18] In this sense, Christian conservatives who claim that the nation was founded on Christian principles are right to note the influences of old-time religion on Madison. After all, he attended an evangelical school geared toward training evangelical ministers, and many of his earlier teachers were clergy or active laypeople. "Though he did not long continue to express them in the same way as his teachers, it is not possible to understand the purpose and earnestness of Madison's public life without sensing its connection with the Christian atmosphere in which he was raised," biographer Ralph Ketcham has written.[19] For instance, like Adams and Franklin, Madison seemed to accept the sinful nature of human beings and consider it when constructing government institutions. As he stated, in Federalist No. 51, "What is government itself but the greatest of all reflections on human nature? If men were angels, no government would be necessary."

Those who claim he was influenced by Enlightenment ideas of rationality and science are right, too, because these were a key part of Madison's education. He learned about republics by studying Rome; about citizenship from Plutarch. And from John Locke he took not only a passion for religious tolerance but also the epistemological point that the very makeup of man—the way we process information through our senses—pretty much guarantees a diversity of viewpoints and perspectives.[20] Rationalist, evangelical, liberal Protestant, and classical—Madison took in all of them, integrated them, and created a philosophy of government that bore the marks of each. Man's sinful nature required governmental checks and balances; his yearning for spiritual exploration required freedom of conscience.

A DISPASSIONATE FAITH

While the world would ultimately learn much about Madison's public philosophy, it learned little of his personal faith. Frustratingly, the man who had the most profound impact on religious freedom was the most reticent to discuss his personal spirituality. Unlike Jefferson, Adams, and Franklin, who spelled out their theology over and over at different stages, Madison left only small clues. From these we can conclude that he was friendlier to organized religion than some of his founding brothers. Nowhere in his writings do we find the generalized hostility to clergy that we see with Adams, Jefferson, or Franklin. In fact, he seemed to respect those of his friends who selected that calling. When his friend William Bradford reported in 1772 that he'd decided not to become a minister, Madison applauded the choice but warned him that "a watchful eye must be kept on ourselves lest while we are building ideal monuments of Renown and Bliss here we neglect to have our names enrolled in the Annals of Heaven." He warned his friend that while he studied history and science, he ought to "season them with a little divinity now and then, which, like the philosopher's stone, in the hands of a good man, will turn them and every lawful acquirement into the nature of itself, and make them more precious than fine gold."[21] An early letter indicates that Madison found some of the Deists and skeptics to be "loose in their principles, encouragers of free enquiry even such as destroys the most essential truths, enemies to serious religion."[22]

The most explicitly Christian passage we have by Madison came in another letter to Bradford. He again recommended that while following his chosen path, he should "always keep the Ministry obliquely in View whatever your profession be"—but this time he added a most interesting rationale. He suggested that Bradford might want to switch careers back to the ministry later in life; Madison spun a fantasy in which young men like them would pursue careers in the law or commerce then—just at the height of their success—suddenly and publicly become "fervent Advocates in the cause of Christ." Such episodes "have seldom occurred," and therefore "would be more striking" and act as a "Cloud of Witnesses."[23] Brant speculated that Madison contemplated this advice for himself, and that his turning away from the ministry was less related to theological doubts than to personal anxieties—his "incapacity for public speech and physical weakness."[24] (In fact, after returning from college, young Jemmy was so frail that he predicted he would not enjoy a "long or healthy life.")[25]

Madison never seemed to lose his view that Christianity was, on some level, the superior religion. In December 1821, when he was seventy years old, he referred to the "genius and courage of Luther";[26] in 1832 he called Christianity the "best & purest religion."[27] In his "Memorial and Remonstrance," written during the religious liberty fights in Virginia, he stated that Christianity didn't need help—that it would thrive thanks to its "innate excellence" and the "patronage of its Author."[28]

Though Madison was in some ways more warmly disposed to religion than Franklin, Jefferson, or Adams, there's something oddly unspiritual about his writings. The others waxed emotional and personal; Madison remained forever intellectual. In a letter he wrote to Frederick Beasley in 1825, he seemed to depict religious belief as a phenomenon rather than a personal reality: The "mind prefers" the idea of a "self-existing cause to that of an infinite series of cause and effect." The belief in an all-powerful God "is so essential to the moral order of the World and to the happiness of man" that it should be encouraged.[29] Madison saw God as good for the world, but it's not clear whether he saw God as transforming his own soul.

Is it paradoxical that someone so spiritually dispassionate became the nation's most zealous champion of religious liberty? On the contrary, Madison in some ways had the perfect combination of personal characteristics to play this role. Because he deeply respected religious people and religion—studying it avidly—he wanted to preserve its expression and health. But because he wasn't intensely attached to a particular approach, he could embrace pluralism and the marketplace of spiritual ideas. And, perhaps most important, he was humble. While other Founders used their formidable minds to comprehend God and His ways, Madison seemed, earlier than the others, to resign himself to accepting the limitations of his understandings. "In religion itself there is nothing mysterious to its author," Madison wrote in 1792. "The mystery lies in the dimness of the human sight."[30] If it is ultimately impossible for mortals to know God's mind, the history of persecution becomes cosmically tragic—two thousand years of dogmatic men burning one another over religious ideas whose veracity only God can know.

"a diabolical persecution"

A WAVE OF BIGOTRY IN MADISON'S BACKYARD CHANGES HISTORY

WHEN MADISON RETURNED TO ORANGE COUNTY, VIRGINIA, after college, he found something that would help shape the course of the struggle for religious freedom. Officials of the Anglican Church had unleashed a wave of persecution against area Baptists. "That diabolical, hell-conceived principle of persecution rages among some," he fumed in a January 24, 1774, letter to his friend William Bradford. "And, to their eternal infamy, the clergy can furnish their quota of imps for such purposes." Specifically, Madison reported, "There are, at present in the adjacent county not less than five or six well-meaning men in close jail for publishing their religious sentiments, which in the main, are very orthodox." In another letter, he told Bradford that he envied him for living in tolerant Philadelphia. "I want again to breathe your free air." Please, Madison implored his friend, "I must beg you to pity me, and pray for liberty of conscience to all."[1]

Though much scholarship has gone into assessing which Enlightenment philosophers shaped Madison's mind, what likely influenced him most was not ideas from Europe but persecutions in Virginia. "To one who looked upon the ministry as the highest calling, who had many friends in that profession . . . nothing was more absurd, unwise, and unjust than the spectacle of a moribund Anglican establishment using civil power to imprison 'well-meaning men' who sought no privilege other than to preach their faith to those who would listen," wrote biographer Ralph Ketcham.[2]

What happened in Virginia that so profoundly shaped James Madison?

According to records scoured by historian Lewis Peyton Little in his book *Imprisoned Preachers and Religious Liberty in Virginia,* from 1760 to 1778 there were at least 153 serious instances of persecution involving seventy-eight Baptists—including fifty-six jailings of forty-five different Baptist preachers. At least fourteen instances occurred in Orange County, where James Madison lived, another twenty-five in Culpeper County, about twenty miles away, and seven in Spotsylvania, roughly thirty miles away. In fact, most of the persecution was clustered in exactly the part of Virginia that gave us Madison, Mason, Washington, and Jefferson.

Because this little-known phenomenon so affected Madison—and therefore the birth of religious freedom—it's crucial that we understand the true nature of the persecution, its villains, and its heroes.

"BAULING AS YOU DO"

In fall 1769, two men walked up to the Reverend James Ireland as he preached, grabbed him by the collar, and demanded to know what he was doing.

"I am preaching the Gospel of Christ to them," Ireland said.

"Who gives you the authority to do so?" they demanded.

"He that was the author of the Gospel, had a right to send forth whom he qualified to dispense it."

They told him he would have to stop preaching for twelve months, or go to jail.

If that was the choice, Ireland said, he would go to jail. And he did, for five months. There he preached through the jail's barred window to crowds that began regularly gathering outside. Officials tried to make it difficult, riding horses into the crowds and threatening those who listened. "The poor negroes have been stripped" and whipped, Ireland reported. At one point, two men moved a bench to the window, stood on it, and urinated in Ireland's face. At another, his opponents—who included not only authorities but local bigots as well—created a concoction of Indian pepper and brimstone to send noxious smoke into his cell.[3]

In Caroline County, John Waller was leading a worship service in spring

1771 when the lead Anglican minister of the Drysdale Parish, Andrew Moreton, went up on stage and flipped through the pages of the prayer book. As
Waller tried to continue, Moreton took the butt end of his horse whip and
stuck it in Waller's mouth. Moreton's clerk, Thomas Buckner, then dragged
Waller to the nearby sheriff, who whipped him bloody. After the beating,
Waller staggered back to the stage and resumed his sermon. He told his followers later that he didn't feel the lashes because the Lord had "poured his
love into his soul without measure." In all, Waller spent 113 days imprisoned
in four different colonial jails.[4]

John Weatherford served five months in the Chesterfield County jail and
continued to preach through prison windows so successfully that his keepers
had to go to extraordinary lengths to dampen his impact. As he stuck his
hands through the bars, men outside slashed them with knives; to keep people away, they built a wall more than ten feet tall. Undeterred, Weatherford
and his friends innovated a signal system: If a handkerchief was raised on a
pole above the wall, Weatherford would know people were gathered on the
other side and would boom out his sermon.[5]

The harassment took many forms. David Barrow's service was interrupted
when a mob forced his head into the mud and water until he almost
drowned.[6] Archibald W. Roberts was indicted for using hymns and poems instead of the Psalms.[7] Other examples recorded by Little and other early historians: "dragged from the house," "frequently taken from pulpet—beaten,"
"meeting broken up by a mob," "pulled down and hauled about by hair, hand
etc," "tried to suffocate him with smoke," "severely beaten with a stick," "severely beaten with butt end of large cane," "brutally assaulted by a mob,"
"dragged off stage, kicked and cuffed about," "shot with a shot-gun," "pulled
down while preaching—dragged out," "severely beaten with a whip," "jerked
off stage—head beaten against ground."

When the Baptists were arrested, with what crimes were they charged?
Unofficially, it was simply the crime of being a Baptist minister. But the most
common official charges were preaching without a license and disturbing the
peace. Elijah Craig and four others in Orange County were imprisoned on
charges of being "Vagrant and Itinerant Persons and for Assembling themselves unlawfully at Sundry Times and Places Under the Denomination of Anabaptists and for Teaching & preaching Schismatick Doctrines."[8] The warrant
that placed William Saunders and William McClannahan in the Culpeper
County jail in 1772 declared that their crimes were to "Teach & Preach Contrary to the Laws and usages of the Kingdom of Great Britain, raising Sedition

& Stirring up Strife amongst his Majestie's Liege People."[9] In Orange County in 1770, a magistrate revealed the class component of the anti-Baptist sentiment when he told Saunders that part of his crime was preaching too *loudly*. The dissenters were deemed uncouth. "Bauling as you Do to Be heard for half a mile Round which in my opinion is nothing but ostentation," the official said. "I assure you that I think Loud praying is no more a sign of true godliness than I think Loud Laughing is a sign of Real pleasure."[10]

When six Baptists were placed in the Caroline County jail in August 1771, a local authority explained that they needed to be punished because they undermined the established church and therefore the social order. In "An Address to the Annabaptists imprisoned in Caroline County, August 8, 1771," an anonymous author wrote that by encouraging adult Baptism, the Baptists undermined morality, the theory being that lowlifes would view the immersion as a get-out-of-jail-free card enabling them to sin again. "Having been once dipped in your happy Waters," he said, these men are then "let loose to commit upon us Murders, and every Species of Injury."[11] Finally, the Baptists were loathed and feared because they conducted night meetings among the slaves.[12] As the Reverend John Leland wrote, "Liberty of conscience, in matters of religion, is the right of the slaves, beyond contradiction; and yet, many masters and overseers will whip and torture the poor creatures for going to meeting, even at night, when the labor of the day is over."[13]

One might wonder why preaching without a license would be a particularly worrisome accusation. How hard could it be to get a license? But this process was designed to subordinate the Baptists, and we must briefly wallow in its bureaucratic awfulness to fully grasp why Baptists came to hate even the lighter forms of state regulation. According to William Firstoe, a historian of this period, here was the way it worked:

A would-be Baptist minister had to get a license from Virginia's General Court, which sat twice a year in Williamsburg. Before making the trip, he had much preparation to do. He would pull together a petition signed by twenty people. Two acting justices of the peace had to then certify that the twenty were actually residents. If successful, they proceeded to the General Court, where the Baptist preacher had to pass an examination given by an *Anglican* clergyman. If he passed, and the General Court approved his certificate, the application then went to several leading Episcopalians (for instance, the president of William and Mary) for further inspection.[14] Once granted, the license gave rights to a place, not a person, so the minister of a church could be arrested for preaching outside that particular building.[15] In one case, the General Court refused to grant a license for a Baptist meeting in Richmond on the grounds that the *Presbyterians* already had a church in that county.[16] One surviving document from the period illustrates how the system created a debilitating sense of subservience. The paper listed the signatures of a cowering group of Baptists from Amelia County who "humbly submit the consideration to your worships, hoping you will in mercy grant the same, to us who are in duty bound to always pray for all authorities under God and over us." The official response was written on the back: "Dissenters petition called Baptist, Rejected."[17]

This bureaucratic labyrinth was humiliating and burdensome, but the Baptists felt they had little choice, for the penalty for preaching without a license was jail.[18] Faced with such attacks, Baptists of Virginia at first appealed to the state legislature for changes in laws so that they could be exempted from taxes or their pastors could be allowed to perform marriages.[19] The Baptists of Orange County came to believe that their ministers should engage in civil disobedience against a legal system that required them to obtain licenses to preach. The General Association meeting of the Separate Baptists of Virginia gathered in Blue Run Church in Orange County—less than ten miles from Madison's home—and endorsed a motion censuring those who had accepted a license. Some four thousand people gathered for the meeting, a strong indication of the powerful evangelical sentiment in the area. "The rapid rise and uncompromising style of the New Light Separate Baptists brought on Virginia's first full-scale debate on religious liberty," wrote the historian Rhys Isaac.[20]

There is evidence that Madison was no casual bystander, even as a young man. He wrote to Bradford that he was out of patience because "I have squabbled and scolded, abused and ridiculed so long about it, to so little purpose."[21] Because many of the Orange County records have been lost, there's no official record of Madison representing the dissenters. But *Johnson's New Universal Cyclopaedia*, a popular nineteenth-century book, claimed that Madison had been "repeatedly appearing in the court of his own county to defend the Baptist nonconformists."[22] In his "autobiography" (a short essay he wrote later as an old man), Madison recalled that despite the fact that the Baptists apparently seemed déclassé to the landed aristocracy of Virginia—their "enthusiasms" rendering them "obnoxious to sober opinion"—he had "spared no exertion to save them from imprisonment & to promote their release from it." Apparently, his actions were sufficiently notable that he became known to the Baptists even as a young man. "This interposition tho' a mere duty prescribed by his conscience," Madison wrote, "obtained for him a lasting place in the favour of that particular sect."[23]

Some of the other Founding Fathers likely were aware of this persecution as well. Patrick Henry on numerous occasions defended the dissenters in court, gratis. In fact, when Henry offered to represent the Reverend Weatherford, the preacher wrapped some money to pay for his fee in a bandanna and passed it out the prison window. Henry sent it back, money still there, and thereby became a hero of the dissenters.[24] The Alexandria jail that held Jeremiah Moore was near the courthouse visited frequently by George Washington and George Mason. Henry, perhaps at Washington's request, helped defend Moore, giving an impassioned speech in his defense.[25]

Some of Virginia's other leading men were also aware of the cases—for a different reason: They were defending the church leaders, or collaborating with the persecution. For instance, the attorney general of Virginia, John Randolph, wrote, under a non de plume, that these Baptist preachers were prompting many to "forsake their Church and their cheerful innocent Society of their Friends and Families, and turn sour, gloomy, severe, and censorious . . . Wives are drawn from their Husbands, Children from their Parents, and Slaves from the Obedience of their Masters."[26] The Speaker of the Virginia House of Delegates, Edmund Pendleton, was the judge who presided over some of the imprisonments in Caroline County.[27]

Madison's sympathy for the Baptists translated into an increasing disgust with the Anglican hierarchy. "If the Church of England had been the established and general religion in all the Northern Colonies as it has been among us here," he wrote Bradford, "it is clear to me that slavery and Subjection might and would have been gradually insinuated among us."[28]

When Madison began his career as a legislator, one of the first issues he focused on was religious freedom. In December 1773, we can see his mind translating his personal experience into a legislative plan. He asked Bradford for materials on the history of Pennsylvania's constitution. "Send me a draught of its Origin and fundamental principles of Legislation; particularly the extent of your religious Toleration. Here allow me to propose the following Queries. Is an Ecclesiastical Establishment absolutely necessary to support civil society in a supreme Government?"[29]

His Pennsylvania-envy had grown during his college years. To get to Princeton he passed through Philadelphia, which was ten times bigger than any town he'd ever seen. In fact, with twenty-five thousand people it was the second largest city in the entire British Empire. "Madison saw for the first time such wonders as stone sidewalks and paved streets lighted at night, row on row of three-story brick dwellings, churches of eight different denominations within a few blocks of one another, and many other public buildings, including two libraries, the Pennsylvania Hospital, the Academy of Philadelphia, the State House, and a barracks for nearly two thousand soldiers," wrote Ketcham.[30] Madison started to connect Philadelphia's cultural and economic success and its religious tolerance. Freedom attracts talent, promotes creativity, and stimulates innovation. "Foreigners have been encouraged to settle among you," he wrote Bradford. "Industry and virtue have been promoted by mutual emulation and mutual inspection; commerce and the arts have flourished and I cannot help attributing those continual exertions of genius which appear among you to the inspiration of liberty and the love of fame and knowledge which always accompany it. Religious bondage shackles and debilitates the mind, and unfits it for every noble enterprise, every expanded prospect."[31]

Just two years later, Madison and other freedom fighters began applying their passion for religious liberty in the political world.

the mighty current of freedom

AFTER INDEPENDENCE, THE STATES BEGIN WRENCHING THEMSELVES FROM THE OLD CHURCH–STATE MODELS

A S WASHINGTON ATTEMPTED TO CREATE A NATIONAL ARMY, THE Continental Congress groped toward the creation of an American government. There was no chief executive or national judiciary, so Congress served all functions. Along with managing the war, negotiating treaties, and creating a navy, the Continental Congress also spent time contemplating the symbolism of the new nation. What was the official bird? (Eagle, not turkey.) What was the flag? (Thirteen stars, "representing a new constellation.")[1] And what was the national seal? That final symbolically fraught task fell in 1776 to an able committee of Franklin, Adams, and Jefferson. The results were fascinating and surprising, as each of these philosopher-statesmen tested biblical, as well as classical, themes. Franklin—that freethinking champion of science and the Enlightenment—proposed: "Moses standing on the Shore, and extending his Hand over the Sea, thereby causing the same to overwhelm Pharaoh who is sitting in an open Chariot, a Crown on his Head and a Sword in his Hand. Rays from the Pillar of Fire in the Clouds reaching to Moses, to express that he acts by Command of the Deity." And what motto did this self-proclaimed Deist propose? "Rebellion to Tyrants is Obedience to God."[2] Jefferson—critic of biblical revelation—proposed that one side of the seal would depict the "Children of Israel in the wilderness led by a cloud by day and a pillar of fire by night." The other side would show Anglo-Saxon brothers Hengist and Horsa.[3] Clearly stronger with the written word than the visual image, the three did not come up with an agreeable seal that time. On May 4, 1782, another, more artistically inclined congressional committee tackled the assignment, devising the design we know today—an eagle, with shield. Above the bird is a constellation of sun and stars. The secretary of the Congress, who led the project, explained that "the Eye over it and the Motto allude to the many signal interpositions of providence in favour of the American cause." Indeed, it included the motto *Annuit Coeptis*, or "God has favored our undertakings," which remains on the seal.[4]

Like an adolescent navigating the passage from one set of childhood rules to an entirely different set for adulthood, Congress veered from one approach to another on questions of religious liberty and identity. In its first year, it issued four proclamations requesting a national day of fasting. Writing to Abigail Adams about the proclamation approved July 12, 1775, John Adams declared, "Millions will be upon their knees at once before their great Creator, imploring His forgiveness and blessing; his smiles on American Councils and arms."[5] During the period after the Declaration and before the Constitution, Congress regularly employed explicitly Christian language. A thanksgiving proclamation in 1777 asked Americans to offer "the penitent confession of their manifold sins" in such a way as to "please God, through the merits of Jesus Christ."[6] But as the years went on, Congress shifted toward a more nondenominational and universal approach. In setting up the government for the Northwest Territory, the Continental Congress in 1787 guaranteed general freedom of worship—a virtual necessity if it was to succeed in having the area fully settled—while at the same time encouraging religious education in the area.[7] It was for a similar combination of practical and principled reasons that Congress gave its first indirect acknowledgment to the rights of Catholics. The occasion was a diplomatic crisis in 1783, when the papal nuncio in France, an essential American ally, requested that the French Catholic Church be allowed to appoint a bishop in the United States. Congress instructed Ben Franklin, the ambassador to France, to take the position that they could not agree to such a proposal because "being purely spiritual, it is without the jurisdiction and powers of Congress, who have no authority to permit or refuse it, these powers being reserved to the several states individually."[8] In America, unlike in much of Europe, Catholic bishops would be appointed by the Holy See without approval from the state.

The war itself buffeted Congress in a variety of directions on religious matters. As noted earlier, at one moment the members were attacking Catholics and the next they were offering them religious liberty. Congress showed a similarly schizophrenic attitude toward the Quakers. While some Quakers supported the cause of independence, others believed that their faith required strict neutrality in the conflict, an approach that alienated them from many of their neighbors. And still others had strong allegiance to the Crown, remembering that it was the Stuart king of England who had protected them against religious persecution in Great Britain.[9] Antagonism toward the Quakers was further fueled by their refusal even to sell flour, grain, and cattle to the army on credit[10] or turn a meetinghouse over to the army for use as a hospital.[11] In August 1777, a set of letters came to public attention in which Quaker leaders secretly professed loyalty to the British Crown. The letters were later proven to be forgeries, but at the time they sent Congress into a witch hunt. A committee including John Adams, Richard Henry Lee, and William Duer concluded that many Quakers were "with much rancor and bitterness, disaffected to the American cause"; they would likely "communicate intelligence to the enemy" and "injure the counsels and arms of America." The group called for the arrest of eleven leading Quakers and recommended that states "apprehend all Persons of that Society, and indeed all others, who have evidenced by their Conduct & Conversation a Disposition inimical to the Cause of America." Furthermore, they asked that Quaker meetinghouses be entered and that "the records and papers of the Meetings for Sufferings in the respective states, be forthwith secured and carefully examined," with political bits sent to Congress. The Council of Pennsylvania followed this recommendation and on September 8 did indeed arrest various Quakers.[12] Minutes of Quaker meetings were seized, and then returned after nothing treasonous was discovered.[13]

After hearing protests from many Quakers, Pennsylvania on January 29, 1778, passed a resolution saying the prisoners could be discharged if they pledged allegiance to the state. The Friends, who had a theological opposition to the taking of oaths, refused. Eventually, the council relented, but decreed that the cost of arresting and confining the prisoners, sending them to Virginia for imprisonment, and "all other incidental charges" be paid by the prisoners! One of the leading Quakers, Israel Pemberton—he was among the men who had met, along with Isaac Backus, with John Adams in 1774—died in prison.[14]

SMASHING THE SCEPTRE

As Washington and the Continental Congress attempted to chisel a national identity, local governments metamorphosed from colonies into states. Soon after the Declaration of Independence was approved, the states began writing new constitutions, establishing independent powers of taxation and governance—and breaking from the Church of England. The seven states that had formally established the Church of England as the official religion moved quickly to disestablish.[15] "Yield to the mighty current of American freedom," declared the Reverend William Tennent of South Carolina during this wave of disestablishment.[16]

But those swift actions should not be confused with a wholesale embrace of religious liberty. In fact, during the decade after independence was declared, only two of the thirteen colonies adopted religious freedom in a form we might recognize today. New Jersey, Vermont, North Carolina, and Georgia retained their bans on Catholics holding office. Maryland prohibited non-Christians. Delaware required that officeholders subscribe to "Trinitarian" Christianity. Pennsylvania demanded that lawmakers "acknowledge the scriptures of the Old and New Testament to be given by divine inspiration." In Connecticut and Massachusetts, taxes went to support the Congregational Church. South Carolina's constitution declared that "the Christian religion is the true religion." Only Virginia and Rhode Island offered full religious tolerance.

The period from 1776 to 1800 was one of convulsive transformation. Before 1776, the colonists mostly employed the Old World approach to religion: Choose an official religion, regulate it, and support it. By 1800, most would embrace the idea that government should only minimally regulate or support religion. This adolescent period was full of experimentation, inconsistency, emotion, and tremendous maturation. Many of the most important struggles occurred at the state level.[17] Conveniently, Adams, Jefferson, Madison, and Franklin played critical roles in these battles—each trying a different approach.

MASSACHUSETTS—A CHRISTIAN STATE

In 1779, the Massachusetts legislature assigned the task of writing a new constitution to a subcommittee of three—James Bowdoin, Sam Adams, and John Adams.[18] The Massachusettsans declared that religion was fundamentally important and therefore must be *supported* by the state.[19] "As the happiness of a people, and the good order and preservation of civil government, essentially depend upon piety, religion and morality; and as these cannot be generally diffused through a community, but by the institution of the public worship of GOD, and of public instructions in piety, religion and morality," therefore, the legislature would require localities to pay for "the institution of the public worship of GOD, and for the support and maintenance of public protestant teachers of piety, religion and morality." This constitution not only demanded that government support the church but also required that the citizens show up on Sunday.[20]

In a bow to tolerance, the Massachusetts constitution stated that localities could decide what particular "sects" to support—meaning, significantly, that the Congregational Church no longer would have a monopoly—and that "every denomination of Christians, demeaning themselves peaceably, and as good subjects of the Commonwealth, shall be equally under the protection of the law; And no subordination of any one sect or denomination to another shall ever be established by law."[21] In fact, in the period from the Declaration until the end of the eighteenth century, the most common approach in New England was to have some taxpayer support of religion, but usually nondenominational Protestantism determined on the local level.[22]

Massachusetts counties that commented on the new constitution seemed to accept the basic logic that religion would flourish more if actively supported by the state. Boston's officials, for instance, declared that were government to cease its support for "morality, religion and Piety," the normal laws attempting to regulate human behavior would be impotent—"feeble barriers opposed to the uninformed lusts of Passions of Mankind."[23] The Massachusetts constitution allowed the state to regulate religious behavior in ways that today would be unthinkable. For instance, it was a crime to "willfully blaspheme the holy name of God, by denying, cursing, or contumeliously reproaching God, his creation, government or final judging of the world." Blasphemy against Jesus Christ, the Holy Ghost, or the Bible was also outlawed. The guilty would be sentenced to sitting in a pillory, being whipped, or sitting on the gallows with a rope around the neck.[24]

The legislature did establish a mechanism under which non-Congregationalists could petition to avoid paying taxes to the Congregational Church, but this procedure entailed deep governmental involvement in the operations of churches and the behavior of individuals. After a group of Baptists tried to avoid paying taxes to the Congregational Church, the state's

Supreme Judicial Court ruled that the request could be granted only if the person "had been dipped." In other words, Baptists need not pay taxes to the Congregationalists if they were *good* Baptists—as defined by the state. In 1800, lawmakers clarified that the genuineness of someone's religious commitment would be determined by gaining a certificate from his minister that the petitioner attended church regularly.

We should be clear: The Massachusetts constitution did not create a Christian commonwealth, it created a Protestant one. It required the "antipapist oath,"[25] in which officeholders swore that no foreign "prelate" could have "any jurisdiction, superiority, preeminence, authority, dispensing or other power, in any matter, civil, ecclesiastic or spiritual within this Commonwealth."[26] Sixty-three of the 181 towns that wrote in with comments about the constitution demanded that the office of governor be limited to Protestants. At the time, there were only about six hundred Catholics in the state, so the Protestants carried the day.[27]

PENNSYLVANIA—FRANKLIN'S COMPROMISE

Ben Franklin's chance to directly define religious freedom in the new America came at his state's constitutional convention in 1776, which he chaired. In most ways, Franklin and the Pennsylvanians were closer to the Virginians than the Massachusettsans, advocating a stricter separation of church and state than would the US Constitution. Pennsylvania's constitution sweepingly declared:

> That all men have a natural and unalienable right to worship Almighty God according to the dictates of their own consciences and understanding. And that no man ought or of right can be compelled to attend any religious worship, or erect or support any place of worship, or maintain any ministry, contrary to, or against, his own free will and consent: Nor can any man, who acknowledges the being of a God, be justly deprived or abridged of any civil right as a citizen, on account of his religious sentiments or peculiar mode of worship.[28]

Protecting people from having to attend a worship service would seem to restrict even prayers at graduations or the Ten Commandments being posted in a courthouse. Of course, Pennsylvania prohibited state support of particular faiths. This accords well with Franklin's view that government support for religion would prop up unworthy preachers and was almost contrary to God's wishes. "When a religion is good, I conceive it will support itself, and when it does not support itself, and God does not take care to support it, so that its professors are obliged to call for help of the civil powers, 'tis a sign, I apprehend, of its being a bad one."[29]

But advocates of a strong separation of church and state cannot claim Franklin fully as one of their own, either. The Pennsylvania constitution, it must be noted, guaranteed citizenship rights only to a person "who acknowledges the being of a God." That's right: Only *theists* were full citizens. The convention illustrated another ever-present reality of these fights: Religious and ideological diversity forced lawmakers into a constant state of coalition building and compromise. For instance, Franklin wanted men of any faith to be able to serve in the legislature. But one of the leading German ministers of the state, the Reverend Henry Muhlenberg, objected that under such a liberal approach, "A Christian people were [to be] ruled by Jews, Turks, Spinozists, Deists [and] perverted naturalists."[30] Lacking the votes to prevail, Franklin accepted a provision requiring members of the assembly to take the following oath: "I do believe in one God, the creator and governor of the universe, the rewarder of the good and the punisher of the wicked. And I do acknowledge the Scriptures of the Old Testament and New Testament to be given by Divine inspiration." As a concession, Franklin got a second sentence inserted promising that no additional tests would ever be added.

But he was not pleased. He compromised to get the constitution through—reminding us that these foundational documents were not sent from the pens of a handful of Founding Fathers straight to the National Archives. They had to be approved by literally thousands of other men in legislatures or state ratification assemblies. The Founding Fathers were not only spiritual beings or philosophers, but also politicians who learned that they had to count votes.

VIRGINIA—THE ENLIGHTENMENT-EVANGELICAL ALLIANCE

The most significant fight was in Virginia. At first, Jefferson led the charge. When Edmund Pendleton proposed an immigration law "for the encouragement of foreign Protestants," Jefferson crossed out "foreign Protestants" and inserted the word *foreigners.*[31] In June 1776, he unsuccessfully attempted to eliminate the Anglican establishment and ban ministers from holding office. He then went off to Philadelphia to attend the Continental Congress while another convention gathered to frame Virginia's new Declaration of Rights and constitution. The draft was written by the esteemed statesman George Mason, who drew especially from John Locke's Letter Concerning Toleration. "All men should enjoy the fullest toleration in the exercise of religion, according to the dictates of conscience, unpunished and unrestrained by the magistrate, unless, under color of religion, any man disturb the peace, the happiness, or safety of society, or of individuals," Mason wrote. It was the "mutual duty of all, to practice Christian forebearance, love and charity towards each other."[32]

As fate would have it, the convention was also attended by twenty-five-year-old James Madison, who had been unable or unwilling to join the Continental army thanks to the "unsettled state of his health" and "discourageing feebleness of his constitution."[33] His presence at the state constitutional convention, the beginning of his political career, proved momentous. Madison believed that Mason's language did not go nearly far enough. Mason had allowed for restrictions on religious practice that would "disturb the peace, the happiness, or safety of society, or of individuals"; Madison thought that loophole too broad. (After all, many Baptists had been thrown in jail on the flimsy pretext of disturbing the peace.) Discovering he lacked support for a direct attack on the Anglican establishment, Madison focused instead on the explication of a radical abstract principle. He proposed "that all men are equally entitled to the free exercise of religion, according to the dictates of conscience, unpunished, and unrestrained by the magistrate, unless"—and note how much more limited were his exceptions—"the preservation of equal liberty and the existence of the State are manifestly endangered."[34]

The change from "toleration" to "free exercise of religion, according to the dictates of conscience" made religious liberty a fundamental human right, no longer subject to definition by those in power but inherent, immutable, and inalienable. Once, religious freedom was a privilege granted by a generous potentate. With time and progress, it became what John Locke and George Mason had suggested: a sensible right offered by an enlightened democratic majority. Madison reached higher still, and landed religious liberty on the loftiest possible plane. It became a freedom so fundamental, and so important, that the state—whether in the hands of the most ignoble monarch or a populist legislature—would simply have no authority to curtail. When in his eighties, Madison dictated a brief autobiographical essay skimming through various moments large and small of his long life. Though

mostly transcribed by a young man (probably Madison's nephew), there were
a few words that had been underlined by a shakier hand, likely that of the ail-
ing Madison himself. The new language, Madison explained, turned freedom of conscience into a *"natural and absolute right."* That phrase in the
Virginia Declaration of Rights would influence key documents in other
states, become a rallying cry for Virginia Baptists—and shift the terms of debate from toleration to liberty.[35]

Ironically, while the spirit of freedom pervaded many debates on many
topics, there was a countervailing concern present in Virginia. Many came to
fear that during the Revolution, real-life religion had gone into decline.
Church buildings had been destroyed by the war. It was thought that worship
attendance was declining, immorality rising, and the clergy struggling. A
friend wrote to Jefferson that one preacher "has been almost starved"; another
gave up his job to avoid starving.[36] The solution was a proposal, in 1784, to tax
Virginians to support Christian churches and clergy, and its champion was
Patrick Henry. Recently returning to the legislature after three years as governor, Henry was the most popular figure in the state and a known champion
of personal liberty. Why would this famous scourge of the Anglican establishment lead the charge on their behalf? Some theorize that Henry took up this
cause because after years of only occasional church attendance, he had more
recently become religious. He had taken to carrying around, and giving out
as gifts, copies of two pious works: Joseph Butler's *Analogy of Religion, Natural and Revealed, to the Course and Constitution of Nature* and a less famous tract called *View of the Internal Evidence of Christianity.*[37] He wanted
to help religion in particular and virtue in general. But the most important
thing to realize is that although the idea of taxpayer-financed religion seems
reactionary today, it was at the time—and, in all likelihood in Patrick Henry's
mind—a *liberal* reform.[38] Like the men who pushed similar measures in other
states, Henry was not attempting to create a formal establishment of the Anglican Church, and obviously Henry was no royalist. He was taking the view that
Christianity *in general* should be aided. Under his proposal, voters could desig-
nate the denomination or even the specific church that their tax dollars would
go to. Baptists could give money to the Baptist Church, Presbyterians to their
own church, and so on. Even Quakers would benefit. Henry's bill eventually
went so far as to allow that those who didn't want to support religion could target their tax dollars toward education more broadly. All in all, as these things
went, Henry's was a broad-minded, tolerant, and pluralistic proposal.

The measure, "A Bill for Establishing a Provision for the Teachers of the Christian Religion," gained wide support. It was premised on the very practical and popular notion that "the general diffusion of Christian knowledge hath a natural tendency to correct the morals of men, restrain their vices, and preserve the peace of society." This gentle and flexible approach would encourage religion—surely an important goal—while remaining consistent with the libertarian spirit of the Revolution. A petition sent in by citizens in Amelia, Virginia, declared that "As every Man in the state partakes of the Blessings of Peace and Order"—and peace and order flow directly from the morality produced by religion—"every Man should be obliged to contribute as well to the Support of Religion." Richard Henry Lee argued that it was the least the citizens of Virginia could do, since "avarice is accomplishing the destruction of religion for want of legal obligation to contribute something to its support."[39] John Marshall, the future Supreme Court chief justice, supported Henry's plan, and so did George Washington.[40]

Madison disagreed. He believed that the proposal was not only unnecessary and unwise but in fact villainous—and, far from being liberal-minded, actually posed a severe threat to religious freedom.

On November 11, 1784, the battle was joined in the House of Delegates in Richmond between the tall, charismatic Patrick Henry and Madison, five feet, six inches, with a wispy voice and a pasty complexion. Though no record of Henry's comments exist, he likely argued that virtue was an important part of democracy and that nations that had neglected religion had suffered and declined. The notes Madison used to guide him through the debate have survived, and reveal the rigor of his mind and his style of battering opponents with an unrelenting blizzard of arguments. His notes, in tiny handwriting on the back of a letter, are below in italics, accompanied by my interpretation of what he probably meant:

What is Christianity? Courts of law to Judge.
   Once civil authority is brought in to aid religion, it must necessarily *define* religion. Going down this road therefore means state involvement in delicate theological matters.

   What edition, Hebrew, Septuagint, or vulgate? What copy—what translation . . . What books canonical, what apochryphal? The papists holding to be the former what protestants the latter, the Lutherans the latter what other protestants & papists the former

Don't kid yourselves into thinking that there is a consensus around even the basic tenets of the majority religion. Even Christians disagree over key elements, and dragging government in as the referee will invariably burn them.

In What light are they to be viewed, as dictated every letter by inspiration, or the essential parts only? Or the matter in generall not the words? . . . Is it salvation by faith or works also

If the state were to teach the Bible, would it declare scripture inerrant or metaphorical? Would it be the Calvinistic interpretation emphasizing faith or the more Unitarian (and Catholic) emphasis on works?

What clue is to guide Judge thro' this labyrinth? When the question comes before them whether any particular Society is a Christian society . . . ? What is orthodoxy, what heresy?

Once we ask civil authorities to become involved, *they* will be the ones to assess what is real Christianity and what is apostasy.

Tendency of Estabg. Christianity 1. to project of Uniformity 2. to penal laws for supporting it.

The assessment bill would create a law, and laws must be enforced with punishments and by police. The state would therefore, by necessity, apply criminal penalties for some religious behaviors.

True question not—Is Rel. neccsy.? Are Rellis. Estabts. Neccsy. For Religion? No

This notation summarizes the essence of Madison's attack—and the principal way culture warriors misunderstand him. He believed that proponents of the general assessment had put forth a great non sequitur by arguing that since religion is important, it must therefore be supported by the state. He believed that religion was important but that tax support for religion—which he referred to as a religious "establishment"—was unnecessary and unwise. Why?

Experience shows Relig: corrupted by Estabt.

Not only did religion not need government help; it would be harmed by it.

Case of Pa. Explained
Pennsylvania, on the other hand, showed that liberty led to economic *and* religious vitality.

Case of primitive Christianity
This should come as no surprise since Christianity itself was at its most vibrant when it was in its most primitive state, before Constantine gave it state support.

promote emigrations from State
An assessment would make some Virginians feel unwelcome.

prevent immigration = into it as asylum
And the state would lose the opportunity to attract talented settlers.

Necessity of Esbts. Inferred from State of Conty
Responding to the argument made by assessment supporters that the sad state of religion in the country necessitated strong action, Madison countered that the real cause of religious stagnation was the war. With peace at hand, religion would now recover.
And finally,

Probably defects of Bill dishonor Christianity.
Yes, Madison's grand finale was that supporting Christianity with government funds would dishonor it.[41]

Madison lost the first test. By a vote of forty-seven to thirty-two, the delegates passed a resolution declaring in principle that the people of the commonwealth "ought to pay a moderate tax or contribution annually for the support of the Christian religion." Madison had to think quickly to forestall the passage of the final bill. At some point during this session, he made a shrewd tactical move: He flip-flopped and accepted a proposal "incorporating" the Episcopal Church, thereby allowing it to keep the land that it had been given (at taxpayer expense) during the years of the Anglican establishment. We know from later writings that Madison fervently opposed the idea of incorporation, so why did he agree to it? He apparently was able to secure a delay on the final assessment vote in exchange for such a concession. "I consider the passage of the Act however as having been so far useful as to have parried for the present the Genl. Assesst. which would have otherwise certainly been saddled upon us," he wrote to his father on January 6, 1785.[42]

Second, he hoped that allowing incorporation would break apart the incipient alliance between the Episcopalians and the Presbyterians. At first, the Presbyterians—more evangelistic in spirit and theology than the Episcopalians—had been sympathetic to Madison's side. But when Presbyterian leaders learned that the general assessment would send money their way, too, their opposition mysteriously softened. The Presbyterian opportunism disgusted Madison. "I do not know of a more shameful contrast" than the Presbyterian change, Madison wrote to his friend James Monroe.[43] But just as Madison had hoped, the Presbyterians were frightened by the incorporation bill, which showed that the intervention of the state would inevitably accrue to the benefit of the semi-official church—the Episcopalians—over all others. Indeed, the Episcopalians blocked similar status for the Presbyterians.[44] "I am glad the Episcopalians have again shewn their teeth & fangs," his co-conspirator Thomas Jefferson wrote from Paris. "The *dissenters* had almost forgotten them."[45] Madison seemed to think his divide-and-conquer strategy had worked. He wrote to Jefferson, "The mutual hatred of these sects has been much inflamed by the late act of incorporating the latter. I am far from being sorry for it as a coalition between them could alone endanger our religious rights and a tendency to such an event had been suspected."[46]

Nonetheless, the bill still had strong support, which prompted Jefferson to suggest calling in the Big Gun against their enemy, Patrick Henry: "What we have to do I think is *devoutly to pray for his death*."[47] Madison had a friendlier and more cunning plan: He worked to help get Henry elected governor and, therefore, out of the legislature.[48] One can almost hear the snicker as Madison writes Monroe that Henry's ascent to the governorship was "a circumstance very inauspicious to his offspring"—his offspring being the assessment bill.[49]

During an ensuing legislative hiatus, Madison tried to turn public opinion against the assessment by writing one of the most important documents in the history of American religious freedom, his fifteen-point "Memorial and Remonstrance Against Religious Assessments." It was not a Deist document or an evangelical document or an economic one, but rather a politically unifying synthesis of *all* the major arguments against an assessment and, more broadly, against any government involvement in religion:

The document declared, "The Religion then of every man must be left to the conviction and conscience of every man; and it is the right of every man to exercise it as these may dictate. This right is in its nature an unalienable right. It is unalienable, because the opinions of men, depending only on the evidence contemplated by their own minds cannot follow the dictates of other men." Each person should not only be free to follow his own conscience but also recognize that his neighbor's spiritual journey is sacred. "We maintain therefore that in matters of Religion, no man's right is abridged by the institution of Civil Society and that Religion is wholly exempt from its cognizance." Note that the close of the sentence is not "interference" or "regulation" or "establishment"—but "cognizance." Madison was suggesting the radical argument that religion should not even be in the sphere of consciousness of civil authorities. It wasn't a matter of good regulation or bad, intrusive or liberal, hostile or helpful, heavy-handed or dainty. Religion should be simply and thoroughly off limits.

From that transcendent mountaintop, Madison hurled a litany of more practical arguments: This new tax will drive people from the state at a time when they're trying to attract settlers (Point 10). The bill will cause strife and violence (11), and most people don't support the idea anyway (14). He unveiled an argument he would return to throughout his life: that one must be vigilant about principles, even if the examples seem small. And in the assessment bill, Madison saw a veritable mountain range of slippery slopes. The assessment must be seen as a step toward more persecution, leading inevitably to "the Inquisition from which it differs only in degree" (9). By establishing government authority to help one religion, the assessment gives government authority to regulate religion *in general*. "Who does not see that the same authority which can establish Christianity, in exclusion of all other religions, may establish with the same ease any particular sect of Christians, in exclusion of all other sects?" (3). In fact, if we can start to chip away and qualify freedom of religion, we will be able to erode other freedoms (15). Soon unscrupulous tyrants will use religious leaders as tools to make their mischief. "Rulers who wished to subvert the public liberty, may have found an established Clergy convenient auxiliaries."

Several of Madison's arguments emphasized not that the assessment was bad for the state or religious minorities, but that it was bad for religion. The bill, he said, was "an offence against God, not against Man"—and previous efforts throughout history to provide financial support for religion had backfired. "During almost fifteen centuries has the legal establishment of Christianity been on trial. What have been its fruits? More or less in all places, pride and indolence in the Clergy, ignorance and servility in the laity, in both, superstition, bigotry and persecution." Stated more positively, Christianity is so magnificent that it doesn't need government support, and those who say otherwise will make people suspicious that Christians "are too conscious of its fallacies to trust it to its own merits."

In a section that smells condescending today, Madison also criticized the bill on the grounds that, by making Christianity the official religion, it would discourage people from other faiths from moving to Virginia, where they might be positively influenced by the "light of Christianity." "The first wish of those who enjoy this precious gift ought to be that it may be imparted to the whole race of mankind. Compare the number of those who have as yet received it with the number still remaining under the dominion of false Religions; and how small is the former! Does the policy of the Bill tend to lessen the disproportion? No; it at once discourages those who are strangers to the light of revelation from coming into the Region of it. . . ." Bold, self-confident Christians ought to welcome people of different faiths rather than, through a love of uniformity, scare away potential converts. This law would make it harder for the majesty of Christianity to be seen. "Instead of Levelling as far as possible, every obstacle to the victorious progress of Truth, the Bill with an ignoble and unchristian timidity would circumscribe it with a wall of defence against the encroachments of error."

Most powerfully, Madison argued that state support for religion would wound religion because real faith must flow from a free mind, without even an ounce of coercion. Whether we like it or not, believers have no right or ability to force belief upon others. "Whilst we assert for ourselves a freedom to embrace, to profess and to observe the Religion which we believe to be of divine origin, we cannot deny an equal freedom to those whose minds have not yet yielded to the evidence which has convinced us." Faith coerced is not true faith. "If this freedom be abused, it is an offence against God, not against man."

Thirteen copies of "Memorial" circulated around Virginia, ultimately garnering 1,552 signatures. The document was designed to appeal to those in the western part of the state who didn't want their taxes increased; Enlightenment thinkers who wanted Virginia to be sophisticated; and evangelicals who feared persecution. More than merely a lawyer's brief against the bill, "Memorial and Remonstrance" was a rallying cry for religion unfettered and entirely voluntary—a powerful argument that church and state must be strictly separated, in part, so that the greatness of Christianity could triumph throughout the world. We must not be forced to follow God, he said, because that would be an insult to God.

Madison did have allies in his radical view that even a gentle assessment constituted a threat to religious freedom: the evangelical Baptists. Consider one petition apparently drawn up by Elder Jeremiah Walker, one of the Baptist preachers who had been imprisoned, and signed by John Young, who served four months in the Caroline County jail. Even though tax support was noncoercive and could directly benefit the Baptists, their petition stated that the measure "Departed from the Spirit of the Gospel and from the bill of Rights." They, too, pointed to Pennsylvania, which offered no state support of religion, and asked, "can any of the Neighboring states boast of men of better morals And more upright Characters."[50] Finally, they contended that one of the arguments for assessment—that heretical views such as Deism were spreading—was unpersuasive since the virtuous religions would win in a marketplace of faith. "Let their Doctrines be scriptural and their lives Holy, then shall Religion beam forth as the sun and Deism shall be put to open shame."[51]

Like Madison, the Baptists further argued that Patrick Henry's approach ignored an important lesson of Christian history: that the greatest flowering of Christianity occurs *without* government support. Let's not misunderstand our own history, they were saying. State support may have indeed given us respite from persecution once upon a time, but even then it came with a spiritual cost. "The Blessed author of the Christian Religion not only maintained and supported his gospel in the world for several Hundred Years, without the aid of Civil Power but against all the Powers of the Earth, the Excellent Purity of its Precepts and the unblamable behaviour of its Ministers made its way thro all opposition," one petition declared. "Nor was it the Better for the church when Constantine the great first Established Christianity by human Laws. True there was rest from Persecution, but how soon was the Church Over run with Error and Immorality."[52] Some inverted the argument that state support succored lazy pastors, arguing that the lack of state support brought forth leaders inspired by the Holy Ghost.[53] As for the mechanics of how a small erosion of principle might transform into major constraints, a Baptist group meeting held in Dupuy's Meetinghouse in Powhatan County offered a sophisticated projection. Because money would be collected through the tax system, the "Sheriffs, County Courts and public Treasury are all to be employed in the management of money levied for the express purpose of supporting Teachers of the Christian Religion."[54]

Evangelical opposition to state aid was not driven merely by fear of persecution. Rather, evangelicals believed that Christ demanded this position. Christians were to render unto Caesar what was his—in other words, the religious and political spheres were meant, by Jesus, to be separate. The Baptist General Association in Orange County, Virginia, declared that the idea that government should help religion was "founded neither in Scripture, on Reason, on Sound Policy; but is repugnant to each of them."[55] In all, some twenty-eight counties sent in petitions arguing that the Gospel itself required rejection of the assessment.[56]

The Quakers and Methodists, a new denomination that had broken off from the Anglicans just one year earlier, worked against the assessment— and, most important, the Presbyterian groups switched sides and came out against the bill. This law was "best calculated to destroy Religion," declared one petition from Presbyterians in Rockbridge. They brought to vivid life the subsidized-minister-is-a-lazy-minister argument by predicting that, should this bill become law, the state would be "swarming with Fools, Sots and Gamblers." The Hanover Presbytery, one of the first products of the Great Awakening in Virginia, came out against assessment, too, in part because many members were of Scots-Irish descent and therefore carried an instinctive distrust of the Church of England and its progeny. Historian William Miller has argued that some Presbyterians came to feel that the idea of state-supported clergy would take power away from the laity by making ministers insufficiently dependent on the congregants.[57]

When the legislators returned to Richmond to vote on the measure, the tide had shifted. "The steps taken throughout the Country to defeat the Gnl. Assessment had produced all the effect that could have been wished," Madison reported. "The table was loaded with petitions and remonstrances from all parts against the interposition of the Legislature in matters of Religion."[58] At that point, two-thirds of the people in the state were dissenters, and only one-third Episcopalians.[59] The result: There were twelve hundred pro-assessment signatures on petitions and ten thousand signatures opposed.[60]

During recent church–state fights, many conservatives have argued that the Founders merely wanted to eliminate the formal establishments, the official state religions. Therefore, almost any other state support of religion— from prayer in school to the Ten Commandments in the courtroom to government subsidies for religious schools—would be perfectly fine. And they're partly right: Some opponents of state "establishments" were truly focused on avoiding an official church religion, no more. But not Madison. The general assessment fight makes crystal clear that he and his evangelical allies viewed any use of taxpayer money to support religion as being an establishment. Throughout the debate, Madison used the terms *establishment* and *general assessment* virtually interchangeably. That's right: For Madison, a tax designed to help religion—all religion—was morally equivalent to the establishment of a single official church.

Having won the assessment fight, Madison then moved boldly to further enshrine religious liberty, this time by pulling from a pile of moribund legislation Bill Number 82, the Virginia Statute for Religious Freedom. Written and originally submitted by Jefferson in 1779, he would list it on his tombstone as one of his greatest accomplishments, but under his legislative leadership the measure died in the committee. In 1785, when the change in public opinion had made passage plausible, Jefferson was in Paris as the American ambassador, and the challenge fell to his young friend Madison.

Compared with "Memorial and Remonstrance," the statute placed a greater emphasis on the rationalist approach to religious freedom. "Almighty God hath created the mind free and manifested his supreme will that free it shall remain by making it altogether insusceptible of restraint," the measure declared. In fact, Jefferson argued, it is an essential aspect of the Lord's way— He chooses to allow humans to find their way to Him, not through revelation or blind faith but through reason: The "holy author of our religion, who being lord both of body and mind, yet chose not to propagate it by coercions on either, as was in his Almighty power to do, but to exalt it by its influence on reason alone." While Madison's "Memorial" paid tribute to piety developed through experience, faith, *or* reason, Jefferson seemed to believe that true religion *only* set roots in a vigorous mind. The legislature apparently believed Jefferson went too far with that emphasis, deleting his contention that religion would extend "by its influence on reason alone."[61]

While Madison and the Baptists argued that state support led to violent religion and lame clergy, Jefferson added an intellectual twist: It would also prop up bad theology. It is the alliance of sword and cross that has promulgated "false religions over the greatest part of the world and through all time." The statute substituted a concept that today seems obviously in tune with our free market sensibility but was novel then: False religious ideas will lose as long as there is a free exchange of ideas. As Jefferson put in one of the most memorable lines in the statute, "Truth is great and will prevail if left to herself."[62]

Whereas "Memorial and Remonstrance" had defeated one particular plan for state-supported religion, the Statute for Religious Freedom attempted to make the principle permanent. "To compel a man to furnish contributions of money for the propagation of opinions which he disbelieves, is sinful and tyrannical." Jefferson and Madison were in full agreement: Tax-financed aid to religion was morally the same as forcing a man to attend an alien church or utter prayers to an inauthentic God.

Some religious conservatives have argued that the statute's reference to the "holy author of our religion" showed that even Jefferson was referring to Christianity. At first glance, they have a point. Surely it could not have been accidental that a pluralist such as Jefferson chose to use the singular form of the words *author* and *religion*. He himself cleared up the ambiguity in his autobiography. He reported that an amendment had been offered to change that phrase from "holy author of our religion" to "Jesus Christ" but that "the insertion was rejected by a great majority, in proof that they meant to comprehend, within the mantle of its protection, the Jew and the Gentile, the Christian and Mahometan, the Hindoo, and infidel of every denomination."[63] Madison had another explanation for why he had fought to keep out references to Christianity—revealing a fascinating difference between his worldview and Jefferson's. To do otherwise, Madison wrote, would "profane it by making it a topic of legislative discussion, and particularly by making His religion the means of abridging the natural and equal rights of all men in defiance of His own declaration that His Kingdom was not of this world."[64] Jefferson sought to encourage pluralism; Madison also to protect the integrity of Christianity.[65] And allied with both of them were evangelical Christians, especially the Virginia Baptists, indomitable foot soldiers in the battle for religious freedom.

The alliance between Enlightenment thinkers and evangelical Christians is sometimes described as a marriage of convenience. The erudite Founders and the spirit-drenched evangelicals shared a hatred of the Church of England and a desire for freedom. But the connection runs deeper. Both believed that individual liberty was the highest value. For Madison and Jefferson, individual liberty trumped the rights of kings or governments. For evangelicals, an individual's personal relationship with God was more important than church and clerical authority. "Every man must give an account of himself to God," wrote the Reverend John Leland, "and therefore every man ought to be at liberty to serve God in a way that he can best reconcile to his conscience." Let's remember who will provide the final assessment of a life well lived. "If government can answer for individuals at the day of judgment, let men be controlled by it in religious matters," Leland wrote. "Otherwise, let men be free."[66]

––––––

What's to be learned from the schizophrenic approaches in the States and Continental Congress during this period? That, as Madison and his colleagues turned to writing the Constitution, there was no national consensus about how to define religious liberty or separation of church and state. The momentum was moving away from official state establishments—but for some Americans, including those in Virginia, that meant a strict separation of church and state, while for others, like the citizens of Massachusetts, it meant a broad-minded government support of Christianity. There were divergent opinions among the state legislatures and within the Continental Congress. And there was division even among the most prominent Founding Fathers. Adams was inclined to have more state support for religion. Washington didn't go quite as far but, at least in his role as commander of the Continental army, employed the power of the state to aggressively promote religion among the troops. Madison and Jefferson, on the other hand, had already begun to embrace the view that a strict separation of church and state was necessary.

In explaining historic shifts, some scholars focus on sweeping forces such as demography or technological advances. Others highlight the roles of decisive leaders who, by sticking in their oar at the right moment and in the right way, are able to alter the current's course. Looking at the aforementioned forces in the young America without the benefit of hindsight, it's not entirely clear what the outcome might be. But with hindsight it's clear that individual leadership did indeed play a decisive role in birthing religious liberty. For we know that there was a Constitution to be written and a Bill of Rights to be crafted and a political fight over the ratification of both, and that the dominant figure was not to be Patrick Henry or John Adams, Ben Franklin or Thomas Jefferson, or even George Washington. It was to be the diffident legislative tactician, one who forged the intellectual consensus and political alliance between the evangelicals and the philosophes, James Madison.

forgetting the "powerful friend"

THE FOUNDERS REJECT 150 YEARS OF HISTORY

—◆—

T HOSE WISHING TO PORTRAY THE FOUNDING FATHERS AS DEVOUT— and the nation as born of a divine intervention—point to the following extraordinary moment on June 28, 1787.

The Constitutional Convention had been meeting for five weeks, and had hit a perilous deadlock. The large states were insisting that congressional representation be based on population; the smaller states wanted a one-state-one-vote rule. The entire effort to create a stronger union was in jeopardy.

Then eighty-one-year-old Benjamin Franklin, quiet during most of the deliberations, addressed the group. Franklin already had mythic stature as philosopher, inventor, entrepreneur, and scientist, so it must have been stunning when this personification of the Enlightenment explained to the illustrious lawmakers that the most important step they could take was not to debate or read or study . . . but to pray.

"We indeed seem to feel our own wont of political wisdom, since we have been running about in search of it," he began in a soft voice that seemed directed almost intimately toward the convention's chairman, George Washington.[1] Franklin noted that while the collected men had studied ancient history and modern, and looked at faraway models and those close to home, they had not yet "thought of humbly applying to the Father of lights to illuminate our understanding." During the war, he said, Congress had asked for divine protection daily—and the nation had succeeded. "Our prayers, Sir, were heard, and they were graciously answered." The evidence could be found in the many instances when outnumbered Americans triumphed over stronger opponents. "All of us who were engaged in the struggle must have observed frequent instances of a Superintending providence in our favor." If we sought and received God's help to win the war, why were we not turning to him for help now? "Have we now forgotten that powerful friend? Or do we imagine that we no longer need His assistance?"

The man who had once described himself as a Deist then declared his belief that God intervened in life and history. "I have lived, Sir, a long time and the longer I live, the more convincing proofs I see of this truth—that *God governs in the affairs of men*. And if a sparrow cannot fall to the ground without his notice, is it probable that an empire can rise without his aid?"

If they didn't beseech God's help, Franklin warned, the men attempting to write a Constitution would fare "no better than the Builders of Babel." He moved, therefore, that every morning the group begin with prayers "imploring the assistance of Heaven."[2]

Some conservatives note that the logjam at the convention soon thereafter *did* break, and the Constitution we now revere was produced. Many attribute that to the power of prayer. One problem: Franklin's motion was *not* accepted. It wasn't even voted on, prompting knowing snickers from some liberal writers. Isaac Kramnick and Laurence Moore, in *The Godless Constitution*, explained that the delegates ignored the proposal because they were more concerned about "worldly matters like Shays rebellion and America's financial instability."[3] Could that really be the explanation? Given the ubiquity of prayers in other venues, such as the Continental Congress, the failure to pass such a predictable proposal—offered by a living legend—must be more meaningful than that.

One theory was that such a move would reek of desperation. Alexander Hamilton and others argued that even if prayer had been a good idea at the beginning of the convention, employing it now would "lead the public to believe that the embarrassments and dissensions within the Convention, had suggested the measure."[4] Hugh Williamson of North Carolina offered another rationale: "The convention had no funds." To me, another explanation more closely hits the mark. The men attending the convention represented eight different denominations.[5] Whereas the Continental Congress of 1775 had felt no qualms about championing Christianity explicitly, the convention meeting twelve years later seemed more conscious of religious diversity in the land. While in 1775 the appointment of a chaplain was viewed primarily as something that could unite the Congress, many now feared that an official invocation of religion might *divide* this group.[6]

THE RELIGIOUS SIGNIFICANCE OF A RELIGION-FREE DOCUMENT

The topic of religion came up three times during the convention, according to Madison's notes. At one point, Madison and Charles Pinckney of South Carolina proposed that Congress be given the power "to establish an University, in which no preferences or distinctions should be allowed on account of religion." Gouverneur Morris argued that Congress could do so with or without such a clause, and the proposal lost by a vote of six states to four. This failed motion hints at the radical nature of Madison's views about religion and state, since, at the time, most major colleges were connected to a Christian denomination.[7]

As part of his larger alternative Constitution, Pinckney also proposed that Congress "shall pass no Law on the subject of Religion," but that provision died with the rest of his plan.[8]

And it was the thirty-year-old Pinckney again who offered what would become the most significant clause related to religious freedom in the original Constitution. On August 20, he proposed that "no religious test or qualification shall ever be annexed to any oath of office under the authority of the US." The amendment was referred to the Committee of Detail, which ignored it.[9] So ten days later, Pinckney brought it to the full convention. Roger Sherman of Connecticut resisted it on the myopic grounds that "the prevailing liberality" would be "a sufficient security against such tests."[10] The resolution passed easily, apparently eleven states to one.[11] The Committee on Style changed it to what we now know as Article VI, clause 3: "No religious test shall ever be required as a qualification to any office or public trust under the United States."

This clause is often ignored as a constitutional no-brainer that doesn't relate to today's discussions about church and state. After all no one now advocates a religious test for public office. But the clause was remarkable. At the time, eleven of the thirteen states *did* limit public office to people of particular faiths or beliefs. This makes manifest a point that was obvious to the convention but often forgotten today. Most delegates assumed that the Constitution would govern the laws of Congress, not the states. That the eleven states didn't try to impose a religious test on the national government reflected a pragmatic reality: If there were one, what religion would it be? Would it be Protestant-only, as in Massachusetts, and ignore the role that Catholics had played in bringing independence? Would it be for Trinitarians, as in the Delaware constitution—ignoring the presence of non-Trinitarians like Ben Franklin in their midst? At that moment, no one church accounted for more than a fifth of the population, so no practitioners could have confidence that religious tests would be to their liking.[12] Thanks to religious diversity, a national religious test was impossible.

More controversial than the lack of tests is the absence of something else from the Constitution—God. Thanks are not offered for His past blessings. Protection is not beseeched for future trials. The rights, we are told in the first three words, come from "we the people," not God the Almighty. He simply makes no appearance at all. Like two psychiatric patients looking at the same inkblot, today's conservative and liberal writers offer dramatically different interpretations of the silence. Conservatives have argued that despite the absence of religious language, the document was infused with Judeo-Christian values, and that many of its framers were quite religious. "The Constitution was designed to perpetuate a Christian order," declared the conservative religious group Focus on the Family.[13] Liberal scholars and activists point to the lack of theistic rhetoric as proof that the Founders believed religion should play no official role in the governing of the republic. The Constitution, wrote Kramnick and Moore, "is a godless document" that was "self-consciously designed to be an instrument with which to structure the secular politics of individual interest and happiness." Why else, they ask rhetorically, would the authors "refuse to assign government . . . any responsibility for promoting religion?"[14]

Neither side has it quite right. Conservatives are wrong in describing the Constitution as a religious document. Yes, it incorporates certain biblical principles, such as the rule of law, but by that standard we should also celebrate the influence of Zeus and Dionysius since the founders so clearly incorporated many principles from ancient Rome and Greece. More important, compared with the Declaration of Independence ("endowed by our Creator"), the Articles of Confederation ("It hath pleased the Great Governor of the World"), numerous proclamations from the Continental Congress ("the supreme and impartial Judge and Ruler of the Universe"), and almost all of the state constitutions ("the Christian religion is the true religion"), the US Constitution is stunningly secular. It doesn't mention Jesus, God, the Creator, or even Providence.[15] In light of the unbroken record of invoking God's name in foundational documents throughout the world, throughout the colonies, and throughout history, the stubborn refusal of the US Constitution to invoke the Almighty is abnormal, historic, radical, and not accidental.

But liberals miss a basic point, too: The framers of the Constitution were not contemplating the role of "government" in religion. They were debating the role of the *national* government in religion. Remember this, and the story of the US Constitution—the drafting, the ratification, the Bill of Rights—suddenly looks very different. Some have asserted that since Madison was a staunch supporter of strict separation of church and state, and he helped shape the Constitution, therefore it must embody his views on the matter. But Madison often lost at the Constitutional Convention, and the one feature he felt was most important for guaranteeing religious freedom, he did not get.

Madison feared that the greatest threat to liberty was not the executive—whether a king, a president, or a governor—but rather the majority imposing its will on the minority in the states. He'd seen the legislatures approve laws postponing the collection of taxes or limiting the ability of creditors to seek payment. Most important, he'd seen Virginia just two years earlier almost impose a tax to support the Christian religion. His work at the Constitutional Convention, it must be remembered, came immediately after his fights for religious liberty in Virginia. He wrote to Jefferson that the state legislatures regularly demonstrated their proclivity toward tyranny: "The injustice of them has been so frequent and so flagrant as to alarm the most stedfast friends of Republicanism."[16] Couldn't piety or good citizenship or the powers of reason check ignoble tendencies? Hardly. The very assemblies that had acted wantonly had done so after each legislator had sworn an oath to God, Madison noted. "The conduct of every popular Assembly, acting on oath, the strongest of religious ties, shews that individuals join without remorse in acts [against] which their consciences would revolt, if proposed to them separately in their closets." Even well-meaning individuals turn ignoble when joined together in a gang, mob, or legislature. "The inefficacy of this restraint [religion] on individuals is well known." Indeed, he noted solemnly, far from being a check on legislative excess, religion "has been much oftener a motive to oppression than a restraint from it."[17]

Ultimately, at the Constitutional Convention, Madison offered two ways to protect minorities and, by implication, religious freedom. The most important safeguard was the presence of a "multiplicity" of interests. He made this point about power in general, offering the contrarian view that a large nation would be more likely to sustain a republic than a small one because of its competing factions and interests. In Federalist No. 51, he wrote that champions of all freedom could learn from the battles over religious liberty. "The security for civil rights must be the same as that for religious rights. It consists in the one case of the multiplicity of interests and in the other in the multiplicity of sects. The degrees of security in both cases will depend on the number of interests and sects." He had concluded that it was the divisions among the Baptists, Presbyterians, and Anglicans that had kept Patrick Henry's damaging assessment bill from becoming law. The "multiplicity of sects" would therefore protect religious liberty. In that sense, each faith owes its power and freedom to the vitality of other faiths. Those seeking the one True Way must tolerate the vibrancy of "false" faiths.

But Madison had another, more direct tool for protecting minorities and liberties: Give Congress the power to veto state laws. The national government could be a "disinterested & dispassionate umpire in disputes between different passions & interests in the State and [curb] the aggressions of interested majorities on the rights of minorities and of individuals."[18] This was as dramatic as it sounded. "Only by abolishing the states altogether could Madison have moved to alter the structure of the Union more radically," wrote historian Jack Rakove.[19] Madison's plan was defeated soundly, seven states to three, in part because southern lawmakers saw immediately that this could lead to Congress outlawing slavery.

After Madison moved into sales mode—trying to get the states to ratify the Constitution—he never again publicly expressed his deep concerns about this flaw in it. But privately he initially wondered whether the failure of the national veto would doom it. He wrote to Jefferson that the Constitution "will neither effectually answer its national object nor prevent the local mischiefs which everywhere excite disgusts [against] the state governments."[20] By the time he wrote the Federalist Papers in 1787 and 1788, Madison had rationalized that at least state tyranny could only subjugate the people in one particular realm at a time, so religious oppression could be effectively quarantined. "The influence of factious leaders may kindle a flame within their particular States, but will be unable to spread a general conflagration through the other States," he wrote in Federalist No. 10.

To fully appreciate how depressing a defeat this must have been to Madison, remember that at the time of ratification, few states had religious liberty of the sort Madison wanted. All but two states had religious tests banning Jews, Unitarians, and agnostics from public office.[21] Taxpayers supported the churches and ministers in Massachusetts, New Hampshire, Connecticut,

New Jersey, Georgia, North Carolina, and South Carolina.[22] In some states, only Trinitarian Protestants could vote or testify in trials. It was considered blasphemy, and therefore illegal in some states, to criticize, reproach, or deny Christianity, the Trinity, Jesus Christ, or the Bible. Nontheists were restricted from owning property or giving money to certain charities; schools required religious services; and people were regularly prosecuted for not observing the Sabbath.[23]

All that, the US Constitution let stand.

RATIFICATION—A POPE AS PRESIDENT?

The framers left Philadelphia on September 17, 1787, and submitted the Constitution to the states for ratification. Though conservatives today hail the religious influences on the founding documents, many at the time bemoaned the lack of religion in the Constitution. A writer in the *Virginia Independent Chronicle* commented on the "cold indifference towards religion";[24] and a New Hampshire delegate predicted that under this Constitution, "congress might deprive the people of the use of the holy scriptures."[25] A Boston writer warned that the absence of God could draw His wrath. Read your Bible and behold that Americans would suffer the same fate as the biblical King Saul: "Because thou hast rejected the word of the Lord, he hath also rejected thee."[26] Some state delegates tried to rectify the God blackout. A delegate to the Connecticut ratifying convention, William Williams, proposed that the Constitution's preamble be amended to read, in part, "We the people of the United States in a firm belief in the being and perfection of the one living and true God, the creator and supreme Governor of the World." But the convention did not agree.[27]

The ban on religious tests raised fears among some that the Constitution would allow for a heathen takeover. One conflicted writer from western Massachusetts complained that the document didn't guarantee religious freedom enough—but then, without sensing any contradiction, griped that "there is a door opened for the Jews, Turks, and Heathens to enter into publick office."[28] Luther Martin of Maryland suggested that "it would be at least decent to hold out some distinction between the professor of Christianity and downright infidelity or paganism."[29] Not surprisingly, fear and loathing of Catholics once again became an animating argument. Major Thomas Lusk, a Massachusetts delegate, declared that under this Constitution, "Popery and the Inquisition may be established in America."[30] The arguments at times became quite far-fetched. As North Carolina delegate Henry Abbott warned, citizens now feared that without a ban on Catholic officeholders, some nation could, through force, compel us to adopt Catholicism as the official religion. The ban on religious tests, Abbott declared, also made it possible that "pagans, deists, and Mahometans might obtain offices among us"—and he wondered "to whom will they swear support—the ancient gods of Jupiter, Juno, Minerva, or Pluto?" The Reverend David Caldwell argued for a new, improved test that would block "Jews and pagans of every kind."[31]

Most vividly, a writer in the *New York Daily Advertiser* offered this creatively paranoid analysis that was reprinted in Connecticut, New Hampshire, and Massachusetts: "1st. Quakers who will make the blacks saucy, and at the same time deprive us of the means of defense—2dly. Mahometans, who ridicule the doctrine of the Trinity—3dly. Deists, abominable wretches—4thly. Negroes, the seed of Cain—5thly. Beggars, who when set on horseback will ride to the devil—6thly. Jews etc. etc." And should the president be Jewish, "our dear posterity may be ordered to rebuild Jerusalem."[32] At least he was thoroughly thinking through the possibilities.

We shouldn't conclude from these extreme instances that most people thought the Constitution bad for religion. Far from it. Baptist leader John Leland praised it for following the broad principle that government stay out of religion. At the Massachusetts convention, the Reverend Isaac Backus declared that religious tests had been the "greatest engine of tyranny in the world," and praised the revolutionary new document for recognizing that "Nothing is more evident both in reason and the Holy Scriptures, than that religion is ever a matter between God and individuals; and, therefore no man or men can impose any religious test without invading the essential prerogatives of our Lord Jesus Christ."[33] After Pennsylvania ratified, Philadelphia sponsored a celebratory parade. Watching from the side, Dr. Benjamin Rush noticed a rabbi and two Christian ministers marching arm in arm and thought it a perfect symbol of the Constitution's ban on religious tests. "There could not have been a more happy emblem contrived of that section of the new constitution, which opens all its power and offices alike, not only to every sect of Christians, but to worthy men of every religion."[34]

The absence of God from the Constitution was pro-religion, but in a way that was not obvious to all. Much of the population had been raised to believe that to ensure a religion's health, the state must support it. The Constitution demanded a paradigm shift, away from public responsibility and toward private. In his own diplomatic way, George Washington tried to awaken people to the change. Responding to a letter from a group of Presbyterian churches in New England about the moral perils of a godless Constitution, Washington encouraged them to stop relying on government for religious leadership and suggested instead that "to the guidance of the Ministers of the Gospel this important object is, perhaps, more properly committed." While Jefferson had denounced religion so weak that it needed the crutch of the state, Washington offered a gentler formulation of a similar point, suggesting that the virtue of faith was sufficiently obvious that government aid was superfluous. "The path of true piety is so plain as to require but little political direction."[35]

But while some praised the document's neutrality, many advocates of religious freedom felt it had not gone far enough. What was needed was not just the absence of state-written religious dogma but an affirmative declaration on the primacy of religious and other freedoms. They demanded a Bill of Rights.

At first, Madison and most of the other Federalists who framed the Constitution resisted a Bill of Rights. Not only was such an addition unnecessary, they believed, it was dangerous. As James Wilson put it in a speech at the Pennsylvania statehouse, the national government could exercise only powers given by "positive grant." So if the Constitution didn't give Congress permission to regulate religion, Congress was literally powerless to touch it at all. Adding a Bill of Rights might muddy the message.[36] Mention some rights and you leave the unmentioned more vulnerable; those not important enough to warrant explicit protection will surely seem to be inferior rights. To make this point, Noah Webster mocked one amendment proposed at the Pennsylvania convention affirming the "liberty to fowl and hunt in seasonable times." If hunting in seasonable times was protected, did that mean hunting in bad weather wasn't? If they were going to add rights, they had better be thorough, so he sarcastically suggested amending the Constitution to declare "Congress shall never restrain any inhabitant of America from eating and drinking, at seasonable times, or prevent his lying on his left side, in a long winter's night, or even on his back, when he is fatigued by lying on his right."[37] When it came to religious liberty, Federalists throughout the country put forth the argument that the Constitution was already crystal clear: Congress could not, declared James Iredell of North Carolina, interfere in "the establishment of any religion whatsoever; and I am astonished that any gentleman should conceive they have." Congress was prohibited from touching religion in any way. "Is there any power given to Congress in matters of religion? . . . If any future Congress should pass an act concerning the religion of the country, it would be an act which they are not authorized to pass, by the Constitution, and which the people would not obey." Richard Dobbs Spaight, who had been a delegate at the Constitutional Convention, echoed the argument: "No power is given to the general government to interfere with it [religion] at all. Any act of Congress on this subject would be a usurpation."[38] So before there was even a First Amendment, many believed that the Constitution required Congress to abstain from passing *any* laws related to religion—and that a Bill of Rights might constitute a step backward.

At first, the ratification campaign went well for the Federalists. Delaware, New Jersey, and Georgia ratified unconditionally without proposing any amendments. Massachusetts, which still had a clear religious establishment, also apparently had little debate on the subject, even though Isaac Backus and twenty Baptists attended the convention as delegates. In Connecticut and Pennsylvania, some delegates discussed the need for a Bill of Rights, but they nonetheless approved the Constitution without recommended amendments.

Still, it soon became clear that the lack of a Bill of Rights concerned many Americans, to the point of endangering ratification. Where were the guarantees for a free press and jury? What would stop the new government from seizing their property? And how could they be sure religious freedom was truly safe? New York's convention recommended that "no Religious Sect or Society ought to be favored or established by Law in preference of others."[39] Most important, it looked as if the lack of a Bill of Rights imperiled ratification in Virginia . . . and a loss in Virginia would trigger a loss in North Carolina, probably incapacitating the Constitution.[40]

Madison got the bad news from his father. James Madison Sr. informed his son in 1788 that the Baptists back home—Madison's old allies—were turning against the Constitution.[41] Apparently, they'd been convinced that without explicit protections, the new government would impose a national religion of some sort.[42] Madison had not intended to campaign for ratification until he received a letter from Joseph Spencer, a Continental army captain and Baptist who had himself been imprisoned. Spencer informed Madison that the candidate for the ratification convention, Colonel Thomas Barber, was actively misrepresenting the situation in a "horrid" way—and that it was working. "The preachers of that Society [Baptists] are much alarm'd fearing Religious Liberty is not Sufficiently secur'd." He suggested that Madison would be wise to personally court the Baptist leadership, especially John Leland, who was planning to submit himself as a delegate to the convention in opposition to ratification. A protégé of Isaac Backus, Leland had moved to

Virginia in 1775 at the age of twenty-one in part to join the fight for religious freedom there. "Mr. Leeland Lyes in your way home from Fredricksburg to Orange would advise you'd call on him and Spend a few Howers in his Company."[43] Spencer enclosed a copy of the objections that Leland had formally laid out, which Madison no doubt studied carefully. Leland wrote: "What is clearest of all—Religious Liberty, is not sufficiently secured. No Religious test is Required as a qualification to fill any office under the United States, but if a Majority of Congress with the President favour one System more than another, they may oblige all others to pay to support their System as much as they please."[44]

Under an oak tree on Leland's farm outside Orange, the two men debated the issue. Based on their public positions, we can imagine that the meeting between Madison and Leland went something like this: The preacher explained his position; Madison replied that he shared the sentiment, but demanding amendments before the Constitution was ratified—as Patrick Henry and Richard Henry Lee wanted—would only serve to kill the constitution itself. Leland held firm. A guarantee was essential. So Madison privately promised that if Leland withdrew his objection to the Constitution, he would work to add amendments guaranteeing religious liberty, but only after the Constitution had been ratified.[45] Leland agreed, and allowed Madison instead of him to represent the county at the ratification convention.[46]

Patrick Henry, still wildly popular in the state, led the charge against ratification. He charged that the Constitution—with its tax-levying Congress and its powerful president—would create a monstrously powerful central government. "The sovereignty of the States will be relinquished," he warned. They'd recently witnessed what might happen to Virginians should a strong union be formed: Northern states had signed off on a potential treaty with Spain that would have cut off Virginia's rights to navigate the Mississippi. And who knew where the national tyranny might end? Though Henry said he personally was discomfited by slavery, he warned that the new Constitution would give the federal government, rather than the states, the power to decide this question. "They'll take your niggers from you," he said to laughter in the chamber.[47] But his most potent attack was over the absence of a Bill of Rights. "The rights of conscience, trial by jury, liberty of the press, all your immunities and franchises, all pretensions to human rights and privileges, are rendered insecure, if not lost."[48] He mocked the legalistic argument that Congress would only exercise powers explicitly delegated to it. What a flimsy foundation for freedom, he suggested. "This sacred right ought not to depend on constructive logical reasoning." If the men who secretly huddled at the Constitutional Convention cared so much about rights, why not just state it clearly?

Speaking so softly the official scribe often could not make out his words, Madison tried to rebut Henry's incendiary charges. Clause by clause, he explained how the separation of powers—the balance between central and state governments, legislative and executive—safeguarded freedom. But Madison refused to accept the idea that the state legislatures would best protect freedom. After all, despite the grandiose defenses of religious liberty in the Virginia Declaration of Rights, some in the state—that is, Patrick Henry—had still come close to imposing a tax to support religious organizations. No, Madison said, what was far more likely to protect religious freedom than "parchment barriers" was religious diversity: the proliferation of a "multiplicity of sects, which pervades America, and which is the best and only security for religious liberty in any society. For where there is such a variety of sects, there cannot be a majority of any one sect to oppress and persecute the rest."[49] As for the document itself, Madison reiterated the view that what Congress is not empowered to do, it is not allowed to do. "There is not a shadow of right in the general government to intermeddle with religion," he declared. "Its least interference with it would be a most flagrant usurpation."[50]

Realizing he didn't have the votes, Madison and his allies offered a compromise: They would agree to amendments as long as the Constitution was first ratified. Henry rejected this proposal and suggested that it was more than just Patrick Henry who disagreed with Madison: God Himself opposed ratification. "I see the awful immensity of the dangers with which it is pregnant. I see it—I feel it," he declared. "I see *beings* of a higher order anxious concerning our decision." As if on cue, and at his personal command, the skies grew dark, the windows rattled, and a momentous thunderstorm broke out.[51]

Henry wanted the delegates to submit amendments to the other states *before* agreeing to ratification. On this crucial procedural matter, Henry lost and Madison won. The convention rejected by a vote of eighty-eight to eighty Henry's amendment and then approved the Federalist resolution eighty-nine to seventy-nine.[52] The convention ultimately *recommended* that the Constitution only be approved if it had a Bill of Rights that, among other things, protected religious freedom.

Even though Madison agreed to the amendments for the sake of political expediency, he soon learned that it was not only his political foes who wanted a Bill of Rights. After the Virginia ratification vote, Madison received a passionate letter from his good friend and the American ambassador to France, Thomas Jefferson, who said he wanted a Bill of Rights that guaranteed the freedom of religion "without the aid of sophisms." That line must have stung Madison, who had been among those making the argument that the freedoms were implied. Jefferson was blunt. "A bill of rights is what the people are entitled to against every government on earth, general or particular, & what no just government should refuse or rest on inference."[53] In reply, Madison (disingenuously) claimed that "my own opinion has always been in favor of a bill of rights provided it be so framed as not to imply powers not meant to be included in the numerous,"[54] though he also said he thought their absence was not a "material defect."

In this correspondence, Madison shared with Jefferson a fear that he had not publicly expressed about a possible Bill of Rights. It was possible, he said, that when it got down to writing a specific declaration of religious freedom, they would discover that their broad-minded approach was not shared by the majority. "There is great reason to fear that a positive declaration of some of the most essential rights could not be obtained in the requisite latitude." If we have a public debate on the specific meaning of religious freedom, he was suggesting, we might lose. "I am sure that the right of Conscience in particular, if submitted to public definition, would be narrowed much more than they are likely ever to be by an assumed power." Being vague, in other words, might better protect religious freedom than would being explicit. As the one who would be guiding through the legislation, Madison was perhaps more vividly aware than Jefferson that the explication of rights would be shaped by an intensely political process. After all, Madison noted, enemies of religious freedom were already pushing for a more regressive view. "One of the objections in New England was that the Constitution by prohibiting religious tests opened a door for Jews, Turks & infidels." He was, in effect, telling Jefferson: If we go down this path, let's not kid ourselves that it will be like the Declaration of Independence or the Virginia Statute for Religious Freedom. This time, we might not be the ones defining what the "rights" really mean.

Furthermore, he argued to Jefferson, it is not like the state declarations of rights had succeeded in protecting liberties anyway. "Repeated violations of these parchment barriers have been committed by overbearing majorities in every state. In Virginia I have seen the bill of rights violated in every instance where it has been opposed to a popular current."[55]

Jefferson was not persuaded. "Half a loaf is better than no bread," he wrote back. "If we cannot secure all our rights, let us secure what we can." Jefferson reassured Madison that the federal judiciary would thankfully be there to interpret the Constitution and protect rights. It was not only his hope but also his expectation that judges would actively define the meaning of constitutional liberties. All in all, Jefferson said, "the Declaration of rights is like all other human blessings alloyed with some inconveniences, and not accomplishing fully its object. But the good in this instance vastly outweighs the evil."[56]

There was something else gnawing at Jefferson. He was convinced that although the War of Independence and its afterglow had made America and its leaders unusually tolerant, this golden moment soon would end—so they'd better enshrine these rights while they could. "The time for fixing every essential right on a legal basis is while our rulers are honest, and ourselves united," he wrote in 1782 in *Notes on the State of Virginia*. "From the conclusion of this war we shall be going down hill." Both the leaders and the people themselves would soon forget the importance of these principles and stop fighting for their preservation. "The shackles, therefore, which shall not be knocked off at the conclusion of this war, will remain on us long, will be made heavier and heavier, till our rights shall revive or expire in a convulsion."

14

the first amendment compromise

BUILDING A WALL THAT LOOKS GOOD FROM ALL SIDES

——◆——

AFTER THE CONSTITUTION WAS RATIFIED IN 1788, THE STATES set to work determining who would be their representatives in the first Congress. One would think that the leading author of the Constitution would have no trouble getting elected to the Congress he had just created. But James Madison was in trouble, for Patrick Henry now had it in for him. First Henry blocked Madison's appointment to be Virginia's first US senator, declaring that his election would send "rivulets of blood throughout the land."[1] Henry believed that the Constitution was dangerous, as was its chief proponent.

Madison decided then to serve in the new House of Representatives. But Henry, then governor of Virginia, was determined to stop that, too. When creating the House districts, he carved from the hills and valleys of Virginia a district that would be dominated by Anti-Federalist towns.[2] Some of Madison's friends suggested he run from friendlier counties, but Henry had anticipated such a move by requiring that any candidate be a resident of the district for twelve months prior to the election.[3] To make sure that Madison wouldn't be able to campaign, Henry had the assembly reappoint him to a lame-duck session of Congress in New York. And if all that wasn't enough to keep Madison out, Henry had one more gambit: He recruited as Madison's opponent a war hero and member of one of Virginia's finest families—Colonel James Monroe, the future president. More than six feet tall, with broad shoulders, Monroe had literally crossed the Delaware with Washington.[4] He had been wounded in the battle of Trenton when an enemy musket ball blasted through his shoulder as he charged a nest of cannon.[5]

By contrast, the frail Madison was short on wartime heroics, and associated with a Constitution unpopular in his own district. He despised even the "spirit of electioneering,"[6] having once lost an election to a state convention over his prim refusal to liquor up the voters at a campaign event. (As he put it, he declined to beseech them through "the corrupting influence of spirituous liquors and other treats.")[7] His campaign for the House got off to a terrible start thanks to an affliction even more painful than Henry's machinations—hemorrhoids. He wrote George Washington (!) that he had a serious case of the "piles" and worried that the long carriage ride from New York would be excruciating.[8] But his allies back home told him to get off his rear and start campaigning, because Monroe had already begun blanketing the district with personal letters.[9]

The main campaign issue was the Constitution itself. Monroe argued that Madison, as an author of the highly flawed document, would stand in the way of needed fixes. Madison's friends urged him to stop being so gentlemanly. "When we find there are evil minds using every measure which Envy or Malice can Suggest to our prejudice it frees us from that restraint we otherwise should feel," wrote David Jameson Jr., who represented Culpeper in the House of Delegates.[10] Apparently, Monroe's allies were telling voters that Madison, believing the Constitution to be perfect, opposed amendments, a position he had by then abandoned. Madison complained to Washington that he was being portrayed as "dogmatically attached to the Constitution in every clause, syllable and letter."[11] What's more, Henry's allies specifically worked to rile up the Baptists—a key voting bloc—into thinking that Madison, of all people, had gone soft on religious freedom.[12] Madison, they said, had "ceased to be a friend to the rights of Conscience."[13]

This was a big problem for Madison, who was counting on support from the growing Baptist community. (By 1790, the 204 Baptist churches in the state had more than twenty thousand members.) Though Madison continued to be ambivalent about amendments, he'd come to believe that the bigger threat was that Anti-Federalists would succeed in calling a second convention and then scrap the whole Constitution. Given that television attack ads were some two hundred years in the future, Madison instead wrote private letters, likely with the expectation that they would become public. The most important was to the Reverend George Eve, the pastor of the Blue Run Church in Orange County, near Madison's Montpelier home. While conceding that he didn't always see a need for a Bill of Rights, Madison admitted in the January 2, 1789, letter that "circumstances are now changed." Whereas before, the campaign for amendments was geared toward killing the Constitution, the document had now been ratified and could be safely amended through the proper process.

Then he made his read-my-lips pledge: "It is my sincere opinion that the Constitution ought to be revised, and that the first Congress . . . ought to prepare and recommend to the States for ratification the most satisfactory provisions for all essential rights, particularly the rights of Conscience in the fullest latitude, the freedom of the press, trials by jury, security against general warrents & c."[14] It was one of the most important campaign promises in American history.

The charismatic Monroe wasn't leaving the evangelical vote to Madison; he campaigned at churches, too. They made several joint appearances, including at the Hebron Lutheran Church in Culpeper on January 26, 1789.[15] After worship services ended, Madison and Monroe stood outside in the windy, freezing cold and debated their visions for the new nation. Madison was bemused that the audience seemed to view them as two combatants. "They stood it out very patiently—seemed to consider it a sort of fight, of which they were required to be spectators."[16] On the way home, Madison's nose froze, and he carried a frostbite scar for the rest of his life.[17] The campaign had left its marks on Madison from top to bottom.

It soon became clear that the evangelicals would, once again, deliver for Madison. At one meeting in Culpeper, an Anti-Federalist named Joel Early told the crowd that Madison believed the Constitution "had no defects." The Reverend George Eve rose to Madison's defense, reminding the crowd of Madison's heroic role in strengthening the religious liberty clause of the Virginia Declaration of Rights. Religious voters, especially those in the minority like evangelicals and Baptists, owed Madison, Eve told the crowd.[18]

On January 30, 1789, three days before the election, it began snowing and didn't stop until ten inches had fallen. Men had to ride on horseback or carriages for hours to get to their polling places, but 44 percent of the eligible voters did. When the results were counted, Madison won 57 to 43 percent (1,308 votes to 972), with special assistance from a lopsided victory in the heavily Baptist Culpeper County as well as his home county of Orange.[19]

Patrick Henry had tried to block him, but Madison had parried by making a solemn campaign promise—especially to the evangelical Christians—that he would work to pass a Bill of Rights, and particularly a guarantee for religious freedom.

THE FIRST AMENDMENT IN THE SAUSAGE GRINDER

The Bill of Rights was written not by the federal Constitutional Convention or by any of the state ratifying conventions that had recommended amendments, but by the newly created Congress. And like all measures going through Congress, it was shaped by a series of tussles and compromises. The sixteen words on religious freedom would forever after be analyzed by scholars and activists trying to divine, or assert, their true meaning. So it's worth going through the process step by step to see the flurry of changes, adjustments, and compromises that gave us the First Amendment. As you're reading, keep in mind that the issue that has bedeviled scholars and culture warriors for the last two-hundred-plus years has been whether the First Amendment was meant to block only the creation of an official national religion or whether it was intended to more generally restrict government involvement with, and even support of, religion.

Many of Madison's Federalist allies were in no rush to promote the amendments, pressing ahead with other business once the new Congress convened. They believed that, having successfully gotten the Constitution ratified without conditions, they were under no obligation to do more. Technically, that was true, but Madison believed it both morally required—he'd made a promise—and politically wise to do so, in order to suck away the energy from the Anti-Federalist forces. Some Federalists cynically referred to his amendments as the "tub to the whale"—a reference to Jonathan Swift's *Tale of a Tub*, in which sailors tossed an empty tub overboard to distract a threatening whale.[20]

On June 8, 1789, to fulfill his pledge to secure a Bill of Rights, Madison went to the floor of the House of Representatives, meeting at Federal Hall in New York, and proposed a series of amendments.[21] His presentation was anything but dynamic; "his person is little and ordinary," Fisher Ames, a fellow member of Congress, commented.[22] Madison continued to assert that these were probably not necessary but that they would help to "quiet the minds of people." Instead of hearing the criticisms of Anti-Federalists and reveling in his ability to defeat them—he did have the votes—Madison declared his desire to assuage their concerns. On principles of "amity and moderation" he aspired to convince those who believed the Constitution would lead to "aristocracy or despotism" that he would not deprive them of the "liberty for which they valiantly fought and honorably bled."[23] Rather than squelch his opponents, his goal with the Bill of Rights was to firmly cement them to the new union.

The rights of conscience and freedom of press were the "choicest flowers," he stated, and should, along with trial by jury, be placed "out of the power of the Legislature to infringe them." He proposed inserting into the body of the Constitution (not as a separate Bill of Rights) the phrase: "The civil rights of none shall be abridged on account of religious belief or worship, nor shall any national religion be established, nor shall the full and equal rights of conscience be in any manner, or on any pretext, infringed." At the time, Madison did not offer any explanation for what he meant by such phrases as *national religion* or *established*.

Just as significant, and often forgotten, Madison then also proposed something radical—that the key elements of the Bill of Rights be applied to the states, not just to Congress. "No State shall violate the equal rights of conscience, or the freedom of the press, or the trial by jury in criminal cases."[24] The states had urged Congress to adopt many different amendments. This was *not* one of them; it grew from Madison's personal conviction that state tyranny was as grave a threat as national tyranny.

Finally, in a little-known provision related to religious freedom (apparently borrowed from George Mason's proposed bill of rights[25]), Madison also proposed that the clause protecting the right to bear arms include the caveat "but no one religiously scrupulous of bearing arms, shall be compelled to render military service in person." Given the antagonism directed toward Quakers during the War of Independence, it is yet further evidence of Madison's commitment to freedom of conscience.[26]

Madison's amendments were referred to a select committee comprising a representative from each state, with Madison representing Virginia. The committee deliberated one week and produced a version that read: "No religion shall be established by law, nor shall the equal rights of conscience be infringed."[27] They offered no official rationale for the changes. Why was "national religion" changed to just "religion"? Why didn't they like Madison's "civil rights" language? And how did Madison feel about the pruning away of his effusive extra-guarantees that the "full and equal" rights could not be infringed "in any manner" or "on any pretext"—did he view this as a literary effort to reduce redundancy or a watering down? It's impossible to tell.[28]

The full House of Representatives on August 15 then had what is the only public and (somewhat) recorded debate about the drafting of the First Amendment. The discussion ignored the free-exercise clause—"Congress shall make no law respecting an establishment of religion, *or prohibiting the free exercise thereof*"—and it's worth pausing on the fact that this revolutionary concept was now so noncontroversial as to need no debate. Members instead focused on language related to religious "establishment," which touched on the gray area of how and why the government should regulate, aid, constrain, touch, mangle, discourage, or encourage religion.

The *Annals of Congress*,[29] a semi-official record of the deliberations, provided a *paraphrased* version of the debate's highlights.[30]

Peter Sylvester of New York said that the current language differed in meaning from what was intended by the committee, and "He feared it might be thought to have a tendency to abolish religion altogether." What on earth did he mean? How could our hallowed First Amendment "abolish religion altogether"? Sylvester apparently feared that the amendment would give Congress the power to abolish the *state* establishments of religion.

John Vining of Delaware, the chairman of the select committee, responded with a willingness to alter the language to clarify the meaning.

Elbridge Gerry of Massachusetts—who had refused to sign the Constitution and may have been mischievously trying to delay the amendments—"said it would read better if it was, that no religious doctrine shall be established by law."

Roger Sherman of Connecticut, a signer of the Constitution and initial opponent of the idea of a Bill of Rights, reiterated his view that the amendment was unnecessary, "inasmuch as Congress had no authority whatever delegated to them by the Constitution to make religious establishments." He suggested they eliminate the amendment entirely.[31]

Daniel Carroll of Maryland, one of the few Catholics in Congress, said that explicit protection of religion was justified because concern about religious liberty had been expressed by "many sects"; an amendment on this topic would therefore "tend more towards conciliating the minds of the people to the government than almost any other amendment he had heard proposed."

Madison then spoke. The reporter's paraphrase of his comments read: "Mr. Madison said, he apprehended the meaning of the words to be, that Congress should not establish a religion, and enforce the legal observation of it by law, nor compel men to worship God in any manner contrary to their conscience."

Before parsing these words too carefully—*Look! He said "a religion," not "religion" generally!*—it's worth remembering that this was a paraphrase done by someone without the benefit of tape recorders or the foresight to know that countless law school moot courts would someday revolve around the word *a*.

Madison apparently still held on to the idea that the amendments weren't technically needed but were now politically required. "Whether the words are necessary or not . . . they had been required by some of the State Conventions." Some at the ratifying conventions seemed to fear that without a Bill of Rights Congress might interpret its general authority to execute the Constitution as enabling it "to make laws of such a nature as might infringe the right of conscience, and establish a national religion."

Like Vining of Delaware, Benjamin Huntington of Connecticut declared that while he agreed with Madison's interpretation of the words, the amendment could actually "be extremely harmful to the cause of religion." He said he feared that it might force federal courts to disallow local religious establishments, such as the one in Connecticut. "The ministers of their congregations to the Eastward were maintained by contributions of those who belonged to their society; the expense of building meeting-houses was contributed in the same manner." If the Bill of Rights forbade establishments in general, wouldn't it wipe out their admirable local practice of providing tax support for their ministers? He noted that someone in Connecticut could refuse to pay taxes to support the local church and justify it on the grounds that so doing would constitute a forbidden religious establishment. (Note again that he viewed tax support for religion as being the same thing as an "establishment.") Clearly, Congress ought to let states regulate these things. Otherwise the federal lawmakers might give inadvertent legitimacy to "those who professed no religion at all."

Then, the reporter stated, Madison tried to assuage Huntington that the amendment referred only to national activity and suggested again putting back the word *national*: "Mr. Madison thought, if the word national was inserted before religion, it would satisfy the minds of honorable gentlemen. He believed that the people feared one sect might obtain a pre-eminence, or two combine together, and establish a religion to which they would compel others to conform. He thought if the word national was introduced, it would point the amendment directly to the object it was intended to prevent."[32] Though Madison himself preferred the national government having the ability to alter state laws, it appears that by this time he realized that passing a Bill of Rights meant assuaging states' rights lawmakers that state power was secure.

Samuel Livermore of New Hampshire was not satisfied. He proposed instead a wording—suggested by the New Hampshire state ratifying convention—that went further than Madison had in restricting the national government's involvement in religion: "Congress shall make no laws *touching* religion, or infringing the rights of conscience."

At this point, Madison withdrew his motion and accepted Livermore's. Madison may have had a don't-throw-me-in-the-briar-patch moment, taking on Livermore's amendment as a concession when actually it was probably more to his liking than his own original wording—because it added the word *touching*. This wording not only banned a formal federal establishment, as Madison's original proposal had, but also banned the federal government from even legislating on the *topic* of establishments—whether to support or oppose them. That language would seem to reflect Madison's and Sherman's view that Congress had no power to meddle with religion at all. The House approved Livermore's broader wording thirty-one to twenty.

Alas, the matter did not rest there. A few days later, on August 20, the House again convened and accepted another amendment, this time from Fisher Ames of Massachusetts, the state with one of the strongest records of promoting government regulation of, and support for, religion. His version, reportedly written by Madison, seemed to give Congress more leeway to legislate on religion, as it prevented Congress not from "touching" religion but "establishing" religion: "Congress shall make no law establishing religion, or to prevent the free exercise thereof, or to infringe the rights of conscience."[33] Congress had already zigged, zagged, and zigged thrice on the extent of federal powers to influence religion.

On September 3 through 9, the Senate considered the amendments that had been passed by the House. No record exists of what was said, but we do know that some senators were not thrilled with the House proposal, and they debated several alternatives. (My emphasis is added to highlight the differences between proposals.)

First, one senator moved that the amendment should read: "Congress shall make no law establishing *one religious sect or society in preference to others.*" This further narrowed the amendment's scope, allowing government to regulate religion in a variety of ways as long as it didn't endorse or create specific religious entities. The motion was defeated.

A second proposal prohibited Congress from "infringing the rights of conscience, or establishing any religious sect or society." By deleting "in preference to others," this proposal put a slightly different twist: that Congress couldn't create religious entities even if it was evenhanded about it. But it still would have allowed Congress to legislate on religion in many other ways. The motion was defeated.

Finally, a senator proposed banning Congress from making laws "establishing any particular *denomination* of religion *in preference to another.*" That motion was also defeated.

Having blocked three efforts to allow more federal involvement with religion than the House proposal had, the Senate then tentatively adopted the language offered by the House: "Congress shall make no law establishing religion." But the senators weren't quite satisfied, either. Meeting six days later, the Senate changed its mind and approved a version that shifted back in the direction of allowing Congress more power over faith: "Congress shall make no law establishing *articles of faith or a mode of worship,* or prohibiting the free exercise of religion." As the official record noted, the Senate had decided to erase from the clause the words "nor shall the rights of Conscience be infringed."[34]

Madison was not happy. He believed the amendments had lost their positive impact and at one point harrumphed that he'd rather have no amendments at all than the ones birthed by the Senate.[35] An Anti-Federalist senator wrote to Patrick Henry that the Senate had "so mutilated and gutted" the amendments that they were now "good for nothing, and . . . will do more harm than benefit."[36] They likely viewed the wording as too narrow, since it could allow government support for, or regulation of, religion as long as doctrine wasn't explicitly dictated. Perhaps they bristled at the Senate's removal of the sweeping phrase *rights of conscience* or the word *touching,* which had reflected the more hands-off approach espoused by Madison and Sherman.

In any event, the House rejected the Senate position.

And the Senate held its ground.

A conference committee was appointed to work out the differences. Madison led the House conferees and was joined by Roger Sherman and John

Vining. Oliver Ellsworth, William Paterson, and, significantly, Charles Carroll, a Catholic, represented the Senate. Four of the six had been at the Constitutional Convention.

Apparently, horse trading ensued. The Senate conferees agreed that if the
House would accept the Senate versions on some of the other amendments,
the Senate would follow the House wording on religious freedom. It is a sign
of the importance that Madison placed on freedom of religion, press, and
speech that he led the House to accept the Senate's language on sixteen different amendments in order to get the stronger language on the First Amendment.[37]

They all agreed that the wording should be: "Congress shall make no laws
respecting an establishment of religion, or prohibiting the free exercise
thereof." Not only could Congress not establish a religion, it also could not
pass a law "respecting an" establishment. There is no official explanation
from any of the parties about why those two words were added. On September 24, the House accepted the language; the next day the Senate did, too.
The First Amendment was born.[38]

Putting aside for a moment the meaning of the final wording, what's clear
is that Congress had several opportunities to give itself more freedom to regulate or support religion and at least one chance to restrict its authority ("no
law touching religion"). It ended up with something in between.

And what happened to Madison's two other amendments bearing on religious freedom? During a debate in the House in August 1789, Representative
Thomas Scott of Pennsylvania complained that Madison's proposal exempt-
ing conscientious objectors would be exploited by the irreligious to avoid service, thereby gutting the local militias. "My design is to guard against those
who are of no religion"—who, he said, would now have "recourse to these
pretexts to get excused" from service.[39] Representative Elias Boudinot of New
Jersey countered that men who were so opposed to taking up arms, they
"would rather die than use them," would be unreliable soldiers anyway. He
noted that bias against conscientious objectors during the Revolutionary War
had led to "several instances of oppression," and that this new government
ought to "let every person know that we will not interfere with any person's
particular religious profession." The House approved the amendment. The
Senate then deleted the provision, presumably on the grounds that such matters should be up to the state legislatures.

And what happened to Madison's more radical amendment declaring,
"No State shall violate the equal rights of conscience"? In introducing the

amendment, Madison bluntly declared that the biggest threat was not a tyrant or the national government but the local "community." "The prescriptions in favor of liberty ought to be levelled against that quarter where the greatest danger lies, namely, that which possesses the highest prerogative of power. But this is not found in either the executive or the legislative departments of Government, but in the body of the people, operating by the majority against the minority."[40]

On August 17, 1789, the House debated that amendment. Representative Thomas Tucker opposed it, arguing, "It will be much better, I apprehend, to leave the state governments to themselves, and not to interfere with them more than we already do; and that is thought by many to be rather too much."

No, no, no, Madison fought back: This was "the most valuable amendment in the whole list."[41]

Remarkably, Madison was able to muster the two-thirds vote in the House required to pass the amendment.[42] But his hopes were dashed in the Senate, which eliminated the amendment. It would not be until after the passage of the Fourteenth Amendment in 1868 that states would fall under the restrictions of the US Constitution's Bill of Rights. One can only wonder how American history might have changed if the Constitution had given Congress the right to overturn state laws that violated individual rights.

THROUGH A GLASS DARKLY

What are we to make of this? Scholars, Supreme Court justices, and culture warriors have picked over this basic chronology for signs of the Founders' intent. What did they mean by *establishment* and *national*? Is it meaningful that the word *a* disappeared between the words *establish* and *religion*?

Allow me to first provide an absurdly truncated summary of the different schools of thought.

Most conservatives argue that the Founders had a very limited conception of the First Amendment; that it was designed specifically to prevent the establishment of an official national religion, and no more. Government support for religion is fine—even worthy—as long as it doesn't favor one religion over another. In legal circles, these scholars are sometimes called accommodationists because they believe the Constitution can accommodate a fair amount of church–state intermingling. "Pluralism and liberty—not secularism or separation—define the relations between church and state under the Constitution," wrote scholar Michael McConnell.[43] Other times they're called nonpreferentialists, since they believe government can aid religion as long as it doesn't prefer one denomination to another. The word *establishment*, this camp argues, is quite clearly a reference to the practice common in some of the states (and many European countries) of designating a single denomination or religion for state support through taxes and other preferences. Former chief justice William Rehnquist looked at the legislative history and concluded that Madison had no intention of separating church and state. "His original language 'nor shall any national religion be established' obviously does not conform to the 'wall of separation' between church and state idea which latter-day commentators have ascribed to him." Rehnquist pointed specifically to the account of Madison explaining the meaning of his amendment—"that Congress should not establish a religion, and enforce the legal observation of it by law." The fact that Madison replied to Representative Huntington's desire to protect state establishments by suggesting the insertion of the word *national* would seem to back up Rehnquist's point. "It seems indisputable from these glimpses of Madison's thinking, as reflected by actions on the floor of the House in 1789, that he saw the Amendment as designed to prohibit the establishment of a national religion, and perhaps to prevent discrimination among sects," Rehnquist wrote. "He did not see it as requiring neutrality on the part of government between religion and irreligion."[44]

The accommodationists note that in the very same session in which Congress passed the First Amendment, it went on to mingle church and state with seeming abandon. It appointed congressional chaplains and, on the very day the House of Representatives passed the Bill of Rights, approved a resolution for a "day of public thanksgiving and prayer to be observed . . . [for] the many signal favors of Almighty God." This was not lost on everyone even back then. Thomas Tucker of South Carolina argued that this resolution conflicted with the Bill of Rights. "This . . . is a business with which Congress have nothing to do; it is a religious matter, and, as such, is proscribed to us." But Tucker was, in fact, in the minority.[45]

There is a second camp that might be called Christian accommodationists. These religious conservatives—often affiliated with the Religious Right—argue that the First Amendment allows not only for government support of religion in general but even "preferential" support for a particular religion, Christianity. Usually this argument is preceded by a recitation of the various Christian beliefs of the Founders and the Christian roots of the settlers.[46] This group goes as far as to say that separation of church and state is a "myth."[47]

The liberal argument—sometimes called the separationist view—looks at the legislative give-and-take and concludes that the First Amendment requires a strict separation of church and state. First, it's noted that the legislators defeated efforts to limit government involvement in religion. Supreme Court justice David Souter wrote in 1992, "What is remarkable is that, unlike the earliest House drafts or the final Senate proposal, the prevailing language is not limited to laws respecting an establishment of 'a religion,' 'a national religion,' 'one religious sect,' or specific 'articles of faith.' The Framers repeatedly considered and deliberately rejected such narrow language and instead extended their prohibition to state support for 'religion' in general."[48] Separationists argue that Madison and others were acutely aware that in many states there had been efforts to use tax dollars to support religion; thus when they opposed "establishments," they meant any official support of religion. Certainly Madison himself, during the assessment fight in Virginia, had indeed equated tax support for religion with an establishment. As historian Leonard Levy has argued, "An establishment of religion in America at the time of the framing and ratification of the Bill of Rights meant government aid and sponsorship of religion, principally by impartial tax support of the institutions of religion, all the churches."[49]

To me, the best explanation of what happened was offered by Levy when he stepped away from the textual microanalysis and looked at the broader context. The entire point of the Bill of Rights, he argued, was to *restrict* government power, not expand it. The drive for a Bill of Rights, he reminded us, was encouraged by Anti-Federalists who believed that the unadorned Constitution gave too much power to the government. He returned to Madison's statement when he introduced the Bill of Rights—that their point was to "limit and qualify the powers of Government."[50] Remember Madison's comment during the ratification fight for the Constitution in Virginia, when he responded to Patrick Henry's concerns by declaring point-blank: "There is not a shadow of right in the general government to intermeddle with religion. Its least interference with it would be a most flagrant usurpation."[51] If Madison believed that about the Constitution sans Bill of Rights, then surely he felt the same about the Constitution as amended. Therefore, Levy concluded, "The First Amendment, no matter how parsed or logically analyzed, was framed to deny power, not to vest."

Thus, many conservatives have it backward. In effect, the conservative ac-commodationists say that while Congress cannot set up an official state reli-gion, anything else is fair game, since nothing else is prohibited. Madison wanted us to think of it the other way around: Just because Congress is explic-itly forbidden from doing one thing (establishing a national religion), that *doesn't* mean that everything else is acceptable. Madison wanted the opposite assumption—that any actions not mentioned and specifically sanctioned are *prohibited.* This concept doesn't apply just to restrictions on religion but to help for religion, too. If Congress wasn't explicitly granted power to aid reli-gion, then it cannot. Congress is not allowed to interfere, restrict, establish, discourage, or encourage religion. In Madison's mind, Congress had one simple assignment when it came to religion: Stay away.

Remember how Madison was afraid that if he explicitly protected any freedoms, it might imply that those unmentioned were unprotected? Well, over time that's exactly what has happened. He agreed to prohibit what he viewed as the most egregious form of state oppression—the creation of a na-tional state church. But instead of that being viewed as the extreme example that must be mentioned just to be safe, it has now become (in the eyes of many conservative scholars) the *only* thing Congress had meant to restrict. Madison's fears have been realized.[52]

Constitutional scholars can amuse themselves for hours parsing these things, but the rest of us might be tempted to reach back in time, slap Mr. Madison (gently, as he was a frail man), and ask him: *Why did you agree to language that could be interpreted in so many different ways? Surely you un-derstood that such ambiguity would bedevil the next generations. Why not just clarify what the hell you meant?*

Because he needed the votes.

I believe there's ample evidence that Madison wanted a strict separation of church and state. He wanted it locally; he wanted it nationally. But here's the point that all of us Founding Father Lovers forget: It is not only their views that matter. Madison was in the business of building a political majority. We today may not pay attention to the other members of his legislative majority, but Madison surely did.

Remember that he originally didn't even want to articulate precise lan-guage on religious freedom. He wanted to leave the Constitution silent be-cause he thought *that* would mean the strictest possible separation of church and state and therefore, in his mind, the greatest chance for religious free-dom. No mention meant no power. He had confided in Jefferson that when it came to drafting language, others would not approach the topic with such liberality as they would. But he pushed an amendment anyway, because he needed the votes—the votes of the ratifying convention in Virginia, the votes of his constituents in Orange County, and the votes of the evangelical Christians who feared the lack of explicit protection. The language he came up with was vague enough to allow for broad support.

He allowed for most of these decisions to be left to the states. Recall again that Madison had wanted desperately to give the federal government the power to protect citizens from state tyranny. But he didn't prevail. On the contrary, he ended up pivoting and then having to convince members of Congress that the beauty of the First Amendment language was that it *did* allow the states to regulate religion.

As a result, we see different men likely voting for the amendment for entirely different reasons. Take Fisher Ames, the man who formally proposed the language that became the First Amendment. He was from Massachusetts, the state that historically considered government support of religion essential. Ames believed that the republic was based on biblical principles and advocated that the Bible should be taught in primary schools. "Should not the Bible regain the place it once held as a schoolbook? Its morals are pure, its examples are captivating and noble," he once wrote. It's highly unlikely that Ames shared Madison's views that government shouldn't even aid religion at the local level. In fact, he probably supported the First Amendment in part for something close to the *opposite* reason—to make sure the federal government would not interfere with Massachusetts's ability to regulate religion as it saw fit.[53]

Samuel Livermore of New Hampshire was the one who proposed the language first approved by the House, that "Congress shall make no laws touching religion, or infringing the rights of conscience." This language would have limited government support or restraint of religion the most. He would seem, therefore, to be an ardent separationist. Yet Livermore was the president of the New Hampshire convention that produced its revised constitution, which had both sweeping guarantees of freedom of conscience *and* authorized taxpayer support of "protestant teachers of piety, religion, and morality."[54]

And look, too, at Benjamin Huntington of Connecticut. The New Englander had expressed the fear that the amendment might actually "be extremely harmful to the cause of religion" by undermining the states' laws. Madison assuaged him by suggesting the insertion of the word *national*, an assurance that the federal Constitution would not upend state laws—even state laws with which Madison disagreed.[55] Madison supported the First

Amendment because he wanted church and state separated as much as possible, while Huntington hoped it would ensure the opposite.[56] Huntington also wanted assurances that this amendment would not "patronize those who professed no religion at all." Perhaps Madison had compromised again—allowing religion to be privileged over irreligion throughout the states—to gain votes.

Or take Roger Sherman. A signer of the Declaration of Independence and the Constitution, Sherman was described by John Adams as an "old Puritan." As a member of the Continental Congress, he had opposed the War Committee's rule allowing the army to give five hundred lashes to delinquent soldiers on the grounds that Deuteronomy prescribed only forty.[57] He had seconded Ben Franklin's motion to begin the Constitutional Convention sessions with a prayer. He had supported the concept of the official Congregational establishment in Connecticut, and he took a very different approach to church and state than did Madison. In today's parlance, he would have been a conservative accommodationist. Yet he went even further than Madison in declaring that Congress had no power to touch religion.[58] For him, the radical separationist view on the national level gave him space to be an accommodationist on the state level.

What we do know is this: The First Amendment was a grand declaration that the *federal government* couldn't support or regulate religion—but it was also a grand declaration that *states absolutely could.* That was part of the compromise that enabled the First Amendment to gain widespread support. Madison's first proposal established a broad right—"nor shall the full and equal rights of conscience be in any manner, or any pretext infringed"—and by the end, the amendment was written as a limitation on Congress only.

The deliberations on the First Amendment didn't really end until 1866 when, in the aftermath of the Civil War, Congress passed the Fourteenth Amendment prohibiting states from enacting laws that infringed on citizens' liberties. Over the subsequent 130-plus years, the courts interpreted this to mean that the Bill of Rights applied to the states—a doctrine called incorporation. While we take this for granted now, we must remember that at the time the Bill of Rights was passed, the lawmakers cobbling together the delicate compromise didn't know that the Fourteenth Amendment would later apply the First Amendment to state and local matters. They did not fret over whether the First Amendment would ban prayer in schools because they assumed that would be decided on the local level. Had they known that the language they'd written—"establishments" and "respecting"—would end up regulating every nook and cranny of American life, the political dynamic would have been different. For instance, it's hard to imagine Fisher Ames voting for the First Amendment if he'd known it would ban prayer from the village school. And if Fisher Ames had objected on those grounds, would Madison have altered the amendment's wording to secure his vote? We'll never know for sure, but we do know that several lawmakers were more worried about Congress negating the state establishments than about the federal government creating a national religion. The sheer religious diversity of the nation at that point made the idea of a national religion preposterous. The more real threat was that the federal government would upend the state policies.

Because all the major players agreed that the states would regulate religion, the First Amendment could pass even though there was *no consensus* about the philosophical matter of how separate church should be from state. Some lawmakers, like Madison, supported the First Amendment because they wanted separation of church and state at all levels of American life. Some, like Huntington, wanted local government support of religion and believed the First Amendment language protected the states' rights to continue the practice. Yes, some supported the First Amendment because they wanted more separation of church and state, while others supported it because they wanted less.

This is all terrible news for culture warriors hoping to find clarity in the words and actions of the Founding Fathers: The debates over the First Amendment were so grounded in a states' rights context that they allowed those involved to *not* resolve the meta questions about the proper relationship between church and state. As scholar Akhil Reed Amar has put it, the First Amendment "is not antiestablishment but pro-states' rights" and officially "agnostic on the substantive issue of establishment versus nonestablishment."[59]

Once the Fourteenth Amendment applied the Bill of Rights to the states, judges were left to figure out what the Founders would have done about things like prayer in school, when in fact such issues were far from the Founders' minds. The brutal reality is that we cannot necessarily determine their views on the separation of church and state on the local level from their attitude about the First Amendment.

So the common sport of divining "the Founders'" intent on the First Amendment is absurd. It's impossible to determine what they meant by the First Amendment because it was a classic political compromise that was *designed* to have different meanings to different people. We have no choice but

to consider Fisher Ames and Benjamin Huntington to be Founders just like
Madison. And their intent was different from Madison's. While Madison had
strong, clear views about religion-and-government on the local level, the First
Amendment did not.

There was one, and only one, area in which the members of Congress intended to pass judgment: the ability of the *national* government to meddle
with religion. And based on the origins of the First Amendment, what can we
conclude was their intent on that limited question?

In my view, on this narrow point, the separationists have the better case.
The Bill of Rights intended to restrict government power, not expand it. And
clearly Madison, at least, meant the word *establishment* to be quite broad and
refer to any government involvement with, or even aid for, religion. But I
have to admit that accommodationists make a good point when they ask, in
effect, that if most Founders had wanted to restrict more than just formal religious establishments, they could have said so. We know Madison ascribed a
certain meaning to *establishment*, but he must have known that others in the
chamber might interpret it a different way. It's certainly not far-fetched to interpret the word *establishment* as referring to an official state religion.

This is maddening. Confronted with national discord on such fundamental issues, we desperately want guidance from our Founding Fathers. Just as
we turn to sacred texts—ancient wisdom from sages and God—to help us live
our lives, we want to feel that studying the American holy texts—the words of
our secular sages—will guide us, too. But just as the Bible cautions us that if
we try to comprehend God's intent we will be looking through "a glass
darkly," our efforts to divine the Founding Fathers' intent by looking only at
their sacred texts leads us to a similar place.

Surely—*surely*—there must be some way of understanding what the
Founding Fathers meant by the First Amendment, and whether they believed
that separating church and state would promote, or hinder, religious liberty.

Fortunately, there is another way. As it happens, four of the most important Founding Fathers who'd tried to articulate the need for religious freedom
then had the privilege and burden of serving as president of the United
States. As Washington, Adams, Jefferson, and Madison struggled to interpret the Constitution and act accordingly, they didn't need to speculate on
intent—they'd been the ones doing the intending. And what did they do
when they had the chance to sort this out once and for all?

They disagreed.

practicing what they preached

THE FIRST PRESIDENCIES BRING INSPIRING RHETORIC, DIRTY POLITICS, AND SHARP DISAGREEMENT AMONG THE FOUNDERS

THE WASHINGTON PRESIDENCY

In the opening days of the first Congress and the first presidency, God's assistance was requested explicitly and repeatedly.

In his inaugural address, George Washington declared that there was an "Invisible Hand" that "conducts the affairs of men," and we must therefore offer prayers to "that Almighty Being who rules over the universe, who presides in the councils of nations, and whose providential aids can supply every human defect."[1]

The House of Representatives then responded to Washington's speech by joining in the call for a "fervent supplication for the blessings of Heaven on our Country."[2]

Washington wrote back with more religion-soaked rhetoric. To the House, he declared that he would surely rely on "a continuance of the blessings of Heaven on our beloved country."[3] To the Senate, he revealed himself as "inexpressibly happy in a belief that Heaven, which has done so much for our infant Nation will not withdraw its Providential influence before our political felicity shall have been completed." The "great Arbiter of the Universe," he declared, would help in the task of "attempting to make a Nation happy."[4]

It's fascinating that the different stations of government would share such a Calvinistic view of God as intervener in events just months before Congress would pass the First Amendment to the Constitution. One cannot help but wonder how the great advocate for separation of church and state, Congressman James Madison, must have felt about those statements.

Actually, we need not speculate, since each of those statements was probably written by . . . James Madison. Washington's first inaugural speech, it is believed by most historians, was in part drafted by Madison, who by then was a trusted adviser to the new president. But Madison was also a leader of the House of Representatives, where he crafted the official reply to Washington. And when Washington responded to the House statements, he again turned to Madison to draft the language.

This conversation between Madison, Madison, and Madison helped establish the precedent for what scholars would come to call "public religion" or, as journalist Jon Meacham has called it, the "American gospel." In other words, certain religious principles had such widespread acceptance that they could be articulated by elected officials in public venues. The language crafted by Washington and Madison fit this description because it was inclusive and nonsectarian, but nonetheless had meaty religious content. That Madison himself was the one to initiate this tradition in the new republic proves that even the most ardent separationists thought certain forms of religious rhetoric—even spoken by the president in official settings, standing in official buildings—were appropriate and valuable. The first statements by Washington/Madison shared the characteristics of "public religion": They were broad enough to appeal to all Americans, and they assumed that God not only watches over but indeed *favors* America.

Other points of consensus about God and government were quickly established during Washington's two terms. Washington took office by putting his hand on a Bible and declaring "So help me God," and many presidents since have done the same. The House of Representatives' building was used for worship services during the presidencies of Washington, Adams, Jefferson, and Madison. On the other hand, the new government abandoned the practice of the Continental Congress of officially referring to the United States as a "Christian nation." The clarifying occasion was a dispute between Tripoli, a Muslim nation, and the US over freedom of the seas. A treaty negotiated during the Washington administration, and ratified by the Senate during the presidency of John Adams, attempted to assuage Tripoli that America was not pursuing a religious war against it: "As the Government of the United States of America is not, in any sense, founded on the Christian religion; as it has in itself no character of enmity against the laws, religion, or tranquillity, of Mussulmen; and, as the said States never entered into any war, or act of hostility against any Mehomitan nation. . . ."[5] The treaty was ratified by the Senate and signed by Adams.

Not all of the precedents established under Washington were noncontroversial. The new Congress continued the Continental Congress's practice of providing congressional chaplains and military chaplains. Madison later said he opposed this. "The Constitution of the US forbids everything like an establishment of a national religion," he wrote, making it clear once again that he had a broad definition of what he'd meant by *establishment* when he had guided the First Amendment through Congress. "The law appointing chaplains establishes a religious worship for the national representatives, to be performed by Ministers of religion, elected by a majority of them; and these are to be paid out of the national taxes." He declared that this practice was "a palpable violation of equal rights, as well as of Constitutional principles: The tenets of the chaplains elected [by the majority] shut the door of worship against the members whose creeds & consciences forbid a participation in that of the majority. To say nothing of other sects, this is the case with that of Roman Catholics & Quakers." He then offered a hypothetical that at least shows how far we have come as a nation: "Could a Catholic clergyman ever hope to be appointed to a Chaplain?"

What would Madison make of today's congressional chaplaincy, which consists not only of Catholic priests but Jewish rabbis and Muslim imams? He would likely applaud the progress but then start naming the other religious denominations still not represented. For him, the principle was sacred. Furthermore, he said, if the members of Congress wanted chaplains, they could pay for them out of their own pocket—"how noble in its exemplary sacrifice to the genius of the Constitution; and the divine right of conscience." Madison privately also criticized the appointment of military chaplains during the Washington administration. He acknowledged the appeal of providing moral or spiritual support for our men in harm's way: "The object of this establishment is seducing; the motive to it is laudable. But is it not safer to adhere to a right principle, and trust to its consequences, than confide in the reasoning however specious in favor of a wrong one." Shifting to a practical argument, he then suggested that there was no evidence that armies with chaplains fought any better than those without. It's not that he didn't think religion was important; he just didn't think that a chaplain would do much to spiritualize a secular soldier. "If such be not the spirit of armies, the official services of their Teachers are not likely to produce it."[6] But significantly, despite harboring serious reservations, Madison apparently did *not* try to block the practice during the Washington administration when he was a leader in Congress. By the time he became president, then, the precedent was well established. Nowhere does he explain why, but he likely concluded that the popularity of these measures made them impossible to dislodge.

Washington's faith-based rhetoric set a powerful and enduring precedent. He continued the practice he started as general of the Continental army of invoking God regularly—and sometimes in service of a very particular political cause. When he gave his sixth annual message to Congress, for instance, he had just put down the Whiskey Rebellion, in which a group of western settlers defied the federal government's taxing authority by engaging in an armed revolt. Washington solemnly declared, "Let us unite, therefore, in imploring the Supreme Ruler of Nations to spread his holy protection over these United States; to turn the machinations of the wicked to the confirming of our Constitution; to enable us at all times to root out internal sedition and put invasion to flight."

Washington's farewell address was important for what it both did and did not say about religion. He began by restating a conviction of his, and of most of the other Founders: "Of all the dispositions and habits which lead to political prosperity, religion and morality are indispensable supports." He declared that it would be literally unpatriotic to attack religion. "In vain would that man claim the tribute of patriotism, who should labor to subvert these great pillars of human happiness, these firmest props of the duties of men and citizens." The rule of law would disintegrate without religion because the legal system relies on the taking of oaths. Furthermore, popular government required "virtue or morality," and morality required religion. For someone occasionally described as a Deist, Washington was sharp in his attack on educated secularists: "Whatever may be conceded to the influence of refined education on minds of peculiar structure, reason and experience both forbid us to expect that national morality can prevail in exclusion of religious principle."

What came next was a specific call for action but, significantly, *not* a call for government support of religion. Rather, Washington said, "Promote then, as an object of primary importance, institutions for the general diffusion of knowledge" so that "public opinion should be enlightened." The best way to improve morality and religion was to encourage general education.[7]

Ironically, one of the most controversial steps he took during his presidency was to give thanks. At the request of Congress, he issued two thanksgiving proclamations. Some critics believed that Washington not only was calling on Americans to pray but was also literally leading them in prayer. The president described his vision of God—"author of all the good that was, that is, or that will be"—asked His help with myriad practical problems, and thanked Him for concrete accomplishments. This was no throw-the-religious-folk-a-bone one-liner:

> Now, therefore, I do recommend and assign Thursday, the 26th day of November next, to be devoted by the people of these States to the service of that great and glorious Being who is the beneficent author of all the good that was, that is, or that will be; that we may then all unite in rendering unto Him our sincere and humble thanks for His kind care and protection of the people of this country previous to their becoming a nation; for the signal and manifold mercies and the favorable interpositions of His providence in the course and conclusion of the late war . . . and, in general, for all the great and various favors which He has been pleased to confer upon us.
>
> And also that we may then unite in most humbly offering our prayers and supplications to the great Lord and Ruler of Nations, and beseech Him to pardon our national and other transgressions; to enable us all, whether in public or private stations, to perform our several and relative duties properly and punctually . . . ; to promote the knowledge and practice of true religion and virtue, and the increase of science among them and us; and, generally, to grant unto all mankind such a degree of temporal prosperity as He alone knows to be best.[8]

In 1795, Washington again, in effect, led the nation in prayer. He thanked "the Great Ruler of Nations for the manifold and signal mercies which distinguish our lot as a nation." Interestingly, this time he tempered the triumphalism with a caution. In a statement unlikely to come from the mouth of a modern politician, he thanked God for "unexampled prosperity" and yet beseeched Him to "preserve us from the arrogance of prosperity."[9]

Finally, Washington made history by extending the definition of American religious legitimacy beyond Christians. For much of the previous decades, the discussion about toleration for all practical purposes referred to freedom for a variety of Protestants and, occasionally, Catholics. There was little mention (or tolerance) of non-Christians. So it was of great consequence when Washington visited the Touro Synagogue in Newport, Rhode Island, and then wrote this follow-up letter declaring full religious equality for Jews:

> It is now no more that toleration is spoken of, as if it was by the indulgence of one class of people, that another enjoyed the exercise of their inherent natural rights. For happily the Government of the United States, which gives to bigotry no sanction, to persecution no assistance, requires only that they who live under its protection, should demean themselves as good citizens, in giving it on all occasions their effectual support.

As he moved to close, one can almost imagine Rabbi Washington, arms outstretched, on the bima, blessing a Jewish congregation:

> May the Children of the Stock of Abraham, who dwell in this land, continue to merit and enjoy the good will of the other inhabitants, while every one shall sit in safety under his own vine and fig tree, and there shall be none to make him afraid. May the father of all mercies scatter light and not darkness in our paths, and make us all in our several vocations useful here, and in his own due time and way everlastingly happy.[10]

For more than two centuries, Americans have celebrated George Washington's courage, wisdom, and leadership. To that list of attributes, we ought to add another: a preternatural, daring, and deeply felt belief in religious equality.

THE ADAMS PRESIDENCY

Of the first four presidents, John Adams was the most overtly Christian from his bully pulpit. In his inaugural address, he expressed "a veneration for the religion of a people who profess and call themselves Christians," and a belief that "Christianity [was] among the best recommendations for the public service."[11] In a thanksgiving proclamation, issued March 23, 1798, Adams asked for "His infinite grace, through the Redeemer of the World, freely to remit all our offenses, and to incline us by His Holy Spirit to that sincere repentance and reformation."[12]

The proclamation enlisted Almighty aid not only in cosmic struggles but also for the more pedestrian battles of his administration. He urged Americans to ask God's help to: "arrest the progress of that impiety and licentiousness . . . prosper our commerce, manufactures, and fisheries. . . . smile on our colleges, academies, schools, and seminaries of learning, and make them nurseries of sound science, morals, and religion. . . . bless all magistrates [and] . . . make them a terror to evil doers. . . . and extend the blessings of knowledge, of true liberty, and of pure and undefiled religion throughout the world."

He appeared to be asking God to side with the Federalists in the growing war with the Jeffersonians. The country was divided over the French revolution and Jefferson was cast as enamored with the revolutionaries, including their hostility to churches, clergy, and organized religion. While asking for a national fast, Adams declared that the United States was "still held in jeopardy by the hostile designs and insidious acts of a foreign nation" that was "subversive of the foundations of all religious, moral, and social obligations." A few months before the passage of the notorious Sedition Act, Adams asked God to "withhold us from unreasonable discontent, from disunion, faction, sedition, and insurrection."

Madison would later point out that the inclusion of specific policy disagreements—and political jabs—in prayer proclamations had politicized a solemn act "to the scandal of religion as well as the increase of party animosities."[13] Even Washington's proclamations were viewed that way, he said. The proclamation probably backfired on Adams. He later wrote that this thanksgiving decree was recommended by a Presbyterian assembly—a fact that "allarmed and alienated" a variety of religious minorities, including "Quakers, Anabaptists, Mennonists, Moravians, Swedenborgians, Methodists, Catholicks, protestant Episcopalians, Arians, Socinians, Armenians, & & &, Atheists and Deist." Therefore, he wrote, "A general Suspicon prevailed that the Presbyterian Church was ambitious and aimed at an Establishment of a National Church." Ironically, the Unitarian Adams was cast as leader of a Presbyterian takeover. "I was represented as a Presbyterian and at the head of this political and ecclesiastical Project. The secret whisper ran through them 'Let us have Jefferson, Madison, Burr, any body, whether they be Philosophers, Deists, or even Atheists, rather than a Presbyterian President.' This principle is at the bottom of the unpopularity of national Fasts and Thanksgivings. Nothing is more dreaded than the National Government meddling with Religion." Amazingly, Adams said that it was the thanksgiving fast more than anything else that led to his electoral defeat in 1800. "The National Fast, recommended by me turned me out of office."[14]

Adams and the Federalists provided more ammunition to Jefferson and Madison when they enacted the Alien and Sedition Acts of 1798. Though usually explained in history books as an assault on free speech, the acts also made Adams seem a foe of religious liberty. By requiring residents to live in America for fourteen years instead of five before naturalization, the Alien Acts were intended to limit the impact of immigration from Irish Catholics.[15] The Alien Acts and the Sedition Act of July 14, which made it a crime to criticize the government, were also targeted at Jeffersonian critics and their French allies. From Adams's vantage point, the threat from Catholic France was substantial and related to religious freedom in a completely different way: France could never be a successful republic because it was Catholic. "Is there any instance of a Roman Catholic monarchy of five and twenty million at once converted into a free and rational people?" he once asked Dr. Joseph Priestley, a philosopher and Francophile. "No, I know of no instance like it."[16]

In fighting the Alien and Sedition Acts, Jefferson and Madison argued that the Adams administration's attacks on free press and speech would lead to restrictions on freedom of religion, and proposed the Kentucky and Virginia resolutions, which asserted that each state had the right to disobey inappropriate federal laws. "Liberty of conscience and freedom of the press were *equally* and *completely* exempted from all authority whatever of the United States," declared the resolution drafted by Madison.[17]

THE ELECTION OF 1800—THE HERETIC VERSUS THE TYRANT

Reading Thomas Jefferson's private comments on religion, one can't help but think, *Boy, if even a small fraction of those ruminations had become public, his political opponents would have pummeled him.* Well, a small fraction did become public, and the election of 1800 gave us our first major test of the political resilience of religious freedom. Would concepts embedded in the Bill of Rights and the Statute for Religious Freedom still shine brightly when covered with political mud?

At the beginning of the republic, Washington kept the deep political divisions from erupting into formal parties, but the incipient splits were substantial. On one side were the Federalists, led ideologically by Secretary of the Treasury Alexander Hamilton, who envisioned an America that was rapidly industrializing, urban, and allied with Great Britain. The Republicans, led by Jefferson and Madison, imagined a more agrarian America, allied with France. The Federalist candidate in 1800 was the president, John Adams. The Republican candidate was the vice president Thomas Jefferson.

Little of the truly anti-religious material that Jefferson had written privately was well known at that point. In fact, he was scrupulous to keep his religious views private. But the Federalists felt they had enough to prove that Jefferson was dangerous, and the Virginian's religious views soon became a major issue in the campaign. For instance, William Linn, a Dutch Reformed minister from New York, wrote of Jefferson: "Though there is nothing in our constitution to restrict our choice, yet the open and warm preference of a manifest enemy to the religion of Christianity, in a Christian nation, would be an awful symptom of the degeneracy of that nation, and a rebellion against God."[18]

Jefferson's support for the French revolutionaries wasn't just about foreign policy. It was about worldview, character, and even piety. Yale's president Timothy Dwight warned that if they were not careful, Americans, too, would "see the Bible cast into a bonfire, the vessels of the sacramental support borne by an ass in public profession, and our children united in chanting mockeries against God."[19] As historian Frank Lambert has put it, "The French revolution was to them a case study of what happens when infidels gain control: churches ransacked, divine revelation ridiculed, and Christ mocked by a 'goddess of Reason.' "[20] Through pamphlets, newspaper articles, and speeches, the Federalists pushed the idea that Jefferson would undermine Christianity and, therefore, morality. Alexander Hamilton, the tactical leader of the Adams campaign, attacked French revolutionary leaders and urged that the nation do whatever was necessary to prevent "an Atheist in Religion and a *Fanatic* in politics from getting possession of the helm of the State."[21]

They were no less skillful than today's political operatives at taking an opponent's comments out of context. A few passages from *Notes on the State of Virginia* had provided Federalists the ammunition. Jefferson had written that efforts to create religious uniformity would corrupt religion, hide truth, and make millions of people—those who wanted to fit in with the prevailing sentiment even if they didn't believe it—into miserable hypocrites. "Is uniformity attainable? Millions of innocent men, women, and children, since the introduction of Christianity, have been burnt, tortured, fined, imprisoned; yet we have not advanced one inch towards uniformity. What has been the effect of coercion? To make one half the world fools, and the other half hypocrites. To support roguery and error all over the earth." It's not hard to see how Jefferson could be cast as hostile to Christianity and contemptuous of Christians. Ironically, it was one of his most ringing defenses of religious liberty that caused him the most trouble. He had been explaining that freedom of conscience was a natural right not subject to governmental control. "The rights of conscience we never submitted, we could not submit. We are answerable for them to our God. The legitimate powers of government extend to such acts only as are injurious to others. But it does me no injury for my neighbour to say there are twenty gods, or no god. It neither picks my pocket nor breaks my leg."

One can almost imagine Adams's campaign operatives licking their lips when they read that twenty-gods line, easy proof that Jefferson was a non-Christian or worse. Linn pointed also to Jefferson's questioning of the biblical flood, his suggestion that children shouldn't be taught the Bible as they were "not mature enough for religious inquiry," and his notion that the Native Americans, being a distinct race, proved that we did not descend from a single pair.[22] Linn conceded that Jefferson was talented but suggested that that made him all the more dangerous—"the greater will be his power and the more extensive his influence in poisoning mankind."[23]

The Federalist *Gazette of the United States* newspaper in September 1800 declared that Jefferson was "an enemy to pure morals and religion, and consequently an enemy to his country and his God."[24] Those who voted for Jefferson, it asserted, were not only unwise but, since they were insulting God, probably damned. "What can screen such wretches from the just vengeance of insulted heaven!" Then, plucking from the type case some large chunks of lead, the newspaper defined the election as a choice:

THE GRAND QUESTION STATED.
    At the present solemn and momentous epoch, the only question to be asked by every American, laying his hand on his heart, is "Shall I continue in allegiance to
    GOD—AND A RELIGIOUS PRESIDENT
    ; or impiously declare for JEFFERSON AND NO GOD!!!"

Jefferson's election would lead to moral mayhem, they asserted. Electing "an open enemy" to "their Redeemer" would mean the triumph of the "morality of devils, which would break in an instant every link in the chain of human friendship, and transform the globe into one equal scene of desolation and horror, where fiend would prowl with fiend for plunder and blood," declared Presbyterian minister John Mitchell Mason.[25] But not just plunder and blood—rampant sex, too. If Jefferson was elected, we would see a devastation of "those morals which protect our lives from the knife of the assassin—which guard the chastity of our wives and daughters from seduction and violence."[26]

As more proof of his depravity, critics pointed to Jefferson's church attendance record. "It is a well established fact that Mr. Jefferson never has attended public worship during a residence of several years in New York and Philadelphia," wrote David Dagett, a New Haven Federalist.[27] And Jefferson's loosey-goosey attitude toward people of other faiths meant he would oppose laws regulating blasphemy or "profanity of any kind." It would be open season on the Bible. "Alas! The religion of the bible, the saviour of sinners, the God of the universe, may be prophaned, derided or blasphemed, with impunity."[28]

The Federalists even attempted to convince some Jewish voters that having a Christian like Adams would be better than an "atheist" like Jefferson. In a letter to *The Philadelphia Gazette*, a man named Moses S. Solomons declared his support for Adams and urged other Jews to make "common cause" with Christians. The letter proved unpersuasive when a few days later the one synagogue in Philadelphia published a statement that "no such man as Moses S. Solomons has *ever been*, or is now a member of the Hebrew congregation in this city."[29] The dirty trick backfired.

Jefferson's side fought back.

Some allies defended his personal religiosity. Abraham Bishop, a lawyer from New Haven, cited Jefferson's line that liberties are a "gift of God" and then asked, "Is this the language of atheist?"[30] Some got right down in the gutter and questioned the Federalists' values. One newspaper printed a poem called "The Triumph of Infidelity" about Adams's running mate, Charles Cotesworth Pinckney, who had impregnated, and then left, a Parisian "female of a respectable family." A less-than-subtle piece of satire, the poem has Pinckney declare:

> I am the first of men in the ways of evil,
> The truest, thriftiest servant of the Devil;

Born, educated, glory to engross
And shine confess'd the Devil's Man of Ross.
Here's three to one I beat even him in pride;
Two whores already in my chariot ride.[31]

But the more effective counterattack was to recast the contest, in exaggerated terms, as one between oppression and freedom. Adams's election would bring "an established church, a religious test, and an order of Priesthood," while Jefferson stood for "religious liberty, the rights of conscience, no priesthood, truth."[32] Another Republican declared that Jefferson's election would mean "Good government without the aid of priestcraft, or religious politics."[33]

The Jeffersonians implied that Adams would support the establishment of a national religion. The Alien and Sedition Acts "had given to the clergy a very favorable hope of obtaining an establishment of a particular form of Christianity thro' the US," wrote Jefferson.[34] Some noted that Adams's state of Massachusetts still had an establishment and limited public office to Protestants. If he allowed that kind of nefarious meddling in his home state, how could we be sure that he wouldn't impose restrictions on all of America?[35] Some threw in a bit of crowd-pleasing anti-Catholic rhetoric for good measure, saying that New England clergy who wanted religious tests were akin to "Romish priests" in Catholic countries who push "test-acts, oaths and inquisitions, as so many state-engines to subordinate mankind to the great and little tyrants."[36] The Federalists' attacks on the Virginian's religion, the Jeffersonians suggested, were a silly diversion from the real threat—a presidency that used the power of the state to promote religion. Voters, Bishop predicted, would figure out that the real danger was that "religion should suffer under a new administration," which would be "using it as a state engine."[37]

The evangelical Baptists—who had rescued Madison's fledgling political career—now did the same for Jefferson. The election coincided with the beginnings of a religious revival that would threaten the remaining establishments. This fueled the growth of the dissenting sects, which viewed Jefferson as their protector, and Adams as a threat. While Jefferson appealed to the evangelicals, he also, ironically, appealed to the irreligious. In 1776, only 17 percent of Americans were members of a church, according to Frank Lambert. Though most elites did belong, popular piety may have been at a low ebb during the Revolutionary era. Jefferson's live-and-let-live philosophy fit the zeitgeist.

When the votes were counted, Jefferson defeated Adams and both sides drew lessons about religious liberty. Adams himself ascribed his loss to voters viewing the election as a choice between an establishment and religious liberty. He noted that dissenting religions had been scared into thinking an Adams election would lead to their subjugation. The Reverend John Leland had a different explanation:

> This exertion of the American genius, has brought forth the *man of the People*, the defender of the rights of man and the rights of conscience, to fill the chair of state. . . . Pardon me, my hearers, if I am over-warm. I lived in Virginia fourteen years. The beneficent influence of my hero was too generally felt to leave me a stoic. What may we not expect, under the auspices of heaven, while Jefferson presides, with Madison in state by his side. Now the greatest orbit in America is occupied by the brightest orb.[38]

THE JEFFERSON PRESIDENCY

Soon after the election, those cows of Cheshire, Massachusetts, got to work. On the morning of July 20, 1801, the congregants in John Leland's Baptist church gathered in their Sunday best, carried around pails of milk and tubs of curd, and sang hymns.[39] Nine hundred cows produced enough milk to make the mammoth cheese that would soon be given to President Jefferson.[40] Leland's views were well known: Any intermingling of church and state came from the same "rotten nest-egg, which is always hatching vipers: I mean the principle of intruding the laws of men into the kingdom of Christ."[41] His cheese was famous before it even arrived in Washington, extolled by Republicans and mocked by Federalists. An "Epico-Lyrico Ballad" published in September 1801 in the Boston *Mercury and New-England Palladium* captured the rapture.

> From meadows rich, with clover red,
> A thousand heifers come;
> The tinkling bells the tidings spread,
> The milkmaid muffles up her head,
> And wakes the village hum.
>
> Then Elder J. with lifted eyes
> In musing posture stood,

Invoked a blessing from the skies
To save from vermin, mites and flies,
And keep the bounty good.[42]

But another poem offered a rebuttal, casting the cheese as a pungent symbol of Jefferson's ethical moldiness and made Jefferson's voice contemptible in this equally subtle verse:

In this great cheese I [Jefferson] see myself portray'd,
My life and fortunes in this useless mass,
I curse the hands, by which the thing was made,
To them a cheese, to me a looking-glass.

Like to this cheese, my outside, smooth and sound,
Presents an aspect kind and lasting too;
When nought but rottenness within is found,
And all my seeming rests on nothing true.[43]

The Reverend Leland delivered the cheese to Jefferson, who thanked him[44] and invited him to preach a service in the Hall of the House of Representatives on Sunday, January 3. Neither of the two great defenders of religious liberty apparently thought anything wrong with turning a Capitol podium into a pulpit. With Jefferson in the audience, Leland preached a classically emotive, evangelical sermon—much to the disgust of some of the traditionalists in the audience.[45] In an account that reveals not only the Federalist–Republican tensions but also class-based roots of the New England contempt for Baptists, the Reverend Dr. Mannasseh Cutler, a Federalist congressman and Congregationalist minister from Massachusetts, described the scene:

Last Sunday, Leland, the cheesemonger, a poor, ignorant, illiterate, clownish preacher (who was the conductor of this monument of human weakness and folly to the place of its destination), was introduced as the preacher to both Houses of Congress, and a great number of gentlemen and ladies from I know not where. The President, contrary to all former practice, made one of the audience. Such a performance I never heard before, and I hope never shall again. The text was, "And behold a greater than Solomon is here [Matthew 12:42; Luke 11:31]." The design of the preacher was principally to apply the allusion, not to the person intended in the text, but to *him* who was then present. Such a farrago, bawled with stunning voice, horrid tone, frightful grimaces, and extravagant gesture, I believe, was never heard by any decent auditory before. Shame or laughter appeared in every countenance. Such an outrage upon religion, the Sabbath, and common decency, was extremely painful to every sober, thinking person present.[46]

Why *did* Jefferson ostentatiously bring a Baptist preacher before Congress? For one thing, it happens that this ardent separationist regularly attended religious services held in the Capitol and raised no church–state objections. More intriguingly, though, James Hutson of the Library of Congress has argued that Jefferson invited Leland because he knew something the audience didn't: He had already received an interesting letter from the Baptists of Danbury, Connecticut, and two days earlier had written a reply that would become one of the most important—and controversial— statements on religious liberty. It was in that letter to the Danbury Baptists that Jefferson wrote that the American people had approved the Constitution, "thus building a wall of separation between Church & State."

These words, religious conservatives often point out, appear in no official documents. Not the Constitution or the Declaration or the Virginia statute. Yet when the Supreme Court first in 1879 (*Reynolds v. United States*) and then more famously in 1947 and 1948 (*Everson v. Board of Education* and *McCollum v. Board of Education*) cited that phrase as its guidepost for deciding cases about church and state, it became the governing metaphor that would shape public debate for decades to come. Advocates of separation of church and state cite it as a seminal founding document, while conservative Christians wax furious over the importance the letter has taken on.

Let's therefore examine the real story of Jefferson's letter to the Danbury Baptists.

The Danbury Baptist Association was founded in 1790 as a coalition of about twenty-six churches in the Connecticut Valley. Connecticut, it should be remembered, had established Congregationalism as its official state religion. The Baptists therefore had to pay taxes to support the salaries of Congregational ministers. Baptist ministers were not legally authorized to conduct marriages. Their ministers faced harassment and limits on where they could preach.[47] It was as a persecuted religious minority that they wrote to President Jefferson with congratulations, praise, and a plea for help. The letter began with a declaration of the basic philosophy that Baptists and Jefferson shared: "Our Sentiments are uniformly on the side of Religious Liberty—That Religion is at all times and places a Matter between God and Individuals—That no man ought to suffer in Name, person or effects on account of his religious Opinions—That the legitimate Power of civil Government extends no further than to punish the man who *works ill to his neighbour.*"

They explained that, the Declaration of Independence notwithstanding, as Baptists in Connecticut *their* rights were grudgingly provided "as favors granted, and not as inalienable rights." To secure those favors they must take "degrading" steps "inconsistent with the rights of freemen." They expressed shock and sympathy that Jefferson, a freedom fighter, would be attacked by such people just because he knew the proper role of government and therefore "dares not assume the prerogative of Jehovah and make Laws to govern the Kingdom of Christ."

They then mustered the courage to ask a favor. While acknowledging that the president "cannot destroy the Laws of each State," they wondered if there might be something he could do to hasten the demise of the religious establishment in Connecticut. "Our hopes are strong that the sentiments of our beloved President, which have had such genial Effect already, like the radiant beams of the Sun, will shine & prevail through all these States and all the world till Hierarchy and Tyranny be destroyed from the Earth."

The letter that prompted the most famous declaration of church–state separation closed, "And may the Lord preserve you safe from every evil and bring you at last to his Heavenly Kingdom through Jesus Christ our Glorious Mediator."

Jefferson took careful note of the letter. In fact, historian Daniel Dreisbach has demonstrated that Jefferson's response was not some throwaway courtesy note but the product of careful deliberation involving several of his top advisers. We know this with some certainty thanks to help from none other than . . . the FBI. In 1998, the FBI used state-of-the-art forensic methods to determine what Jefferson had inked out.[48] By looking at Jefferson's deletions, historians were able to get a much more nuanced sense of Jefferson's thought process. According to Dreisbach and James Hutson, here's what happened.

Jefferson believed the Danbury letter would afford him the opportunity to explain to the world "why I do not proclaim fastings & thanksgivings, as my predecessors did."[49] His first draft of the letter therefore explained that he was prohibited from "even occasional performances of devotion" unlike, he said, the way it is "practiced indeed by the Executive of another nation as the legal head of its church." Hutson argued that this was, in his genteel way, Jefferson getting some payback against the British and Federalist Anglophiles. "Jefferson took the gloves off," Hutson said, by making "it clear that he regarded religious proclamations as yet more British weeds that needed to be pulled from the American political system."[50]

Jefferson asked his attorney general, Levi Lincoln of Connecticut, to review his response for political landmines. "You understand the temper of those in the North, and can weaken it therefore to their stomachs," the president noted.[51] Lincoln replied that Jefferson's draft was too combative. By criticizing the proclamations, Jefferson would potentially insult not only Federalists but Republicans as well—as the custom is "venerable being handed down from our ancestors," Lincoln cautioned. Thanks to the FBI, we can now see that Jefferson responded to Lincoln's warning by cutting out the offending passage. So the final letter to the Baptists ended up without the portion on proclamations—the ostensible reason he wrote the letter in the first place. But the rest of it proved momentous anyway.

First, Jefferson thanked the Baptists and acknowledged that while "my duties dictate a faithful and zealous pursuit of the interests of my constituents," it is all the more gratifying when he hears that people have faith in him. He restated their, and his, central belief "that religion is a matter which lies solely between Man & his God, that he owes account to none other for his faith or his worship, that the legitimate powers of government reach actions only, & not opinions."

And then he tied that belief quite clearly to the passage of the Constitution. "I contemplate with sovereign reverence that act of the whole American people which declared that *their* legislature should 'make no law respecting an establishment of religion, or prohibiting the free exercise thereof,' thus building a wall of separation between Church & State." Responding to their Christian benediction with a more Unitarian formulation, Jefferson closed, "I reciprocate your kind prayers for the protection & blessing of the common father and creator of man."

Those who believe Jefferson was describing a wall of separation that would, say, keep prayer out of public schools should look again at the word *their*—which he underlined. In responding to the Baptists' complaint about the Connecticut government, Jefferson said merely that the *national* legislature—the Congress of "the whole American people"—had, at least, created a wall of separation. He did not offer any help in battling the Connecticut law, except to say that he expects to see "the progress of those sentiments" of freedom. In other words, just as Madison had in creating the First Amendment, Jefferson was clear here (as he was in later correspondences) that he viewed it as applying only to the federal government and not to the states. This is how he could have taken this posture on federal proclamations even though he himself had issued one when he was governor of Virginia. As he stated in his second inaugural address, "I have therefore undertaken on no occasion to prescribe the religious exercises suited to it, but have left them, as the Constitution found them, under the direction and discipline of the church or *state* authorities acknowledged by the several religious societies" (my emphasis).

Many conservatives, meanwhile, argue that separation of church and state is a myth created by a liberal twentieth-century misreading of Jefferson's letter. But a plain reading of it—especially in the context of whom he was writing to and why—makes it quite clear that Jefferson did indeed mean that the First Amendment built a wall between the church and the (national) state. One can disagree with Jefferson's interpretation, but he was clear about what *he* thought the First Amendment meant. Conservatives also claim that Jefferson only intended to build a wall protecting religion from the state, and not the other way around. But the context of this letter makes it clear that Jefferson wanted to limit not only government interference but government *encouragement* of religion as well. In fact, given Jefferson's seething bitterness about the role that New England clergy had played in attacking him during the 1800 election—and given his voluminous writings on the damage done society by "priests"—it's likely that when he wrote the letter, he was more concerned about the effect of religion on the polity than the other way around.

Jefferson and Madison both believed that it was nearly impossible for government to help religion without simultaneously harming it. Madison was very clear about that in Virginia when he characterized a program to provide more money to religions as a form of tyranny. And Jefferson believed that issuing religious proclamations was harmful in part because it made him into a Preacher in Chief. He explained in a letter in 1808 that the federal government has "no power to prescribe any religious exercise." Some suggested at the time that it might be okay if the president merely recommended rather than required a day of prayer or fasting. Jefferson said that this, too, would violate the Constitution. Why? Because a presidential recommendation would carry extra influence and therefore "some degree of proscription, perhaps in public opinion."[52] Even public opinion itself—directed against religions that didn't want to follow that particular exercise—is a form of "penalty," he said.

Jefferson apparently drew his own sometimes inscrutable distinction between official proclamations that entailed the president acting in the role of preacher, and general religious rhetoric. "May that Infinite Power which rules the destinies of the universe, lead our councils to what is best, and give them a favorable issue for your peace and prosperity," he said in ending his first presidential address.[53] He didn't describe God's intervention in American affairs as frequently or effusively as Washington and Adams had, but he did on occasions allude to a higher power.

There were a few other instances of Jefferson departing from his strict separationist views. He agreed to a provision paying a Catholic missionary to help work with Indians. (This was not exactly heavy-duty support of religion, as the Indians had already converted and the money was going to help "civilize" them.)[54] And he did attend services held in the House of Representatives and Senate, apparently viewing the mere provision of a locale as not entailing government meddling with religion. Through these actions he illustrated that despite his expansive rhetoric, he was comfortable with many forms of church–state mingling. But on balance, Jefferson distanced himself from Washington and, especially, Adams—instead articulating a vision of government and church spaciously apart.

THE MADISON PRESIDENCY

Now we come to James Madison—Father of the Constitution and chaperone of the First Amendment. Surely if anyone would know how, as chief magistrate, to implement and interpret that document, it would be Madison.

What did he do?

In almost every action, he conveyed support for strict separation of church and state. And he once again made it clear that he viewed the First Amendment as preventing many forms of federal government *support* for religion, *not* just blocking the creation of an official state church favoring one denomination. His actions and contemporaneous statements made this pretty clear, but any ambiguity should have been removed by the startling discovery in 1946 of a heretofore unknown private memo by Madison. In the files of one of Madison's earliest biographers was found a document in Madison's handwriting explaining his views on a wide variety of issues—especially religious freedom. In this "Detached Memoranda," thought to have been written between 1817 and 1832, Madison gave his reasoning for his positions and actions on a variety of church–state issues.

For instance, in 1811, Congress passed a law establishing a church in the District of Columbia. It did not provide tax support or establish it as an official church but merely gave formal legal standing, akin to a government license.

Madison vetoed the bill. At the time, he said that it "exceeds the rightful authority to which governments are limited by the essential distinction between civil and religious functions, and violates in particular the article of the Constitution of the United States which declares that 'Congress shall make no law respecting a religious establishment.' "[55] Later, in the "Detached Memoranda," he explained that the trend of providing incorporation to religious bodies not only violated separation of church and state but had an additional negative consequence: making it more likely that religious organizations would become wealthy. This was bad news. He noted the vast wealth accumulated by the Catholic Church in Europe, and while he acknowledged that churches in America were far from rich, he argued that even minimal government financial help for the church should terrify Americans. Be very wary of big principles being violated in small doses, Madison warned. "The people of the US owe their Independence & their liberty, to the wisdom of decrying in the minute tax of 3 pence on tea, the magnitude of the evil comprised in the precedent." Americans who complain about the ACLU nitpicking small church–state infringements have to reckon with the views of Madison, who praised the Americans for starting a Revolution over a tea tax: "Let them exert the same wisdom, in watching against every evil lurking under plausible disguises, and growing up from small beginnings."[56]

Another example: In 1811, Congress passed a law helping a particular Baptist church in Mississippi. This was not a case of creating an official religion or giving official status—or even of helping the majority religion—but rather a provision of some land for a church, representing a minority sect, no less. Madison vetoed this bill, too. He said it violated the establishment clause and would set a negative "principle and precedent for the appropriation of funds of the United States for the use and support of religious societies, contrary to the article of the Constitution which declares that 'congress shall make no law respecting a religious establishment.' "[57]

Though he didn't actually do anything about it as president, Madison also wrote in the "Detached Memoranda" about his opposition to congressional and military chaplains. And in 1810, he signed the law requiring delivery of mail on the Sabbath.[58]

How did Madison deal with religious proclamations? Early in his life, he seemed to think that declarations of prayer days did not violate freedom of conscience or separation of church and state. In the Virginia legislature, he introduced a bill—authored by Jefferson—for "Appointing Days of Public Fasting and Thanksgiving" and even issuing fines against lackadaisical preachers.[59]

But he came to dislike most presidential religious proclamations, viewing them as "shoots from the same root" as the laws regarding chaplains, giving land to churches, or church incorporation. Madison resisted Congress's request that he issue presidential proclamations of thanksgiving and fasting. "They seem to imply and certainly nourish the erroneous idea of a *national* religion," he wrote. If Americans want to band together to pray, he said, they should do so, but to bring about such prayer or gathering through the political process was "doubly wrong." He suggested that once the practice was begun, there would be a tendency toward promoting a majority religion, and gave as evidence the Christian tone of John Adams's thanksgiving call for Christian worship. Madison reported that he had received many private letters urging him to follow the pattern of Adams and Washington, prompting him to fear that Americans "have lost sight of the equality of *all* religious sects in the eye of the Constitution."[60]

On a few occasions—for instance, during the War of 1812—he did issue proclamations that, sure enough, were deemed political. When he asked for prayers that God would "animate their patriotism" and "bestow a blessing on their arms," Federalists who opposed the war felt Madison had invoked God in support of an unjustified conflict.[61] But Madison's approach differed from that of Washington and Adams in one way. Rather than calling the nation to prayer, he designated particular days on which different religions could devise prayers of their own—if they wished—"according to their own faith and forms."[62]

Perhaps to assuage his conscience, Madison used his July 9, 1812, call to prayer as an occasion to also reassert his views about freedom of conscience and even separation of church and state. One of the blessings he thanked God for was "a political Constitution" guaranteeing "those sacred rights of conscience so essential to his present happiness and so dear to his future hopes." And he practically ordered people *not* to participate in the day of prayer if they didn't believe in it. God will only listen, he said, if "those who join in it are guided only by their free choice, by the impulse of their hearts and the dictates of their consciences." He hailed "freedom from all coercive edicts" as a model for "Christian nations" to emulate, rather than the "unhallowed connection" between religion and state that "corrupts religion into an instrument or an usurper of the policy of the state."

The popular conservative idea that separation of church and state is a concept invented by twentieth-century courts is breathtakingly wrong—at least if we go by the actions and ideas of "the father of the Constitution" and chaperone of the Bill of Rights. Madison could not have been more clear: He thought more separation was better than less, and strict separation—"perfect separation"—was the best of all. He reported in 1822 that there was still "a strong bias toward the old error, that without some sort of alliance or coalition between Gov & Religion neither can be duly supported." This is a "danger [that] cannot be too carefully guarded against," and every instance in which separation had been enforced was a victory for freedom. "Every new & successful example therefore of a perfect separation between ecclesiastical and civil matters, is of importance," he wrote to Edward Livingston. "And I have no doubt that every new example, will succeed, as every past one has done, in shewing that religion and Gov[ernment] will both exist in greater purity, the less they are mixed together."[63]

At another point, he said it was "settled opinion here" that "religion is essentially distinct from civil government, and exempt from its cognizance; that a connexion between them is injurious to both; that there are causes in the human breast, which ensure the perpetuity of religion without the aid of law."[64]

Madison even had problems with the far more defensible idea that the nation had "Christian principles." Jasper Adams, the president of the College of Charleston, sent to many notable figures a pamphlet he'd written arguing that Americans "have retained the Christian religion as the foundation of their civil, legal, and political institutions." John Marshall, the chief justice of the United States, praised the treatise and declared, "The American population is entirely Christian and with us, Christianity and religion are identified." But Madison wouldn't bite even on that general idea. Instead, he reframed the debate. The question, Madison wrote Jasper Adams, was not whether Christianity is a glorious religion but whether it therefore deserved or benefited from support or sanction by the government. "The simple question to be decided is whether a support of the best & purest religion, the

Xn religion itself" ought to come from the government or be "left to the voluntary provisions of those who profess it." He said "experience will be an admitted Umpire" on this question and proceeded to trace the history of church–state intermingling, concluding with his belief that the nations that supported religion least saw religion blossom most.[65]

Madison was emphatic, passionate, and clear. But he lived through many battles on the subject and knew full well that other great men—men with equal commitment to religious freedom—had come to different conclusions. In the letter to the Reverend Adams the eighty-three-year-old Madison struggled to lay out his thoughts on the matter one last time. Noting that rheumatism "makes my hand and fingers as everse to the pen as they are awkward in the use of it," he conceded that Adams—who advocated government support and aid of religion—had "very ably" made his case. Madison seemed to realize that he had bequeathed the next generation a certain amount of ambiguity. "I must admit moreover that it may not be easy, in every possible case, to trace the line of separation between the rights of religion and the Civil authority with such distinctness as to avoid collisions and doubts on unessential points." Madison acknowledged what we all have discovered in the subsequent centuries: There are many gray areas.

But Madison had a solution for dealing with these difficult cases: Err on the side of separation. "The tendency to a usurpation on one side or the other, or to a corrupting coalition or alliance between them will be best guarded against by an entire abstinence of the Government from interference," Madison said, "in any way whatever."

16

friends in heaven

THE FOUNDERS END THEIR SPIRITUAL JOURNEYS AND PREPARE
TO CONTINUE THE CONVERSATION IN THE NEXT LIFE

FREEDOM OF CONSCIENCE MEANS NOT ONLY THE FREEDOM TO believe but also the freedom to change—not only the right to practice one faith but also the right to a spiritual journey. The Founders didn't just champion religious freedom—they used it. Franklin, Washington, Jefferson, Adams, and Madison never stopped examining—passionately, combatively, wisely—life's deepest questions. Each journey was distinctive, but they ended up in similar places, still deeply spiritual but with an ever-shortening list of required religious creeds. The older they got, the simpler their faith became.

Born a Puritan, Franklin had, at one point, idolized Cotton Mather. Over time, he experimented with other philosophies, from Deism to polytheism. At the age of eighty-three, just five weeks before his death, he was challenged by his friend Ezra Stiles to summarize his "Christian convictions." Franklin responded with a more universal declaration:

> Here is my Creed. I believe in one God, Creator of the Universe. That he governs the World by his Providence. That he ought to be worshipped. That the most acceptable Service we can render to him, is doing good to his other Children. That the Soul of Man is immortal, and will be treated with Justice in another life, respect[ing] its Conduct in this. These I take

to be the fundamental Principles of all sound Religion, and I regard them as you do, in whatever Sect I meet them.[1]

Like Jefferson, he came to admire Jesus without worshipping him. In another example of selective quoting, *America's God & Country*, a conservative encyclopedia of quotations, cited this letter from Franklin ostensibly showing his Christian passion: "As to Jesus of Nazareth . . . I think the System of Morals and his Religion, as he left them to us, is the best the World ever saw, or is likely to see."[2] The editor ends the quote there, ignoring what Franklin wrote two sentences later: "but I apprehend it has received various corrupting Changes and I have, with most of the present Dissenters in England, some Doubts as to his Divinity." In characteristic fashion, Franklin added that he saw "no harm" in people believing Jesus was son of God, "tho' it is a question I do not dogmatize upon, having never studied it." Besides, he said, it was futile for him to now "busy himself" with the question of Jesus's divinity "when I expect soon an Opportunity of knowing the Truth with less Trouble."

George Washington died just two years after he left office, depriving him of the years of agrarian contemplation afforded the others. His latter years were much like his earlier: He showed perfunctory interest in the rituals and sacraments of religion—church attendance and communion—but had a strong belief that God had intervened in his own life and the course of the nation. He retained a sense of deep humility about man's capacity to understand God's ways. Just a few months before his death, Washington noted that "the ways of Providence are inscrutable, and can not be scanned by short sighted man, whose duty is submission."[3] The most direct end-of-life summary of his spiritual approach came in a letter he wrote on Christmas 1795, four years before his death. "In politics, as in religion, my tenets are few and simple; the leading one of which, and indeed that which embraces most others, is to be honest and just ourselves, and to exact it from others; meddling as little as possible in their affairs where our own are not involved. If this maxim was generally adopted, wars would cease and our swords would soon be converted into reap-hooks and our harvests be more peaceful, abundant and happy."[4] Be honest, be good, and leave others alone—his core faith was as universal as Franklin's.

For James Madison, there are signs that his affection for orthodox Christianity faded, too, as the years went on. Although his wife, Dolley, and his mother, Nelly Conway Madison, were both confirmed, Madison himself never was.[5] He did not kneel at prayer[6] or scrupulously keep the Sabbath.[7] In a letter to Frederick Beasley on November 20, 1825, Madison referred to "Nature's god" but didn't mention Jesus, the Bible, or the church. "Madison's letter seems more the response of a Deist than that of an orthodox Christian," concluded historian David Holmes.[8]

Little is known about the possible effect of Dolley Madison on James Madison's spirituality or approach to religious liberty: He was Episcopalian, and Dolley was raised Quaker. While Quakers were no longer being hanged as heretics, they were still considered abnormal.[9] As expected, when Dolley and James wed, the Quaker Meeting House "read her out" of the community. Later in life, she was confirmed as an Episcopalian but continued to offer "panegyrics" about Quakerism. There appear to be no letters or even second-hand comments on what influence Dolley's spirituality might have had on James, but it would stand to reason that his proximity to someone of such a different upbringing would have further sensitized him to religious differences.

Like Franklin, the more John Adams studied, the more convinced he became that religion could be boiled down to a few principles. First, he came to believe that good deeds were the *only* determinant of heavenly reward. "The great result of all my researches has been a most diffusive and comprehensive charity. I believe with Justin Martyr, that all good men are Christians." He was therefore also highly skeptical of the idea that those not familiar with Christianity would go to hell. In a letter to Jefferson, he claimed that nine-tenths of the population was not schooled in Christianity and therefore would, according to Christian doctrine, suffer for eternity. Why does God allow "innumerable millions to make them miserable, forever"? The explanation often given, said Adams, was, "For his Own Glory." This answer disgusted him. "Wretch! . . . Is he vain?" he asked about God. "Tickled with Adulation? Exulting and triumphing in his Power and the Sweetness of his Vengeance? Pardon me, my Maker, for these Aweful Questions. My Answer to them is always ready: I believe no such Things."[10]

Adams continued to praise the basic moral teachings of Jesus—the Sermon on the Mount, love thy neighbor—but as he aged he became more interested in universal truths that transcended religions. The son of Puritans said he had spent time reading about Hinduism and found much he admired. "Where is to be found Theology more orthodox or Phylosophy more profound than in the Introduction to the Shast[ra]? 'God is one, creator of all, Universal Sphere, without beginning, without End.' " He called these doctrines "sublime if ever there were any sublime."[11] He even offered the hope that there soon would be available more English translations of the sacred books of the "persians, the Chinese and the Hindoos" so that "our grandchildren and my great-grandchildren may compare notes and hold fast all that is good."

He wasn't threatened by exposure to other faiths; nor did he believe that open-minded people needed to hide their pride in their own faith. "I am, therefore, of opinion that men ought (after they have examined with unbiased judgments every system of religion, and chosen one system, on their own authority, for themselves), to avow their opinions and defend them with boldness."[12] In the end, he even softened his views on state aid to religion. At age eighty, Adams participated in the 1820 Massachusetts convention that rewrote the state constitution. And Adams—who had once told Isaac Backus that the establishment would fall when the solar system reorganized—proposed that the state no longer recognize particular religious sects.[13] The man who once attacked Catholics as villainous, Quakers as troublemakers, and Jeffersonians as infidels wrote to Jefferson in old age that what he now treasured most was "universal toleration."[14]

He conceived of God as all-powerful, but over time grew less chauvinistic about our place in His designs. "There is no special Providence for us," he wrote in 1812. "We are not a chosen people that I know of."[15] And he, too, became more modest about his own ability to divine the Divine. "Admire and adore the Author of the telescopic universe, love and esteem the work, do all in your power to lessen ill, and increase good; but never presume to comprehend."[16]

Adams boiled down his life's learning to a few principles, similar to Franklin's: "The Ten Commandments and The Sermon on the Mount contain my Religion."[17] Then he condensed his personal theology even further. "I have learned nothing of importance to me, for they have made no Change in my moral or religious Creed, which has for 50 or 60 years been contained in four short Words 'Be just and good.' "

Thomas Jefferson ended his life more enamored than ever of Jesus's teachings and yet just as enraged at Christianity's focus on doctrinal disputes, ritual, miracles, and holy wars. Like Adams, he became convinced that Unitarianism was the closest to the truth, as it rejected the doctrine of the Trinity, threw the Bible to the side, emphasized good works, and urged a simple love of a singular God. "I trust that there is not a young man now living in the United States who will not die an Unitarian," he wrote in 1822.[18]

But the greatest spiritual program, he concluded, consisted of the tenets agreed to by all the world's religions. "Were I to be the founder of a new sect," he told Thomas Parker in 1819, "I would call them Apriarians, and, after the example of the bee, advise them to extract the honey of every sect."[19] In 1813, Jefferson wrote to William Canby that if one merely abides by the basic principles embodied in *all* religions, one "will never be questioned at the gates of heaven."[20]

Jefferson succinctly laid out his creed in 1822:

1. That there is one God, and he all-perfect
2. That there is a future state of rewards and punishments
3. That to love God with all thy heart and thy neighbor as thyself, is the sum of religion.[21]

In a letter to Thomas Jefferson Smith, the son of a friend, on February 21, 1825, he offered this advice on how to lead a life that would earn salvation: "Adore God. Reverence and cherish your parents. Love your neighbor as yourself, and your country more than yourself. Be just. Be true. Murmur not at the ways of Providence. So shall the life into which you have entered, be the portal to one of the eternal and ineffable bliss."[22]

It is impossible to read the letters of Jefferson in his declining years and come away without a sense that the man who said faith should be guided by reason and scientific analysis very much believed he would soon be welcomed into the afterlife. He yearned for the day when he could reunite with his friends, less frail, to observe the activities of the earth and reminisce. His vision of Heaven seemed concrete and enthralling. To Abigail Adams, he wrote, "Our next meeting must then be in the country to which they [other mutual friends] have flown, a country, for us, not now very distant."[23]

Most poignant of all was this stunningly wise and spiritual condolence letter that Jefferson wrote to John Adams on November 13, 1818, after he heard that Abigail had died.

The public papers, my dear friend, announce the fatal event of which your letter of October 20. had given me ominous foreboding. Tried myself, in the school of affliction, by the loss of every form of connection which can rive the human heart, I know well, and feel what you have lost, what you have suffered, are suffering, and have yet to endure. The same trials have taught me that, for ills so immeasurable, time and silence are the only medicines. I will not therefore, by useless condolences, open afresh the sluices of your grief nor, altho' mingling sincerely my tears with yours, will I say a word more, where words are vain, but that it is of some comfort to us both that the term is not very distant at which we are to deposit, in the same cerement, our sorrows and suffering bodies, and to ascend in essence to an ecstatic meeting with the friends we have loved and lost and whom we shall still love and never lose again. God bless you and support you under your heavy affliction.[24]

Jefferson and Adams, once great friends, then bitter enemies, and then friends again in old age, continued to correspond—and explore, vent, bond, and confess—as they approached their ends. They talked about politics, old times, the future, and, often, about religion. They found themselves in increasing agreement—about the outrages of the clergy, the silliness of many religious disputes, the handful of divine truths that shine amid them all, and the blessings of religious freedom. And they shared a conviction that their friendship would carry on in the next life. Like two old gents bickering in the park over current events, they continued to banter by letter. After reviewing world events in a letter to Adams on September 4, 1823, Jefferson painted an image of the two of them standing at the windows of heaven, blissfully reminiscing and peering below, without the burdens of responsibility. "You and I shall look down from another world on these glorious achievements to man," Jefferson wrote, "which will add to the joys even of heaven."[25]

they were right

———•———

WHAT WOULD THE FOUNDERS MAKE OF TODAY'S DEBATES? Before offering comment, they would surely want a quick briefing on what happened in the subsequent two hundred years. There have been thousands of battles, local and national, over the proper role of religion in American life. Though all of the states had disestablished their official churches by 1833, many had continued to allow for varying degrees of government support for religion. The pendulum has swung back and forth, approaches varying state by state, town by town. But a few seismic shifts stand out.

The most important was the Civil War. The Northern victors concluded that the basic relationship between the states and the federal government needed to be changed—as it related not only to blacks and enslavement but to all citizens and all liberties. As a result, they passed the Fourteenth Amendment: "No state shall make or enforce any law which shall abridge the privileges or immunities of citizens of the United States; nor shall any state deprive to any person life, liberty, or property without due process of law; nor deny to any person within its jurisdiction the equal protection of the laws."

As interpreted by twentieth-century court rulings, the Fourteenth Amendment applied the principles of the First Amendment to the states eighty years after Madison had tried unsuccessfully to do the same. That's why we have fights over prayer in school, crèches in the town square, and the Ten Commandments in the state courthouse.[1] Scholars debate whether the framers of the Fourteenth Amendment intended to apply the First Amendment to the states in quite the manner that subsequent courts decided. But there is evidence that, at a minimum, these nineteenth-century Founding Fathers—the authors of the Fourteenth Amendment—did intend to take the essence of the liberties guaranteed under the First Amendment and apply them at all levels of society. Robert Bingham, the Ohio congressman who proposed the Fourteenth Amendment, declared on the floor of the House that the new amendment encompassed "all the sacred rights of person—those rights dear to freeman and formidable only to tyrants—and of which the fathers of the Republic spoke, after God had given them the victory." Until that point, Bingham declared, when states trampled constitutional rights, citizens were powerless. "They restricted the rights of conscience," he said, "and he had no remedy."[2] So while the Founding Fathers had decided in the 1780s that the Constitution did not apply religious freedom to the states, the leaders in the 1860s decided that it did—or at least that's the recent interpretation of the Supreme Court. I suspect that were they alive today, some of the Founding Fathers would be thrilled—Madison always feared state tyranny most—and others would be disappointed that the Fourteenth Amendment was passed and subsequently interpreted in a way that applied separation of church and state at the local level. But I also believe that Robert Bingham would be pleased, and his views are as important as Madison's, since the Fourteenth Amendment supersedes the First.

Those who passed the Fourteenth Amendment, and the courts that later interpreted it, concluded, in effect, that it no longer mattered whether Madison—or Adams or Fisher Ames or Patrick Henry—wanted his views on religious freedom applied to the states. The men who ratified the Fourteenth Amendment decided that, with the benefit of hindsight, the basic principles the Founders had envisioned just for the federal government should now be applied to the states. In that sense, those who are angry that God has been "kicked out" of the public schools shouldn't blame the ACLU or, for that matter, Thomas Jefferson—but Abraham Lincoln and General Grant. The decisive blow against prayer in school came when Lee surrendered at Appomattox.

The second major change resulted from immigration. The religious makeup of the population of the United States in 1789 was 99 percent Protestant. Today, it is 52 percent Protestant.[3] The John Adams of 1776 would be appalled that the largest denomination in America right now is Catholicism.

Waves of immigration before the Civil War and then again in the beginnings of the twentieth century brought millions of Catholics to America, and they now represent roughly a quarter of the population. More recently, we've seen significant immigration of non-Christians. Today America is home to more Hindus than Unitarians, more Muslims than Congregationalists, and more Buddhists than Jews. In fact, there are more than twelve million non-Christians in America—about four times the entire population of the colonies when the Constitution was ratified.[4] Immigration combined with continuous splintering of existing denominations to create a breathtaking diversity of sects. These "facts on the ground" reinforce the Founders' pluralistic impulse and forever shut the door on the possibility that America could be, in any official sense, deemed a Protestant, or even a Christian, nation.

Another important event was the publication in 1859, just twenty-six years after Madison's death, of *The Origin of Species* by Charles Darwin. This had an indirect but profound effect on church–state issues. During the eighteenth century, as in earlier years, there was, to be sure, a raging conflict between rationalists and theists. Church fathers loathed Deism, for instance, as a great threat because it denied the infallibility of the Bible and thereby undermined pillars of organized religion. But rationalists of that era were *not* usually atheists. They were men such as Jefferson and John Locke who argued fervently that rationalism and science proved the *existence* of God.

Darwin and the rise of evolutionary theory more directly pit science against God. Over the years, many more scientists would view religion as superstition. Even this can be, and usually is, vastly overstated. Many scientists believe in God, including some of the most acclaimed like Albert Einstein, who famously said, "Science without religion is lame, religion without science is blind."[5] But rightly or wrongly, many religious Americans came to fear that the advance of science threatened their faith. What's more, many now believe that science and secularism undermined morality and, therefore, insulted God. These three phenomena—the rise of Darwinism, the growth of religious diversity, and the incorporation of the Bill of Rights—progressed on parallel tracks.

Then three rulings of the US Supreme Court further transformed the church–state battle. In 1962, in *Engel v. Vitale,* the Court ruled that school officials in New York State could not compose a prayer to be recited by students. The next year, in *Abington Township School District v. Schempp,* the Court ruled that schools could not sponsor or lead Bible reading or recitation of the Lord's Prayer. These were the decisions that "kicked God out of the schools." And in 1973, in *Roe v. Wade*, the Court ruled that there was a right to privacy that included the right to an abortion. Though *Roe* was not a church–state case, many religious Americans viewed it as tragically connected to the earlier rulings. God was ejected from the public sphere and the state of morality plummeted, the most egregious example being the legalization of abortion. That this period also saw higher crime, drug use, divorce, and out-of-wedlock birth only convinced many that God had been so affronted by the ejection of His word from school that He had withdrawn his protection.[6]

In 1979, a Southern Baptist minister named Jerry Falwell created the Moral Majority. Born in Lynchburg, Virginia—about a two-hour drive from where John Leland had once preached[7]—Falwell helped lead a fundamental shift in the way that Baptists, evangelicals, and ultimately conservative Christians viewed the role of politics and religion. Whereas the eighteenth-century Baptists said Jesus wanted the religious and temporal worlds separated, this twentieth-century Baptist and the movement he helped create believed that society had become so degraded, God wanted believers to take back the political sphere to reassert His values. Religious conservative leaders convinced millions that the wall separating church and state was not only too high but in fact illegitimate and ahistorical—a myth. It is now the case that among conservative evangelical Protestants, the dominant view is one that Isaac Backus and John Leland would have rejected: that serving God means putting Him—His words, His scriptures, His prayers—in the public sphere as much as possible.

Meanwhile, significantly, the relationship between conservative Protestants and Catholics improved. For much of the nineteenth and twentieth centuries, separation of church and state was sustained in part as a way of reducing the power of immigrant Catholics. Conservative Protestants enthusiastically supported the "Blaine Amendments" that prohibited state support for Catholic parochial schools.[8] But as Catholics became more mainstream and politically conservative, evangelical Christians in the decades after 1980 came to focus more on what they had in common—opposition to abortion and secularism, for instance—and became less concerned about the possibility that government would aid Catholicism. This ecumenism on the right led to a larger and more potent coalition demanding less separation of church and state.

Simultaneously, an important change occurred in the approach of *supporters* of separation of church and state. Usually this is described as "secularization," but that misses the mark; after all, most of the significant church–state cases that fortified the wall between church and state were brought by religious people. Rather, what happened was a heightened emphasis on the rights of religious minorities. As a result, most public debates, especially on TV, cast the conflict as between those who are pro-religion— and therefore against separation of church and state—and those who are either "secular" or protecting religious minorities, and therefore in favor of separation of church and state. This was certainly part of the Founders' interest, too, but civil libertarians and the news media have become so focused on the rights of minorities that they have lost a crucial element of the Founders' philosophy—that separation of church and state was good for religion *in general*. This is a rather profound idea that's been forgotten.

BREAKING THE CULTURE-WAR LENS

That brings us back to today's culture wars, one facet of which is the cherry-picking of Founding Father quotes to prove almost anything. As I hope I've shown throughout this book, activists have made a number of false or misleading assertions about the Founding Fathers, the separation of church and state, and the birth of religious freedom.

Among the commonly promoted ideas that are mistaken:

Liberal Fallacy 1:
Most Founding Fathers were Deists or secular.
Deism held that God created the laws of nature and then receded from action. Most of the Founders agreed with the first part of that sentence but disagreed with the second. They rejected the idea that the Bible was inerrant but, to a person, believed in an omnipotent God who intervened in the lives of men and nations. That means they were either not Deists at all or were a flavor of Deist not typically imagined when the word is used. Some wanted secular government, but none of them was a secular individual. Also, many of the other men who were instrumental in the Revolution and the Continental Congress were orthodox Christians, including: Patrick Henry, Sam Adams, John Hancock, John Witherspoon, Roger Sherman, and many more. These men represented viewpoints that had to be heeded by the likes of Jefferson and Madison, who were not just philosophers but also politicians who assembled coalitions. It is even clearer that *none* of these Founders was a "secular humanist"; they believed in God and that He shaped their lives and fortunes.

Conservative Fallacy 1:
Most Founding Fathers were serious Christians.

Of course it depends on how we define the term, but if we use the definition of *Christianity* offered by those who make this claim—conservative Christians—then the Founders studied in this book were not Christians. Jefferson and Franklin overtly rejected the divinity of Jesus. Jefferson loathed the entire clerical class and what had become of Christianity. Adams became an active Unitarian, rejecting much Christian doctrine. And Franklin, Jefferson, and Adams abhorred the Calvinist idea that salvation was determined by divine preference rather than good works. Madison and Washington remained the most silent on matters of personal theology and continued to attend Christian churches, but in their voluminous writings never seemed to speak of Jesus as divine. If they must wear labels, the closest would be *Unitarian*.

Liberal Fallacy 2:
The Constitution demanded strict separation of church and state throughout the land.

Actually, the original Constitution called for the *federal* government to keep out of religious affairs but allowed states—which governed most matters—to mingle church and state as much as they wanted. Had the original Constitution attempted to impose separation of church and state throughout the land, it probably would not have been ratified. Liberals can certainly argue for strict and pervasive separation, but they cannot claim all the Founders as agreeing.

Conservative Fallacy 2:
Separation of church and state is a twentieth-century invention of the courts.

Not all Founders wanted rigorous separation, but a few rather important ones did. James Madison, a man who knew a thing or two about the Constitution, strongly supported separation of church and state. For him, the higher the wall, the better. Jefferson agreed. Not everyone agreed with Madison and Jefferson, but clearly this was not a myth concocted two hundred years later by activist judges. Nor is it true that "the Founders" were protecting religion from the state and not the other way around, as is often maintained by Christian conservatives. Different Founders had different emphases. Madison and the Baptists tended to speak more about the negative effects of church–state entanglements on religion. But Jefferson more often emphasized the destructive effects of church–state cooperation on the functioning of a democracy. As a collective, they believed that separation of church and state was good for both.

Liberal Fallacy 3:
Separation of church and state was designed mostly to protect religious minorities.

That was certainly part of the goal, but just as important was the idea that the wall would allow for religion in general—including the majority religion—to flourish. Indeed, Madison and others hoped that the separation of church and state would help spread Christianity.

Conservative Fallacy 3:
Advocates of separation are anti-religion.

Actually, the separation of church and state resulted from an alliance of eighteenth-century rationalists such as Jefferson and evangelical Christians like Isaac Backus and John Leland, who were most certainly pro-religion.

Common Fallacy 4:
The Founders figured this all out.

The Founders crafted a revolutionary compromise that took huge steps toward separating religion and government at the national levels. But they disagreed with one another on the particulars, and even some of the core principles. They did not, alas, resolve many of the most difficult issues.

History seen through the lens of the culture war is history distorted. In their righteous advocacy for the cause, some activists on both sides have warped facts and the motives of their opponents. In the spirit of Adams's and Jefferson's rapprochement, it's time for each side to appreciate that its enemies are right on key points. We all have our biases, but as someone who respects many of the players on both sides of the culture wars, I would like to summarize my own views of what likely transpired:

America *was* settled to be a Christian nation. To be more precise, it was settled to be a Protestant nation. Inhabitants of most colonies prior to the Revolution were not interested in religious pluralism or tolerance. They wanted society based on Protestant principles, with a strong mingling of church and state and vigilant antagonism toward Catholicism. Almost all of the colonies tried some variant on state-supported religion, and every one of those experiments failed. Perhaps the most important flare-ups of persecution came in a few Virginia counties, where they were witnessed by a thoroughly disgusted young James Madison. He and several other Founders looked at the wreckage of these experiments and concluded that official state religions led to oppression of minority religions *and* lethargy among the majority religions. Meanwhile, the Great Awakening created vibrant new denominations independent of and hostile to the official religions. These religious revivals also spawned a generation of Americans accustomed to fighting authority in search of higher principles.

The break from Great Britain had many causes, but the desire for religious freedom was one of them. In the South, the Church of England was the official religion, even though the majority of the population by that point was not Anglican. The oppressiveness of the Church seemed part and parcel of the royal tyranny. In the North, the Church of England was even more despised, and patriots stirred fears that freedom of religion would soon be curtailed. In one of the little-known, and less admirable, aspects of the struggle, rebels exploited fear of Catholics to help fuel antagonism to British rule.

The War of Independence further transformed colonial attitudes toward religious freedom. It created from a collection of colonies a single nation — and forced, for the first time, its leaders to confront the growing religious diversity. George Washington imposed tolerance throughout the Continental army. The Continental Congress became ever more aware of the differences among its own members. Demographic facts and strategic wartime needs coincided with a growing philosophical movement emphasizing individual liberty.

Beginning in 1776 with Virginia and ending with Massachusetts in 1833, all of the states discontinued the practice of having an official religion. Many people of goodwill believed that while official establishments were ill advised, government financial support of religion was still important and necessary. This view, typified by people like Patrick Henry, ended up losing — thanks to an unusual alliance between Enlightenment rationalists and evangelical Christians. Enlightenment rationalists believed that reason, not revelation, was the key to morality and a good life, and they therefore loathed anything that enlisted state power to prop up religious doctrine. They believed that in a free marketplace of ideas, reason would prevail. Evangelicals believed that church–state alliances had not only oppressed them but also conflicted with the teachings of Jesus, who specifically declared himself to be ruler of a different kingdom. They believed that in a free marketplace of ideas and religion, the truth would prevail, and that that truth would be the word of Jesus Christ.

On some fundamental points, a broad consensus developed:

- Government—certainly not the federal government, and probably not the state government—should never establish an official religion.
- Freedom of conscience is an inalienable right—not a privilege generously offered by those in power, but a fundamental right, granted by God—that simply cannot be abridged.
- Elected officials could and should use broad, nonsectarian religious language in public pronouncements.
- Religious diversity and pluralism are among the most important guarantors of religious freedom.

Most of the Founders would agree with all of these statements.

On other points, the Founders disagreed. Some believed that government could and should support religion because a vibrant faith sector was essential to a functioning democracy. Others—most notably James Madison and Thomas Jefferson—believed that government support for, or use of, religion would invariably harm both, and that the wisest route was to always err on the side of strict separation.

The US Constitution and the First Amendment did *not* resolve this disagreement. They were approved with support from people on both sides, thereby leaving to future generations the battles we fight today. Over the years, some communities have decided the issues in ways that Patrick Henry would applaud—we had *state-written* prayer in school right up until 1962. Others have opted for Madison's approach.

Is it, therefore, useless to study the Founding Fathers? Not at all—if we know how to use them properly. It's time we stopped using the Founders as historical conversation stoppers—as in *I'm right and you can tell, because the Founding Fathers agree with me.* Instead, we must pick up the *argument* that they began and do as they instructed—use our reason to determine our views. The mind, as Jefferson reminded us, is the only oracle God gave us. Jefferson wanted people less dependent on the Bible; I would extend the idea, and urge us to be less dependent on Jefferson. Many modern church–state questions fall into a constitutional gray zone, and squinting at the founding documents with greater intensity will not change that.

We need to ask a different question—not *Are these practices constitu-tional?* but *Are they wise?*

To help answer that question, let's play that popular parlor game of WWFFD—what would the Founding Fathers do? For starters, their views would depend on what government office they were occupying at the moment. If they were president of the United States and there had never been a Fourteenth Amendment, they would have defended the right of the states to do pretty much whatever they wanted—from putting a crèche on the town square, to hanging a Ten Commandments plaque in the local courthouse, to leading prayers in school.

But what if they were governors of a state that was considering placing the Ten Commandment plaque? Ah, now that's different. Each of these five men may have taken a different approach. Governor Madison, I believe, would have opposed the idea. He would have argued that as much as he liked the Decalogue, government endorsing it would not only harm those who didn't believe it, but tarnish the Decalogue itself. Governor Jefferson would reassert the *right* of the state to do this but would also declare that, in the end, it was a bad idea. Adams, or at least Adams of the 1776 mind-set, would likely have gone along with the plaque. He'd view complaints from the evangelicals as a bit picayune and suggest that as long as the court is not actually restricting the religions of others, there's no harm in publicly declaring allegiance with bib-lical principles. Washington would likely have agreed with Adams's approach but fretted that the plaque was citing material from the Bible instead of broader, more unifying principles. He might have suggested a more general statement that God wants us to follow certain universal moral laws. Franklin would have caused the most mischief by agreeing to the posting of the Ten Commandments but only if all of the other religions in the area also got rep-resentation. Under Governor Franklin, the courthouse would have become a museum to all religious traditions—passages from the Quran and Bhagavad Gita side by side with the Ten Commandments.

What about prayer in school? You'd have to explain to the Founders that most Americans were now educated in public schools. Once they realized that public schools were funded by tax dollars and run by the government, they would scratch their powdered wigs. Adams, I believe, would have been fine with it. As for Washington, it's worth remembering that he supported Patrick Henry's assessment until he saw how it upset many Virginians. He would certainly have extolled the benefits of prayer—look how often he invoked the divine in his own public pronouncements—and, I believe, would have sought a compromise allowing for moments of prayer, especially if not officially proscribed. Jefferson would have supported the constitutional right of the school to do this but opposed the practice, as he believed education should be focused on the dissemination of scientific and historical information. Initially, he even opposed having theology taught at the University of Virginia. Madison would have sided with Jefferson—especially if someone whose salary was paid by taxpayers led the prayer. He would have likely invoked his general rule that when it comes to gray areas, it's best to err on the side of separation of church and state.[9]

These hypotheticals reinforce a few points. First, the Founders differed from one another. Even in their own time, they recognized that there were perplexing dilemmas about which they and their contemporaries disagreed. If the Founders who wrote the Constitution or witnessed its creation disagreed about what it meant, then we should all cut each other some slack. When we argue that our adversaries are wrong, we should remember that mostly they are likely wrong (or right) at the margins. They are inaccurate, not corrupt; mistaken, not evil.

Since the US Supreme Court decided that state and local governments had to guarantee freedom of religion, courts have wrestled with a seemingly unlimited supply of new questions. Can students organize a Bible study on school property? What if it's after school? What if secular groups are also meeting? Can a prayer be said at graduation? What if it's led by the principal? What if other faiths are represented, too? Could a cross be put on the town square? What if it was put up by the KKK? What if there's a menorah nearby?

Many of the most important Supreme Court cases focused not on the establishment clause but the other religion clause in the First Amendment, that guaranteeing the "free exercise" of religion. While the establishment-clause cases focused on issues of state support or endorsement of religion, the free-exercise cases have focused on a different question: When is it permissible to restrict religious practice? Though these cases are invariably controversial, they have not cleaved public opinion along the same culture-war fault lines as the establishment-clause cases. After all, is it liberal or conservative, red or blue, to favor the rights of religious minorities to practice their faith? But in terms of the development of religious freedom, these cases are just as important. Courts have tended to distinguish between freedom of thought—

which has nearly impervious protection—and freedom of action, which sometimes may be restrained. For instance, early in the twentieth century, the Supreme Court concluded that freedom of religion could not be used by members of the Church of Latter Day Saints to justify polygamy. Courts have struggled to define when a community has enough of a "compelling interest" that it can regulate someone's religious behavior. Jehovah's Witnesses can believe what they want to believe, but what if they start knocking on doors? What if someone's religion requires ritual animal sacrifice? What if it involves taking hallucinogenic drugs? It's not the purview of this book to review all the free-exercise cases, but the bottom line is that the courts have considered religious liberty to be one of the highest American principles, placed strict limits on how and when it can be infringed, and allowed for the government to make special efforts to ensure that individuals and groups feel able to practice their faith as freely as possible. Over the years, the courts have allowed Americans to: get unemployment benefits if they quit their jobs for religious reasons; skip jury duty if it conflicts with their faith; leave public school during the day to get supplementary religious education from their churches; obtain the services of government-financed chaplains in prison; decline to salute the flag if doing so conflicts with a religious creed; ask employers to make "reasonable accommodations" of their faith; and avoid military service on religious grounds. Religious institutions have been granted enormous tax advantages, and exemption from certain civil rights and labor laws. All of this was done in the spirit of the Founders' view that religious liberty was among the "choicest flowers" and required special protection.[10]

I believe that if the Founders were reviewing the decisions, what would strike them is not what we are fighting over but what we are not fighting over. Relative to the world the Founders lived and died in, America today provides a breathtaking amount of religious freedom. Government doesn't dictate religious doctrine. Ministers can preach without getting approval from the state, let alone the leadership of other religions. Our tax dollars rarely pay the salaries of ministers who preach abhorrent beliefs. People of every possible religious view can find others who share theirs and worship together.

Yes, there are still problems: nearly every faith, from pagans to evangelical Christians, claims that it's being discriminated against, and often this is technically true. But a Christian who is not allowed to run a Bible study group on public school property is still allowed to worship in church, at home, in the car, on the street, at a rock concert, plugged into an iPod, or surfing on the Internet. What's most striking is how rarely we see religious liberty fundamentally under assault in the United States.

America is religiously free. The Founding Fathers tried a radical new approach—and it worked.

MADISON'S SOLUTION

This triumph was the product of demographic forces, revolutionary ideas, and the bold actions of many men and women: the people who fought for the Constitution and those who, by opposing it, birthed the Bill of Rights; the courageous members of religious minorities, such as Mary Dyer, Isaac Backus, John Leland, or Charles Carroll; the Catholic soldiers who fought in the Revolutionary War despite growing up as second-class citizens; the brilliant philosopher-statesmen like Jefferson and Franklin who changed the way Americans thought about religious freedom; and George Washington, who concluded that religious tolerance was as important a prerequisite for building a nation as a flag, an army, or a dollar bill.

But it is James Madison who deserves the greatest thanks.

It was Madison who developed the most holistic understanding of what was likely to help both faith and society. While Adams and Washington generally approved of religious freedom, they held on to lingering hopes that, because of its importance, religion should be encouraged by government. Patrick Henry went even further and pushed to have it actively supported. Jefferson went in the other direction—though I believe he came out on the right side of most of the policy issues, his arguments tended to be dominated by a rationalist vision of a world without superstition or faith. Much of his writing focused on protecting the state from religion, rather than the other way around. He viewed religious ritual as anachronistic, and predicted that eventually everyone would be a Unitarian. In the end, he misunderstood the power of old-fashioned religion—the tradition, ritual, and sheer nonrational spiritual power of faith.

Madison, however, embraced and integrated the arguments of both Jefferson *and* the Baptists—that separation of church and state was essential for the functioning of democracy *and* for the flowering of faith. He best articulated and understood the obvious threat of government restraint and the less obvious menace of government support for religion. He believed that government assistance to faith was, or would invariably become, a debilitating force. Madison believed government help would hurt.

He saw that when colonial establishments existed, aid for one particular denomination led, inexorably, toward disabilities for the other faiths. If one religion got first-class treatment, the rest, by definition, were second-class. This process unfolded differently in each state, but a common scenario Madison witnessed was that when one particular religion had official status, the others had to get permission for their preachers, which meant they had to justify themselves to men who often held their faith in contempt.

When Madison was fighting Patrick Henry's assessment bill—which was, we must remember, liberal and fair-minded as these things went—he noted that after government offers its help, it then sets rules to administer that aid. And when it creates rules, it must enforce them. And enforcing rules requires a policing mechanism and a set of penalties. And while the initial application of this statist regimen—in the hands of the well-meaning people who birthed it—may be benign, it would eventually end up controlled by people of less liberal dispositions.

Madison (and Jefferson) believed that even presidential proclamations of fasting or thanksgiving were wrong because they made the commander in chief into the preacher in chief. Madison's most important insight was that it would lead to a distrust of religion. It would be assumed, Madison suggested, that the invocation of religion by a politician was, well, political. He and his Baptist allies would be mystified by the assumption that being pro-separation means being anti-God. How on earth does it follow that if you treasure religion, you'd want government touching it? Church and state, when married, bring out the worst in each other, Madison would say. If God is powerful, he does not need the support of the Treasury.

Indeed, to equate support for religion in the public square with love of God is not only an insult to those God-fearing people on the other side of the debate, but also expresses a profound lack of confidence in God and a disconcerting shallowness of personal faith.

Since that may sound harsh, allow me to elaborate. One of the reasons that men such as Isaac Backus and John Leland and, ultimately, Madison embraced separation of church and state was that they had supreme confidence that, in a free marketplace of ideas, their religion would win. I don't know whether Backus would have wanted prayer in public schools or not, but I imagine he would be saddened by the emphasis placed on that cause by many of today's religious conservatives. I can hear Backus shout: How tepid is your faith if you think it can be easily shaken without constant reinforcement by a government-run school! How ineffective must be the churches—and parents—if you rely on the public schools as the only way to keep your children away from depravity! Crutches are for the weak or ill. Backus and Leland would exhort: God does not need the support of government to triumph.

When Jefferson was preparing for a debate over the official church in Virginia, he made a simple notation about a common objection and the answer he would offer up in rebuttal:

> Obj: Religion will decline if not supported
> Ans. Gates of Hell shall not prevail. . . .

How is it that even Jefferson seemed to have more confidence in the power of Christianity to defeat the forces of evil than many modern Christians? Madison and the Baptists believed that free markets in divine ideas worked the same way as commercial markets. Freedom allows for strong faiths to thrive. Government interference—even well-meaning support—allows weak faiths to survive. What's more, government involvement turns people away from faith, revealing its practitioners to be lacking the courage of their own convictions—a surefire way to botch your spiritual sale.

Did the Founders believe that their radical approach to religious freedom had succeeded? Jefferson had his doubts. On January 22, 1821—in the midst of a new wave of religious revivalism—he wrote to Adams that "this country, which has given to the world the example of physical liberty, owes to it that of moral emancipation also. For, as yet, it is but nominal with us. The inquisition of public opinion overwhelms in practice the freedom asserted by the laws in theory."[11]

But Madison grew more optimistic. After he left office, he looked around and became convinced that separation of church and state had indeed spawned more religious liberty, which in turn spurred more, and better, spiritual practice. "No doubt exists that there is much more of religion among us now than there ever was before the change," he wrote. "This proves rather more than that the law is not necessary to the support of religion." Madison felt that his views on religious freedom and separation of church of state—ahead of their time when he first advocated them—had been proven right, and the best evidence of all was found in the churches. "Religious instruction is now diffused throughout the Community by preachers of every sect with almost equal zeal. . . . The qualifications of the Preachers, too among the new

sects where there was the greatest deficiency, are understood to be improv-
ing."[12] On the question of whether clergy could survive without state support,
the jury was in: "the number, the industry, and the morality of the Priesthood,
and the devotion of the people have been manifestly increased by the total
separation of the Church from the State."[13] Historians have indicated that
Madison's observations were factual. By 1850, the percentage of the population connected to a church was 34 percent, double what it was in 1776, fueled
largely by the growth of the Baptists and Methodists, who proliferated as the
establishments crumbled.[14]

In 1833, when Madison was eighty-two years old, he wrote a letter to the
Reverend Jasper Adams admitting that the radical approach to religious freedom had been an experiment. Some countries in Europe had tried different
formulas, but it "remained for North America to bring the great & interesting
subject to a fair, and finally to a decisive test." Again he concluded: Separation of church and state had helped create true religious freedom, which
had, in turn, increased the quality and intensity of faith.[15]

Today Madison would be even prouder. The United States is among the
most religious *and* most tolerant of nations. Compared with our past, and
with most other countries, we have relatively little religious conflict and have
seen one barrier after another fall. Religious "sects" once persecuted as false
and heretical—Quaker, Catholic, Unitarian, Jehovah's Witness, and Southern Baptist—later sent men to the White House.[16] At various points in recent
years, we've had five Catholic Supreme Court justices,[17] five Jewish Cabinet
secretaries,[18] and five Mormon US senators[19]—and stunningly little controversy resulted. As anti-Semitism has risen around the world, it has not in the
United States. We've witnessed a Ramadan dinner at the White House; a
Hindu priest opening a session of the House of Representatives; and a Buddhist sworn in as navy chaplain.[20] The diversity that the Founders hoped for
has continued to grow. As of 2004, there were at least twelve different Christian denominations with more than 1.5 million adherents in the US,[21] and
five different religions with more than a million.[22]

Has this been as good for the country as Madison predicted? It would be
hard to prove that our personal morality has consistently soared, and it's impossible to catalog the vast extent to which faith has given strength, wisdom,
or goodness to individual Americans. But this much can be demonstrated:
Most major American social reform movements that improved the status of
the disenfranchised or maltreated were fueled by religious faith. The efforts
to abolish slavery, end child labor, conserve the environment, create an eight-

hour day, promote civil rights for blacks, enfranchise women, establish public schools, create a social safety net—all were driven in large part by people
of faith and religious organizations.[23] Many of the most enduring and important institutions of civil society dedicated to social progress have religious
origins. It's hard to imagine a functioning charitable sector without organizations like the YMCA, Salvation Army, the Red Cross, Catholic Charities,
Habitat for Humanity, Boy Scouts, Goodwill, and Alcoholics Anonymous.
The Founders believed that religion would enable republican government to
survive by keeping officeholders honest and voters virtuous. In many ways,
that's been true. When society has degenerated, and passive or regressive political leaders have protected the immoral status quo, it has often been religious men and women—inspired by faith-driven moral missions and
operating independently of the state—who have crusaded for change.

Of course, there are still problems. The US Supreme Court has heard
scores of religious freedom cases over the last two hundred years, each of
which dealt with difficult questions of how to define religious freedom. Conservatives point out that certain expressions of personal religiosity are now
frowned upon and occasionally punished in public schools or other public
venues. Atheists can cite the huge tax breaks and legal preferences that aid religion in general. Religious minorities can point to the invocation of Jesus
Christ at George W. Bush's inaugural and other examples to show that Christianity still maintains a privileged position. Rather than adjudicate who has
the better case, I'd like to emphasize a different point: The forms of "persecution" felt by Christians and secularists today are minor inconveniences relative to the indignities that concerned the Founders. There are occasional
cases of Christians having to put away their Bibles in the school cafeteria, but
those children have nearly total freedom to worship in every other part of
their life. There are occasional misuses of government funds, but there are
many more examples of well-meaning citizens crafting ways to help people of
faith without distorting religion—for instance, by providing financial aid to
students attending Notre Dame or poverty assistance grants through Catholic
Charities. And those religious minorities who feel uncomfortable with the
majoritarian imposition of Christian rhetoric or ritual nonetheless live at a
time and in a place where religious minorities enjoy more protection than
ever. The Founders would see America as even more free than they expected—and they would be pleased.

Madison, I suspect, would also be delighted by surveys showing that, compared with most developed nations, Americans believe in God more, pray

more, and attend worship services more frequently.[24] Tolerance and pluralism has led to religious vibrancy. His Founding Faith has proved to be justified.

Madison would not be surprised that such religious vitality has flourished in the context of increasing tolerance, diversity, and freedom. This, he would say, is no coincidence. Religious freedom provides each American an unobstructed path to God, Who especially treasures the adoration that is offered without duress or cajoling. Conversely, restrictions on religious freedom — including, in Madison's mind, government aid for religion — drain faith of its spiritual force. Madison had it right. Were he alive today, he would conclude, with awesome pride, that we are the most religiously vibrant nation on earth not despite separation of church and state — and religious freedom — but because of it.

acknowledgments

I'm deeply indebted to the many historians who have spent their lives im-
mersed in various aspects of religious history and the Founding Fathers.
Among those who influenced me greatly were: Mark Noll, Frank Lambert,
James Hutson, Derk Davis, George Marsden, Edwin Gaustad, William
McLoughlin, Paul Boller, David Holmes, Rhys Isaac, Jack Rakove, Martin
Marty, Jon Butler, and Daniel Dreisbach. I'm grateful that Lambert, Hutson,
Randall Ballmer, and Walter Isaacson reviewed portions of the manuscript.
Extraordinarily helpful edits also came from one of America's best magazine
editors, Paul Glastris, who worked through the structure paragraph by paragraph and helped me to see themes I would have missed; Jeff Janus, who
sharpened my writing and thinking throughout the entire manuscript;
Michael Waldman, who offered tremendous insight about presidential religious rhetoric; David Kuo, who helped steer me through rocky theological
shoals; John Zimmerman, who helped me better understand the role of religion in modern social movements; Arthur Goldwag, who gave great literary
and marketing advice; Elizabeth Sams, who carefully read the manuscript
when I was too embarrassed to show it to anyone else; Charles Peters, who
kept me intellectually honest; and Alyson Lipner, my research assistant, who
waded through zillions of footnotes. Rafe Sagalyn, my agent, helped keep me
sane, solvent, and focused, while the talented team at Random House—Will

Murphy (my editor), Lea Beresford (assistant editor), Steve Messina (production editor), Laura Jorstad (copy editor), and designers Casey Hampton, Victoria Wong, Gene Mydlowski, and Kathleen DiGrado—all demonstrated a persistent commitment to high quality. I want to especially thank my parents and wife. In addition to being the most loving and supportive parents a boy could want, Martin and Sandra Waldman also happen to be skilled writers and editors. Mom still circles grammatical errors on restaurant menus, and Dad has become a one-man truth squad about media sloppiness. Their help throughout the process was invaluable. Most important, my wife, Amy Cunningham, performed the ultimate wifely sacrifice of listening to me read the entire manuscript aloud in the car, at a lake, and in three restaurants, making careful and inspired edits as we went. Being married to a brilliant wordsmith makes writing a book more fun and more plausible.

Though they may not realize it, the webmasters who created certain online archives made this project possible. Special thanks to whoever assembled the material for the online archives on the Founding Fathers and religious freedom (see the full list at the beginning of the Bibliography). These anonymous souls have performed an enormous public service by putting so much Founding Father material online.

Finally, I thank my family profusely. Because of my responsibilities as CEO of Beliefnet.com, I was not able to take off any significant time to work on this book. All of my research and writing was therefore done at night, on weekends, and during vacations. Joe and Gordon were far more understanding of Daddy's time-consuming obsession than I had any right to expect. I am very grateful to both of them.

bibliography

In addition to the hundreds of outstanding books on religious freedom and the Founding Fathers, there are now some deep, authoritative online collections. Many of the seminal works are now collected at www.beliefnet.com/foundingfaith.

For this book, I drew heavily from:

The Library of Congress *American Memory* collection—this includes a vast number of documents related to the founding, including:

- Papers from the Continental Congress—memory.loc.gov/ammem/collections/continental/bdsdcoll2.html
- Constitutional Convention—memory.loc.gov/ammem/collections/continental/bdsdcoll3.html
- Correspondence from delegates to the Continental Congress—lcweb2.loc.gov/ammem/amlaw/lwdg.html
- The George Washington Papers—lcweb2.loc.gov/ammem/gwhtml/gwhome.html
- Thomas Jefferson Papers—memory.loc.gov/ammem/collections/jefferson_papers
- Jamestown records—memory.loc.gov/ammem/collections/jefferson_papers/mtjessay2.html
- Early Congressional debates—memory.loc.gov/ammem/amlaw/lwjrnl.html

There are many PDFs of the original documents, too (memory.loc.gov/ammem/collections/continental/subject.html)

The *Avalon Project* at Yale Law School—www.yale.edu/lawweb/avalon/. This includes a vast collection of historical documents, including earlier state and colonial constitutions; Madison's notes from debates of the Constitutional Convention; presidential papers of Washington, Adams, Jefferson, and Madison; and much more.

The *Thomas Jefferson Digital Archive*—etext.virginia.edu/jefferson/. Created by the University of Virginia Library, this has more than seventeen hundred examples of writings by Jefferson, including most of his correspondence.

The *James Madison Papers* at the Library of Congress—memory.loc.gov/ammem/collections/madison_papers/index.html. Pretty much everything Madison wrote, including his correspondence, autobiography, and Constitutional Convention notes.

The Papers of Benjamin Franklin—www.franklinpapers.org/franklin/. A digital collection sponsored by the American Philosophical Society, Yale University, and the Packard Humanities Institute.

The *Adams Family Papers* digital archive—www.masshist.org/digitaladams/aea/index.html. This archive, created by the Massachusetts Historical Society, includes correspondence between John and Abigail, his autobiography, and his diary.

The Papers of George Washington—gwpapers.virginia.edu/documents/index.html. Archived by the University of Virginia under "the joint auspices of the University and the Mount Vernon Ladies' Association of the Union."

The Founders' Constitution—press-pubs.uchicago.edu/founders/tocs/amendI_religion .html. This is a digital version of the extraordinary five-volume collection assembled by Philip Kurland and Ralph Lerner. It includes a wide range of documents related to each part of the Constitution, including the First Amendment and the religious test clause. In my footnotes, I've listed items in this collection by document number rather than page number so readers can look them up either in the books or, more conveniently, online at the website created by the University of Chicago Press.

Important "paper-based" books include:

Adams, Dickinson W. *Jefferson's Extracts from the Gospels*. Princeton, NJ: Princeton University Press, 1983.

Adams, John Quincy, and Charles Francis Adams. *John Adams: Volume One*. New York: Cosimo Classics, 2005.

Ahlstrom, Sydney E. *A Religious History of the American People*. New Haven, CT: Yale University Press, 1972.

Aldridge, Alfred Owen. *Benjamin Franklin and Nature's God*. Durham, NC: Duke University Press, 1967.

Allen, Brooke. *Moral Minority: Our Skeptical Founding Fathers*. Chicago: Ivan R. Dee, 2006.

Alley, Robert S. *James Madison on Religious Liberty*. New York: Prometheus Books, 1985.

Allgor, Catherine. *A Perfect Union: Dolley Madison and the Creation of the American Nation*. New York: Henry Holt, 2006.

Amar, Akhil Reed. *Bill of Rights: Creation and Reconstruction*. New Haven, CT: Yale University Press, 1998.

Ames, Seth. *Works of Fisher Ames*. Indianapolis: Liberty Classics, 1983.

Backus, Isaac. *A History of New England Baptists*, Volume 1 of 2. Newton, MA: Backus Historical Society, 1871.

Bailyn, Bernard. *The Ideological Origins of the American Revolution*. Cambridge, MA: Harvard University Press, 1967.

———, editor. *The Debate on the Constitution*. New York: Library of America, 1993.

Banning, Lance. *The Sacred Fire of Liberty: Madison and the Founding of the Federal Republic*. Ithaca, NY: Cornell University Press, 1995.

Barton, David. *America's Godly Heritage*. Aledo, TX: WallBuilder Press, 1993.

———. *The Myth of Separation*. Aledo, TX: WallBuilder Press, 1992.

———. *Original Intent*. Aledo, TX: WallBuilder Press, 1999 (Coral Ridge Ministries edition).

Becker, Carl L. *The Declaration of Independence*. New York: Vintage Books, 1958. (Originally published 1922.)

Beeman, Richard R. *Patrick Henry*. New York: McGraw-Hill, 1974.

Berens, John F. *Providence and Patriotism in Early America, 1640–1815*. Charlottesville: University of Virginia Press, 1978.

Berns, Walter. *The First Amendment and the Future of American Democracy*. New York: Basic Books, 1976.

Bishop, George. *New England Judged by the Spirit of the Lord*. London: T. Sowle, 1703, reprinted by Kessinger Publishing's Rare Reprints.

Boller, Paul F., Jr. *George Washington and Religion*. Dallas: Southern Methodist University Press, 1963.

Bonomi, Patricia U. *Under the Cope of Heaven: Religions, Society, and Politics in Colonial America*. New York: Oxford University Press, 1986.

Boorstin, Daniel J. *The Americans*. New York: Vintage, 1958.

——. *The Lost World of Thomas Jefferson*. Chicago: University of Chicago Press, 1948.

Borden, Morton. *Jews, Turks and Infidels*. Chapel Hill: University of North Carolina Press, 1984.

Bowen, Catherine Drinker. *John Adams and the American Revolution*. Boston: Little, Brown, 1950.

——. *Miracle at Philadelphia*. Boston: Little, Brown, 1966.

Braden, Bruce. *"Ye Will Say I Am No Christian": The Thomas Jefferson/John Adams Correspondence on Religion, Morals, and Values*. Amherst, NY: Prometheus Books, 2006.

Brant, Irving. *James Madison: Father of the Constitution, 1787–1800*. Indianapolis: Bobbs-Merrill Company, 1950.

——. *James Madison: The Virginia Revolutionist*. Indianapolis: Bobbs-Merrill Company, 1941.

Brenner, Lenni, editor, *Jefferson and Madison: On the Separation of Church and State*. Fort Lee, NJ: Barricade Books, 2004.

Brauer, Jerald C., Sidney E. Mead, and Robert N. Bellah. *Religion and the American Revolution*. Philadelphia: Fortress Press, 1976.

Breitweiser, Mitchell Robert. *Cotton Mather and Benjamin Franklin*. Cambridge, UK: Cambridge University Press, 1984.

Bremer, Francis J. *The Puritan Experiment: New England Society from Bradford to Edwards*. Hanover, NH: University Press of New England, 1995.

Bridenbaugh, Carl. *Mitre and Sceptre*. London: Oxford University Press, 1962.

Bullock, Steven C. *Revolutionary Brotherhood: Freemasonry and the Transformation of the American Social Order, 1730–1840*. Chapel Hill: University of North Carolina Press, 1996.

Bumsted, J. M., editor. *The Great Awakening*. Waltham, MA: Blaisdell Publishing Company, 1970.

Bunson, Maggie. *Founding of Faith: Catholics in the American Revolutionary Era*. Boston: Daughters of St. Paul, 1977.

Burgess, Robert S. *To Try the Bloody Law: The Story of Mary Dyer*. Burnsville, NC: Celo Valley Books, 2000.

Butler, Jon. *Becoming America*. Cambridge, MA: Harvard University Press, 2000.

Butler, Jon, Grant Wacker, and Randall Balmer. *Religion in American Life*. New York: Oxford University Press, 2000.

Butterfield, Lyman H. "Elder John Leland, Jeffersonian Itinerant. *American Antiquarian Society Proceedings* 62, 1952, reprinted in William L. Lumpkin, *Colonial Baptists and Southern Revivals*. New York: Arno Press, 1980.

——, editor. *The Adams Papers: The Earliest Diary of John Adams*. Cambridge, MA: Harvard University Press, 1966.

——. *The Adams Papers*, Volume 1: *December 1761–May 1776*. New York: Atheneum, 1965.

Buxbaum, Melvin H. *Benjamin Franklin and the Zealous Presbyterians*. University Park: Pennsylvania State University Press, 1975.

Cappon, Lester J. *The Adams–Jefferson Letters*. Chapel Hill: University of North Carolina Press, 1959.

Carr, William G. *The Oldest Delegate: Franklin in the Constitutional Convention*. Newark: University of Delaware Press, 1990.

Chadwick, Bruce. *George Washington's War*. Naperville, IL: Sourcebooks, 2004

Cobb, Sanford H. *The Rise of Religious Liberty in America*. New York: Cooper Square Publishers, 1902.

Cohen, J. M., editor and translator. *The Four Voyages of Christopher Columbus*. New York: Penguin Books, 1969.

Conley, Patrick T., and John P. Kaminski. *The Bill of Rights and the States*. Madison, WI: Madison House, 1992.

Connell, Janice T. *Faith of Our Founding Father: The Spiritual Journey of George Washington*. New York: Hatherleigh Press, 2004.

Cousins, Norman. *In God We Trust.* New York: Harper Brothers and Company, 1958.

Cross, Arthur Lyon. *The Anglican Episcopate and the American Colonies.* New York: Longmans, Green and Co., 1902, reprinted by Kessinger Publishing's Rare Reprints.

Curry, Thomas J. *Farewell to Christendom.* New York: Oxford University Press, 2001.

———. *The First Freedoms.* New York: Oxford University Press, 1986.

Davis, Derek H. *Religion and the Continental Congress, 1774–1789.* Oxford: Oxford University Press, 2000.

Dawson, Joseph Martin. *Baptists and the American Republic.* Nashville: Broadman Press, 1956.

DeMar, Gary. *America's Christian Heritage.* Nashville: Broadman & Holman Publishers, 2003.

———. *America's Heritage.* Fort Lauderdale: Coral Ridge Ministries, 2002.

Dershowitz, Alan. *America Declares Independence.* Hoboken, NJ: John Wiley & Sons, 2003.

Dolan, Jay P. *The American Catholic Experience.* South Bend, IN: University of Notre Dame Press, 1992.

Dreisbach, Daniel L. *Thomas Jefferson and the Wall of Separation Between Church and State.* New York: New York University Press, 2002.

Eckenrode, H. J. *Separation of Church and State in Virginia: A Study in the Development of the Revolution.* Richmond, VA: Department of Archives and History, 1910.

Eidsmoe, John. *Christianity and the Constitution: The Faith of Our Founding Fathers.* Grand Rapids, MI: Baker Book House, 1987.

Ellis, John Tracy. *Catholics in Colonial America.* Baltimore: Helicon Press, 1965.

Ellis, Joseph J. *His Excellency: George Washington.* New York: Alfred A. Knopf, 2004.

Evans, Bette. *Interpreting the Free Exercise of Religion: The Constitution and American Pluralism.* Chapel Hill: University of North Carolina, 1997.

Falwell, Jerry. *Listen, America!* New York: Bantam Books, 1981. (Originally published 1980.)

Federer, William J. *America's God and Country: Encyclopedia of Quotations.* St. Louis: Amerisearch, 2000.

Feldman, Noah. *Divided by God.* New York: Farrar, Straus and Giroux, 2005.

Finke, Roger, and Rodney Stark. *The Churching of America, 1776–1990: Winners and Losers in Our Religious Economy.* New Brunswick, NJ: Rutgers University Press, 1992.

Fitzpatrick, John C. *George Washington Himself.* Indianapolis: Bobbs-Merrill Company, 1933.

Flexner, James Thomas. *George Washington: Anguish and Farewell (1793–1799).* Boston: Little, Brown, 1969.

———. *Washington: The Indispensable Man.* Boston: Little, Brown, 1969.

Foot, Michael, and Isaac Kramnick. *The Thomas Paine Reader.* New York: Penguin, 1987.

Ford, Paul Leicester, editor. *The Writings of Thomas Jefferson,* Volumes 1–10. New York: G. P. Putnam's Sons, 1892–99.

Franklin, Benjamin. *The Autobiography of Benjamin Franklin.* Mineola, NY: Dover Publications, 1996.

Frost, William J. *A Perfect Freedom: Religious Liberty in Pennsylvania.* University Park: Pennsylvania State University Press, 1990.

Gaustad, Edwin. *Church and State in America.* New York: Oxford University Press, 2003.

———. *Faith of Our Fathers.* San Francisco: Harper & Row, 1987.

———. *Historical Atlas of Religion in America.* New York: Harper & Row, 1962.

———. *Sworn on the Altar of God: A Religious Biography of Thomas Jefferson.* Grand Rapids, MI: William B. Eerdmans, 1996.

Gaustad, Edwin S., and Mark A. Noll, editors. *A Documentary History of Religion in America to 1877.* Grand Rapids, MI: William B. Eerdmans, 1982.

Grant, James. *John Adams: Party of One.* New York: Farrar, Straus and Giroux, 2005.

Greene, Evarts B. *Religion and the State: The Making and Testing of an American Tradition.* Ithaca, NY: Cornell University Press, 1941.

Grigsby, Hugh Blair. *The History of the Virginia Federal Convention of 1788: With Some Account of the Eminent Virginians of That Era Who Were Members of the Body.* Volume 1. Richmond: Virginia Historical Society, 1891.

Hall, Timothy L. *Separating Church and State.* Urbana: University of Illinois Press, 1998.

Hansen, Chadwick. *Witchcraft at Salem.* New York: George Braziller, 1969.

Hart, Benjamin. *Faith and Freedom: The Christian Roots of American Liberty.* Springfield, VA: Christian Defense Fund, 1997.

Hawke, David. *The Colonial Experience.* Indianapolis: Bobbs-Merrill Company, 1966.

Healey, Robert M. *Jefferson on Religion in Public Education.* Hamden, CT: Archon Books, 1970. (Originally published 1962.)

Heimert, Alan. *Religion and the American Mind: From the Great Awakening to the American Revolution.* Cambridge, MA: Harvard University Press, 1968.

Heimert, Alan, and Perry Miller, editors. *The Great Awakening.* Indianapolis: Bobbs-Merrill Company, 1967.

Hill, Frances. *The Salem Witch Trials Reader.* Cambridge, MA: Da Capo Press, 2000.

Hoffman, Ronald, and Peter J. Albert. *Religion in a Revolutionary Age.* Charlottesville: United States Capitol Historical Society and the University Press of Virginia, 1994.

Hogeland, William. *The Whiskey Rebellion.* New York: Scribner, 2006.

Holmes, David L. *The Faiths of the Founding Fathers.* New York: Oxford University Press, 2006.

Hovey, Alvah. *A Memoir of the Life and Times of the Rev. Isaac Backus, A.M.* Harrisburg, VA: Gano Books, 1991.

Howe, Mark DeWolfe. *The Garden and the Wilderness.* Chicago: Phoenix Books, 1965.

Hunt, Gaillard, editor. *Writings of James Madison.* New York: G. P. Putnam's Sons, Volumes 1–8, 1900–1908.

Hutson, James H., editor. *Religion and the New Republic.* Lanham, MD: Rowman and Littlefield, 2000.

Isaac, Rhys. *The Transformation of Virginia 1740–1790.* Chapel Hill: University of North Carolina Press, 1982.

Isaacson, Walter. *Franklin.* New York: Simon & Schuster, 2003.

Jacoby, Susan. *Freethinkers: A History of American Secularism.* New York: Henry Holt, 2004.

Jayne, Allen. *Jefferson's Declaration of Independence: Origins, Philosophy, and Theology.* Lexington: University Press of Kentucky, 1998.

Jeffers, H. Paul. *The Freemasons in America.* New York: Citadel Press, 2006.

Jefferson, Thomas. *Jefferson's "Bible": The Life and Morals of Jesus of Nazareth.* Grove City, PA: American Book Distributors, 1996.

——. *Notes on the State of Virginia.* Chapel Hill: University of North Carolina Press, 1982.

——. *The Works of Thomas Jefferson,* Federal Edition. New York and London: G. P. Putnam's Sons, 1904–5.

Kammen, Michael, editor. *The Origins of the American Constitution.* New York: Penguin, 1986.

Ketcham, Ralph. *The Anti-Federalist Papers and the Constitutional Convention Debates.* New York: Signet Classics, 1986.

——. *James Madison: A Biography.* Charlottesville: University of Virginia Press, 1990.

Koch, Adrienne. *Power, Morals and the Founding Fathers.* Ithaca, NY: Cornell University Press, 1961.

——, editor. *Notes of the Debates in the Federal Convention of 1787 Reported by James Madison.* New York: W. W. Norton, 1966.

Koch, Adrienne, and William Peden. *The Life and Selected Writings of Thomas Jefferson.* New York: Modern Library, 1998.

Kramnick, Isaac, and R. Laurence Moore. *The Godless Constitution: The Case Against Religious Correctness.* New York: W. W. Norton, 1996.

Kurland, Philip B., and Ralph Lerner. *The Founders' Constitution,* Volumes I–V. Indianapolis: Liberty Fund and University of Chicago Press, 1987.

Kurtz, Stephen G., and James H. Hutson, editors. *Essays on the American Revolution.* Chapel Hill: University of North Carolina Press, 1973.

Labunski, Richard. *James Madison and the Struggle for the Bill of Rights.* Oxford: Oxford University Press, 2006.

LaHaye, Tim. *Faith of Our Founding Fathers.* Brentwood, TN: Wolgemuth & Hyatt, 1987.

Lambert, Frank. *The Founding Fathers and the Place of Religion in America.* Princeton, NJ: Princeton University Press, 2003.

———. *Inventing the "Great Awakening."* Princeton, NJ: Princeton University Press, 1999.

———. *"Pedlar in Divinity": George Whitefield and the Transatlantic Revivals.* Princeton, NJ: Princeton University Press, 1994.

Lawson, Edward J. *A Magnificent Catastrophe: The Tumultuous Election of 1800, America's First Presidential Campaign.* New York: Free Press, 2007.

Levy, Leonard W. *The Establishment Clause.* Chapel Hill: University of North Carolina Press, 1994.

Lipscomb, Andrew A., and Albert Ellery Bergh, editors. *The Writings of Thomas Jefferson,* Volumes 1–19. Washington, DC: Thomas Jefferson Memorial Association of the United States, 1903–7.

Little, Lewis Peyton. *Imprisoned Preachers and Religious Liberty in Virginia.* Lynchburg, VA: J. P. Bell Company, 1938.

Mac, Toby, and Michael Tait. *Under God.* Bloomington, MN: Bethany House Publishers, 2004.

Madison, James. "Autobiography." In Douglass Adair, "James Madison's Autobiography," *The William and Mary Quarterly,* 3rd Series, Volume 2, Number 2 (April 1945), 191–209.

Madison, James, Alexander Hamilton, and John Jay. *The Federalist Papers.* New York: Penguin, 1987.

Maier, Pauline. *American Scripture: Making the Declaration of Independence.* New York: Vintage Books, 1997.

Main, Jackson Turner. *The Antifederalists: Critics of the Constitution.* Chapel Hill: University of North Carolina Press, 1961.

Mansfield, Stephen. *Forgotten Founding Father: The Heroic Legacy of George Whitefield.* Nashville: Highland Books, 2001.

Marcus, Jacob Rader. *Early American Jewry.* Philadelphia: Jewish Publication Society of America, 1961.

Marsden, George M. *Jonathan Edwards.* New Haven, CT: Yale University Press, 2003.

Marshall, Peter, and David Manuel. *The Light and the Glory.* Grand Rapids, MI: Baker Book House, 1977.

Marty, Martin E. *Pilgrims in Their Own Land.* New York: Penguin, 1984.

Mather, Cotton. *Essays to Do Good Addressed to All Christians Whether in Public or Private Capacities.* New York: Whiting and Watson, 1815, republished by Kessenger Publishing's Rare Reprints.

Mayer, Henry. *Son of Thunder: Patrick Henry and the American Republic.* New York: Grove Press, 1991.

McBrien, Richard P. *Caesar's Coin.* New York: Macmillan Publishing Company, 1987.

McCrackan, W. D. *The Huntington Letters.* New York: Appleton Press, 1897.

McCullough, David. *John Adams.* New York: Simon & Schuster, 2001.

McDonald, Forrest. *Novus Ordo Seclorum: The Intellectual Origins of the Constitution.* Lawrence: University Press of Kansas, 1985.

McLoughlin, William G. *Isaac Backus and the American Pietistic Tradition.* Boston: Little, Brown, 1967.

———. *New England Dissent, 1630–1833: The Baptists and the Separation of Church and State.* Cambridge, MA: Harvard University Press, 1971.

Meacham, Jon. *American Gospel.* New York: Random House, 2006.

Mead, Sidney E. *The Nation with the Soul of a Church.* New York: Harper & Row, 1975.

———. *The Old Religion in the Brave New World.* Berkeley: University of California Press, 1977.

Metzger, Charles H. *Catholics and the American Revolution.* Chicago: Loyola University Press, 1962.

Meyer, Donald H. *Democratic Enlightenment.* New York: Capricorn Books, 1976.

Miller, Perry. *The New England Mind.* Cambridge, MA: Harvard University Press, 1939.

Miller, William Lee. *The First Liberty.* Washington, DC: Georgetown University Press, 2003.

Morgan, Edmund S. *Visible Saints: The History of a Puritan Idea*. Ithaca, NY: Cornell University Press, 1963.

Morison, Samuel Eliot. *Builders of the Bay Colony*. Boston: Houghton Mifflin, 1930.

Morrison, Jeffry H. *John Witherspoon and the Founding of the American Republic*. South Bend, IN: University of Notre Dame Press, 2005.

Nash, Gary. B. *Quakers and Politics*. Boston: Northeastern University Press, 1968.

Needleman, Jacob. *The American Soul: Rediscovering the Wisdom of the Founders*. New York: Jeremy Tarcher/Putnam, 2002.

Noll, Mark A. *America's God: From Jonathan Edwards to Abraham Lincoln*. New York: Oxford University Press, 2002.

———. *Christians in the American Revolution*. Grand Rapids, MI: Christian University Press and Christian College Consortium, 1977.

———, editor. *Religion and American Politics: From the Colonial Period to the 1980s*. New York: Oxford University Press, 1990.

Noll, Mark A., Nathan O. Hatch, and George M. Marsden. *The Search for Christian America*. Colorado Springs: Helmers & Howard, 1989.

Noonan, John T., Jr. *The Lustre of Our Country*. Berkeley: University of California Press, 1998.

Novak, Michael. *On Two Wings*. San Francisco: Encounter Books, 2002.

Novak, Michael, and Jana Novak. *Washington's God*. New York: Basic, 2006.

Palm, Daniel C., editor. *On Faith and Free Government*. Lanham, MD: Rowman and Littlefield, 1997.

Pelikan, Jaroslav. *Interpreting the Bible and the Constitution*. New Haven, CT: Yale University Press, 2004.

Peterson, Merrill D. *Adams and Jefferson*. Oxford: Oxford University Press, 1976.

Peterson, Merrill D., and Robert C. Vaughan. *The Virginia Statute for Religious Freedom*. Cambridge, MA: Cambridge University Press, 1988.

Rakove, Jack N. *Declaring Rights: A Brief History with Documents*. Boston: Bedford Books, 1998.

———. *James Madison and the Creation of the American Republic*. New York: Longman, 2002.

———. *Original Meanings*. New York: Vintage Books, 1996.

———, editor. *Interpreting the Constitution: The Debate over Original Intent*. Boston: Northeastern University Press, 1990.

Reichley, A. James. *Religion in American Public Life*. Washington, DC: Brookings Institution, 1985.

Royster, Charles. A *Revolutionary People at War: The Continental Army and American Character, 1775–1783*. Chapel Hill: University of North Carolina, 1979.

Rutman, Darren. *American Puritanism*. Philadelphia: J. B. Lippincott, 1970.

Sanford, Charles B. *The Religious Life of Thomas Jefferson*. Charlottesville: University of Virginia Press, 1984.

Schwartz, Barry. *George Washington: The Making of an American Symbol*. New York: Free Press, 1987.

Shaw, Peter. *The Character of John Adams*. Chapel Hill: University of North Carolina Press, 1976.

Sheridan, Eugene. *Jefferson and Religion*. Charlottesville: Thomas Jefferson Memorial Foundation, 1998.

Smith, Elwyn A. *The Religion of the Republic*. Philadelphia: Fortress Press, 1971.

Smith, James Morton, editor. *George Washington*. New York: Hill and Wang, 1969.

———. *Seventeenth-Century America*. Chapel Hill: University of North Carolina Press, 1959.

Smith, Page. *John Adams*, Volume 1: 1735–1784. Garden City, NY: Doubleday and Company, 1962.

———. *John Adams*, Volume 2: 1784–1826. Garden City, NY: Doubleday and Company, 1962.

Sparks, Janred, editor. *Writings of George Washington*, Volumes 1–9. Boston: American Stationers Company, 1837.

Steiner, Franklin. *The Religious Beliefs of Our Presidents*. Amherst, NY: Prometheus Press, 1995.

Stokes, Anson Phelps. *Church and State in the United States*, Volumes 1–3. New York: Harper and Brothers, 1950.

Stokes, Anson Phelps, and Leo Pfeffer. *Church and State in the United States: One-volume Edition*. New York: Harper and Row, 1950.

Stout, Harry S. *The New England Soul: Preaching and Religious Culture in Colonial New England*. New York: Oxford University Press, 1986.

Stout, Harry S., and D. G. Hart. *New Directions in American Religious History*. New York: Oxford University Press, 1977.

Sweet, William Warren. *Religion in Colonial America*. New York: Charles Scribner's Sons, 1942.

Taylor, Robert J. *Massachusetts, Colony to Commonwealth: Documents on the Formation of Its Constitution, 1775–1780*. New York: W. W. Norton, 1961.

Thomas, Cal, and Ed Dobson. *Blinded by Might*. Grand Rapids, MI: Zondervan Press, 1999.

Thompson, C. Bradley. *John Adams and the Spirit of Liberty*. Lawrence: University Press of Kansas, 1998.

Thornton, John Wingate. *The Pulpit of the American Revolution, or the Political Sermons of the Period of 1776*. New York: Burt Franklin, 1860, reprinted 1970.

Tuveson, Ernest Lee. *Redeemer Nation: The Idea of America's Millennial Role*. Chicago: University of Chicago Press, 1968.

Veit, Helen E., Kenneth R. Bowling, and Charlene Bangs Bickford. *Creating the Bill of Rights*. Baltimore: Johns Hopkins University Press, 1991.

Walters, Kerry S. *Benjamin Franklin and His Gods*. Urbana: University of Illinois Press, 1999.

Wampler, Dee. *The Myth of Separation Between Church and State*. Enumclaw, WA: WinePress Publishing, 2002.

Washington, George. *The Writings of George Washington*, Volume 5, 1776–77. New York: G. P. Putnam's Sons, 1890.

Washington, H. A., editor. *Writings of Thomas Jefferson*, Volume 7. Washington, DC: Taylor & Maury, 1854.

Willison, George F. *Patrick Henry and His World*. Garden City, NY: Doubleday and Company, 1969.

Wills, Garry. *Inventing America*. Boston: Houghton Mifflin, 1978.

———. *Under God*. New York: Simon & Schuster, 1990.

Wilson, John F. *Church and State in American History*. Boston: D. C. Heath and Company, 1965.

Wirt, William. *Sketches of the Life and Character of Patrick Henry*. Birmingham, AL: Palladium Press, 2002, originally published in 1818 by James Webster.

Witte, John, Jr. *Religion and the American Constitutional Experiment*. Boulder, CO: Westview Press, 2005.

Wood, Gordon S. *The Creation of the American Republic, 1776–1787*. New York: W. W. Norton, 1969.

———. *The Radicalism of the American Revolution*. New York: Vintage Books, 1991.

Wright, Conrad. *The Beginnings of Unitarianism in America*. Boston: Starr Press, 1955.

notes

Introduction

1. Throughout the book, I use the term *evangelical* when referring to certain groups and movements of the eighteenth and nineteenth centuries. This is somewhat anachronistic, as neither the leaders nor followers of these movements used that term. Even today there is much debate about who counts as "evangelical" versus "born again" versus "fundamentalist." Many Americans whom pollsters classify as evangelicals do not refer to themselves that way. Some modern historians have referred to the leaders of the Great Awakening and the eighteenth-century Baptists as evangelicals; some have not. It seems to me that in at least two cases, it is quite justifiable and helpful to think of certain eighteenth-century groups as evangelicals or proto-evangelicals. The Baptists of that era are the direct spiritual ancestors of the modern Southern Baptists, most of whom are today called evangelicals. In addition, they stylistically resemble modern evangelicals with their emphasis on God's grace, personal salvation, and a desire to bring the unsaved into the fold. Similarly, George Whitefield, the leader of the Great Awakening, was very much a proto-evangelical as well. His theology was similar to modern evangelicals—and just as important, so was his style: using the latest media technology to spread the word, ignoring denominational categories, and offering a more hope filled and emotional appeal. In the case of other denominations, such as Presbyterians, I have tended to view those described as "Old Lights" as not being evangelical and those as "New Lights" as being akin to modern evangelicals. It is sometimes difficult to apply modern labels to such movements; I have attempted to conservatively apply the term based on assessment of theology, style, and cultural position.
2. Jerry Falwell, *Listen America!* (Garden City, NY: Doubleday and Company, 1980), Bantam Books paperback, 25.
3. Tim LaHaye, *Faith of Our Founding Fathers* (Brentwood, TN: Wolgemuth & Hyatt, 1987), 29.
4. Brooke Allen, "Our Godless Constitution," *The Nation*, February 21, 2005, posted February 3, 2005, www.thenation.com/doc/20050221/allen (accessed 2006).
5. I came across the non sequitur numerous times. As evidence that the Founders didn't support strict separation of church and state, some religious conservatives cite examples about

the faithfulness of the Founders themselves. Often they don't even attempt to make a logi-cal connection proving that their faith led them to have a certain viewpoint on separation of church and state. Rather, it is simply assumed that someone who is religious or believes religion is important for a flourishing republic would, by definition, oppose separation of church and state. One of many examples comes in M. Stanton Evans, "Faith of Our Fa-thers," *American Spectator*, February 2007. Evans refers to the "absurdly false" reasoning of various Supreme Court rulings upholding separation. "While the proofs of this are many, among the simplest ways of grasping the truth of the matter is to consult the views of lead-ing politicians in the revolutionary-constitutional epoch. In this respect the obvious place to start is with George Washington, military hero of the War of Independence, presiding of-ficer at the Constitutional Convention, and first president of the new republic. Far from being a secularist or skeptic, Washington throughout his public life was a staunch sup-porter of the view that religious piety was essential to the well-being of the country."

6. In describing most Founders as Deists, most people forget the aspect of Deism that as-sumed a distant, uninvolved God who would not hear prayers or influence history. Histo-rian David Holmes has compared Deist views with those of traditional Christians who worshipped the biblical God. "He was a God whom the Bible depicts as acting in history and hearing prayers. In place of this Hebrew God, Deists postulated a distant deity. . . . Deism inevitably undermined the personal religion of the Judeo-Christian tradition. In the worldview of the typical Deist, humans had no need to read the Bible, to pray, to be bap-tized or circumcised, to receive Holy Communion, to attend church or synagogue, or to heed the words or ministrations of misguided priests, ministers, or rabbis." David L. Holmes, *The Faith of the Founding Fathers* (Oxford: Oxford University Press, 2006), 47.

1. *Christian America*

1. Roberto Rusconi and Blair Sullivan, *The Book of Prophecies Edited by Christopher Colum-bus* (Eugene, OR: Wipf & Stock, 1997), 67–73. His calculation of the end of the world was based on St. Augustine's predictions as analyzed by contemporary theologians: "From the creation of the world or from Adam until the coming of Our Lord Jesus Christ there are 5,343 years and 318 days, according to the calculation made by King Alfonse (the Wise). . . . Adding to this number 1,500 years, and one not yet completed, gives a total of 6,845 years counted toward the completion of this era. By this count, only 155 years remain of the 7,000 years in which, according to the authorities cited above, the world must come to an end."

It's long been understood that converting the natives to Christianity was an important goal for Columbus. Isabella and Ferdinand had just vanquished the Muslim Moors from Spain. In his ship logs on his first voyage he explained that the monarchs had instructed him to go to India and "consider the best means for their conversion." He signed his letters "Xpo Ferens" or "Christoferens," which means Christ-bearer, as he was dedicated to carry-ing the message of Christ across the seas.

More recent scholarship has highlighted the role of apocalyptic motivations. In 1501, he wrote the *Libros de las profecías*, or Book of Prophecies, a collection of Bible passages and prophetic writings that he believed showed how his discoveries were part of an apoca-lyptic plan. The book had been dismissed by early historians as the ramblings of a madman or a con job to impress the religious Isabella. More recent historians have argued that the book was a continuation of a lifelong interest in end times. He was convinced that his dis-covery of these new lands had fulfilled a stage of prophecy. "In this voyage to the Indies, Our Lord wished to perform [a] very evident miracle in order to console me and others in the matter of this voyage to the Holy Sepulchre [Jerusalem]," he wrote (Delno C. West and August Kling, editors and translators, "Introductory Letter," *Christopher Columbus: Libro de las profecías* (Gainesville: University of Florida Press, 1991). At another point he wrote, "God made me the messenger of the new heaven and the new earth of which he spoke in the Apocalypse of St. John [Rev. 21:1] after having spoken of it through the mouth of Isaiah; and he showed me the spot where to find it." Even his famous obsession with accumulating gold was at least in part driven by his religious views, too: He believed that to bring Christ's return, the Spanish would have to conquer Jerusalem back from the Muslims, a task that would require vast sums of money. Columbus declared that he hoped that upon returning to the islands he "would find a barrel of gold that those who were left would have acquired by exchange; and that they would have found the gold mine and the spicery, and those things in such quantity, that the sovereigns before three years will undertake and prepare to conquer the Holy Sepulcher." Historian Pauline Watts concludes that his voyage to the West Indies was connected to his desire to liberate the Holy Lands. "His apocalypticism must be recognized as inseparable from his geography and cosmology," she wrote in "Prophecy and Discovery: On the Spiritual Origins of Christopher Columbus's 'Enterprise of the Indies,' " *American Historical Review* 90, no. 1 (1985), 74. Other informative essays on this topic: Delno C. West, "Wallowing in a Theological Stupor or a Steadfast and Consuming Faith: Scholarly Encounters with Columbus," Proceedings of the First San Salvador Conference, October 30–November 3, 1986; Pauline Moffitt Watts, "Science, Religion, and Columbus's Enterprise of the Indies," OAH *Magazine of History* 5, no. 4 (Spring 1991), 14–17; Kevin A. Miller, "Why Did Columbus Sail?" in *Christian History* XI, no. 3, issue 35.

2. "Letter of Columbus to Various Persons Describing the Results of His First Voyage and Written on the Return Journey," in *Christopher Columbus: The Four Voyages* (New York: Penguin Books, 1969), 117–118.

3. "Digest of Columbus's Log Books" in *Christopher Columbus,* 56. A succinct summary of Columbus's religious motives is provided in Martin E. Marty, *Pilgrims in Their Own Land* (New York: Penguin Books, 1984).

4. Jon Butler, Grant Wacker, and Randall Balmer, *Religion in American Life* (Oxford: Oxford University Press, 2000), 27.

5. Frank Lambert, *The Founding Fathers and the Place of Religion in America* (Princeton, NJ: Princeton University Press, 2003), 47. Many history books neglect the importance of religion for the first wave of settlers, those who settled Jamestown. While faith was not the only motivator—money and European geopolitics were probably big ones—religion was a key element. "In their own conception of themselves, they are first and foremost Christians, and above all militant Protestants," wrote Perry Miller, the foremost American scholar of colonial history. "Religion, in short, was the really energizing power in this settlement, as in the others."

6. Ibid., 46.

7. William Warren Sweet, *Religion in Colonial America* (New York: Charles Scribner's Sons, 1942), 3. This was from a promotional book called *Discourse of Western Planting* by Richard Hakluyt, the Anglican chaplain to Britain's ambassador to France.

8. Lambert, *Founding Fathers,* 46. According to historian Jon Butler, another tract advertising the colony trumpeted the Christian missions "to recover out of the arms of the Devil, a number of poor and miserable souls, wrapped up unto death, in almost invincible ignorance." Jon Butler, *Becoming America: The Revolution Before 1776,* (Cambridge, MA: Harvard University Press), 53.

9. David Freeman Hawke, *The Colonial Experience* (Indianapolis: Bobbs-Merrill Company, 1966), 95. "Many fed on the corpses of dead men, and one who had gotten insatiable, out of custom to that food, could not be restrained until such time and was executed for it," recounted Hawke.

10. John F. Wilson, *Church and State in American History,* Studies in History and Politics (Lexington, MA: D. C. Heath and Company, 1965), 11.

11. Butler et al., *Religion in American Life,* 68.

12. Marty, *Pilgrims,* 56.

13. Evarts B. Greene, *Religion and the State: The Making and Testing of an American Tradition* (Ithaca, NY: Cornell University Press, 1941), 34.

14. Patricia U. Bonomi, *Under the Cope of Heaven: Religion, Society, and Politics in Colonial America* (New York: Oxford University Press, 1986), 16.

15. Greene, *Religion and the State,* 35.

16. Lambert, *Founding Fathers*, 46.

17. Ibid., 68.

18. Ibid., 70–71. Relations degenerated so much — including raids by the Indians — that the legislature required every family to bring to church on Sundays "one fixed and serviceable gun with sufficient powder and shott." In fact, Lambert argued that the settlers came to view the Indians and the Catholics similarly, and that some of the same soldiers who fought in Oliver Cromwell's army against the loathsome Irish Catholics came to Virginia and employed the same language and attitude toward the Indians. As a result, "guns, not Bibles became the primary means of dealing with Indians."

19. Marty, *Pilgrims*, 86.

20. Jacob Rader Marcus, *Early American Jewry: The Jews of New York, New England and Canada 1649–1794*, Volume 1, (Philadelphia: Jewish Publication Society of America, 1951), 4.

21. Thomas J. Curry, *The First Freedoms: Church and State in America to the Passage of the First Amendment* (New York: Oxford University Press, 1986), 1.

22. Edmund S. Morgan, *Visible Saints: The History of a Puritan Idea* (Ithaca, NY: Cornell University Press, 1965), 7.

23. Lambert, *Founding Fathers*, 40.

24. Ibid., 42.

25. Marty, *Pilgrims*, 61.

26. Sydney Ahlstrom, *A Religious History of the American People* (New Haven, CT: Yale University Press, 1972), 124.

27. Curry, *First Freedoms*, 4.

28. Hawke, *Colonial Experience*, 71. Blocking the advance of Catholicism was clearly also a motive. As John Winthrop, the Bay Colony's first governor, explained in 1639, the settling would "helpe on the comminge of the fullnesse of the Gentiles, and to raise a Bulworke against the kingdome of Anti-Christ which the Jesuites labour to reare up in those parts." Edwin S. Gaustad and Mark A. Noll, editors, *A Documentary History of Religion in America to 1877* (Grand Rapids, MI: William B. Eerdmans, 2003), 66.

29. Daniel J. Boorstin, *The Americans: The Colonial Experience* (New York: Vintage Books, 1958), 3.

30. As historian Perry Miller wrote, "They would have expected laissez faire to result in a reign of rapine and horror. The state to them was an active instrument of leadership, discipline, and wherever necessary, of coercion; it legislated over any or all aspects of human behavior, it not merely regulated misconduct but undertook to inspire and direct all conduct." *Errand into the Wilderness*, excerpted in Wilson, *Church and State*, 26.

31. Morgan, *Visible Saints*, 35.

32. Ibid., 114.

33. Curry, *First Freedoms*, 14.

34. Gaustad and Noll, *Documentary History*, 114. This contains excerpts of an act passed in New York on August 9, 1700.

35. Curry, *First Freedoms*, 13.

36. Lambert, *Founding Fathers*, 96.

37. Wilson, *Church and State*, 26, quoting Miller.

38. Marty, *Pilgrims*, 81. Here is the exchange between Hutchinson and court officers regarding her revelations:

> "How do you know that that was the spirit," one officer of the court asked.
>   "How did Abraham know that it was God that bid him offer his son, being a breach of the sixth commandment?" she replied.
>   "By an immediate voice," said another officer.
>   "So to me by an immediate revelation."
>   "How! An immediate revelation," the officer said.
>   "By the voice of his own spirit to my soul," she said. "You have the power

over my body but the Lord Jesus hath power over my body and soul . . . if you go on in this course you begin, you will bring a curse upon you and your posterity, and the mouth of the Lord hath spoken it."

Gaustad and Noll, *Documentary History*, 98.

39. Frances Hill, *The Salem Witch Trials Reader* (Cambridge, MA: Da Capo Press, 2000), 25.
40. George Bishop, *New England Judged by the Spirit of the Lord* (London: Printed and sold by T. Sowle, 1703), 9. In 1656, the government of Massachusetts issued the following declaration:

> We thought it requisite to declare, that about three years since divers persons, professing themselves Quakers, of whose pernicious opinions and practices we had received intelligence from good hands, from Barbadoes to England, arrived at Boston, whose persons were only secured to be sent away the first opportunity, without censure or punishment; although their professed tenets, turbulent and contemptuous behaviour to authority, would have justified a severer animadversion; yet the prudence of this Court was exercised only in making provision to secure the peace and order here established against their attempts, whose design—we were well assured by our own experience, as well as by the example of their predecessors in Munster—was to undermine and ruin the same.

41. Ibid., 222–223. Other examples included: Deborah Wilson, "being a young woman of a very modest and retired life, and of sober conversation . . . [was taken] through your town of Salem naked." She, her mother, and her sister were tied to a cart and dragged through town. Humphrey Norton, a priest traveling en route to New Haven, was captured, whipped, [and] imprisoned for twenty days in the cold of winter. His hand was "burned very deep with a red-hot iron . . . with the letter H for heresy."
42. Ibid., 232. They were taken from town to town to be whipped. "Under cruelty and sore usage, the tender women traveling their way through all, was a hard spectacle to those who had in them anything of tenderness; but the presence of the Lord was so with them, that they sung in the midst of the extremity of their sufferings, to the astonishment of their enemies."
43. Much of the account of Mary Dyer's martyrdom is from Robert S. Burgess, *To Try the Bloody Law: The Story of Mary Dyer* (Burnsville, NC: Celo Valley Books, 2000).
44. Butler et al., *Religion in American Life*, 64.
45. Lambert, *Founding Fathers*, 98.
46. Hill, *Salem Witch Trials*, 294.
47. Francis J. Bremer, *The Puritan Experiment: New England Society from Bradford to Edwards*, revised edition (Hanover, NH: University Press of New England, 1995), 182.
48. Ibid., 44. They subscribed to the views expressed in John Foxe's *Book of Martyrs* that there were five distinct periods of church history, the first four of which had passed. They were living in the fifth period, begun by the Reformation, in which the "forces of Christ and the forces of Antichrist were locked in battle."
49. Excerpted in Hill, *Salem Witch Trials*, 223. The evidence against Burroughs, according to Mather, was: "He was Accused by five or six of the Bewitched, as the Author for their Miseries; he was Accused by eight of the Confessing Witches, as being an Head Actor at some of the Hellish Randezvouzes, and one who had the promise of being a King in Satans Kingdom, now going to be Erected: he was Accused by nine persons for extraordinary Lifting, and such Feats of Strength, as could not be done without a Diabolical Assistance." Quoted in Gaustad and Noll, *Documentary History*, 98.
50. Hill, *Salem Witch Trials*, 34.
51. Anson Phelps Stokes and Leo Pfeffer, *Church and State in the United States* (New York: Harper & Row, 1950, 1964), 6, 14–15. Because Williams wrote that the "garden and the wilderness" should be kept separate by a "wall," some have assumed that Jefferson borrowed the phrase from him. There is no evidence, however, that Jefferson knew of

Williams's writings. Williams's influence on the history of separation of church and state, therefore, was indirect: He founded the Baptist faith in America, instilling it with a commitment to separation of church and state. He also founded Rhode Island as an island of religious tolerance. Though apparently less influential to the founders than the Pennsylvania example, it nonetheless provided a second instance of a pluralistic approach in action.

52. Ibid., 28.
53. Marty, *Pilgrims*, 69.
54. Gaustad and Noll, *Documentary History*, 47.
55. Marcus, *Early American Jewry*, 32.
56. Stokes and Pfeffer argued that the colonies that had been set up primarily for commercial purposes—such as New York, New Jersey, Georgia, Maryland, and the Carolinas—tended toward greater religious tolerance than those set up for religious or ideological purposes. The former needed to attract as many settlers as possible and therefore could not afford to alienate potential religious groups. "Merchant proprietors with much land for sale in America . . . found it a matter of necessity to insure a measure of toleration," 28.
57. Marty, *Pilgrims*, 69.
58. Marcus, *Early American Jewry*, 29.
59. Ibid., 30.
60. Marty, *Pilgrims*, 71.
61. John Tracy Ellis, *Catholics in Colonial America* (Baltimore: North Central Publishing Company, 1965), 159. From 1684 to 1688, Thomas Dongan, an Irish Catholic, was British colonial governor of New York.
62. Ibid., 367–369. It almost goes without saying that Indians were treated even worse. During a battle between settlers and Indians on Staten Island in 1640, soldiers tore infants from the breasts of their mothers, tying some to small boards and stabbing them. A witness described the shrieks of dying Indians and the sight of "adultes trying to escape while holding their own exposed entrails in their arms." Right after the savagery, the leader "piously called a day of fasting and prayer to deal with Dutch suffering under the Indians." Marty, *Pilgrims*, 68.
63. Butler et al., *Religion in American Life*, 54.
64. Curry, *First Freedoms*, 38; Ellis, *Catholics in Colonial America*, 336. The new government quickly clamped down on Catholics. Two priests, Fathers White and Copley, were seized, put in chains, and shipped to England for the crime of being a priest in Maryland.
65. Marty, *Pilgrims*, 84.
66. Wilson, *Church and State*, 15. The law defined blasphemy as language that would "curse him, or deny our Saviour Jesus Christ to be the Son of God, or shall deny the holy Trinity . . . , or the Godhead of any of the said three persons of the Trinity or the Unity of the Godhead, or shall use or utter any reproacheful speeches, words or language concerning the said holy Trinity, or any of the said three persons thereof."
67. Curry, *First Freedoms*, 41.
68. Ellis, *Catholics in Colonial America*, 339. The zeal to punish Catholics was so strong that it even managed to unite the Puritans and Anglicans, who were usually too busy oppressing each other. The Puritans in Maryland were joined by men like John Yeo, an Anglican minister, who wrote to the Archbishop of Canterbury that the papists and Quakers were turning Maryland into "a Sodom of uncleanness & a Pest house of iniquity."
69. Curry, *First Freedoms*, 48.
70. Ellis, *Catholics in Colonial America*, 345–347.

2. Benjamin Franklin

1. Walter Isaacson, *Benjamin Franklin: An American Life* (New York: Simon & Schuster, 2003), 11. He became a tallow chandler, transforming animal fat into candles and soap.
2. Ibid., 11–13.

3. Kerry S. Walters, *Benjamin Franklin and His Gods* (Urbana: University of Illinois Press, 1999), 19.

4. Ibid.

5. Ibid., 14.

6. Stokes and Pfeffer, *Church and State,* 23.

7. Isaacson, *Benjamin Franklin,* 26.

8. Cotton Mather, *Essays to Do Good Addressed to All Christians Whether in Public or Private Capacities* (1815; reprint, New York: Kessinger Publishing, 2003), 51. Franklin's views of Mather may also have softened in 1721 when the HMS *Seahorse* brought from the West Indies a new case of smallpox that would, within a few months, wipe out nine hundred people, roughly 9 percent of the population (equivalent to fifty-four thousand people in today's Boston). Mather had studied the disease when it struck his own household in 1702 and learned from his own slave that the practice of inoculation was commonly employed in Africa. So he campaigned to have Boston's children inoculated, too. And it was James Franklin, Benjamin's older brother, who led the opposition to the new scientific technique.

9. Benjamin Franklin, "Silence Dogood, Number 9," *New England Courant* 51 (printed July 23, 1722), *The Papers of Benjamin Franklin,* a digital collection sponsored by the American Philosophical Society, Yale University, and the Packard Humanities Institute, www.franklinpapers.org.

10. Benjamin Franklin, *The Autobiography and Other Writings,* edited by L. Jesse Lemisch (New York: Penguin Books, 1961), 35.

11. Ibid. According to Walters in *Franklin and His Gods,* while in London, Franklin became exposed to a cast of characters whose behavior altered his theology. There was his generous Roman Catholic landlady and another "Maiden Lady of 70," also Catholic, who gave almost every penny she earned to charity. There was Thomas Denham, a Quaker businessman who became like a father figure to Franklin and died in 1728. At the same time, Franklin himself almost died of pleurisy. Historian Kerry Walters has argued that his exposure to nonsatanic Catholics, the pain of losing Denham, and a brush with his own mortality all pushed Franklin to the "painful realization that the impersonal clockmaker god of his Dissertation was spiritually as well as ethically bankrupt."

12. Benjamin Franklin, "Articles of Belief and Acts of Religion," November 20, 1728. Historians have debated what on earth we're supposed to make of this. Was Franklin really a polytheist? Alfred Owen Aldridge said yes, pointing to other instances in which Franklin invoked multiple gods and arguing that his views were similar to those of Isaac Newton. Kerry Walters, on the other hand, has argued that Franklin was writing metaphorically: These multiple Gods grew from his growing sense of religious pluralism—that each person will conjure a manifestation of God that is most accessible, appropriate, and spiritually useful. My view is that Franklin meant it literally when he wrote it, but that over time he became a solid monotheist with deep respect for the "other Gods" worshipped by other religions.

13. Benjamin Franklin, Letter to George Whitefield, June 6, 1753:

> The faith you mention has certainly its use in the world. I do not desire to see it diminished, nor would I endeavor to lessen it in any man. But I wish it were more productive of good works, than I have generally seen it; I mean real good works; works of kindness, charity, mercy, and public spirit; not holiday-keeping, sermon-reading or hearing; performing church ceremonies, or making long prayers, filled with flatteries and compliments, despised even by wise men, and much less capable of pleasing the Deity. The worship of God is a duty; the hearing and reading of sermons may be useful; but if men rest in hearing and praying, as too many do, it is as if a tree should value itself on being watered and putting forth leaves, though it never produced any fruit.
>
> Your great master thought much less of these outward appearances and professions, than many of his modern disciples. He preferred the doers of the

word, to the mere hearers; the son that seemingly refused to obey his father, and yet performed his commands, to him that professed his readiness, but neglected the work; the heretical but charitable Samaritan, to the uncharitable though orthodox priest and sanctified Levite; and those who gave food to the hungry, drink to the thirsty, raiment to the naked, entertainment to the stranger, and relief to the sick, though they never heard of his name, he declares shall in the last day be accepted; when those who cry Lord,! Lord! who value themselves upon their faith, though great enough to perform miracles, but have neglected good works, shall be rejected. He professed, that he came not to call the righteous, but sinners to repentance; which implied his modest opinion, that there were some in his time so good, that they need not hear even him for improvement; but now-a-days we have scarce a little parson, that does not think it the duty of every man within his reach to sit under his petty ministrations; and that whoever omits them offends God.

I wish to such more humility, and to you health and happiness, being your friend and servant,

B. FRANKLIN PHILADELPHIA, 6, June, 1753.

14. Benjamin Franklin, *Poor Richard's Improved Almanack* (1753).
15. Benjamin Franklin, "Dialogue Between Two Presbyterians," *Pennsylvania Gazette* (printed April 10, 1735). *The Papers of Benjamin Franklin, Volume 2, January 1, 1735, through December 31, 1744, 27.*
16. Alfred Owen Aldridge, *Benjamin Franklin and Nature's God* (Durham, NC: Duke University Press, 1967), 16.
17. Benjamin Franklin, *A Defence of the Rev. Mr. Hemphill's Observations* (Philadelphia: Printed and Sold by B. Franklin at the New Printing-Office near the Market, 1735), *The Papers of Benjamin Franklin*, Volume 2, 90. In April 1735, Hemphill was found guilty, in part because he had plagiarized some sermons.
18. "A Narrative of the Late Massacres, in Lancaster County, of a Number of Indians, Friends of This Province, by Persons Unknown with Some Observations on the Same," January 1764, *The Papers of Benjamin Franklin*, Volume 11.
19. Benjamin Franklin to Peter Collinson, Philadelphia, May 9, 1753, *The Papers of Benjamin Franklin*, Volume 4, 477.
20. Franklin to unknown recipient, December 13, 1757. *The Papers of Benjamin Franklin*, Volume 7.
21. The full list of virtues to be cultivated was:

   1. Temperance. Eat not to dullness; drink not to elevation.
   2. Silence. Speak not but what may benefit others or yourself; avoid trifling conversation.
   3. Order. Let all your things have their places; let each part of your business have its time.
   4. Resolution. Resolve to perform what you ought; perform without fail what you resolve.
   5. Frugality. Make no expense but to do good to others or yourself; i.e., waste nothing.
   6. Industry. Lose no time; be always employed in something useful; cut off all unnecessary actions.
   7. Sincerity. Use no hurtful deceit; think innocently and justly, and, if you speak, speak accordingly.
   8. Justice. Wrong none by doing injuries, or omitting the benefits that are your duty.
   9. Moderation. Avoid extremes; forbear resenting injuries so much as you think they deserve.
   10. Cleanliness. Tolerate no uncleanliness in body, clothes, or habitation.

11. Tranquility. Be not disturbed at trifles, or at accidents common or unavoidable.
12. Chastity. Rarely use venery but for health or offspring, never to dullness, weakness, or the injury of your own or another's peace or reputation.
13. Humility. Imitate Jesus and Socrates.

In his autobiography, Franklin noted that his original list lacked Humility but that "a Quaker friend" had "kindly informed me that I was generally thought proud; that my pride showed itself frequently in conversation; that I was not content with being in the right when discussing any point, but was overbearing and rather insolent." He added Humility to the list.

22. Here are the before-and-after versions of the Lord's Prayer as published in Benjamin Franklin, "A New Version of the Lord's Prayer" (1768), *The Papers of Benjamin Franklin*, Volume 15, 299.

REASONS FOR THE CHANGE OF EXPRESSION

Old Version. *Our Father which art in Heaven.*
New V. *Heavenly Father,* is more concise, equally expressive, and better modern English.

Old. *Hallowed be thy Name.* This seems to relate to an Observance among the Jews not to pronounce the proper or peculiar Name of God, they deeming it a Profanation so to do. We have in our Language no *proper Name* for God; the Word *God* being a common or general Name, expressing all chief Objects of Worship, true or false. The Word *hallowed* is almost obsolete: People now have but an imperfect Conception of the Meaning of the Petition. It is therefore proposed to change the Expression into
New. *May all revere thee.*

Old V. *Thy Kingdom come.* This Petition seems suited to the then Condition of the Jewish Nation. Originally their State was a Theocracy: God was their King. Dissatisfied with that kind of Government, they desired a visible earthly King in the manner of the Nations round them. They had such King's accordingly; but their Happiness was not increas'd by the Change, and they had reason to wish and pray for a Return of the Theocracy, or Government of God. Christians in these Times have other Ideas when they speak of the Kingdom of God, such as are perhaps more adequately express'd by
New V. *And become thy dutiful Children and faithful Subjects.*

Old V. *Thy Will be done on Earth as it is in Heaven.* More explicitly,
New V. *May thy Laws be obeyed on Earth as perfectly as they are in Heaven.*

Old V. *Give us this Day our daily Bread.* Give us what is *ours,* seems to put in a Claim of Right, and to contain too little of the grateful Acknowledgment and Sense of Dependance that becomes Creatures who live on the daily Bounty of their Creator. Therefore it is changed to
New V. *Provide for us this Day, as thou hast hitherto daily done.*

Old V. *Forgive us our Debts as we forgive our Debtors.* Matthew. *Forgive us our Sins, for we also forgive every one that is indebted to us.* Luke. Offerings were *due* to God on many Occasions by the Jewish Law, which when People could not pay, or had forgotten as Debtors are apt to do, it was proper to pray that those Debts might be forgiven. Our Liturgy uses neither the *Debtors* of Matthew, nor the *indebted* of Luke, but instead of them speaks of *those that trespass against us*. Perhaps the Considering it as a Christian Duty to forgive Debtors, was by the Compilers thought an inconvenient Idea in a trading Nation. There seems however something presumptious in this Mode of Expression, which has the Air of proposing ourselves as an Example of Goodness fit for God to imitate. *We hope you will at least be as good as we are*; you see we forgive one another, and therefore we pray that you would forgive us. Some have considered it in another Sense, *Forgive us* as *we forgive others*; i.e. If we do not forgive others we pray that thou wouldst not forgive us. But this being a kind of conditional *Imprecation* against ourselves, seems improper in such a Prayer; and therefore it may be better to say humbly and modestly

New V. *Forgive us our Trespasses, and enable us likewise to forgive those that offend us.* This instead of assuming that we have already in and of ourselves the Grace of Forgiveness, acknowledges our Dependance on God, the Fountain of Mercy, for any Share we may have of it, praying that he would communicate of it to us.

Old V. *And lead us not into Temptation.* The Jews had a Notion, that God sometimes tempted, or directed or permitted the Tempting of People. Thus it was said he tempted Pharaoh; directed Satan to tempt Job; and a false Prophet to tempt Ahab, &c. Under this Persuasion it was natural for them to pray that he would not put them to such severe Trials. We now suppose that Temptation, so far as it is supernatural, comes from the Devil only; and this Petition continued, conveys a Suspicion which in our present Conceptions seems unworthy of God, therefore might be altered to

New V. Keep *us* out of *Temptation*.

23. Aldridge, *Franklin and Nature's God*, 167. The devout might be even more appalled to learn that Franklin's collaborator was an eccentric English nobleman named Sir Francis Dashword, who presided over meetings of something called the Order of Saint Francis. The group held ceremonies in which a high priest, dressed up as a Franciscan monk, had sex with a prostitute dressed as a nun.
24. Franklin, letter to Ezra Stiles, Philadelphia, March 9, 1790, *The Papers of Benjamin Franklin.*
25. Franklin, letter to Abiah Franklin, Philadelphia, April 12, 1750, *The Papers of Benjamin Franklin*, Volume 37.
26. Franklin, letter to Abiah Franklin, Philadelphia, October 16, 1747, *The Papers of Benjamin Franklin*, Volume 37, 179.
27. Franklin, letter to Samuel Johnson, August 23, 1750, *The Papers of Benjamin Franklin*, Volume 4, 37.
28. Franklin, letter to Elizabeth Hubbart, February 22, 1756, *The Papers of Benjamin Franklin*, Volume 6, 406.
29. Franklin, letter to George Whitefield, June 19, 1764, *The Papers of Benjamin Franklin*, Volume 11, 231.
30. Benjamin Franklin, "Remarks Concerning the Savages of North America" (1784, unpublished), *The Papers of Benjamin Franklin.*
31. J. William Frost, A *Perfect Freedom: Religious Liberty in Pennsylvania* (University Park: Pennsylvania State University Press, 1990), 5.
32. Isaacson, Benjamin Franklin, 56.
33. Lambert, *Founding Fathers*, 119. The Pennsylvania model was not without its flaws. Jews in Pennsylvania, as in the other colonies, were not allowed to hold office for some of the colonial period, and the Quaker refusal to swear oaths created persistent problems for officeholders. Some Anglicans complained that the Quakers had imposed their faith on *them* by banning cockfights and other entertainments.
34. Frost, *Perfect Freedom*, 34.

35. Isaacson, *Benjamin Franklin*, 123.
36. Benjamin Franklin, "Plain Truth: or, Serious Considerations on the Present State of the City of Philadelphia, and Province of Pennsylvania by a Tradesman of Philadelphia" (printed November 17, 1747), *The Papers of Benjamin Franklin*, Volume 37.
37. Edmund S. Morgan, *Benjamin Franklin* (New Haven, CT: Yale University Press, 2002), 68.
38. Conrad Weiser, letter to Governor Morris in Berks County, November 19, 1755, Pennsylvania Archive Series 1, Volume 2, 503.

3. *The Evangelical Revolution*

1. Frank Lambert, *Inventing the "Great Awakening"* (Princeton, NJ: Princeton University Press, 1999), 73. In 1737, some ministers believed they saw proof of God's attention when the balcony at a church collapsed without anyone dying.
2. Ibid., 98.
3. Nathan Cole, account from October 23, 1740. Quoted in Gaustad and Noll, *Documentary History*, 164–165.
4. Lambert, *Inventing the "Great Awakening,"* 113.
5. Frank Lambert, *"Pedlar in Divinity": George Whitefield and the Transatlantic Revivals* (Princeton, NJ: Princeton University Press, 1994), 120.
6. Mark A. Noll, Nathan O. Hatch, and George M. Marsden, *The Search for Christian America* (Colorado Springs: Helmers and Howard, 1989), 51–52.
7. Aldridge, *Franklin and Nature's God*, 106.
8. Walters, *Franklin and His Gods*, 144.
9. Benjamin Franklin, *Autobiography*, part 11, *The Papers of Benjamin Franklin*.
10. From *George Whitefield's Journals* (Gainesville, FL: Scholars' Facsimiles & Reprints, 1756), quoted in Roger Finke and Rodney Stark, *The Churching of America, 1776–1990: Winners and Losers in Our Religious Economy* (New Brunswick, NJ: Rutgers University Press, 1997), 51.
11. William G. McLoughlin, "The Role of Religion in the Revolution: Liberty of Conscience and Cultural Cohesion in the New Nation," in Stephen G. Kurtz and James H. Hutson, editors, *Essays on the American Revolution* (New York: W. W. Norton, 1973). One of the best historians on this topic is Frank Lambert in *Inventing the "Great Awakening."*

4. *John Adams*

1. Page Smith, *John Adams*, Volume 1, 1735–1784 (Garden City, NY: Doubleday and Company, 1962). "I shall never forget the rows of venerable heads ranged along those front benches which, as a young fellow, I used to gaze upon," he wrote as an old man (page 5).
2. Catherine Drinker Bowen, *John Adams and the American Revolution* (Boston: Little, Brown, 1950), 22.
3. C. Bradley Thompson, *John Adams and the Spirit of Liberty* (Lawrence: University Press of Kansas, 1998), 53.
4. Smith, *John Adams*, Volume 2, 1079.
5. John Adams, *John Adams Autobiography*, Part 1, "John Adams," through 1776, sheet 3 of 53 (electronic edition). *Adams Family Papers: An Electronic Archive*, Massachusetts Historical Society, www.masshist.org/digitaladams. He later explained to another friend that "people are not disposed to inquire for piety, integrity, good sense or learning in a young preacher" but instead sought out "stupidity (for so I must call the pretended sanctity of some absolute dunces)."
6. Thompson, *John Adams and the Spirit of Liberty*, 19.
7. John Adams, letter to John Taylor, 1814, quoted in Norman Cousins, editor, *In God We Trust: The Religious Beliefs and Ideas of the American Founding Fathers* (New York: Harper and Brothers, 1958), no. 31, 108.

8. John Adams, August 15, 1756, *John Adams's Diary* 1, 18 November 1755–29 August 1756 (electronic edition). *Adams Family Papers: An Electronic Archive*, Massachusetts Historical Society, www.masshist.org/digitaladams/aea.

9. Adams's diary, quoted in Cousins, *In God We Trust*, 80.

10. Adams, letter to Thomas Jefferson, September 14, 1813, in Lester J. Cappon, editor, *The Adams–Jefferson Letters: The Complete Correspondence Between Thomas Jefferson and Abigail and John Adams* (Chapel Hill: University of North Carolina Press, 1987), 372.

11. From the website of the United First Parish Church of Quincy, Massachusetts (www.ufpc.org/history/summary.htm).

12. Adams, letter to F. A. Van der Kemp, December 27, 1816.

13. Adams, letter to Samuel Quincy, April 22, 1761, in Cousins, *In God We Trust*, 93.

14. Adams, letter to Jefferson, September 14, 1813, in Cappon, *Adams–Jefferson Letters*, 373.

15. Adams, letter to Abigail Adams, October 9, 1774 (electronic edition). *Adams Family Papers*. Though his contempt for Catholicism was the most intense, Adams's views on other religions, particularly early in his life, were intolerant, too. He was distrustful of Quakers and said that while "The Hebrews have done more to civilize men than any other nation . . . I cannot say that I love the Jews very much neither, nor the French, nor the English, nor the Romans, nor the Greeks. We must love all nations as well as we can, but it is very hard to love most of them." Adams, letter to F. A. Van der Kemp, February 16, 1809, quoted in Cousins, *In God We Trust*, 103.

    While his views on many things softened over the years, his anger at the Catholic Church persisted. Writing to Jefferson in 1816 about a recent revival of the Catholic order of Jesuits, Adams said, "This Society has been a greater Calamity to Mankind than the French Revolution or Napoleon's Despotism or Ideology. It has obstructed the Progress of Reformation and the Improvements of the human Mind in Society much longer and more fatally."

16. www.deism.org/foundingfathers.htm (accessed 2006).

17. Adams, letter to Jefferson, April 19, 1817, quoted in Cappon, *Adams–Jefferson Letters*, 509. Conservatives have misquoted Adams as well. M. Stanton Evans in *The American Spectator*, February 2007, quoted Adams as saying, "Statesmen may plan and speculate for liberty, but it is Religion and Morality alone which can establish the principles upon which freedom can securely stand. A patriot must be a religious man." The quote comes from a letter Adams wrote on June 21, 1775, to Zabdiel Adams, a clergyman cousin. The actual quote was:

    > Who would not Exchange the discordant Scenes of Envy, Pride, Vanity, Malice, Revenge, for the sweet Consolations of Philosophy, the serene Composure of the Passions, the divine Enjoyments of Christian Charity, and Benevolence?
    >
    > Statesmen my dear Sir, may plan and speculate for Liberty, but it is Religion and Morality alone, which can establish the Principles upon which Freedom can securely stand. . . . The only foundation of a free Constitution, is pure Virtue, and if this cannot be inspired into our People, in a greater Measure, than they have it now, They may change their Rulers, and the forms of Government, but they will not obtain a lasting Liberty.

    Adams did not write, "A patriot must be a religious man." His wife, Abigail, did make comments close to that, though: "A patriot without religion, in my estimation, is as great a paradox as an honest man without the fear of God," she wrote her friend Mercy Warren on November 5, 1775.

18. Letter to Benjamin Rush, August 28, 1811, quoted in Cousins, *In God We Trust*, 102. Throughout the last part of the eighteenth century and first part of the nineteenth, a liberal wing of the Congregational Church in Massachusetts began to break away from the stand-

ing order. Sometimes called Arminians, they rejected the idea that only the elect could be saved and believed that good works would help shape one's ultimate fate. Eventually, the divisions hardened into a permanent rift and the creation of the Unitarian denomination. A concise description of the theological and political underpinnings of Unitarianism comes from Conrad Wright, *The Beginnings of Unitarianism in America* (Boston: Starr King Press, 1955). Wright summarized the "liberal movement which developed within with the congregational churches of New England" and resulted in Unitarianism. It combined a skepticism about Trinitarian doctrine, a commitment to reason as a key element in spiritual quest, and Arminianism. Between 1735 and 1805, "two generations of religious liberals, commonly called Arminians, rejected traditional Calvinistic patterns of thoughts and developed a new set of basic assumptions about human nature and human destiny. . . . Arminianism asserted that men are born with the capacity both for sin and for righteousness; that they can respond to the impulses toward holiness as well as the temptation to do evil; and that life is a process of trial and discipline by which, with the assistance God gives to all, the bondage to sin may be gradually overcome" (pages 3–4).

19. Adams, letter to Benjamin Rush, January 21, 1810, quoted in Cousins, *In God We Trust*, 101.
20. Adams diary, July 26, 1796, quoted in ibid., 99, and in *Adams Family Papers*.
21. Adams diary, February 22, 1756, quoted in Cousins, 80–81, and in *Adams Family Papers*. While Adams most often rhapsodized about Christian ethics, he also was in awe of God the Creator—not just his goodness but his greatness, too. "He has hung up in the heavens over my head, and spread out in the fields of nature around me, those glorious shows and appearances with which my eyes and my imagination are extremely delighted." He created flowers and forests and creatures and smells. "I am thrown into a kind of transport when I behold the amazing concave of heaven, sprinkled and glittering with stars." Adams diary, August 22, 1756, *Adams Family Papers*.
22. From a draft of "Dissertation on Canon and Federal Law," in Adams diary, February 21, 1765, *Adams Family Papers*, Adams diary, part 10, page 11.
23. Adams, letter to Abigail, January 20, 1796, *Adams Family Papers*.
24. *Defence of the Constitutions of Government of the United States of America, 1788*, Volume 3, quoted in Cousins, *In God We Trust*, 97.
25. Adams, letter to Benjamin Rush, August 1, 1812, in *Old Family Letters* (Philadelphia: J. B. Lippincott, 1892), digitized by Google.
26. Adams, letter to Abigail, November 18, 1775, *Adams Family Papers*.
27. Adams diary, August 14, 1796, quoted in Cousins, *In God We Trust*, 99.
28. Adams, letter to F. A. Van der Kemp, December 27, 1816, quoted in ibid., 104.
29. While we now see that there is indeed evidence of Adams's traditionalism, it is also true that some culture warriors have gone too far. In *America's Godly Heritage*, David Barton quoted John Adams thusly:

> "The general principles on which the fathers achieved independence were . . . the general principles of Christianity. . . . I will avow that I then believed, and now believe, that those general principles of Christianity are as eternal and immutable as the existence and attributes of God."

Barton concluded: "Now that's a strong statement—right to the point." David Barton, *America's Godly Heritage: A Transcript of the Video and Audio by the Same Title* (Aledo, TX: WallBuilders, 1993).

Actually, it's not that simple. Adams was referring to a statement made by a group of young men in Philadelphia who had invoked certain principles of the Founders. "And what were these *general Principles?*" Adams wrote. "I answer the general Principles of Christianity, in which all those Sects were united." What sects is he referring to? Earlier in the letter, he listed the probable religious affiliations of the people who had issued the statement: "Roman Catholicks, English Episcopalians, Scotch and American Presbyterians, Methodists, Moravians, Anababtists, German Lutherans, German Calvinists Universalites,

Arians, Priestleyans, Socinians, Independents, Congregationals, Horse Protestant and House Protestants, Deists and Atheists; and 'Protestan qui ne croyent rien' [Protestants who believe nothing]."

So the "general principles" of Christianity to which Adams was referring—and which Barton quoted—were those that Deists and Calvinists could all agree to. Adams doesn't actually list those principles, but suffice it to say they probably don't constitute a creed that Barton would view as real Christianity.

30. Adams, letter to Abigail, October 29, 1775, *Adams Family Papers*. One other thought might occur when reading Adams's angry rejection of various religious doctrines and practices combined with his strong sense that religion was essential for a governing Republic: Perhaps he viewed religion as a regulator of the masses, something that was important for the hoi polloi who couldn't control themselves. Franklin articulated that idea fairly explicitly.

But I do not believe that Adams's support for religion was merely a utilitarian remedy for *other* people. For one thing, his private correspondence is full of invocations of Providence. He referred to God as "my adored Maker," beseeched that "God bless, preserve and prosper" his children, and that "God almighty grant to you and to every Branch of the Family, all the Support that you want!" He signed one letter "God almightys Providence protect and bless you and yours and mine." His comments about the role of Providence in the American Revolution and other events came as much in private diaries and letters as public declarations. It's also worth noting that his faith in God persisted even as he lost some confidence in the ability of religion and morality to regulate behavior. By 1787, he wrote Jefferson that "neither Philosophy, nor Religion, nor Morality, nor Wisdom, nor Interest, will ever govern nations or Parties, against their Vanity, their Pride, their Resentment or Revenge, or their Avarice or Ambition. Nothing but Force and Power and Strength can restrain them." Virtue, he noted in 1814, was "as precarious a foundation for liberty as honor or fear." Instead, government checks and balances loomed more important.

5. The Godly Roots of Rebellion

1. John Adams, letter to Dr. Jedidiah Morse, 1815.
2. Thompson, *John Adams and the Spirit of Liberty*. Full sermon found in John Wingate Thornton, editor, *The Pulpit of the American Revolution* (New York: Burt Franklin, 1860), 9.
3. Alan Heimert, *Religion and the American Mind: From the Great Awakening to the American Revolution* (Cambridge, MA: Harvard University Press, 1966), 421.
4. Ibid., 482.
5. In 1756, evangelical minister Samuel Davies declared the French and Indian War to be the "grand decisive conflict between the Lamb and the beast," which would, after the defeat of the French, usher in "a new heaven and a new earth."
6. Noll, Hatch, and Marsden, *Search for Christian America*, 62.
7. Butler et al., *Religion in American Life*, 149.
8. Paul Boyer, quoted at *Frontline: Apocalypse! Apocalypticism Explained: The American Revolution*, www.pbs.org/wgbh/pages/frontline/shows/apocalypse/explanation/amrevolution .html.
9. Charles H. Metzger, *Catholics and the American Revolution: A Study in Religious Climate* (Chicago: Loyola University Press, 1962), 133.
10. Henry Mayer, *A Son of Thunder: Patrick Henry and the American Republic* (New York: Grove Press, 1991), 245.
11. Elbridge Gerry, letter to John Adams, December 13, 1775, quoted in James Trecothick Austin, *The Life of Elbridge Gerry, with Contemporary Letters to the Close of the American Revolution* (Boston: Wells and Lilly, 1829), 124.
12. Derek H. Davis, *Religion and the Continental Congress 1774–1789: Contributions to Original Intent* (New York: Oxford University Press, 2000), 40.
13. "The Articles of Association," October 20, 1774. *Avalon Project: Journals of the Continental Congress 1774–1779*.

14. Stokes and Pfeffer, *Church and State*, 36.
15. Extracts from the Letter Book of Captain Johann Heinrichs of the Hessian Jaeger Corps, quoted in Metzger, *Catholics and the American Revolution*, 130.
16. This summary was culled primarily from Butler et al., *Religion in American Life*.
17. Stokes and Pfeffer, *Church and State*, 23, quoting W. W. Sweet, in "Church Membership," Dictionary of American History.
18. Finke and Stark, *Churching of America*, 16. Finke and Stark offer another fascinating theory: that there were too many men. Many of those who immigrated from Europe were men, and many who went west were as well. And, they argue, communities with a high ratio of men to women tend to be less religious. Other theories: "Major impediments to the churching of colonial America are common features of all frontier settings: transience, disorder, too many men, too many scoundrels, and too few effective and committed clergy." But they also argued that the presence of the establishments caused lethargy and that affluence caused lack of verve among the dominant congregations (pages 33–39).
19. George F. Willison, *Patrick Henry and His World* (Garden City, NY: Doubleday and Company, 1969), 70.
20. Quoted in Finke and Stark, *Churching of America*, 36.
21. Willison, *Patrick Henry*, 64.
22. Ibid., 67–68.
23. Mayer, *Son of Thunder*, 63.
24. Willison, *Patrick Henry*, 76.
25. Ibid., 80.
26. Carl Bridenbaugh, *Mitre and Sceptre: Transatlantic Faiths, Ideas, Personalities, and Politics, 1689–1775* (New York: Oxford University Press, 1962), 212.
27. Ibid., 11.
28. Ibid., 222.
29. Ibid., 210.
30. Ibid., 226.
31. Ibid.
32. John Adams, "A Dissertation on the Canon and Feudal Law" (1765).
33. Heimert, *Religion and the American Mind*, 369. Another minister declared that the taxes that supported that episcopacy would also sustain the lifestyles of debauched British aristocracy: "The avaricious courtiers of Great Britain, with their numerous train of needy dependants and hangers on, with a whole tribe of dissolute spendthrifts, and [idol bodies]" surrounding the king to aid in "pursuit of pleasure and the boundless luxuries of life."
34. Samuel Adams, *Boston Gazette*, October 5, 1772, Harry Alonzo Cushing, editor, in *The Writings of Samuel Adams*, Volume 2 (1770–1773) (Boston: James R. Osgood and Company, 1883), part 5.
35. Samuel Adams, *Boston Gazette*, April 4, 1768.
36. Bridenbaugh, *Mitre and Sceptre*, 290.
37. Ibid., 345. There was even speculation that the English would limit public offices to Anglicans. These fears were given credence thanks to a plan by New Jersey governor Francis Bernard to establish a formal aristocracy; other efforts to change some of the colonial charters; the New York governor's decision to deny incorporation to the Presbyterian Church; and an English proposal to merge all of North America into four districts.
38. Ibid., 293.
39. Ibid., 307. Their concern was reinforced by the activities of the Society for Propagation of Religion. Mayhew alleged that their goal was not "the converting of heathens to Christianity, but the converting of Christians of *other protestant denominations*, to the faith of *the church of England*."
40. Ruth H. Bloch, "Religion and Ideological Change in the American Revolution," in Mark A. Noll, editor, *Religion and American Politics: From the Colonial Period to the 1980s* (New York: Oxford University Press, 1990), 48.
41. Davis, *Religion and the Continental Congress*, 153. Sam Adams claimed that the snazzy at-

tire of Boston's elites was a sign of decadence, and therefore somehow linked to "the whore of Babylon." John Adams wrote to one friend proudly that Roman Catholics in Braintree "dare not show themselves." He described the "Jesuits" as slick operators who were only now pretending to be good citizens. "To see them bowing, smiling, cringing and seeming cordially friendly to persons whom they openly avowed their malice against two years ago, and whom they would gladly butcher now is provoking yet diverting."

42. *Pennsylvania Gazette*, October 12, 1774, quoted in Metzger, *Catholics and the American Revolution*, 28.

43. Ibid., 32. *The Massachusetts Spy* published a report that a messenger to the British general Thomas Gage in Boston had been captured bearing a note from Gage that "his very good friends the Catholics may be henceforth sent to assist him in cutting the throats of all heretics." The *New York Journal* declared that unless the British were stopped, they would force upon the colonists "the blind, bloody religion of Popery, which is founded in ignorance and superstition, and calculated to promote the present ruin, and eternal destruction of all that embrace it."

44. Ibid., 33.

45. John Lathrop, Thanksgiving sermon, Boston, 1774, quoted in ibid., 38.

46. Samuel West, "Sermon Before the Honorable Council and House of Representatives of Massachusetts Bay, Boston, 1776," quoted in Metzger, *Catholics and the American Revolution*, 38.

47. Heimert, *Religion and the American Mind*, 389.

48. Ibid., 394.

49. Metzger, *Catholics and the American Revolution*, 30.

50. Ibid., 32.

51. From Alexander Hamilton's speech "A Full Vindication," December 15, 1774, quoted in Henry Cabot Lodge, editor, *The Works of Alexander Hamilton* (Federal Edition), 12 volsumes (New York: G. P. Putnam's Sons, 1904), online edition, oll.libertyfund.org/?option= com_staticxt&staticfile=show.php%3Ftitle=1378&chapter=64142&layout=html&Itemid= 27 (accessed October 2007).

52. Sam Adams, in *Writings of Samuel Adams*, volume 3, 213, quoted in Stokes and Pfeffer, *Church and State*, 31.

53. Address to the People of Great Britain, Journals of the Continental Congress, Library of Congress website.

54. The Articles of Association, October 20, 1774, *Avalon Project: The Journals of the Continental Congress 1774–1779*.

55. Metzger, *Catholics and the American Revolution*, 44.

56. James Dana, "A Century Discourse Delivered at the Anniversary Meeting of the Freemen of Wallingford, April 9, 1770," quoted in Davis, *Religion and the Continental Congress*, 156. One preacher noted the pervasiveness of anti-Catholic rhetoric when he said, "Hardly a book or an article of religion has been written; hardly a sermon on any controversial point has . . . been preached; hardly a public debate or private conversation has been held on the subject of religion or politic sin which . . . the parties have not contrived to have a thwack at Popery." Metzger, *Catholics and the American Revolution*, 36, 121, and throughout.

57. Sherwood, 1776, excerpted in Gaustad and Noll, *Documentary History*, 227–228.

58. From *The Tablet*, July 20 and 27, 1912, quoted in Metzger, *Catholics and the American Revolution*, 121. Metzger notes that "Gasquet is not to be regarded as an authority on American history, but he testifies to the persistence of this belief."

59. In Virginia, Bridenbaugh said, "The question of episcopacy merged with problems of toleration and establishment and led without a break to James Madison's religious clause in the celebrated Virginia's Declaration of Rights of 1776, to the bill for disestablishment of the same year, and the final statute for religious freedom passed in 1786."

60. Alvah Hovey, *A Memoir of the Life and Times of Rev. Isaac Backus*, A.M. (Gould and Lincoln, 1858), republished by Gano Books of Harrisonburg, VA, 1991, 44–46. Backus believed that the "Half-Way Covenant" that the Congregationalists had adopted to open their doors and enlarge their ranks was contrary to the Bible's teachings: "At all times the doors of the

church should be carefully kept against such as cannot give a satisfactory evidence of the work of God upon their souls, whereby they are united to Christ."

61. William G. McLoughlin, *Isaac Backus and the American Pietistic Tradition* (Boston: Little, Brown, 1967), 113.

62. Lambert, *Founding Fathers*, 201.

63. McLoughlin, *Isaac Backus*, 114.

64. Ibid., 121. Another example is Backus's plea before the Massachusetts legislature on December 2, 1774: "Must we be blamed for not lying still, and thus let our countrymen trample upon our rights, and deny us that every liberty that they are ready to take up arms to defend for themselves? You profess to exempt us from taxes to your worship and yet tax us every year. Great complaints have been made about a tax which the British Parliament laid upon paper; but you require a paper tax of us annually. . . . We are determined not to pay either of them; not only upon your principle of not being taxed where we aren't to be represented, but also because we dare not render that homage to any earthly power, which I and many of my brethren are fully convinced belongs only to God. We cannot give in the certificates you require, without implicitly allowing to men that authority which we believe in our consciences belongs only to God. Here, therefore, we claim character rights, liberty of conscience. And if any still deny it to us, they must answer it to Him who has said, 'With what measure ye mete, it shall be measured to you again.' If any ask what we would have, we answer: Only allow us freely to enjoy the religious liberty that they do in Boston, and we ask no more." Excerpted in Gaustad and Noll, *Documentary History*, 227.

65. McLoughlin, *Isaac Backus*, 127.

66. Ibid., 125.

67. Ibid., 127.

68. "A Declaration of the Rights, of the Inhabitants of the State of Massachusetts-Bay, in New England," excerpted in Gaustad and Noll, *Documentary History*, 238.

69. McLoughlin, *Isaac Backus*, 130. and Hovey, *A Memoir*, 204–213.

70. Hovey, *A Memoir*, 213. His longtime friend Thomas Baldwin described Backus: "Mr. Backus' personal appearance was very grave and venerable. He was not far from six feet in stature; and in the later part of his life considerably corpulent. He was naturally modest and diffident; which probably led him into a habit which he continued to the day of his death, of shutting his eyes when conversing or preaching on important subjects. His voice was clear and distant, but rather sharp than pleasant." Hovey, *A Memoir*, 311.

71. Adams diary, October 14, 1774, quoted in Cousins, *In God We Trust*, 87.

6. George Washington

1. Described on the website of the architect of the Capitol, www.aoc.gov/cc/art/rotunda/ apotheosis/Overview.cfm (accessed May 2007).

2. D. James Kennedy, *What They Believed: The Faith of Washington, Jefferson and Lincoln* (Fort Lauderdale, FL: Coral Ridge Ministries, 2003), 17.

3. Tim LaHaye, *Faith of Our Founding Fathers*, 110.

4. Ibid., 113

5. Allen, *Moral Minority*, 28.

6. Mason Locke Weems, *A History of the Life and Death, Virtues and Exploits of General George Washington* (Philadelphia: J. P. Lippincott, 1918), chapter 13. Available online at xroads.virginia.edu/~CAP/gw/weems.html.

7. John Eidsmore. *Christianity and the Constitution: The Faith of Our Founding Fathers* (Grand Rapids, MI: Baker Book House, 1987), 129.

8. Paul F. Boller Jr., *George Washington and Religion* (Dallas: Southern Methodist University Press, 1963), 28. Brooke Allen quoted a letter to the editor written by someone who had interviewed a former slave of Washington. This former slave, Ona Judge Staines, apparently reported that "the stories of Washington's piety and prayers, so far as she ever saw or heard while she was his slave, have no foundation. Cardplaying and wine-drinking were the business at his parties, and he had more of such company Sundays than on any other day" (page 31).

9. William White to Colonel Hugh Mercer, Philadelphia, August 15, 1835, from White's memoirs, quoted in Boller, *George Washington and Religion*, 33. One possible interpretation is that Washington was taking to heart Jesus' admonition against taking communion if you had a problem with someone you know. But that certainly wasn't the interpretation that Washington's clergy applied.

10. Ibid., 34.

11. Speech to the Delaware Chiefs at his headquarters in Middle Brook on May 12, 1779, quoted in ibid., 68.

12. Ibid., 77.

13. "After-Dinner Anecdotes of James Madison, Excerpts from Jared Sparks' Journal for 1829–31," *Virginia Magazine of History and Biography*, (April 1952), quoted in ibid., 89.

14. Samuel Miller, *The Life of Samuel Miller* (Philadelphia, 1869), quoted in ibid., 89.

15. This account comes from an undated letter from Arthur Bullis Bradford to B. F. Underwood, quoted in ibid., 83.

16. "Only by the direct intervention of God was [Washington's life] spared," wrote David Barton, *America's Godly Heritage*, 3.

17. Washington to the Inhabitants of Princeton, August 25, 1783, quoted in *George Washington and Religion*, 58.

18. Farewell orders to the army, November 2, 1783.

19. "Address to Congress on Resigning His Commission," Annapolis, December 23, 1783, quoted in Boller, *George Washington and Religion*, 59.

20. Washington's Farewell Address, *Avalon Project*, www.yale.edu/lawweb/avalon/washing.htm.

21. Steven C. Bullock, *Revolutionary Brotherhood: Freemasonry and the Transformation of the American Social Order, 1730–1840* (Chapel Hill: University of North Carolina Press, 1996), 16.

22. Ibid., 141.

23. De Witt Clinton, "An Address Delivered Before Holland Lodge, December 24, 1793," quoted in ibid., 139.

24. Ibid., 147. In fact, Bullock proposed that when Washington suggested "institutions for the general diffusion of knowledge," he was influenced by the Masons.

25. Ibid., 21.

26. Ibid., 26.

27. Ibid., 169.

28. Ibid., 53. The evangelicals of the 1820s, during the Second Great Awakening, turned against Masonry, and modern-day Christian leaders will occasionally take it on as well. Pat Robertson declared that Freemasonry was a key force in promoting anti-religiosity. H. Paul Jeffers, *The Freemasons in America* (New York: Citadel Press, 2006), 177.

29. Bullock, *Revolutionary Brotherhood*, 23.

30. Ibid., 58–62. Men of "all Religions, Sects, persuasions and denominations, of all nations and countries" made up the organizations, creating, in the words of one Boston brother in 1734, "a Paradise or Heaven."

31. Ibid., 59.

32. Ibid., 258.

33. "Letter from George Washington to Rhode Island Masonic lodge in 1790," quoted in Jeffers, *Freemasons in America*.

34. Bullock, *Revolutionary Brotherhood*, 137.

35. "Reprint of the Minutes of the Grand Lodge of Free and Accepted Masons of Pennsylvania," quoted in ibid., 139.

36. George Washington, letter to York, Pennsylvania, Masons, January 3, 1792, *The George Washington Papers at the Library of Congress, 1741–1799*: Series 2 Letterbooks, Letterbook 39, memory.loc.gov/cgi-bin/query/P?mgw:10:./temp/~ammem_y28O:: (accessed 2007).

37. Washington, letter to Robert Sinclair, Philadelphia, May 6, 1792.

7. Holy War

1. Charles Royster, *A Revolutionary People at War: The Continental Army and the American Character, 1775–1783* (Chapel Hill: University of North Carolina Press, 1969), 99.
2. Washington's full message: "As the Contempt of the Religion of a Country by ridiculing any of its Ceremonies, or affronting its Ministers or Votaries, has ever been deeply resented, you are to be particularly careful to restrain every Officer and Soldier from such Imprudence and Folly and to punish every Instance of it." George Washington to Benedict Arnold, September 14, 1775, *The George Washington Papers at the Library of Congress, 1741–1799:* Series 3b, Varick Transcripts, Letterbook 1.
3. George Washington, letter to Arnold, September 14, 1775, quoted in Paul F. Boller, "George Washington and Religious Liberty," in James Morton Smith, editor, *George Washington: A Profile* (New York: Hill and Wang, 1969), 169. "You are to protect and support the free Exercise of the Religion of the Country and the undisturbed Enjoyment of the rights of Conscience in religious Matters, with your utmost Influence and Authority."
4. Orders issued November 5, 1775, quoted in Boller, in *George Washington: A Profile*, 170.
5. Metzger, *Catholics and the American Revolution*, 50.
6. Metzger, *Catholics and the American Revolution*, 52; Heimert, *Religion and the American Mind*, 394.
7. "An Appeal to the Inhabitants of Quebec," Continental Congress, Philadelphia, 1774, www.historicaldocuments.com/AppealtotheInhabitantsofQuebec.htm.
8. Davis, *Religion and the Continental Congress*, 155.
9. Metzger, *Catholics and the American Revolution*, 192.
10. Ibid., 220. In appointing him quartermaster general, John Hancock, the president of Congress, wrote on June 6 that the appointment was made "from a sense of your merit, and attachment to the American cause."
11. "To the Roman Catholics in the United States of America," March 15, 1790, in Boller, *George Washington and Religion*.
12. John Adams, letter to Abigail Adams, quoted in Metzger, *Catholics and the American Revolution*, 64.
13. Ibid., 65.
14. Ibid., 66.
15. General Orders, Headquarters, Valley Forge, May 5, 1778, *The George Washington Papers at the Library of Congress, 1741–1799*, "It having pleased the Almighty ruler of the Universe propitiously to defend the Cause of the United American-States and finally by raising us up a powerful Friend among the Princes of the Earth."
16. The *Journal of Congress* for August 14, 1776, included the resolution, which informed the soldiers that "after they have violated every Christian and moral precept, by invading, and attempting to destroy, those who have never injured them or their country, their only reward, if they escape death and captivity, will be a return to the despotism of their prince, to be by him again sold to do the drudgery of some other enemy to the rights of mankind. . . . Resolved, Therefore, that these states will receive all such foreigners who shall leave the armies of his Britannic majesty in America, and shall choose to become members of any of these states; and they shall be protected in the free exercise of their respective religions, and be invested with the rights, privileges and immunities of natives as established by the laws of these states; and, moreover, that this Congress will provide for every such person; fifty acres of unappropriated lands in some of these states, to be held by him and his heirs in absolute property." This is reprinted in Stokes and Pfeffer, *Church and State*, 467.
17. Davis, *Religion and the Continental Congress*, 163.
18. General Orders, September 17, 1775, *The George Washington Papers at the Library of Congress, 1741–1799,*
19. Washington, communication to the president of Congress, June 8, 1777, quoted in Boller, in *George Washington: A Profile*, 172.

20. There were an estimated 2,005 churches in colonial America. The breakdown, as summarized in Stokes and Pfeffer, *Church and State*, (page 272), was:

> Congregationalists, mostly in New England—658
> Presbyterians, largely in the middle colonies but becoming increasingly prominent in the South—543
> Baptists, especially in Rhode Island, the middle colonies, the Carolinas, and Virginia—498
> Anglicans, mainly in the South and in the larger towns elsewhere—480
> Quakers, mostly in Pennsylvania and North Carolina—298
> German and Dutch Reformed, mainly in the middle colonies—251
> Lutherans, largely in the middle colonies—151
> Roman Catholics, mostly in large eastern towns and Maryland—50
> Miscellaneous minor groups—76

21. Bruce Chadwick, *George Washington's War: The Forging of a Revolutionary Leader and the American Presidency* (Naperville, IL: Sourcebooks, 2004), 112.
22. Ibid., 234.
23. Stokes and Pfeffer further wrote, "They came in contact with men of different religious bodies from different parts of the country and gained respect for them. They increasingly felt that they were fighting not for their colony only but for the united colonies which were to form a new nation. Massachusetts Congregationalists, Rhode Island Baptists, New York Episcopalians and Dutch Reformed, New Jersey Presbyterians, Pennsylvania members of many small Protestant sects with a continental background, Maryland Roman Catholics, and a scattering of Jews from the seaboard cities to give a few examples, met in the same camps and acquired a new idea of the need and possibility of religious tolerance. Such an intermingling of men of different religious faiths and backgrounds had not taken place before in America except in a few of the larger cities, and in three or four small colleges that had broken away, at least in actual practice, from rather narrow local and denominational antecedents. Furthermore, soldiers visiting sections of the emerging independent nation could not fail to be impressed by what they saw of the contributions to the social life of such differing groups as Quakers, Lutherans, Congregationalists, and Anglicans." Stokes and Pfeffer, *Church and State*, 35.
24. Washington, letter to Governor Dinwiddie, June 12, 1757, quoted in Davis, *Religion and the Continental Congress*, 81.
25. Washington, letter to Governor Jonathan Trumbull, Cambridge, December 15, 1775, quoted in Boller, *George Washington and Religion*, 50.
26. General Orders, Saturday March 22, 1783, *The George Washington Papers at the Library of Congress, 1741–1799*.
27. General Orders, Headquarters, Cambridge, March 22, 1783, in *The George Washington Papers at the Library of Congress, 1741–1799*. In his order establishing the chaplain corps on July 9, 1776, he wrote, "The blessing and protection of Heaven are at all times necessary, but especially so in times of public distress and danger."
28. Order from Washington, February 27, 1776, in *The George Washington Papers at the Library of Congress, 1741–1799*.
29. General Orders from Headquarters, New York, July 9, 1776, in *The George Washington Papers at the Library of Congress, 1741–1799*.
30. General Orders, Headquarters, New York, May 2, 1778, in *The George Washington Papers at the Library of Congress, 1741–1799*.
31. General Orders, Headquarters, New York, May 15, 1776, in *The George Washington Papers at the Library of Congress, 1741–1799*.
32. General Orders, Headquarters, near Germantown, Pennsylvania, September 13, 1777. Another example: When the peace treaty was signed in April 1783, Washington declared that victory had occurred "under the Smiles of Providence" and ordered the chaplains to "render thanks to almighty God" for "causing the rage of war to cease among the nations."
33. This was prompted by General Horatio Gates's victory over General Burgoyne at Saratoga.

General Orders, Headquarters, at Wentz's, Worcester Township, October 18, 1777, *The George Washington Papers at the Library of Congress, 1741–1799.*

34. General Orders, October 20, 1781, in *The George Washington Papers at the Library of Congress, 1741–1799.*

35. Royster, *Revolutionary People,* 16.

36. Bonomi, *Under the Cope,* 215.

37. In his diary for November 17, 1774, Yale president Ezra Stiles reported on activity in three Connecticut towns. Recounted in Stokes, *Church and State,* 269.

38. Royster, *Revolutionary People,* 156.

39. Letter from Congress, May 26, 1779, Continental Congress, in *Journals of the American Congress from 1774 to 1788,* Volume III (Washington: Way and Gideon, 1823), 289.

40. Letter to John Parke Custis, January 22, 1777, in *The Writings of George Washington, 1776–77,* Volume V (New York: G. P. Putnam's Sons, 1890), 187.

41. David McCullough, *John Adams* (New York: Simon & Schuster, 2001), 161.

42. Chadwick, *George Washington's War,* 404.

43. John Hunt's diary, May 30 and May 31, 1780, as quoted in ibid., 402.

44. The Continental Congress's thanksgiving proclamation issued November 1, 1777, quoted in Davis, *Religion and the Continental Congress,* 87.

45. Martin Marty, "The Virginia Statute Two Hundred Years Later," in Merrill D. Peterson and Robert C. Vaughan, editors, *The Virginia Statute for Religious Freedom: Its Evolution and Consequences in American History* (New York: Cambridge University Press, 1988), quoting Thomas Jefferson, 9.

8. Thomas Jefferson

1. D. James Kennedy and Jerry Newcombe, *What If America Were a Christian Nation Again?* (Nashville: Thomas Nelson Publishers, 2003), 46. This rumor stems from the fact that the full title of his first effort was: "The Philosophy of Jesus of Nazareth extracted from the account of his life and doctrines as given by Matthew, Mark, Luke, & John. Being an abridgement of the New Testament for the use of the Indians unembarrassed with matters of fact or faith beyond the level of their comprehensions." Some conservative Christians have pointed to this as proof that Jefferson was a good Christian who merely tried to shorten the Bible for use in missionary work, but historian Eugene Sheridan has argued that Jefferson was being ironic and that he had, on earlier occasions, referred to the Federalists as "Indians." Wrote Sheridan, "They were, rather, the Federalists and their clerical allies, whose political and religious obscurantism, as the president saw it, endangered the stability of the Republic and needed to be reformed by a return to the simple, uncorrupted morality of Jesus." More to the point, he never actually used it to help Indians and, most important, even if that had been a goal of the first effort it was clearly not the goal of the second, which produced what we now call the Jefferson Bible.

2. Anson Phelps Stokes and Leo Pfeffer summarized Locke's influence in *Church and State in the United States.* "It was the Englishman John Locke who of all modern philosophers carried the most weight among statesmen such as Thomas Jefferson and James Madison, who in turn laid the framework of our civil and religious liberties. He taught that the magistrate had no authority to rule over souls; that religion must depend on inward conviction, not on external compulsion; and that the rights of conscience in matters of personal religious faith must be treated with respect. He believed in government by consent and maintained that liberty, life, and property or 'estate' were inalienable rights, inherent in or natural to every individual, and thus antedated government" (page 4).

3. Thomas Jefferson, letter to John Adams, August 22, 1813, in Lester J. Cappon, *The Adams-Jefferson Letters* (Chapel Hill: University of North Carolina Press, 1959), 367.

4. Jefferson, letter to William Short, August 4, 1820, in Andrew A. Lipscomb and Albert Ellery Bergh, editors, *The Writings of Thomas Jefferson,* Volume 15 (Washington, DC: Thomas Jefferson Memorial Association of the United States, 1907), 257.

5. Jefferson, letter to William Short, April 13, 1820, in Cousins, *In God We Trust,* 150.

6. Jefferson, letter to Francis Van der Kemp, July 30, 1816, in image on Library of Congress website, memory.loc.gov/cgi-bin/query/P?mtj:33:./temp/~ammem_uE79::.
7. Jefferson, letter to James Smith, December 8, 1822, in Cousins, *In God We Trust*, 159.
8. Jefferson, letter to Adams, April 11, 1823, in Cappon, *The Adams-Jefferson Letters*, 591.
9. Jefferson, letter to Salma Hale, July 26, 1818, image on Library of Congress website, memory.loc.gov/cgi-bin/query/P?mtj:1:./temp/~ammem_HJxv::.
10. Jefferson, letter to Thomas Parker, May 15, 1819, image on Library of Congress website, http://memory.loc.gov/cgi-bin/query/P?mtj:11:./temp/~ammem_I482::.
11. Jefferson, letter to Adams, April 11, 1823, in Cappon, *The Adams-Jefferson Letters*, 591.
12. Jefferson, letter to William Short, August 4, 1820, in Andrew A. Lipscomb and Albert Ellery Bergh, editors, *The Writings of Thomas Jefferson*.
13. Jefferson, letter to John Adams, August 22, 1813, in Cappon, *The Adams-Jefferson Letters*, 367.
14. Jefferson, letter to James Fishback, September 27, 1809, in Dickinson W. Adams, editor, *Jefferson's Extracts from the Gospels: "The Philosophy of Jesus" and "The Life and Morals of Jesus"* (Princeton, NJ: Princeton University Press, 1983), 343.
15. Jefferson, letter to Thomas Whitmore, June 5, 1822, in H. A. Washington, editor, *The Writings of Thomas Jefferson*, Volume 7 (Washington, DC: Taylor & Maury, 1854), 245.
16. Jefferson, letter to Samuel Kercheval, January 19, 1810, in Andrew A. Lipscomb and Albert Ellery Bergh, editors, *The Writings of Thomas Jefferson*, Volume 12 (Washington, DC: Thomas Jefferson Memorial Association of the United States, 1903), 345.
17. Jefferson, letter to Elbridge Gerry, March 29, 1801, in Adams, *Jefferson's Extracts*, 16.
18. Jefferson, letter to Charles Thomson, January 9, 1815, in ibid., 364.
19. Jefferson, "Syllabus of an Estimate of the Merit of the Doctrines of Jesus, compared with Those of Others," in Cousins, *In God We Trust*, 169.
20. Jefferson, letter to William Short, August 4, 1820, in Adams, *Jefferson's Extracts*, 394.
21. Jefferson, letter to John Taylor, Philadelphia, June 4, 1798, in Andrew A. Lipscomb and Albert Ellery Bergh, editors, *The Writings of Thomas Jefferson*, Volume 17 (Washington, DC: Thomas Jefferson Memorial Association of the United States, 1907), 205.
22. Jefferson, letter to Marquis de Lafayette, May 14, 1817, in Andrew A. Lipscomb and Albert Ellery Bergh, editors, *The Writings of Thomas Jefferson*, Volume 15 (Thomas Jefferson Memorial Association of the United States, 1905), 114.
23. Jefferson, letter to Horatio G. Spafford, March 17, 1814, in Andrew A. Lipscomb and Albert Ellery Bergh, editors, *The Writings of Thomas Jefferson*, Volume 13 (Washington, DC: Thomas Jefferson Memorial Association of the United States, 1905), 118.
24. Jefferson, letter to Charles Clay, January 29, 1815, in Andrew A. Lipscomb and Albert Ellery Bergh, editors, *The Writings of Thomas Jefferson*, Volume 14 (Washington, DC: Thomas Jefferson Memorial Association of the United States, 1903–04), 232.
25. Jefferson, letter to Jeremiah Moor, August 14, 1800, in *The Works of Thomas Jefferson*, Federal Edition, Volume 9 (New York and London: G. P. Putnam's Sons, 1904–5).
26. Jefferson letter to Dr. Benjamin Rush, September 23, 1800, in Andrew A. Lipscomb and Albert Ellery Bergh, editors, *The Writings of Thomas Jefferson*, Volume 10 (Washington, DC: Thomas Jefferson Memorial Association of the United States, 1907), 173.
27. Jefferson, letter to Levi Lincoln, August 26, 1801, in ibid., 273.
28. Jefferson, letter to William Short, August 4, 1820, in Lipscomb and Bergh, editors, *The Writings of Thomas Jefferson*, Volume 15, 114.
29. Another vivid Jefferson comment about the priests and their antipathy to him came in his letter to Horatio Gates Spafford, January 10, 1816, in Paul Leicester Ford, editor, *The Writings of Thomas Jefferson*, Volume 10 (New York: G. P. Putnam's Sons, 1899), 12: "You judge truly that I am not afraid of the priests. They have tried upon me all their various batteries, of pious whining, hypocritical canting, lying & slandering, without being able to give me one moment of pain. I have contemplated their order from the Magi of the East to the Saints of the West, and I have found no difference of character, but of more or less caution, in proportion to their information or ignorance of those on whom their interested duperies were to be plaid off. Their sway in New England is indeed formidable. No mind beyond mediocrity

dares there to develope itself. If it does, they excite against it the public opinion which they command, & by little, but incessant and teasing persecutions, drive it from among them."

30. Jefferson, letter to Charles Clay, January 29, 1815, in Lipscomb and Bergh, editors, *The Writings of Thomas Jefferson*, Volume 14, 232.

31. Jefferson, letter to Charles Thompson, January 9, 1816, in Lipscomb and Bergh, editors, *The Writings of Thomas Jefferson*, Volume 14, 385.

32. Jefferson, letter to Dr. Benjamin Rush, April 21, 1803, in Adams, *Jefferson's Extracts*, 331. The Jefferson Bible and "The Philosophy of Jesus" have an interesting history. "The Philosophy of Jesus," which Jefferson worked on in the White House, bore the full name "The Philosophy of Jesus of Nazareth, extracted from the account of his life and doctrines as given by Matthew, Mark, Luke & John. Being an abridgement of the New Testament for the use of the Indians unembarrassed with matters of fact or faith beyond the level of their comprehensions." This document has never been found. However, historians did recover the Bibles from which he cut his favorite passages, specifically two editions of the King James Version printed in Dublin, one in 1791 and the other in 1799. These volumes had been held by Jefferson family members and were donated to the University of Virginia in 1913 by Jefferson's great-granddaughter Martha Jefferson Trist Burke. Historians also have a copy of his "Syllabus" and a "table of texts" he created listing parts of the New Testament he thought most important. Dickinson W. Adams, the historian overseeing the project, then found copies of identical Bibles so he could compare those with the cut-up version and determine what phrases had been sliced out and created a reconstruction of "The Philosophy of Jesus," which is printed in Adams, *Jefferson's Extracts*.

   The Jefferson Bible's full title, handwritten by Jefferson in the front pages of his volume, was "The Life and Morals of Jesus of Nazareth, Extracted Textually from the Gospels in Greek, Latin, French and English." He pasted a map of the ancient world and "Holy Land" in the front. Jefferson likely created it in 1820 but kept it a secret from most people. His own family found out about it only after his death. The book came into the possession of his only surviving child, Martha Jefferson Randolph. After her death, the book passed to her son Thomas Jefferson Randolph. He allowed the biographer Henry S. Randall to publish the title page in his biography in 1858, which was when the existence of the Bible first became public. The Bible then passed from one Jefferson ancestor to another until 1895, when Cyrus Adler, the librarian of the Smithsonian, became aware of it when he came across the mutilated English Bibles Jefferson had used. Adler contacted Jefferson's great-granddaughter Carolina Randolph, who at that point held the book. He purchased it for the government for four hundred dollars. Eventually a Republican congressman named John Lacey became aware of it and read the document and arranged for Congress to have it printed in 1904. Apparently, for some fifty years there was a tradition of giving new members of Congress a copy of the Jefferson Bible upon their swearing-in, according to a foreword by William Murchison in an edition of the Jefferson Bible published by American Book Distributors.

33. Jefferson, letter to F. A. Van der Kemp, April 25, 1816, in Lipscomb and Bergh, editors, *The Writings of Thomas Jefferson*, Volume 15, 118.

34. Ibid.

35. Adams, *Jefferson's Extracts*, 26.

36. Ibid., 27.

37. Jefferson, letter to William Short, October 31, 1819, in Ford, editor, *The Writings of Thomas Jefferson*, Volume 10, 143.

38. Adams, *Jefferson's Extracts*, 28.

39. Jefferson, letter to William Short, August 4, 1820, in Lipscomb and Bergh, editors, *The Writings of Thomas Jefferson*, Volume 15, 114.

40. Edwin S. Gaustad, *Sworn on the Altar of God: A Religious Biography of Thomas Jefferson* (Library of Religious Biography Series) (Grand Rapids, MI: Wm. B. Eerdmans, 2001), 129–130.

41. "The Life and Morals of Jesus," in Adams, *Jefferson's Extracts*.

42. Jefferson, letter to Edward Dowse, April 19, 1803, in Lipscomb and Bergh, editors, *The Writings of Thomas Jefferson*, Volume 10, 376.

43. Jefferson, "Syllabus."

44. Jefferson, letter to William Short, August 4, 1820, in Lipscomb et al., editors, *The Writings of Thomas Jefferson*, Volume 15, 114.

45. Jefferson, letter to Dr. Joseph Priestley, April 9, 1803, in Lipscomb and Bergh, editors, *The Writings of Thomas Jefferson*, Volume 10, 374.

46. It was in a letter to Vine Utley, written on March 21, 1819, that Jefferson mentioned his practice of reading moral materials before bed. As Jefferson put tremendous work into the volume and then kept it secret, Dickinson Adams, the editor of *Jefferson's Extracts from the Gospels*, believes "it was undoubtedly one of the works on morality that he read each evening, for, with the exception of a single important point of doctrine, it was the one in which he finally established to his ultimate satisfaction the authentic deeds and principles of the man he esteemed as the mater moral perceptor of the ages" (page 38).

47. Jefferson, letter to Dr. Benjamin Waterhouse, June 26, 1822, in Bergh, editor, *The Writings of Thomas Jefferson*, Volume 15, 383.

48. Jefferson, letter to Edward Dowse, April 19, 1803, in Lipscomb and Bergh, editors, *The Writings of Thomas Jefferson*, Volume 10, 376.

49. Jefferson, letter to John Adams, August 22, 1813, in Lipscomb and Bergh, editors, *The Writings of Thomas Jefferson*, Volume 13, 376.

50. Jefferson, letter to Levi Lincoln, April 26, 1803, in Paul Leicester Ford, editor, *The Works of Thomas Jefferson*, Federal Edition, Volume 9 (New York and London: G. P. Putnam's Sons, 1904–5).

51. Jefferson, letter to Margaret Bayard Smith, August 6, 1816, in Lipscomb and Bergh, editors, *The Writings of Thomas Jefferson*, Volume 15, 61.

52. Kennedy, *What They Believed*, 36–37.

53. LaHaye, *Faith of Our Founding Fathers*, 13.

54. Jefferson, First Inaugural Address, March 4, 1801.

55. Thomas Jefferson, "First Annual Message to Congress," December 8, 1801, *Addresses, Messages, and Replies, Jefferson, Thomas, 1743–1826*, University of Virginia Library Electronic Text Center.

56. Thomas Jefferson, "Second Annual Message to Congress," December 15, 1802, *Avalon Project*: Jefferson: Reports to Congress (2nd), www.yale.edu/lawweb/avalon/presiden/sou/jeffmes2.htm.

57. Jefferson, letter to Eliza Trist, December 11, 1788, in Lenni Brenner, editor, *Jefferson and Madison on the Separation of Church and State* (Fort Lee, NJ: Barricade Books, 2004), 159.

58. Jefferson, letter to John Page, July 15, 1763, in Albert Ellery Bergh, editor, *The Writings of Thomas Jefferson*, Volume 4 (Washington, DC: Thomas Jefferson Memorial Association of the United States, 1904), 10.

59. Jefferson, letter to the Reverend John Hargrove, March 11, 1801, in Brenner, editor, *Jefferson and Madison on Separation of Church and State*, 159.

60. Jefferson, letter to George Ticknor, November 25, 1817, in Lipscomb and Bergh, editors, *The Writings of Thomas Jefferson*, Volume 10, 95.

61. Jefferson, letter to Peter Carr, August 10, 1787, in Andrew A. Lipscomb and Albert Ellery Bergh, editors, *The Writings of Thomas Jefferson*, Volume 5 (Washington, DC: Thomas Jefferson Memorial Association of the United States, 1904), 326.

62. Jefferson, *Notes on the State of Virginia*, University of Virginia Electronic Text Center, 285.

63. Ibid.

64. Jefferson, letter to John Adams, April 11, 1823, in Lipscomb and Bergh, editors, *The Writings of Thomas Jefferson*, Volume 15, 426.

65. Jefferson, letter to Ezra Stiles Ely, June 25, 1819, Library of Congress website, image 653.

9. *Nature's God Meets the Supreme Judge*

1. Benjamin Rush, letter to John Adams, recounted in McCullough, *John Adams*, 113–114.

2. Alan M. Dershowitz, *America Declares Independence* (Hoboken, NJ: John Wiley & Sons, 2003), 64.

3. "A Day of Fasting, Humiliation and Prayer, with a total abstinence from labor and recreation: Proclamation on April 15, 1775," quoted in William J. Federer, editor, *America's God and Country: Encyclopedia of Quotations* (St. Louis: Amerisearch, 1995), 275.

4. Constitution of Delaware (1776), Article Twenty-two.

5. John Witherspoon, "The Absolute Necessity of Salvation Through Christ" (January 2, 1758), in *The Works of John Witherspoon* (Edinburgh: J. Ogle, 1815), Volume 5, 276, 278.

6. Thanksgiving Proclamation, Continental Congress, November 1, 1777, The Library of Congress *American Memory* collection, memory.loc.gov/ammem/index.html.

7. Samuel Adams, "Proclamation for a Day of Public Thanksgiving," October 17, 1796, in Harry Alonzo Cushing, editor, *The Writings of Samuel Adams*, Volume 4 (1722–1803) (Boston: James R. Osgood and Company, 1883).

8. John Adams, letter to Abigail Adams, July 3, 1776, *Adams Family Papers*.

9. Pauline Maier in *American Scripture: Making the Declaration of Independence* (New York: Alfred A. Knopf, 1997) speculates that it's Richard Henry Lee.

10. Michael Novak, "God's Country *or* Taking the Declaration Seriously," Francis Boyer Lecture, Washington Hilton, February 25, 1999.

11. John Adams, letter to Abigail Adams, September 16, 1774, *Adams Family Papers*.

12. Metzger, *Catholics and the American Revolution*, 186.

13. Ibid., 185.

14. Quoted in Stokes and Pfeffer, *Church and State*, 85. They source it to Ray Allen Billington, "American Catholicism and the Church–State Issue," *Christendom* 3 (1940), quoted in James M. O'Neill, *Religion and Education Under the Constitution* (Cambridge, MA: Da Capo Press, 1972), 33.

15. Thomas Jefferson, letter to Roger C. Weightman, June 24, 1826, *Thomas Jefferson Letters*.

16. There is one other more literal way in which the Declaration dealt with religious liberty. In the litany of charges against King George, the document declared that he had approved legislation "for abolishing the free system of English laws in a neighboring province, establishing therein an arbitrary government, and enlarging its boundaries so as to render it at once an example & fit instrument for introducing the same absolute rule into these states." Historian Pauline Maier says in *American Scripture* that this is a reference to the passage of the Quebec Act of 1774 (page 118).

17. From "Jefferson, a Summary View of the Rights of British America," resolution before the Virginia House of Burgesses, July 1774.

18. The full passage is in *Notes on the State of Virginia*: "And can the liberties of a nation be thought secure when we have removed their only firm basis, a conviction in the minds of the people that these liberties are of the gift of God? That they are not to be violated but with his wrath? Indeed I tremble for my country when I reflect that God is just: that his justice cannot sleep for ever: that considering numbers, nature and natural means only, a revolution of the wheel of fortune, an exchange of situation, is among possible events: that it may become probable by supernatural interference! The Almighty has no attribute which can take side with us in such a contest. — But it is impossible to be temperate and to pursue this subject through the various considerations of policy, of morals, of history natural and civil. We must be contented to hope they will force their way into every one's mind. I think a change already perceptible, since the origin of the present revolution. The spirit of the master is abating, that of the slave rising from the dust, his condition mollifying, the way I hope preparing, under the auspices of heaven, for a total emancipation, and that this is disposed, in the order of events, to be with the consent of the masters, rather than by their extirpation."

19. Thomas Paine, *The Rights of Man*, part 7 of 16, www.ushistory.org/paine/rights/index.htm.

10. *James Madison*

1. Irving Brant, *James Madison: The Virginia Revolutionist* (Indianapolis: Bobbs-Merrill, 1941), 52; Ralph Louis Ketcham, *James Madison: A Biography* (New York: Macmillan, 1971), 13.

2. Brant, *Virginia Revolutionist*, 57.

3. Ketcham, *Madison: A Biography*, 26. Brant, *Virginia Revolutionist*, 59.

4. Brant, *Virginia Revolutionist*, 60.

5. Madison is quoted from his "Autobiography," 197, in Douglass Adair, "James Madison's Autobiography," *William and Mary Quarterly*, 3rd Series, Volume 2, Number 2 (April 1945), 191–209.

6. Ketcham, *Madison: A Biography*, 23.

7. Brant, *Virginia Revolutionist*, 69.

8. Ibid., 70–71.

9. Ketcham, *Madison: A Biography*, 30.

10. From Witherspoon's sermon "The Dominion of Providence Over the Passions of Men," delivered in May 1776, Liberty Fund, oll.libertyfund.org/Texts/LFBooks/Sandoz0385/HTMLs/0018_Pt03_Part2.html.

11. Witherspoon, "The Dominion of Providence." One crucial part of evangelicalism that Witherspoon did retain was the emphasis on the individual. "Witherspoon's evangelical Presbyterianism proclaimed that the supreme good for each person was to find a faith that would give him victory over death." Therefore each person had to make something of life, emphasize humanitarian projects, and be aware that nations would be "held accountable to the final judgment." His sermons emphasized the Law of Love and good works. Topics included "the nature and Extent of Disciple Religion," "Let your light so shine before men that they may see your good works," and "The Trial of Religious truth by Its Moral Influence." Ketcham, *Madison: A Biography*, 47.

12. Ketcham, *Madison: A Biography*, 43. Some Christian commentators have concluded that since Witherspoon was a devout Christian, he therefore wanted "a Christian commonwealth"; see "John Witherspoon: The Forgotten Founding Father," a lecture by Arthur Herman posted on the website of the Family Research Council, www.frc.org/get.cfm?i=WT03K02 (accessed May 2007). As a Scot, however, Witherspoon viscerally opposed the Anglican Church and viewed the establishment of an official religion in the United States as conflicting with religious freedom. In addition, according to historian William Lee Miller, "One of the topics on the Princeton graduation exercises the year before Madison graduated, for just one example, was support for the proposition that 'every religious profession, which does not by its principles disturb the public peace, ought to be tolerated by a wise state.'" William Lee Miller, *First Liberty: America's Foundation in Religious Freedom* (Washington, DC: Georgetown University Press, 2003), 77.

13. Brant, *Virginia Revolutionist*, 114.

14. Ibid., 115.

15. Ibid.

16. James Madison, letter to William Bradford, April 1, 1774.

17. James Madison, "A Poem Against the Tories" (1771), quoted in *Virginia Revolutionist*, 87.

18. Ketcham, *Madison: A Biography*, 54.

19. Ibid., 48. Until recently, it looked as if some Madison writings indicated that, at the end of the day, it was a biblical worldview that animated his government philosophy. A number of conservative Christian books, including David Barton, *The Myth of Separation: What Is the Correct Relationship Between Church and State?* (Aledo, TX: WallBuilder Press, 1992), had quoted Madison as saying, "We have staked the whole future of American civilization, not upon the power of government, far from it. We have staked the future of all of our political institutions upon the capacity of each and all of us to govern ourselves according to the Ten Commandments of God." But it turns out that Madison never said such a thing, and Barton had to issue a retraction.

20. Ketcham, *Madison: A Biography*, 49.

21. Madison, letter to William Bradford, November 9, 1772, ibid.

22. Madison, letter to William Bradford, December 1, 1773.

23. Madison, letter to William Bradford Jr., September 25, 1773. This is a reference to Hebrews 12:1–2, which recalls the ancient prophets and then says, "Therefore, since we are sur-

rounded by so great a cloud of witnesses, let us also lay aside every weight, and sin which clings so closely, and let us run with perseverance the race that is set before us, looking to Jesus the pioneer and perfecter of our faith."

24. Brant, *Virginia Revolutionist*, 118.
25. Madison, letter to William Bradford, November 9, 1772.
26. Madison, letter to F. L. Schaeffer, December 3, 1821.
27. Madison, letter to the Reverend Jasper Adams, 1832, *James Madison Papers*, image 1175.
28. Madison, "Memorial and Remonstrance," reprinted in Philip B. Kurland and Ralph Lerner, editors, *The Founders' Constitution*, Document 43, press-pubs.uchicago.edu/founders/documents/amendI_religions43.html.
29. Madison, letter to Frederick Beasley, November 20, 1825.
30. James Madison, "Who Are the Best Keepers of the People's Liberties?" *National Gazette* (December 22, 1792). In Gaillard Hunt, editor, *The Writings of James Madison, Comprising His Public Papers and His Private Correspondence, Including His Numerous Letters and Documents Now for the First Time Printed* (New York: G. P. Putnam's Sons, 1900), Volume 6.

11. *"A Diabolical Persecution"*

1. Madison, letter to William Bradford, January 24, 1774.
2. Ketcham, *Madison: A Biography*, 58.
3. Lewis Peyton Little, *Imprisoned Preachers and Religious Liberty in Virginia* (Lynchburg, VA: J. P. Bell Company, Inc., 1938), 155.
4. Ibid., 230–231 and 404–408.
5. Ibid., 339–342.
6. Ibid., 461.
7. Ibid., 442.
8. Ibid., 135–140.
9. Ibid., 369.
10. Ibid., 207.
11. Ibid., 261.
12. L. H. Butterfield, "Elder John Leland, Jeffersonian Itinerant," *American Antiquarian Society Proceedings* 62, 1952, in William L. Lumpkin, *Colonial Baptists and Southern Revivals* (New York: Arno Press, 1980), 172.
13. Ibid., 181.
14. Little, *Imprisoned Preachers*, 69.
15. Ibid., 67.
16. Ibid., 68
17. Ibid., 147.
18. Ibid., 68.
19. Miller, *First Liberty*, 8.
20. Rhys Isaac, " 'The Rage of Malice of the Old Serpent Devil': The Dissenters and the Making and Remaking of the Virginia Statute for Religious Freedom," in Peterson and Vaughan, *Virginia Statute*, 142.
21. James Madison, letter to William Bradford, January 24, 1774.
22. Little, *Imprisoned Preachers*, 131.
23. The document is held by the Library of Congress, and an image of it is found on the Library of Congress website, memory.loc.gov/master/mss/mjm/27/0200/0222.jpg (accessed May 2007).
24. Little, *Imprisoned Preachers*, 346.
25. Ibid., 389.
26. Mayer, *Son of Thunder*, 158.
27. Ibid., 159.
28. Madison, letter to William Bradford, January 24, 1774.
29. Madison, letter to William Bradford, December 1, 1773.

30. Ketcham, *Madison: A Biography*, 27.
31. Madison, letter to William Bradford, April 1, 1774.

12. *The Mighty Current of Freedom*

1. Congress referred to it as a "new constellation" in the Flag Act.
2. Davis, *Religion and the Continental Congress*, 138.
3. Ibid., 138–139.
4. A similar division was revealed in a debate over whether the Congress should pay for the publication of Bibles. Because most Bibles had been imported from England, the colonies found themselves with an acute shortage. Some members of Congress, including John Adams, proposed that Congress pay for the printing and distribution of Bibles. Congress was nearly evenly divided on the issue, with New Hampshire, Massachusetts, Connecticut, Rhode Island, New Jersey, Pennsylvania, and Georgia in favor, and New York, Delaware, North Carolina, Virginia, and Maryland opposed—and it tabled the idea. In 1782, Congress did authorize (though didn't pay for) creation of a Bible published by a Philadelphia printer named Robert Aitken. Derek Davis (ibid.) has surmised that "Congress probably did not perceive the project as an improper advancement of religion. It did, however, seem to view as one its primary responsibilities the preservation of the liberty of the various states in things pertaining to religion. Therefore, it is more likely that Congress believed that because of the likelihood that the Aitken Bible would not appeal to all citizens of the various states, it would be an infringement upon the states' liberty for Congress, which represented all of the states, to expend the monies required to publish the needed Bibles" (page 148).
5. Adams, letter to Abigail Adams, July 12, 1775, in *Adams Family Papers*.
6. Congressional Thanksgiving Day Proclamation, November 1, 1777.
7. Section 14, Article 1, of the Northwest Ordinance stated: "No person, demeaning himself in a peaceable and orderly manner, shall ever be molested on account of his mode of worship or religious sentiments, in the said territory." Section 14, Article 3, stated: "Religion, morality, and knowledge, being necessary to good government and the happiness of mankind, schools and the means of education shall forever be encouraged."
8. "Report on Letters from the Ministers in Paris," Continental Congress, December 20, 1783, quoted in ibid., 86.
9. Gaustad and Noll, *Documentary History*, 206.
10. Chadwick, *George Washington's War*, 214.
11. Ibid., 235. The army therefore seized the meetinghouse.
12. Another issue that forced the Continental Congress to declare its collective philosophy on religious liberty was the addition of new land. The Treaty of Paris gave America the Northwest Territory. To ensure that the nation would be able to retain hold of the area, congressmen urgently wanted to populate it. They concluded that religious freedom was a major draw, and in a reflection of the idea that encouraging religion meant supporting religion, they ruled, as noted above, "Religion, morality and knowledge, being necessary to good government and the happiness of mankind, schools and the means of education shall forever be encouraged."
13. Edward Frank Humphrey, *Nationalism and Religion in America 1774–1789* (New York: Russell and Russell, 1965), 147.
14. Ibid., 151.
15. Lambert, *Founding Fathers*, 220.
16. Heimert, *Religion and the American Mind*, 391.
17. In New York, the Constitutional Convention moved toward the free exercise of religion in 1777—after first rejecting, nineteen to ten, an amendment by John Jay that would have excepted "the professors of the religion of the Church of Rome" and banning clergy from holding office on the ground that they ought not be "diverted from their great duties" tending the flock. See Stokes and Pfeffer, *Church and State*, 73. The South Carolina constitution of 1778 declared Protestantism to be the official religion of the state, adding that in

order for a church to be incorporated, its members must agree "that there is one eternal God, and a future state of rewards and punishments." Ibid., 79, and *Avalon Project.*

18. Robert J. Taylor, editor, *Massachusetts, Colony to Commonwealth: Documents on the Formation of the Constitution, 1775–1780* (Chapel Hill: University of North Carolina Press, 1961), 113.

19. Ibid., 128. The document stated:

> As the happiness of a people, and the good order and preservation of civil government, essentially depend upon piety, religion and morality; and as these cannot be generally diffused through a community, but by the institution of the public worship of GOD, and of public instructions in piety, religion and morality: Therefore to promote their happiness, and to secure the good order and preservation of their government, the people of this Commonwealth have a right to invest their legislature with power to authorize and require, and the legislature shall, from time to time, authorize and require, the several towns, parishes, precincts, and other bodies politic, or religious societies, to make suitable provision, at their own expense, for the institution of the public worship of GOD, and for the support and maintenance of public protestant teachers of piety, religion and morality, in all cases where such provision shall not be made voluntarily.
>
> And the people of this Commonwealth have also a right to, and do, invest their legislature with authority to enjoin upon all subjects an attendance upon the instructions of the public teachers aforesaid, at stated times and seasons, if there be any on whose instructions they can conscientiously and conveniently attend.
>
> Provided notwithstanding, that the several towns, parishes, precincts, and other bodies politic, or religious societies, shall, at all times, have the exclusive right of electing their public teachers, and of contracting with them for their support and maintenance.
>
> And all monies paid by the subject to the support of public worship, and of the public teachers aforesaid, shall, if he require it, be uniformly applied to the support of the public teacher or teachers of his own religious sect or denomination, provided there be any on whose instructions he attends; otherwise it may be paid towards the support of the teacher or teachers of the parish or precinct in which the said monies are raised.
>
> And every denomination of Christians, demeaning themselves peaceably, and as good subjects of the Commonwealth, shall be equally under the protection of the law; And no subordination of any one sect or denomination to another shall ever be established by law.

20. John T. Noonan Jr., "Quota of Imps," in Peterson and Vaughan, *Virginia Statute,* 180.

21. John Leland mocked this provision by arguing, "Should not government protect all kinds of people, of every species of religion, without showing the least partiality? Has not the world had enough proofs of the impolicy and cruelty of favoring a Jew more than a Pagan, Turk or Christian; or a Christian more than either of them? Why should a man be proscribed, or . . . disgraced, for being a Jew, a Turk, a Pagan, or a Christian of any denomination, when his talents and veracity as a civilian, entitle him to the confidence of the public." Butterfield, "Elder John Leland," 210.

22. As William McLoughlin noted in his essay "The Role of Religion," the precise approaches differed as to "whether the tax was to be laid by the local unit (parish or town) or by the state legislature, whether it was to support Christianity generally or only Protestant Christianity, and whether it was to support only 'learned' ministers or any minister" (Kurtz and Hutson, *Essays on the American Revolution,* 214). Significantly, even when states directly supported religion, they preferred doing so through the churches and ministers as opposed to denom-

inational organizations. Doing the latter would have smacked more of colonial-style establishment.

23. Taylor, *Colony to Commonwealth*, 150.
24. Noonan, in Peterson and Vaughan, *Virginia Statute*, 171.
25. Noonan, in ibid., 176.
26. Noonan, in ibid. This was, by the way, consistent with John Locke, who excluded atheists from office because they denied the foundation of government, and Catholics because they "subordinated the state to the pope."
27. Noonan, in ibid., 191.
28. Constitution of Pennsylvania, September 28, 1776, in *Avalon Project*.
29. Franklin, letter to Richard Price, October 9, 1780, *The Papers of Benjamin Franklin*.
30. Morton Borden, *Jews, Turks, and Infidels*. (Chapel Hill: University of North Carolina Press, 1984), 11.
31. Brenner, *Jefferson and Madison*, 39.
32. Brant, *Virginia Revolutionist*, 244. The original draft is in the Library of Congress.
33. Madison, "Autobiography," 199.
34. Brant, *Virginia Revolutionist*, 246. The full text reads: "That Religion or the duty we owe to our Creator, and the manner of discharging it, can be directed only by reason and conviction; not by force or violence; and therefore, that all men are equally entitled to the free exercise of religion, according to the dictates of conscience, unpunished, and unrestrained by the magistrate, unless the preservation of equal liberty and the existence of the State are manifestly endangered. And that is the mutual duty of all, to practice Christian forbearance, love and charity towards each other."
35. Madison, "Autobiography," JPEG at *James Madison Papers*, memory.loc.gov/ammem/collections/madison_papers/index.html.
36. Robert Rutland, "James Madison's Dream: A Secular Republic," in Robert S. Alley, editor, *James Madison on Religious Liberty* (Buffalo, NY: Prometheus Books, 1985), 201.
37. Willison, *Patrick Henry and His World*, 383.
38. And it was a liberal reform being employed in several states. In his essay "Role of Religion" (Kurtz and Hutson, *Essays on the American Revolution*), William McLoughlin summarized the landscape. The Maryland Declaration of Rights in 1776 declared, after promising religious liberty, "Yet, the legislature may, in their discretion, lay a general and equal tax for the support of the Christian religion, leaving each individual the power of appointing the payment over of the money collected from him to the support of any particular place of worship or minister or for the benefit of the poor." The Maryland plan exempted any "Jew or Mohamedan who made a declaration of his belief before two justices" (page 223). The four New England states (and the District of Maine) "transformed their old Congregational establishments into general-assessment systems for the support of Protestant churches during the Revolutionary years" (page 214). Significantly, even when states directly supported religion, they preferred doing so through the churches and ministers as opposed to denominational organizations.

The theologically most explicit constitution was that of South Carolina, passed in 1778, which required that Protestant churches, to be officially sanctioned, needed to subscribe to this creed: "1st. That there is one eternal God, and a future state of rewards and punishments. 2d. That God is publicly to be worshipped. 3d. That the Christian religion is the true religion. 4th. That the holy scriptures of the Old and New Testaments are of divine inspiration and are the rule of faith and practice. 5th. That it is lawful and the duty of every man being thereunto called by those that govern, to bear witness to the truth." The southern states in particular were watching the Virginia outcome closely, noted McLoughlin. "Had the debates on this plan in Maryland and Virginia produced a majority in favor, doubtless other states would have followed their examples."

39. H. J. Eckenrode, *Separation of Church and State in Virginia* (Richmond, VA: Department of Archives and History, 1910), 75.
40. Ibid., 105.

41. Alley, *Madison on Religious Liberty*, 55.
42. James Madison, letter to James Madison Sr., January 6, 1785, in Robert Rutland and William Rachel, editors, *The Papers of James Madison*, Volume 8 (Chicago: University of Chicago Press, 1973), 217.
43. Madison, letter to James Monroe, April 12, 1785, quoted in Alley, *Madison on Religious Liberty*, 67.
44. Marvin K. Singleton, "Colonial Virginia as First Amendment Matrix: Henry, Madison, and Assessment Establishment," in ibid., 163.
45. Thomas Jefferson, letter to Madison, December 8, 1784, quoted in ibid., 65.
46. Madison, letter to Jefferson, August 20, 1785, in James Morton Smith, editor, *The Republic of Letters*, Volume 1 (New York: W. W. Norton, 1995), 374.
47. Jefferson, letter to Madison, December 8, 1784, quoted in Alley, *Madison on Religious Liberty*, 65.
48. Ketcham, *Madison: A Biography*, 163.
49. Madison, letter to James Monroe, November 27, 1784, in Gaillard Hunt, editor, *The Writings of James Madison*, Volume 2, (New York: G. P. Putnam's Sons, 1901), 94.
50. Little, *Imprisoned Preachers*, 487.
51. Ibid.
52. The petition is copied from Thomas J. Curry, *Farewell to Christendom: The Future of Church and State in America* (New York: Oxford University Press, 2001), 123–124. Prince George County Petition, November 28, 1785.
53. Rhys Isaac, " 'The Rage of Malice of the Old Serpent Devil': The Dissenters and the Making and Remaking of the Virginia Statute for Religious Freedom," in Peterson and Vaughan, *Virginia Statute*, 152.
54. Eckenrode, *Separation of Church and State*, 108.
55. Ibid.
56. Isaac, " 'The Rage of Malice of the Old Serpent Devil,' " 150.
57. Miller, *First Liberty*, 39.
58. Madison, letter to Jefferson, January 22, 1786, in Hunt, *Writings of James Madison*, 214.
59. Willison, *Patrick Henry and His World*, 380.
60. Eckenrode, *Separation of Church and State*, 111–112.
61. Miller, *First Liberty*, 50.
62. Stokes and Pfeffer, *Church and State*, 70. The full quote is: "That truth is great and will prevail if left to herself; that she is the proper and sufficient antagonist to error, and has nothing to fear from the conflict unless by human interposition disarmed of her natural weapons, free argument and debate; errors ceasing to be dangerous when it is permitted freely to contradict them."
63. Jefferson's autobiography, in *Avalon Project*.
64. James Madison, "Monopolies Perpetuities Corporations Ecclesiastical Endowments," quoted in Alley, *Madison on Religious Liberty*, 89.
65. One final dispute over religious freedom illustrates the differences between Jefferson and Madison. In 1788, Jefferson had proposed that the Virginia constitution ban clergy from holding public office. New York, North Carolina, South Carolina, Maryland, and Georgia had similar laws, New York's explaining that clergymen should be "dedicated to the service of god and the cure of souls, and ought not to be diverted from the greater duties of their function." This was viewed as a sensible way of keeping church and state separate and preventing one denomination from dominating state politics. But Madison, despite being second to none in his desire to keep church and state apart, opposed the idea in Jefferson's draft of the Virginia constitution. He thought that it threatened religious freedom. "Does not the exclusion of Ministers of the Gospel as such violate a fundamental principle of liberty by punishing a religious profession with the privation of a civil right," he wrote in a letter labeled "Remarks on Mr. Jefferson's draught of a constitution." "Does it [not] violate another article of the plan itself which exempts religion from the cognizance of Civil power? Does it not violate justice by at once taking away a right and prohibiting a compen-

sation for it?" Jefferson seemed more focused on checking the power of the clergy; Madison, on the principle of freedom. Stokes and Pfeffer, *Church and State*, 160.

66. Butterfield, "Elder John Leland," 199.

13. Forgetting the "Powerful Friend"

1. William G. Carr, *The Oldest Delegate: Franklin in the Constitutional Convention* (Newark: University of Delaware Press, 1990), 96.
2. From James Madison, "The Debates in the Convention of 1787," *Avalon Project*.
3. Isaac Kramnick and R. Laurence Moore, *The Godless Constitution: A Moral Defense of the Secular State* (New York: W. W. Norton, 1997), 34.
4. Carr, *Oldest Delegate*, 99. Hamilton reportedly declared that they were "competent to transact the business and . . . he did not see the necessity of calling in foreign aid," according to another account. But some historians note that this was a secondhand account that seemed an attempt to injure Hamilton's reputation. Roger Sherman disagreed. "Past omission of a duty could not justify a further omission," he said—and surely the benefits outweighed the risks.
5. Ibid., 97. In 1787, the denominational breakdown was as follows:

Religious Affiliation	Number of Delegates
Episcopalian/Anglican	31
Presbyterian	16
Congregationalist	8
Quaker	3
Catholic	2
Methodist	2
Lutheran	2
Dutch Reformed	2

    From www.adherents.com/gov/Founding_Fathers_Religion.html (accessed May 2007). The total is more than 55, the number of delegates, because several were affiliated with more than one denomination.
6. Stokes and Pfeffer, *Church and State*, 84.
7. Ibid., 9; www.yale.edu/lawweb/avalon/debates/914.htm#17.
8. The Records of the Federal Convention of 1787 (Farrand's Records, Volume 3), Appendix D, The Pinckney Plan, memory.loc.gov/cgi-bin/query/r?ammem/hlaw:@field(DOCID +@lit(fr003446)): (accessed May 2007).
9. Leonard W. Levy, *The Establishment Clause: Religion and the First Amendment*, second edition (Chapel Hill: University of North Carolina Press, 1994), 80.
10. Ibid., 80.
11. James Madison, *Notes of Debates in the Federal Convention of 1787 Reported by James Madison* (New York: W. W. Norton, 1987), 561.
12. Stokes and Pfeffer, *Church and State*, 91.
13. Kramnick and Moore, *The Godless Constitution*, 27.
14. Ibid., 45.
15. In an interesting historical footnote, the Constitution of the Confederacy, which was based almost entirely on the US Constitution, did make a few changes. One of them was to add to its preamble the line, "invoking the favor and guidance of Almighty God." Miller, *First Liberty*, 99.
16. James Madison, letter to Thomas Jefferson, October 24, 1787, *James Madison Papers*, image 1580.
17. Ibid. And in his own notes at the Constitutional Convention, Madison recorded himself as having said, "Conscience, the only remaining tie, is known to be inadequate in individuals: In large numbers, little is to be expected from it. Besides, Religion itself may become a motive to persecution & oppression. —These observations are verified by the Histories of every Country antient & modern." James Madison, "The Debates in the Convention of 1787: June 6," *Avalon Project*.

18. Madison, letter to George Washington, April 16, 1787, press-pubs.uchicago.edu/founders/documents/v1ch8s6.html.

19. Jack N. Rakove, *Original Meanings: Politics and Ideas in the Making of the Constitution* (New York: Vintage Books, 1997), 169.

20. Madison, letter to Jefferson, September 6, 1787, Library of Congress website, image number 551.

21. Levy, *Establishment Clause*, 77–78.

22. Stokes and Pfeffer, *Church and State*, 444.

23. Levy, *Establishment Clause*, 77–78.

24. Kramnick and Moore, *Godless Constitution*, 33.

25. Ibid., 35.

26. Ibid., 36.

27. William Williams, letter to the *American Mercury*, February 11, 1788. It was also published in *The Connecticut Courant* on March 3, 1788. Philip B. Kurland and Ralph Lerner, editors, *The Founders' Constitution* (Indianapolis: Liberty Fund and University of Chicago, 1987), Volume 4, Article 6, Clause 3, Document 21.

28. Curry, *First Freedoms*, 195.

29. Luther Martin, "Genuine Information," 1788, in Kurland and Lerner, *Founders' Constitution*, Volume 4, Article 6, Clause 3, Document 18.

30. Samuel Bannister Harding, *The Contest Over the Ratification of the Federal Constitution in the State of Massachusetts* (New York: Longmans, Green and Co, 1896), 70. Another delegate said reports were afoot that the pope could be elected president.

31. Debate in the North Carolina Ratifying Convention, July 30, 1788, in Kurland and Lerner, *Founders' Constitution*, Volume 5, Amendment I, Document 52.

32. Kramnick and Moore, *Godless Constitution*, 33.

33. Isaac Backus, *A History of New England Baptists* (Newton, MA: Backus Historical Society, 1871).

34. "The Federal Procession of 1788," talk delivered to the quarterly meeting of the Carpenters' Company, July 20, 1987, by John C. Van Horne, librarian, Library Company of Philadelphia, www.ushistory.org/carpentershall/history/procession.htm (accessed May 2007).

35. Washington, letter to Presbyterian Church leaders of northern New England, *The Massachusetts Centinel*, December 5, 1789, in Stokes and Pfeffer, *Church and State*, 92.

36. James Wilson, speech to the Pennsylvania State House, October 6, 1787, in Bernard Bailyn, editor, *The Debate on the Constitution*, Part I (New York: Library of America, 1993), 63.

37. Noah Webster ("America"), "Reply to the Pennsylvania Minority," New York *Daily Advertiser*, December 31, 1787, in Bailyn, *The Debate on the Constitution*, 559.

38. Bailyn, "Debate in North Carolina Ratifying Convention, July 30, 1788," in Kurland and Lerner, *Founders' Constitution*, Volume 5, Amendment I, Document 52.

39. New York ratifying convention, July 26, 1788, in Levy, *Establishment Clause*, 91.

40. Ketcham, *Madison: A Biography*, 249.

41. Curry, *First Freedoms*, 195.

42. James Madison Sr., letter to James Madison, January 30, 1788, in Butterfield, "Elder John Leland," 184.

43. Captain Joseph Spencer, letter to Madison, February 28, 1788, in ibid., 186.

44. James H. Smylie, "Protestant Clergy, the First Amendment and Beginnings of a Constitutional Debate, 1781–1791," in Elwyn A. Smith, editor, *The Religion of the Republic* (Philadelphia: Fortress Press, 1971), 120.

45. Ketcham, *Madison: A Biography*, 250; Joseph Martin Dawson, *Baptists and the American Republic* (Nashville: Broadman Press, 1956), 103–117. This meeting has become the stuff of legend. There are now plaques and statues at the spot where Madison and Leland supposedly met. According to Dawson, one account of the meeting came from Eugene Bucklin Bowen of Cheshire, Massachusetts, where Leland later lived. "It was a battle royal," claimed Bowen, "with Leland insisting that there should be an article in the Constitution guaranteeing religious liberty. Madison, however, was afraid to put it in on account of the

opposition of some of the colonies, Massachusetts in particular." Another account by Governor George Briggs says that Leland dropped out not as a result of this meeting but after Madison had "made a two-hour speech from a 'hogshead of tobacco, standing on an end' at the picnic grounds."

46. Stokes and Pfeffer, *Church and State*, 354.
47. Mayer, *Son of Thunder*, 433, citing Hugh Blair Grigsby, a nineteenth-century historian. Grigsby's description can be found in footnote 142 on p. 157 in his book, *The History of the Virginia Federal Convention of 1788*, written in the 1850s: "I was told by a person on the floor of the Convention at the time, that when Henry had painted in the most vivid colors the dangers likely to result to the black population from the unlimited power of the general government, wielded by men who had little or no interest in that species of property, and had filled his audience with fear, he suddenly broke out with the homely exclamation: 'They'll free your niggers!' The audience passed instantly from fear to wayward laughter; and my informant said that it was most ludicrous to see men who a moment before were half frightened to death, with a broad grin on their faces." The substance of the comments about slavery is paraphrased in *Debates in the Several State Conventions on the Adoption of the Federal Constitution*, edited by Jonathan Elliot (Philadelphia: J. B. Lippincott Company, 1891). Elliot paraphrases Henry's comments about "negroes" on June 17, 1788, but does not describe the reactions from the other delegates.
48. Patrick Henry, "Virginia Ratifying Convention," June 5, 1788, press-pubs.uchicago.edu/founders/documents/v1ch8s38.html.
49. Brant, *Virginia Revolutionist*, 100. He notes that the recorder several times wrote, "Here Mr. Madison spoke so low that he could not be distinctly heard."
50. George W. Carey, *In Defense of the Constitution* (Indianapolis: Liberty Fund, 1995), quoted in Alley, *Madison on Religious Liberty*, 71.
51. Ketcham, *Madison: A Biography*, 263.
52. Rakove, *Original Meanings*, 125.
53. Jefferson, letter to Madison, December 20, 1787, quoted in Jack N. Rakove, *Declaring Rights: A Brief History with Documents* (New York: Bedford/St. Martin's Press, 1997), 156.
54. Madison, letter to Jefferson, October 17, 1788, quoted in ibid., 161.
55. Madison, letter to Jefferson, October 17, 1788, in Kurland and Lerner, *Founders' Constitution*, Chapter 17, Document 22.
56. Jefferson, letter to Madison, March 15, 1789, in ibid., Chapter 14, Document 49.

14. The First Amendment Compromise

1. Richard Labunski, *James Madison and the Struggle for the Bill of Rights* (New York: Oxford University Press, 2006), 137.
2. Ibid., 129. The eight counties thrown together had been represented by sixteen delegates to the ratification convention, and of those sixteen only five had voted to ratify the Constitution.
3. Labunski, *James Madison and the Struggle*, 140.
4. He is pictured directly behind Washington in the famous Emmanuel Leutze painting.
5. Labunski, *James Madison and the Struggle*, 142.
6. Lance Banning, *The Sacred Fire of Liberty: James Madison and the Founding of the Federal Republic* (Ithaca, NY: Cornell University Press, 1995), 271.
7. Madison, "Autobiography," 199. "The consequence," he wrote in the third person, "was that the election went against him; his abstinence being represented as the effect of pride or parsimony."
8. As he told George Washington, "I have for some time past been much indisposed with the piles. They have not yet entirely gone off; and may possibly detain me for some days longer." Labunski, *James Madison*, 144.
9. Ibid., 146.
10. David Jameson Jr., letter to Madison, January 18, 1789, in ibid., 157.

11. James Madison, letter to George Washington, January 14, 1789, in Hunt, *Writings of James Madison*, Volume 4, 318.
12. Labunski, *James Madison*, 162.
13. Madison, letter to George Eve, January 2, 1789, in Hunt, *Writings of James Madison*, Volume 5, 319.
14. Ibid., 320.
15. Brant, *Virginia Revolutionist*, 241.
16. Madison's observations, made December 3, 1827, in Labunski, *James Madison*, 166.
17. Ibid.
18. Benjamin Johnson, letter to Madison, January 19, 1789, in Labunski, *James Madison*, 167.
19. Labunski, *James Madison*, 175.
20. Helen E. Veit, Kenneth R. Bowling, and Charlene Bangs Bickford, editors, *Creating the Bill of Rights: The Documentary Record from the First Federal Congress* (Baltimore and London: Johns Hopkins University Press, 1991), xv. The Anti-Federalists first pushed to change the structure of the federal government, diverting more power to the states, but these amendments were defeated.
21. Ketcham, *Madison: A Biography*, 292. One proposed that "no person religiously scrupulous of bearing arms shall be compelled to render military service in person."
22. In a letter from Fisher Ames to George Richards Minot on May 3, 1789, about a different debate, Ames wrote of Madison, "He speaks low, his person is little and ordinary. He speaks decently, as to manner, and no more. His language is very pure, perspicuous, and to the point. Pardon me, if I add, that I think him a little too much of a book politician, and too timid in his politics, for prudence and caution are opposites of timidity." Collected in Seth Ames, editor, *Works of Fisher Ames*, Volume 1 (Indianapolis: Liberty Classics, 1983).
23. Veit, Bowling, and Bickford, *Creating the Bill of Rights*, 77–78; *Congressional Register*, June 8, 1789.
24. "House Debate: June 8, 1789," *Annals* 1:434–436, 440–443.
25. The Virginia ratifying convention proposed a Bill of Rights; the nineteenth clause stated: "That any person religiously scrupulous of bearing arms ought to be exempted, upon payment of an equivalent to employ another to bear arms in his stead."
26. It's not clear what prompted this amendment, but during the ratifying conventions, some delegates in Pennsylvania—which was dominated by Quakers—objected to the failure to provide a way for people to avoid military service if it conflicted with their religious beliefs, noting that therefore the "rights of conscience" may be violated. Ketcham, *Anti-Federalist Papers*, 255.
27. *The Debates and Proceedings in the Congress of the United States*, "History of Congress," 42 volumes (Washington, DC: Gales & Seaton, 1834–1856), debates on August 15, 1789.
28. The committee also recommended a clause that "no person religiously scrupulous shall be compelled to bear arms." This was based on a proposal from Virginia and the Carolinas and had strong support but was mysteriously not included in the final version approved by the House. Stokes and Pfeffer, *Church and State*, 96.
29. According to the explanation on the website of the Library of Congress—www.constitution.org/gmason/amd_gmas.htm—"The *Annals of Congress*, formally known as *The Debates and Proceedings in the Congress of the United States*, cover the 1st Congress through the first session of the 18th Congress, from 1789 to 1824. The *Annals* were not published contemporaneously, but were compiled between 1834 and 1856, using the best records available, primarily newspaper accounts. Speeches are paraphrased rather than presented verbatim, but the record of debate is nonetheless fuller than that available from the *House* and *Senate Journals*."
30. The full text of the House debate on the first amendment is:

> The House again went into a Committee of the whole on the proposed amendments to the constitution, Mr. Boudinot in the chair.
> The fourth proposition being under consideration, as follows:

Article 1. Section 9. Between paragraphs two and three insert "no religion shall be established by law, nor shall the equal rights of conscience be infringed."

Mr. Sylvester had some doubts of the propriety of the mode of expression used in this paragraph. He apprehended that it was liable to a construction different from what had been made by the committee. He feared it might be thought to have a tendency to abolish religion altogether.

Mr. Vining suggested the propriety of transposing the two members of the sentence.

Mr. Gerry said it would read better if it was, that no religious doctrine shall be established by law.

Mr. Sherman thought the amendment altogether unnecessary, inasmuch as Congress had no authority whatever delegated to them by the Constitution to make religious establishments; he would, therefore, move to have it struck out.

Mr. Carroll—As the rights of conscience are, in their nature, of peculiar delicacy, and will little bear the gentlest touch of governmental hand; and as many sects have concurred in opinion that they are not well secured under the present constitution, he said he was much in favor of adopting the words. He thought it would tend more towards conciliating the minds of the people to the Government than almost any other amendment he had heard proposed. He would not contend with gentlemen about the phraseology, his object was to secure the substance in such a manner as to satisfy the wishes of the honest part of the community.

Mr. Madison said, he apprehended the meaning of the words to be, that Congress should not establish a religion, and enforce the legal observation of it by law, nor compel men to worship God in any manner contrary to their conscience. Whether the words are necessary or not, he did not mean to say, but they had been required by some of the State Conventions, who seemed to entertain an opinion that under the clause of the constitution, which gave power to Congress to make all laws necessary and proper to carry into execution the constitution, and the laws made under it, enabled them to make laws of such a nature as might infringe the rights of conscience, and establish a national religion; to prevent these effects he presumed the amendment was intended, and he thought it as well expressed as the nature of the language would admit.

Mr. Huntington said that he feared, with the gentleman first up on this subject, that the words might be taken in such latitude as to be extremely hurtful to the cause of religion. He understood the amendment to mean what had been expressed by the gentleman from Virginia; but others might find it convenient to put another construction upon it. The ministers of their congregations to the Eastward were maintained by the contributions of those who belonged to their society; the expense of building meeting-houses was contributed in the same manner. These things were regulated by bylaws. If an action was brought before a Federal Court on any of these cases, the person who had neglected to perform his engagements could not be compelled to do it; for a support of ministers, or building of places of worship might be construed into a religious establishment.

By the charter of Rhode Island, no religion could be established by law; he could give a history of the effects of such a regulation; indeed the people were now enjoying the blessed fruits of it. He hoped, therefore, the amendment would be made in such a way as to secure the rights of conscience, and a free exercise of the rights of religion, but not to patronize those who professed no religion at all.

Mr. Madison thought, if the word national was inserted before religion, it would satisfy the minds of honorable gentlemen. He believed that the people feared one sect might obtain a pre-eminence, or two combine together, and establish a religion to which they would compel others to conform. He thought if the word national was introduced, it would point the amendment directly to the object it was intended to prevent.

Mr. Livermore was not satisfied with that amendment; but he did not wish them to dwell long on the subject. He thought it would be better if it was altered, and made to read in this manner, that Congress shall make no laws touching religion, or infringing the rights of conscience.

Mr. Gerry did not like the term national, proposed by the gentleman from Virginia, and he hoped it would not be adopted by the House. It brought to his mind some observations that had taken place in the conventions at the time they were considering the present constitution. It had been insisted upon by those who were called antifederalists, that this form of Government consolidated the Union; the honorable gentleman's motion shows that he considers it in the same light. Those who were called antifederalists at that time complained that they had injustice done them by the title, because they were in favor of a Federal Government, and the others were in favor of a national one; the federalists were for ratifying the constitution as it stood, and the others not until amendments were made. Their names then ought not to have been distinguished by federalists and antifederalists, but rats and antirats. Mr. Madison withdrew his motion, but observed that the words "no national religion shall be established by law," did not imply that the Government was a national one; the question was then taken on Mr. Livermore's motion, and passed in the affirmative, thirty-one for, and twenty against it.

31. In *Letters of a Countryman II* in 1787, Sherman wrote, "If you are about to trust your liberties with people whom it is necessary to bind by stipulation, . . . your stipulation is not worth the trouble of writing. No bill of rights ever yet bound the supreme power longer than the *honey moon* of a new married couple, unless the *rulers were interested* in preserving the rights." Quoted in Scott D. Gerber, "Roger Sherman and the Bill of Rights," *Polity* 28, no. 4 (summer 1996), 521–540.

32. Noted political scientist Leo Pfeffer argued that this exchange also proved that Madison was, as he had during the Virginia assessment fight, viewing the term *establishment* to include not only formal incorporation of a particular religion but also taxpayer support for religion in a more general sense. Leo Pfeffer, "Church and State: Something Less Than Separation," *University of Chicago Law Review* 19, no. 1 (autumn 1951), 1–29.

33. "Amendments to the Constitution," June 8, 1789, *Annals* 1:424–450, 661–665, 707–717, 757–759, 766.

34. Senate amendments, September 9, 1789, in Veit, Bowling, and Bickford, *Creating the Bill of Rights*, 45.

35. "Madison says he had rather have none than those agreed to by the Senate," wrote New Hampshire senator Paine Wingate to John Langdon, September 17, 1789, quoted in ibid., 297. Fisher Ames, in a letter to Caleb Strong, September 15, 1789, wrote, "Many in our house, Mr. Madison, in particular, thinks, that they have lost much of their sedative Virtue by the alteration" (ibid.). One historian, Gary Glenn, has argued that one of the key behind-the-scenes battles must have been over the words *rights of conscience*. Madison, Glenn believed, wanted that language in part because he viewed it as providing equal rights to believers and nonbelievers. If true, this would mean that the Senate's decision to eliminate the "rights of conscience" clause was a statement in favor of a governmental preference for religion over irreligion. Gary D. Glenn, "Forgotten Purposes of the First Amendment Religion Causes," *Review of Politics* 49, no. 3 (summer 1987). Others, such as Kenneth Starr, have said that the Founders seemed to view rights of conscience and free exercise of religion interchangeably. See his speech "The Relationship of Church and State:

The Views of the Founding Fathers," delivered to the Supreme Court Historical Society May 18, 1987. The paper was, in May 2007, on the Society's website, www.supreme courthistory.org/04_library/subs_volumes/04_c08_h.html.

36. Senator William Grayson of Virginia, letter to Patrick Henry, September 29, 1789, quoted in Veit, Bowling, and Bickford, *Creating the Bill of Rights*, 300.

37. Stokes and Pfeffer, *Church and State*, 100, quoting the official documents that "the House of representatives had *receded* from their disagreement to the 1st, 3d, 5th, 6th, 7th, 9th, 10th, 11th, 14th, 15th, 17th, 20th, 21st, 22d, 23d, and 24th amendments."

38. Technically, Madison's proposals about religion and speech were in the third amendment of twelve he offered. But over time, the first two amendments, which dealt with legislative apportionment issues, fell away, and what was the third amendment became the First.

39. Veit, Bowling, and Bickford, *Creating the Bill of Rights*, 189; *Gazette of the United States*, August 22, 1789.

40. "Amendments to the Constitution," June 8, 1789, *Annals* 1:424–450, 661–665, 707–717, 757–759, 766.

41. "Amendments to the Constitution, August 17, 1789, *Annals* 1:729–731, 755, 766. Ironically, it was listed as the "fourteenth amendment."

42. The Bill of Rights then went to the states for ratification. Little is known about the debates. Nine states approved the Bill of Rights fairly quickly. Virginia, Massachusetts, Connecticut, and Georgia delayed. Georgia thought it unnecessary. Federalists in Massachusetts thought the rights were too much of a concession to the Anti-Federalists. In Virginia, the Anti-Federalists attacked hard, making a somewhat bizarre set of arguments about the religion clauses. In a formal statement, the eight state senators who opposed the amendment argued that it was not tough enough because, while it prevented the establishment of one religion, it opened the door for them to "levy taxes to any amount, for the support of religion or its preachers." In other words, they said the Bill of Rights was flawed because it would allow for government support of religion.

Madison seemed unfazed. In a letter to George Washington, he predicted that "this marriage of the third articles [the First Amendment], particularly, will have this effect." What he apparently meant was that the senators who opposed the amendment were well-known opponents of the Constitution as a whole and were poking holes in the Bill of Rights as part of their general campaign to undermine support for the new government and Constitution. In fact, some of those senators, such as Patrick Henry, were actually in favor of government support of religion, so their protestations on that point seemed disingenuous.

43. The most influential articulation of this view is Michael W. McConnell, "Accommodation of Religion," *Supreme Court Review* 1985 (1985), 1–59. McConnell proposed that the government should observe the following rules: "1) An accommodation must facilitate the exercise of beliefs and practices independently adopted rather than inducing or coercing beliefs or practices acceptable to the government. . . . 2) An accommodation must not interfere with the religious liberty of others by forcing them to participate in religious observance. . . . 3) An accommodation must not favor one form of religious belief over another." There's much to commend McConnell's approach as a matter of constitutional law. What I believe he neglects, however, is the wisdom of Madison's and the Baptists' central argument that "liberty" is not possible without "separation" of church and state. Madison and the eighteenth-century evangelicals would agree with McConnell in saying that separation isn't the goal—liberty is—but they would argue that history has proven over and over that liberty inevitably erodes if separation isn't preserved.

44. Dissenting opinion in *Wallace v. Jaffree*.

45. Thomas Tucker, quoted in Curry, *First Freedoms*, 217.

46. In his book *Myth of Separation*, David Barton quoted James Madison as saying: "We have staked the whole future of American civilization not upon the power of government, far from it. We have staked the future of all our political institutions upon the capacity of

mankind for self-government, upon the capacity of each and all of us to govern ourselves, to control ourselves, to sustain ourselves according to the Ten Commandments." Alas, Madison scholars attempted to find such a quote in his writings and couldn't, so Barton declared the quote fraudulent. Ahem. But Barton has volumes of other quotes from Founding Fathers showing that they wanted government support for religion and sometimes Christianity specifically, as long as it didn't involve the creation of one official denomination. "The intent of the First Amendment was not to separate Christianity and state," Barton wrote. "Had that been the intent, it would never have been ratified. Even when the state constitutions stated that their citizens had a right to worship God according to their conscience, a statement immediately followed stipulating that it be within Christian standards. In other words, as long as someone was pursuing some form of orthodox Christianity, he was protected in his freedom of worship and conscience." It will shock liberals to learn that Barton's assessment of the state constitutions was basically correct. Christian lawyer Dee Wampler, in *his* book, called *The Myth of Separation of Church and State* (Enumclaw, WA: WinePress Publishing, 2002), declared that "Jefferson believed, as did other Founders, that the First Amendment simply prevented the federal establishment of a single denomination" (page 35).

47. Books claiming that the separation of church and state is entirely or largely a myth or that America is, by design, a "Christian nation," include:

- David Barton, *The Myth of Separation* (Aledo, TX: WallBuilder Press, 1993).
- Dee Wampler, *The Myth of Separation Between Church and State* (Enumclaw, WA: WinePress Publishing, 2002).
- Tim LaHaye, *Faith of Our Founding Fathers* (Brentwood, TN: Wolgemuth & Hyatt, 1987).
- D. James Kennedy, *What They Believed: The Faith of Washington, Jefferson, and Lincoln* (Fort Lauderdale, FL: Coral Ridge Ministries, 2003).
- Gary DeMar, *America's Heritage* (Fort Lauderdale, FL: Coral Ridge Ministries, 2002).
- ———, *America's Christian Heritage* (Nashville, TN: Broadman & Holman, 2003).
- Peter Marshall and David Manuel, *The Light and the Glory: Did God Have a Plan for America?* (Grand Rapids, MI: Baker Book House, 1977).

A number of prominent Christian conservative leaders have stated quite clearly that they believe separation of church and state is a myth. A very small sampling:

"There is no such thing as separation of church and state in the Constitution. It is a lie of the Left and we are not going to take it anymore." —Pat Robertson, November 1993, during an address to the American Center for Law and Justice

"The ACLU and the liberal media have touted the phrase so many times that most people believe the phrase is in the Constitution. Nowhere is 'separation of church and state' referenced in the Constitution. This phrase was in the former Soviet Union's Constitution, but it has never been part of the United States Constitution." —Mathew Staver, Liberty Counsel, "The Myth Behind Separation of Church and State"

"Our Party pledges to exert its influence to restore the original intent of the First Amendment of the United States Constitution and dispel the myth of the separation of Church and State." —Texas Republican Party platform, 2004

According to Deborah Caldwell of Beliefnet.com, David Barton was hired by the Republican National Committee "as a political consultant and has been traveling the country for a year—speaking at about 300 RNC-sponsored lunches for local evangelical pastors. During the lunches, he presents a slide show of American monuments, discusses his view of America's Christian heritage—and tells pastors that they are allowed

to endorse political candidates from the pulpit." www.beliefnet.com/story/154/story_15469
_1.html.

48. *Robert E. Lee, individually and as Principal of Nathan Bishop Middle School et al., Petitioners v. Daniel Weisman etc.* on writ of certiorari, United States Court of Appeals for the First Circuit, June 24, 1992.

49. Levy, *Establishment Clause*, 76.

50. James Madison, "Introduction to the Bill of Rights," June 8, 1789, in Kurland and Lerner, *Founders' Constitution*, Document 11, Bill of Rights.

51. Madison, during the Virginia ratifying convention, June 12, 1788, in ibid., Document 49.

52. Levy, *Establishment Clause*, 142.

53. Russell Kirk, "The First Clause of the First Amendment: Politics and Religion," lecture at the Heritage Foundation, January 28, 1988, www.heritage.org/Research/PoliticalPhilosophy/HL146.cfm (accessed May 2007).

54. The New Hampshire constitution stated:

> ART. IV. Among the natural rights, some are in their very nature unalienable, because no equivalent can be given or received for them. Of this kind are the *rights of conscience.*
>
> ART. V. Every individual has a natural and unalienable right to worship God according to the dictates of his own conscience and reason; and no person shall be hurt, molested, or restrained in his person, liberty, or estate for worshipping God in the manner most agreeable to the dictates of his own conscience, or for his religious profession, sentiments, or persuasion; provided he doth not disturb the public peace or disturb others in their religious worship.
>
> ART. VI. As morality and piety, rightly grounded on evangelical principles, will give the best and greatest security to government, and will lay in the hearts of men the strongest obligations to due subjection; and as a knowledge of these is most likely to be propagated through a society by the institution of the public worship of the Deity, and of public instruction in morality and religion; therefore, to promote those important purposes the people of this State have a right to empower, and do hereby fully empower, the legislature to authorize, from time to time, the several towns, parishes, bodies corporate, or religious societies within this State, to make adequate provisions, at their own expense, for the support and maintenance of public protestant teachers of piety, religion, and morality.
>
> *Provided notwithstanding,* That the several towns, parishes, bodies corporate, or religious societies, shall at all times have the exclusive right of electing their own public teachers, and of contracting with them for their support and maintenance. And no person, or any one particular religious sect or denomination, shall ever be compelled to pay toward the support of the teacher or teachers of another persuasion, sect, or denomination. And every denomination of Christians, demeaning themselves quietly and as good subjects of the State, shall be equally under the protection of the law; and no subordination of any one sect or denomination to another shall ever be established by law. And nothing herein shall be understood to affect any former contracts made for the support of the ministry; but all such contracts shall remain and be in the same state as if this constitution had not been made.

> Reprinted in Kurland and Lerner, *Founders' Constitution* press-pubs.uchicago.edu/founders/tocs/amendI_religion.html.

55. There was no formal roll call on this amendment, so we are left somewhat in the dark about who actually voted for it.

56. Gary Glenn made another argument: that Huntington was wanting to ensure that at least religion was given preference to atheism or "those who professed no religion at all." He

feared, Glenn has argued, that by referring to the "equal rights of conscience," Madison was not only putting all religious people on equal footing but also requiring equal treatment for the religious and nonreligious. That, Huntington argued, could not be allowed. We don't know for sure what impact this argument had on Madison (who *did* want nonbelievers protected), but we do know that the word *equal* was deleted before "rights of conscience" under the amendment offered by Samuel Livermore of New Hampshire. Glenn, "Forgotten Purposes," 350.

57. Christopher Collier, *Roger Sherman's Connecticut: Yankee Politics and the American Revolution* (Middletown, CT: Wesleyan University Press, 1971), 185, quoted in Eidsmore, *Christianity and the Constitution.*

58. There was somewhat of a debate as to whether Sherman was a collaborator or an opponent of Madison. He clearly resisted the idea of a Bill of Rights, but recently it was discovered that he had written a draft of the Bill of Rights himself. Some historians argue that he was just articulating the views of the committee on which he was serving; others say that he was attempting to promote a legitimate, albeit different, version of a Bill of Rights. In any event, the language he used in his draft was, "The people have certain natural rights . . . Such are the rights of Conscience in matters of religion." In Gerber, "Roger Sherman," 521–540.

59. Akhil Reed Amar, *The Bill of Rights* (New Haven, CT: Yale University Press, 1998), 33.

15. Practicing What They Preached

1. "First Inaugural Address of George Washington," April 30, 1789, *Avalon Project.*
2. "Address of the House of Representatives to George Washington, President of the United States," May 5, 1789, in *Compilation of the Messsages and Papers of the Presidents,* Volume 1, published by authority of Congress, 1902, republished by Project Gutenberg, 2004, www.gutenberg.org/files/11314/11314-h/11314-h.htm.
3. James Madison, "George Washington's Reply of the President to the House of Representatives," May 8, 1789.
4. James Madison, "George Washington's Reply of the President to the Senate," May 18, 1789.
5. "The Barbary Treaties: Treaty of Peace and Friendship, Signed at Tripoli November 4, 1796," *Avalon Project.*
6. James Madison, "Detached Memoranda," 1817, in Alley, *Madison on Religious Liberty.*
7. "Washington's Farewell Address," 1796, *Avalon Project.*
8. "Proclamation. A National Thanksgiving," October 3, 1789, *Avalon Project.*
9. "A Proclamation," January 1, 1795, *Avalon Project.*
10. Washington, letter to Moses Seixas of the Hebrew Congregation of Newport, Rhode Island, August 17, 1790, in Cousins, *In God We Trust,* 61.
11. Inaugural address of John Adams, March 4, 1797, *Avalon Project.*
12. The actual proclamation can be found on the Library of Congress website, www.loc.gov/exhibits/religion/vc006493.jpg (accessed May 2007).
13. Madison, "Detached Memoranda," quoted in Alley, *Madison on Religious Liberty,* 93.
14. John Adams, letter to Benjamin Rush, June 12, 1812.
15. Stokes and Pfeffer, *Church and State,* 177.
16. John Adams, letter to Thomas Jefferson, August 15, 1823, quoted in Cappon, *Adams–Jefferson Letters,* 594.
17. Madison's *Report of 1800* on the Virginia resolutions, quoted in Amar, *Bill of Rights,* 40.
18. Lambert, *Founding Fathers,* 266.
19. Gaustad, *Sworn on the Altar,* 91.
20. Lambert, *Founding Fathers,* 266.
21. Ibid., 273.
22. Ibid., 277.
23. The Reverend William Linn, *Serious Considerations on the Election of a President: Addressed to the Citizens of the United States* (New York: John Furman, 1800), quoted in Gaustad, *Sworn on the Altar,* 91.

24. Ibid., 92.
25. John Mitchell Mason, *The Voice of Warning to Christians, on the Ensuing Election of a President of the United States* (New York: G. F. Hopkins, 1800), quoted in Daniel L. Dreisbach, *Thomas Jefferson and the Wall of Separation Between Church and State* (New York: New York University Press, 2002), 20.
26. A short address to the voters of Delaware. [Signed at end] A Christian federalist. Kent County, September 21, 1800, quoted in Lambert, *Founding Fathers*, 93.
27. Lambert, *Founding Fathers*, 277.
28. Ibid., 278, quoting Connecticutensis, *Three Letters to Abraham Bishop* (Hartford, CT, 1800), 28–29.
29. Morton Borden, *Jews, Turks, and Infidels* (Chapel Hill: University of North Carolina Press, 1984), 26.
30. Lambert, *Founding Fathers*, 283.
31. Timothy Dwight, "The Triumph of Infidelity" (1788), quoted in ibid., 280.
32. *General Aurora Advertiser*, Philadelphia, October 14, 1800, quoted in ibid., 277.
33. Ibid., 280.
34. Jefferson, letter to Benjamin Rush, September 23, 1800, *The Thomas Jefferson Digital Archive*, etext.virginia.edu/jefferson/.
35. Gaustad, *Sworn on the Altar*, 95.
36. Lambert, *Founding Fathers*, 283.
37. Abraham Bishop, *Connecticut Republicanism: An Oration on the Extent and Powers of Political Delusion* (New Haven, CT, 1800), 45, in ibid., 284.
38. John Leland, "A Blow at the Root: Being a Fashionable Fast-Day Sermon (Cheshire, 9 April 1801)," in L. F. Greene, editor, *The Writings of the Late Elder John Leland* (New York: Arno Press, 1965 [1845]), quoted in Dreisbach, *Wall of Separation*, 13.
39. We don't know exactly which hymns, but Leland was a prolific hymn writer, so perhaps they sang one of his:

> *If you have a heart lamenting,*
> *And bemoan'd your wretched case,*
> *Come to Jesus Christ repenting;*
> *He will give you gospel grace;*
> *If you want a heart to fear him,*
> *Love and serve him all your days*
> *Come to Jesus Christ and ask him;*
> *He will guide you in his ways.*

Several of his hymns are in Gaustad and Noll, *Documentary History*, 282–285, as well as *Writings of Leland*.
40. Butterfield, "Elder John Leland," 220.
41. A "fashionable fast-day sermon," delivered in 1801, excerpted in Gaustad and Noll, *Documentary History*, 301–302.
42. Dreisbach, *Wall of Separation*, 33.
43. "Reflections of Mr. Jefferson, Over the Mammoth Cheese" (1802), quoted in ibid., 15.
44. As to what happened to the cheese, Butterfield wrote in "Elder John Leland, Jeffersonian Itinerant," "The last of it is said to have been served with hot punch at a presidential reception in 1805; it is also said to have been dumped into the Potomac at a date not known" (page 229).
45. It's not known exactly what he preached, but Leland's views on religious liberty were classically Baptist in their emphasis on the different spheres of governance. "Every man must give an account of himself to God, and therefore every man ought to be at liberty to serve God in a way that he can best reconcile to his conscience. If government can answer for individuals at the day of judgment, let men be controlled by it in religious matters; otherwise, let men be free" (page 199).

46. Dreisbach, *Wall of Separation*, 22, quoting Cutler. Leland was known for his preaching. Butterfield included this wonderful story: "A characteristic one tells how he outdid an Episcopal clergyman in Virginia who argued in favor of state support for ministers because they have to spend so much time preparing sermons. Leland answered that he could expound the Scriptures without special preparation, and the Episcopalian challenged him to preach on a text to be provided just before beginning his sermon. Leland went into the pulpit and was handed a text which proved to be Numbers 22:21, 'And Balaam saddled his ass.' Mr. Leland first commented on the account from which the text was taken, and then said he should divide his subject into three parts: 1st, Balaam, as a false prophet, represents a hireling clergy. 2d, the saddle represents their enormous salaries, and 3d, the dumb ass represents the people who will bear such a load." Butterfield, "Elder John Leland," 168–169.

47. Dreisbach, *Wall of Separation*, 33.

48. James Hutson, " 'A Wall of Separation': FBI Helps Restore Jefferson's Obliterated Draft," June 1998, www.loc.gov/loc/lcib/9806/danbury.html (accessed May 2007).

49. Jefferson, letter to Attorney General Levi Lincoln, January 1, 1802, quoted in Dreisbach, *Wall of Separation*, 147, and *American Memory*, the Thomas Jefferson Papers, Image 561.

50. Dreisbach, *Wall of Separation*, 40.

51. Jefferson, letter to Attorney General Levi Lincoln, January 1, 1802, quoted in ibid., 146.

52. Jefferson, letter to Samuel Miller, January 23, 1808, quoted in Cousins, *In God We Trust*, 137.

53. Jefferson, first inaugural address, March 4, 1801, *Avalon Project*.

54. Dreisbach, *Wall of Separation*, 101.

55. James Madison, "Veto Message to Congress," February 21, 1811, in Hunt, *Writings of James Madison*, Volume 8, 132.

56. James Madison, "Detached Memoranda," 1817, published in *William and Mary Quarterly*, 3d Series, 3 (1946), 534–568, and Kurland and Lerner, *Founders' Constitution*, First Amendment, Document 64.

57. James Madison, "Veto Message to Congress," February 28, 1811, in Hunt, *Writings of James Madison*, Volume 8, 133.

58. "Detached Memoranda." A good history of the controversy over Sunday mail is James R. Rohrer, "Sunday Mails and the Church-State Theme in Jacksonian America," *Journal of the Early Republic* 7, no. 1 (spring 1987), pp. 53–74.

59. "Religion and the Republic: James Madison and the First Amendment," in Alley, *Madison on Religious Liberty*, 241.

60. James Madison, letter to Edward Livingston, July 10, 1822, in Kurland and Lerner, *Founders' Constitution*, Amendment I, Document 66.

61. Madison, Proclamation of Day of Fasting and Prayer, July 9, 1812, in James D. Richardson, editor, *A Compilation of the Messages and Papers of the Presidents*, published by authority of Congress, 1902, republished by Project Gutenberg, 2004, www.gutenberg .org/files/11314/11314-h/11314-h.htm.

62. Madison, letter to Edward Livingston, July 10, 1822, in Alley, *Madison on Religious Liberty*, 82.

63. Ibid.

64. Madison, letter to Edward Everett, March 19, 1823, in ibid., 83.

65. Madison, letter to the Reverend Jasper Adams, 1832, *James Madison Papers*, image 1175.

16. *Friends in Heaven*

1. Benjamin Franklin, letter to Ezra Stiles, March 9, 1790, *The Papers of Benjamin Franklin* and Edwin S. Gaustad, *Faith of Our Fathers: Religion and the New Nation* (San Francisco: Harper & Row, 1987), 64. This was similar to statements he'd made earlier in life. For instance, when he learned that his grandson, a Protestant, wasn't being allowed to marry a friend's daughter, who was Catholic, Franklin offered a lovely metaphor. "In each Religion there are some essential things, & others which are only Forms & Fashions," he said. "As a

piece of Sugar which can be wrapped up in brown or white or blue Paper, & tied with flaxen or wool string, red or yellow; it is always the Sugar which is the essential thing." The truths he listed were:

> 1st. That there is a God who made the World, & who Governs it by his Providence.
> 2nd. That he should be adored, & served[.]
> 3rd. That the best service to God is doing good to men.
> 4th. That the human soul is immortal &
> 5th. That in a future Life if not in the present one, vice will be punished, & Virtue rewarded[.]

2. Federer, ed., *God and Country*, 251.
3. The occasion was the death of Patrick Henry in 1799. Quoted in Gaustad, *Faith of Our Fathers*, 77.
4. George Washington, letter to James Anderson, December 25, 1795, quoted in Chadwick, *George Washington's War*, 487.
5. Holmes, *Faiths of the Founding Fathers*, 94.
6. Meade, quoted in James Hutson, "James Madison and the Social Utility of Religion: Risks vs. Rewards," www.loc.gov/loc/madison/hutson-paper.html (accessed May 2007).
7. Holmes, *Faiths of the Founding Fathers*, 97. In 1835, a cousin wrote Dolley and apologized for a disagreement that arose over Madison's apparent habit, at that point in his life, of not scrupulously keeping the Sabbath. Apparently she was a strict Episcopalian and was "startled" by his lax views on what was permissible on Sunday.
8. Ibid., 96.
9. Dolley's father had been a leader in the Philadelphia meeting—some described him as a "fanatic"—and had even taken the step of freeing his slaves, an act of conscience that likely helped precipitate his economic downfall. Dolley remembered him as "strict," "single-minded," and "exact," according to biographer Catherine Allgor. His business (making starch) began to fail, perhaps because of his decision about slaves, and he was ultimately read out of the Quaker community for failure to pay bills. Dolley married Quaker John Todd, but in the summer of 1793 a horrifying yellow fever epidemic gripped the city. He had Dolley and the children removed to Gray's Ferry while he remained in the city center, "burying the dead, succoring the sick, writing wills for the dying, making brief trips to the Schuylkill to relieve his and his wife's anxiety." On October 2, his father died. On October 12, his mother died. On October 24, he visited Dolley one last time, and then died himself. Dolley became seriously ill and saw their son, William, die before she recovered. Within a year of her husband's death, she was introduced to James Madison (by future vice president Aaron Burr). In deciding to marry Madison, she was choosing not only to return to the life of slave-holding gentry but also to leave her religion. Catherine Allgor, *A Perfect Union: Dolley Madison and the Creation of the American Nation* (New York: Henry Holt, 2006).
10. John Adams, letter to Thomas Jefferson, September 14, 1813, quoted in Cappon, *Adams–Jefferson Letters*, 372.
11. Adams, letter to Jefferson, December 25, 1813, quoted in ibid., 412–413.
12. March 7, 1756, Adams diary entry, quoted in Cousins, *In God We Trust*, 81.
13. Cappon, *Adams–Jefferson Letters*, 569.
14. Adams, letter to Jefferson, December 12, 1816, quoted in ibid., 499.
15. Adams, letter to Benjamin Rush, October 22, 1812, quoted in Joseph Ellis, *Passionate Sage: The Character and Legacy of John Adams* (New York: W. W. Norton, 2001), 107.
16. Quoted in James Grant, *John Adams: Party of One* (New York: Farrar, Straus and Giroux, 2003), 116.
17. Adams, letter to Jefferson, November 4, 1816, quoted in Cappon, *Adams–Jefferson Letters*, 493.
18. Jefferson, letter to Dr. Benjamin Waterhouse, June 26, 1822, *Thomas Jefferson Digital Archive*.

19. Jefferson, letter to Thomas Parker, May 15, 1819.
20. Jefferson, letter to William Canby, September 18, 1813.
21. Jefferson, letter to Dr. Benjamin Waterhouse, June 26, 1822. After stating his creed, he goes on to compare it to what Christianity has become:

> These are the great points on which he endeavored to reform the religion of the Jews. But compare with these the demoralizing dogmas of Calvin.
>
> 1. That there are three Gods.
> 2. That good works, or the love of our neighbor, are nothing.
> 3. That faith is every thing, and the more incomprehensible the proposition, the more merit in its faith.
> 4. That reason in religion is of unlawful use.
> 5. That God, from the beginning, elected certain individuals to be saved, and certain others to be damned; and that no crimes of the former can damn them; no virtues of the latter save.
>
> Now, which of these is the true and charitable Christian? He who believes and acts on the simple doctrines of Jesus? Or the impious dogmatists, as Athanasius and Calvin? Verily I say these are the false shepherds foretold as to enter not by the door into the sheepfold, but to climb up some other way. They are mere usurpers of the Christian name, teaching a counter-religion made up of the *deliria* of crazy imaginations, as foreign from Christianity as is that of Mahomet. Their blasphemies have driven thinking men into infidelity, who have too hastily rejected the supposed author himself, with the horrors so falsely imputed to him. Had the doctrines of Jesus been preached always as pure as they came from his lips, the whole civilized world would now have been Christian. I rejoice that in this blessed country of free inquiry and belief, which has surrendered its creed and conscience to neither kings nor priests, the genuine doctrine of one only God is reviving, and trust that there is not a *young man* now living in the United States who will not die an Unitarian.

22. Jefferson, letter to Thomas Jefferson Smith, February 21, 1825.
23. Jefferson, letter to Abigail Adams, January 11, 1817, in Lipscomb and Bergh, editors, *The Writings of Thomas Jefferson*, Volume 15
24. Jefferson, letter to Adams, November 13, 1818, quoted in Cappon, *Adams–Jefferson Letters*, 529.
25. Jefferson, letter to Adams, September 4, 1823, quoted in ibid., *American Memory, Thomas Jefferson Papers*, Image 1164.

17. They Were Right

1. Some conservative scholars have argued that the Fourteenth Amendment didn't intend to apply the concepts of separation of church and state to the states, but a series of court rulings over the years have gone against them, thereby "incorporating" the First Amendment freedoms to apply to the states. In *Cantwell v. Connecticut*, 310 U.S. 296, 303 (1940), the Court incorporated the "free exercise" clause. In *Everson v. Board of Education*, 330 U.S. 1, 8 (1947), they applied the establishment clause against the states.
2. Bingham, quoted in Amar, *Bill of Rights*, 191. The connection between the Fourteenth Amendment and religious freedom was even more specific than that. One of the arguments Bingham used was that the effort to disenfranchise and degrade Negroes had dragged the basic freedoms—including freedom of worship—through the mud. He pointed out that laws against teaching slaves to read had meant that Christians attempting to teach the Bible had been thrown in jail. A Louisiana law, for instance, banned uttering words from "the pulpit" that might incite "insubordination among the slaves." In North Carolina, an anti-slavery preacher named Jesse McBride was sentenced to a year in prison and twenty lashes for his sermons. In 1859, Daniel Worth was sentenced for his anti-slavery

sermons; then a law was passed saying that such sermons in the future would be punishable by execution. Even after the Civil War, the new Black Codes had made it a crime for free Negroes to "exercise the functions of ministers of Gospel." The leading Senate sponsor of the Fourteenth Amendment, Henry Wilson, accused slavery defenders of hanging "ministers of the living god for questioning the divinity of slavery." Ohio representative Cydnor Tompkins said the Southern effort to stifle anti-slavery speech was criminalizing "the man who dares to proclaim the precepts of our holy religion."

In other words, proponents of the Fourteenth Amendment believed that slavery was a cancer that harmed not only Negroes but also the spirit of the Constitution, including religious liberty. They wanted the principles of the Bill of Rights to be lifted from the mud and held aloft again—and that meant freedom of religion being applied throughout American society. Bingham himself explained the conditions he sought to rectify: "The States did deny to citizens the equal protection of the laws, they did deny the rights of citizens under the Constitution, and, except to the extent of the express limitations upon the States, as I have shown, the citizen had no remedy. They denied trial by jury, and he had no remedy. They took property without compensation, and he had no remedy. They restricted the freedom of the press, and he had no remedy. They restricted the freedom of speech, and he had no remedy. They restricted the rights of conscience, and he had no remedy."

On the other hand, many scholars argue that while it's possible that the Fourteenth Amendment incorporated the free-exercise clause, it is a logical impossibility that the Fourteenth Amendment was intended to incorporate the establishment clause against the states. If the real purpose of the establishment clause was to limit the national government's ability to interfere with state activity, then it would make no sense to force that down the throats of the states. If the original establishment clause was agnostic on the actual merits of the separation of church and state, what does it mean to apply that agnosticism to the states? I have sympathy with this argument. I keep thinking of Fisher Ames or one of the other New Englanders who supported the First Amendment in part because it would allow their states to regulate religion as they saw fit. How would they feel if they found out that courts had now concluded that the principle now applied to local government was separation of chuch and state?

There's no evidence that Representative Bingham grappled with that paradox. Instead, Bingham simply seemed to accept the general notion that the Bill of Rights had originally prevented Congress from trampling on basic freedoms and the time had now come to prevent the states from trampling on those same freedoms. In that sense, Bingham didn't so much "incorporate" the freedoms of the Bill of Rights as redefine them. If Fisher Ames and Robert Bingham could discuss the matter, I imagine Bingham would simply say, "We tried it your way for the first eighty years or so and it didn't work." The basic political pact that gave us the First Amendment is now null and void, and we are siding with Madison's original view that separation of church and state is not so much a doctrine designed to limit national power (as Ames had thought) but rather was now something bigger and more fundamental, an individual right that could not be violated by any branch of government. In effect, Bingham was embracing the spirit of Madison's first proposal that "the civil rights of none shall be abridged on account of religious belief or worship, nor shall any national religion be established, nor shall the full and equal rights of conscience be in any manner, or on any pretext, infringed." Madison had to compromise away some beloved parts of his religious freedom measure. Representative Bingham made Madison's ideas whole again.

3. National Opinion Research Center of University of Chicago, 2002.
4. Henry William Elson, *History of the United States of America* (New York: MacMillan Company, 1904), 198–200. Transcribed by Kathy Leigh. Quoted in www.usahistory.info, www.infoplease.com/ipa/A0004979.html.
5. Albert Einstein, "Science, Philosophy and Religion: A Symposium," 1941.
6. In describing what he viewed as a massive liberal misinterpretation of history, M. Stanton Evans in "Faith of Our Fathers" wrote, "In obedience to lessons allegedly taught in these irreligious histories, archly secularist views have been imparted, and measures taken, se-

verely wrenching the lives and customs of our people. This has in turn led to angry conflict on a host of faith-related issues—abortion, euthanasia, homosexuality, marriage—that now so painfully divide us" (page 22).

7. Leland lived in Orange County, but according to Butterfield in "Elder John Leland, Jeffersonian Itinerant," "He seems to have served from time to time half a dozen churches in Orange, Louisa, Culpeper, and Spotsylvania Counties, some of which he founded" (page 168).

8. In supporting such amendments, conservative Protestants were also overtly buying into separation of church and state on the local level. The original Blaine Amendment declared: "No State shall make any law respecting an establishment of religion, or prohibiting the free exercise thereof; and no money raised by taxation in any State for the support of public schools, or derived from any public fund therefor, nor any public lands devoted thereto, shall ever be under the control of any religious sect; nor shall any money so raised or lands so devoted be divided between religious sects or denominations."

9. Butterfield, "Elder John Leland," 236. And by the way, had John Leland been around for consultation, he likely would have once again embraced the Jeffersonians. Indeed, Leland opposed the ban on Sunday mail delivery on the grounds that such a prohibition entailed state recognition of a particular faith's holy day. "It does not belong to [the state] to establish fixed holy days for divine worship," he said.

10. Most of this summary comes from Michael McConnell's influential article "Accommodation of Religion," *The Supreme Court Review*, Vol. 1985, 1–59. His full list:

> providing unemployment benefits to persons who resign their jobs for religious reasons; exempting self-employed persons from the Social Security system if they are religiously opposed to participation and belong to a religious organization that provides for its dependent members; exempting jurors with a religious objection from jury duty; releasing children from public schools to receive religious education in their own churches; expending trust funds in the discretion of the Secretary of the Interior for sectarian education; exempting members of the Old Order Amish sect from compulsory education laws; providing chaplains in prisons and in the military; exempting adherents to "well-recognized" faiths opposed to participation in war from military conscription; exempting distributors of religious materials from municipal tax on door-to-door vending; exempting non-Sunday Sabbatarians from Sunday closing laws; and requiring employers to make 'reasonable accommodations' to the religious practices of their workers. Examples of accommodations to religious institutions include exempting churches and church-operated schools from certain payroll taxes and exempting pervasively religious private and elementary and secondary schools from labor laws . . . exemptions from the requirement of saluting the flag in public school, instituted at the behest of religious objectors but extended to dissenters on the ground of religion, politics, nationalism, or any other "matters of opinion"; zoning protections for churches and schools; and property tax exemptions for churches and other non profit organizations.

11. Thomas Jefferson, letter to James Madison, January 22, 1821, quoted in Cappon, *Adams–Jefferson Letters*, 569.

12. Madison, letter to Robert Walsh, March 2, 1819, in Hunt, *Writings of James Madison*, 425. According to Stokes and Pfeffer, *Church and State*, independence and separation of church and state had quickly resulted in new religious denominations. "The tendency to divide and multiply denominations was accentuated by several factors: the spirit of freedom that was prevalent; the life of the frontier with its isolated communities; the growing split over slavery, which brought about the division of the larger Protestant churches, with the exception of the Episcopal, into Northern and Southern branches; the Second Awakening, which developed in the first few years of the nineteenth century, and the growing revival of

religion and independent conviction that followed it; and the immigration of groups from northern Europe with strong national traditions and feelings." As subsidies faded away, the churches developed more capacity for self-governance and self-preservation. "The new freedom and the new responsibility, combined with the opening up of new territories, resulted in much emphasis on evangelistic effort." The churches became more democratic in their organization, and toleration spread (pages 209–210).

13. Madison, letter to Frederick Beasley, November 20, 1825, in Cousins, *In God We Trust*, 320.
14. Finke and Stark, *Churching of America*, 54–66.
15. Madison, letter to the Reverend Jasper Adams, spring 1833, quoted in Brenner, *Jefferson and Madison*, 395.
16. Unitarians: John Adams, John Quincy Adams, Millard Fillmore, William Howard Taft; Quakers: Herbert Hoover, Richard M. Nixon; Baptists: Warren G. Harding, Harry S. Truman, Jimmy Carter, William Jefferson Clinton; raised as a Jehovah's Witness: Dwight Eisenhower; Catholic: John F. Kennedy. According to www.adherents.com/adh_presidents .html (accessed May 2007).
17. As of June 2007, the Supreme Court's five Catholics were John Roberts, Anthony M. Kennedy, Antonin Scalia, Clarence Thomas, and Samuel Alito, according to www .adherents.com/adh_sc.html.
18. In 1996, Mickey Kantor, Robert Reich, Donna Shalala, Robert Rubin, and Dan Glickman.
19. In 2005, the five senators who were members of the Church of Latter Day Saints were Michael Crapo (R-ID), Harry Reid (D-NV), Gordon Smith (R-OR), Robert Bennett (R-UT), and Orrin Hatch (R-UT), according to www.adherents.com/adh_congress.html#109.
20. Journalist 1st Class (SW) Hendrick L. Dickson, "Navy Commissions Military's First Buddhis Chaplain," Navy News Service, July 23, 2004, reprinted on www.news.navy.mil/ search/display.asp?story_id=14398 (accessed May 2007).
21. 2001 *American Religious Identification Survey* (ARIS). Reprinted on www.adherents.com/ rel_USA.html#families.
22. Christian, Jewish, Muslim, Hindu, Buddhist, according to www.pluralism.org/resources/ statistics/tradition.php.
23. I've focused on those social movements that are now relatively noncontroversial. Of course, religion has also played a crucial role in more controversial social movements, including the drive to restrict or prohibit abortion and the Prohibition movement.
24. Pulled primarily from two international surveys conducted during 1991 and 1993 by the International Social Survey Program (ISSP), as of May 2007 located at the National Opinion Research Center (NORC) at the University of Chicago. Summarized nicely on www .religioustolerance.org/rel_comp.htm. There's some controversy over whether it's actually true that 44 percent of Americans attend church weekly, as polls show, but most experts do believe that US church attendance is higher than that in most other industrialized countries. A good summary is found on www.religioustolerance.org/rel_rate.htm.

index

ABOUT THE AUTHOR

STEVEN WALDMAN is co-founder, editor in chief, and president of Beliefnet.com, the largest faith and spirituality website. Previously, Waldman was the national editor of *U.S. News & World Report* and a national correspondent for *Newsweek*. His writings have also appeared in *The Atlantic, The Washington Post, The New York Times, Slate, The Washington Monthly, National Review,* and elsewhere. He appears frequently on television and radio to discuss religion and politics. He is also the author of *The Bill,* a book about the creation of AmeriCorps. Waldman lives in New York with his wife, the writer Amy Cunningham, and their children, Joseph and Gordon.

ABOUT THE TYPE

This book was set in Electra, a typeface designed for Linotype by
W. A. Dwiggins, the renowned type designer (1880–1956). Electra
is a fluid typeface, avoiding the contrasts of thick and thin strokes
that are prevalent in most modern typefaces.